D1070882

A Nation Divided

Diversity, Inequality, and Community in American Society

EDITED BY

Phyllis Moen,
Donna Dempster-McClain, AND
Henry A. Walker

CORNELL UNIVERSITY PRESS   ITHACA AND LONDON

First published 1999 by Cornell University Press

First printing, Cornell Paperbacks, 1999

Printed in the United States of America

Cornell University Press strives to use environmentally responsible suppliers and materials to the fullest extent possible in the publishing of its books. Such materials include vegetable-based, low-VOC inks, and acid-free papers that are recycled, totally chlorine-free, or partly composed of nonwood fibers. Books that bear the logo of the FSC (Forest Stewardship Council) use paper taken from forests that have been inspected and certified as meeting the highest standards for environmental and social responsibility. For further information, visit our website at www.cornellpress.edu.

Library of Congress Cataloging-in-Publication Data

A nation divided : diversity, inequality, and community in American society / edited by Phyllis Moen, Donna Dempster-McClain, and Henry A. Walker.
p.   cm.
Includes bibliographical references and index.
ISBN 0-8014-3719-9. -- ISBN 0-8014-8588-6 (pbk.)
1. Social classes--United States.   2. Social Stratification--United States.   3. Pluralism (Social sciences)--United States.   4. United States--Social conditions--1945-   I. Moen, Phyllis.
II. Dempster-McClain, Donna. III. Walker, Henry A.
HN90.S6N37 1999
305.5'0973--dc21   99-15783
                                          CIP

FOR

ROBIN M. WILLIAMS, JR.

Contents

Foreword

I t is always perilous to speculate about the present, but let me suggest nevertheless that we are perhaps traversing a moment in our sociocultural history when this volume's framing terms, diversity and inequality, constitute a particularly urgent interdisciplinary problematic for scholars in the humanities and social sciences. The tension between these terms is exceedingly pronounced in academia—in our own community of scholarship and research, where achieving a form of consensus that respects the diversity of backgrounds, opinions, values, needs, talents, and goals that seek their constitutive places within our collective identity has long been an explicit, clearly articulated objective.

At its core, the institutional question before us seems to replicate straightforwardly the key issue we encounter in a society rent by economic stratification and by the marginalization of the underprivileged: Can we achieve a certain consensus, and thereby a sustained diversity, without fundamental modifications of the communal framework, of the institutional or the social structures that allow us to respect the differences between individuals and groups, that make the patterns of diversity livable and worthy of protection? There is, I submit, no more relevant question for society at large, hence no more relevant question for us in our own social microcosm. The chapter authors are to be commended for their willingness to wrestle with these issues—a willingness that is a further and compelling testimonial to the critical power that the work of Robin M. Williams, Jr., has exercised in our community.

It is fitting that a volume celebrating Williams's work entails a collaboration of scholars of international renown who are bent on reckoning with the forces that shape American society as the twentieth century draws to a predictably uneasy close. It is also fitting that the questions addressed by the chapter authors cover a broad spectrum of reflection that spans the practical and the theoretical, that incorporates quantitative and qualitative analyses, and that reconstructs a dense cluster of concepts and themes that Williams has insisted on apprehending in their complexity and their integrality. All of us should be grateful for the opportunity to engage in the kind of retrospection and stock-taking that this volume affords us.

Philip E. Lewis

Acknowledgments

his volume is testimony to the life-long scholarship of an eminent American sociologist, Robin M. Williams, Jr. Williams joined the Cornell faculty in 1946 and is currently Henry Scarborough Professor of Social Science, Emeritus. His work demonstrates that consensus in American society is based not on homogeneity of cultural values but, rather, on "mutual accommodation." The mutual accommodation theme echoes throughout his research and writing, from *The Reduction of Intergroup Tensions* (1947) to *A Common Destiny: Blacks and American Society* (with Gerald David Jaynes, 1989). It also served as the basis for a 1996 symposium held in his honor at Cornell University.

The chapters in this volume first took shape at that conference. At the symposium and in this volume, prominent social and behavioral scientists pay tribute to his intellectual accomplishments and influence. They report cutting-edge scholarship in areas that Williams's seminal contributions helped to define. We are grateful to the contributors for defining the need for and challenge of mutual accommodation across race, ethnicity, class, gender, sexual preference, and family divides.

We express our gratitude to many people who made the symposium and, therefore, the book a reality. Three Cornell administrators played especially crucial roles in this endeavor. Francille M. Firebaugh, former Dean of the College of Human Ecology, enthusiastically supported the Bronfenbrenner

Life Course Center and campus-wide events such as the symposium. She demonstrated a deep and continuing commitment to crossing boundaries separating departments, disciplines, and colleges to address issues of national concern. Dean of the College of Arts and Sciences, Philip E. Lewis, has promoted and supported sociology not only in his college but also across the campus. Finally, Provost Don Randel's vision for sociology at Cornell is reflected in his support for the development of this volume.

Many others at Cornell and elsewhere made substantial contributions to this project. Marion Van Loan served as the conference coordinator and ably managed symposium logistics together with Sarah Demo, Alice Goh, Erika Pluhar, and others in the Bronfenbrenner Life Course Center. A number of distinguished Cornell scholars participated in the symposium but are not represented in this volume: Ronald L. Breiger, Joan Jacobs Brumberg, Robert Frank, Douglas T. Gurak, Robert L. Harris, Jr., Michael Macy, Victor Nee, and Sidney G. Tarrow. We would like to thank as well participating scholars from outside Cornell: Gerald D. Jaynes, Roy S. Bryce-Laporte, and James Jackson. Crafting the actual volume meant numerous drafts overseen by Joanne Jordan. Our copyeditor, Larry Clarkberg, worked magic in achieving consistency and cohesion. Fran Benson, our editor at Cornell University Press, moved us from a collection of papers to an organic whole. We also thank Kim Langford of Silverchair Science + Communications for overseeing the production of the final product. We appreciate as well the support and endurance of Dick Shore, John McClain, Joyce Walker, and especially Marguerite Williams. Finally, and above all, we gratefully acknowledge the intellectual contributions of Robin M. Williams, Jr., who has been an exceptional colleague, collaborator, mentor, and friend.

A Nation Divided

Introduction

Henry A. Walker, Phyllis Moen, and Donna Dempster-McClain

America is a nation of uncommon racial, ethnic, and cultural *diversity*. It is also characterized by substantial social and economic *inequality*. This book, in an effort to provide a fresh look at diversity, inequality, and community in American society, offers a sociological perspective on the challenges that contemporary intergroup relations pose for life in the twenty-first century.[1]

Diversity and inequality stand at the center of contemporary public policy debates. Can we have one without the other? Will greater diversity accompanying recent changes in the pace and character of immigration benefit or harm the nation? Before the immigration reforms of the 1960s, the overwhelming majority of newcomers were white and European. Today, 80 percent of immigrants come from Asian or Latin American countries. Many Americans express concern that the "new" immigrants will not "fit in." Some even argue that they will disrupt and eventually destroy "the American way of life." This pessimistic view is countered by others who claim that continued immigration is not only beneficial but essential to the nation's vitality.[2]

---

[1] Following Weber (1968), we use the term community to describe a collection of diverse peoples who believe they belong together.

[2] The general populace expresses considerable ambivalence about the role of immigrants in American society. More than three-fourths (77.2%) of respondents to a recent survey agreed that the United States should take stronger measures to stop the inflow of immigrants. On the other hand, more than three-fifths (62.1%) agreed that the presence of immigrants makes Americans more open to (new) ideas and cultures (Davis and Smith 1996).

On the economic front, will rising inequalities further divide and destabilize American society? The evolution of a global marketplace has had paradoxical effects on American society, with the rich getting richer and the poor getting poorer. These developments, along with the concerted efforts of many public officials to reduce social welfare costs, have widened the chasm between those on the lower rungs of the economic ladder and those at the top. Many fear that growing economic disparity divides the national community, fostering not only greater economic inequality but also fueling social unrest and instability.

Diversity and equality are uncomfortable bedfellows. Social and economic inequalities regularly accompany—and are interwoven with—categorical differences among people. Wherever people differ on nominal characteristics (e.g., race, gender), they also possess different amounts of the things societies value. As an example, members of ethnic group A get more or less education, more or less income than those in group B. Charles Tilly (see Chapter 1) calls patterns of this sort *durable inequalities*. Durable inequalities have important effects on life chances and choices, as well as on the prospect for national cohesion and community.

Contributors to this volume examine several key features of American society. Their objectives are (1) to describe and explain durable inequality (i.e., show why diversity and inequality are so often found together), (2) to analyze the connections between durable inequality and social stability, and (3) to discuss strategies designed to reduce or eliminate durable inequality and to promote harmonious social relations.

America: Different by Design?

Can a nation in which inequality is enmeshed with diversity maintain and/or establish a sense of community? The American founders struggled mightily with this question. Their vantage point was the world they had fled—a world in which substantial economic and social inequalities were endemic. Much of the strife that typified European nations in the seventeenth and eighteenth centuries was grounded in ethnic, religious, and class differences.

The founders took two bold steps to ensure that they would live in a far different world. First, they created a society based on a unique set of organizing principles. Its founding documents proclaimed the "natural" equality of its members, possessing "unalienable rights to life, liberty, and the pursuit of happiness." The founders' second initiative was even bolder. They held that the new nation would shelter and nurture a new "race" of people— the Americans—drawing its members from every corner of the globe. In America, every *man* would be free—free to express himself, free of religious favoritism and persecution—and equal. We retain the language of the founders to emphasize a cardinal point: the founders equated Americans with "men," defined as white, free, property owners, aged twenty-one or older. These definitions were disputed *before* they were included in the founding documents and have been subjected since to continuing revision. *Every* debate about admitting new categories of persons to citizenship is a debate about who is to be regarded as an American (see also Bem, Chapter 4).

The founders established the legal equality of (some, but not all) diverse peoples. Any person admitted to citizenship expected—and had the right to demand—civil, social, and political rights (Marshall 1949) equal to those held by any other citizen. Whether the founders took those steps to reduce the potential for intergroup friction and discord is unclear. Obviously, their actions did not eliminate or prevent—and in some case even ensured—the development of durable inequalities across race, class, and gender lines.

As a consequence, the American people are both diverse *and* divided. They differ along common divisions such as race, ethnic heritage, religion, and gender. They differ as well on dimensions that have always existed but have only recently entered the public discourse, dimensions such as sexual orientation and patterns of family life. Many of these categorical differences are linked to durable social and economic inequalities, thus fostering divisiveness. Groups of Americans who have less of some socially valued good than their fellows—whether income or respect—express discontent with their position and, increasingly, disaffection with the American ideal. Their disenchantment has been translated into political action with increasing frequency.[3] This is not to say that American society is coming apart at the seams, but the national fabric may well be in need of repair.

Current divisions exist in part because the founders did not extend legal equality to *all* persons. The denial of legal equality to some categories of persons (e.g., blacks, women, and American Indians) ensured the privileged position of white males as a "protected class." Since its founding, the American nation has come to extend civil, social, and political rights to many groups that were initially denied them. Impetus for the extension of rights lay in the tension between the national ethos and the practical, moral, and legal realities of life in American society. The presence of "Americans" without legal equality created a legitimization crisis—an American dilemma (Myrdal 1944) that called the American creed into question. How does a nation proclaim the "natural" equality of all its members but deny legal equality to some?

---

[3] The persistence and intensity of ethnic politics (e.g., black, Hispanic, or Jewish activism) is extensively documented. More recently, activists who represent other clusters of "different" people (e.g., immigrants and homosexuals but also disenchanted whites like the "Freemen") have appeared on the national scene.

The extension of legal rights to groups that were initially denied them resolved one source of tension in American society. However, the acquisition of full rights of citizenship did not—indeed could not—ensure the elimination of durable inequalities that were a product of that initial legal inequality. Durable inequalities, once established, are difficult to eliminate. As a consequence, some durable inequalities persist despite the legal equality of races, ethnic groups, and women and men.[4]

American society, then, as both diverse and unequal, faces the challenge of fostering a sense of community. Most Americans subscribe to the dictum of *"e pluribus unum"* but differ on how to achieve it. Some presume that reducing or eliminating diversity is the key to establishing social harmony (Schlesinger 1992).[5] Others argue that governments can (and should) encourage *diversity* but eliminate *durable inequality,* thereby creating the conditions for a communal society (e.g., Takaki 1993).

Generalizing across Time and Space

The challenges created by the dynamic tensions between diversity, inequality, and community in American society are not new. Neither are they unique; a number of other nations face these same challenges. Moreover, as globalization proceeds and national and cultural systems converge (Inkeles 1998), the number of nations that face such problems will surely increase.

The founders did not conceive the American Dream in isolation. Two nations—one old and one new—embarked on new beginnings in 1789. Americans declared "diversity, equality, community," and almost simultaneously the French responded *"liberté, égalité, fraternité."* Today, France also confronts the "American" dilemma. France has a heterogeneous population and is saddled with a host of social and economic inequalities that vary with racial and ethnic diversity. French policymakers—like their American counterparts—also debate the possibilities of, and prospects for, maintaining community among persons whose racial and cultural differences are bound together in a system of durable inequalities (see also Williams 1970).

---

[4] Legal equality has not been extended to all groups. Religious groups are a notable exception. We live in an age of great debate about the meaning of religious freedom and about the proper role of religion in politics (Carter 1993). Yet, members of some established religions must restrict their religious practices. As an example, an orthodox Muslim man must restrict himself to one wife in the United States.

[5] Isolation of people by social category (e.g., race) and assimilation satisfy the objective of reducing diversity. It has become fashionable to dismiss those who promote either solution as "racist." Clearly, forced or voluntary separation expresses distaste and intolerance for out-groups. However, categorical discrimination is not required to produce assimilation, as we point out below.

Although there are important differences in the processes that led to the current situations in France and the United States, we will not detail them here. Instead, we focus on their essential similarity. The history of American society makes clear that race, ethnic, and gender divisions have been the rule since the nation's founding. Present-day tensions merely continue a long historical pattern. We note as well that France was wracked with territorial and factional disputes for a substantial period after the Revolution of 1789. The "stable French national identity" (Skocpol 1979) that seems strained by contemporary ethnic relations is as illusory as the idea of a coherent American identity (Witte 1996). As Gerard Noiriel (1996) points out in his analysis of *The French Melting Pot,* old-timers and politicians regularly imagine a much more homogeneous past than ever actually existed. Thus, the United States and France illustrate the processes that link categorical differences, quantitative inequalities, and social unrest. Although durable inequalities tied to ethnic, race, religious, and gender differences are particularly salient examples of such disparities, the processes can extend to other differences that are less "visible."

World historical patterns presage a global society in which durable inequalities based on race and cultural differences are likely to spread to societies that have had largely homogeneous populations. Immigration may trigger the development of durable inequalities, but it is not the sole determinant of the patterns of culturally or racially based inequalities found in contemporary America. As a consequence, whether American society can establish or maintain community also has implications for increasingly diverse societies across the globe.

The Problem of Social Integration

Concerns about the effects of diversity and inequality on social stability illuminate a general sociological issue—the problem of *social integration* (Parsons 1951; Williams 1970). How is society possible (Simmel [1908] 1971)? How can a collection of individuals with different skills, abilities, and interests create an enduring collective life? How does a society achieve social integration (Parsons 1951)? These questions motivated the founders of modern sociology and intrigued their philosopher ancestors.

The first generation of sociologists did not agree about the processes that establish or maintain integrated communities, but they had clear ideas about the forms they take. Early sociologists identified two ideal-typical patterns of cohesive social relationships or societies. Durkheim ([1893] 1964) described them as systems of mechanical and organic solidarity; Tönnies (1957) called them *Gemeinschaft* and *Gesellschaft.* Weber (1968) used the terms "communal and associative relationships." Societies that exhibit mechanical solidarity

(*Gemeinschaft* or communal societies) are generally small and made up of individuals who share a number of personal characteristics, attitudes, beliefs, and so on. Shared interests, beliefs, and actions are presumed to provide the social glue that holds such societies together. Societies characterized by organic solidarity (*Gesellschaft* or associative societies) are larger and contain more complex combinations of persons who differ with respect to a variety of individual characteristics, normative systems, attitudes, and so on. These more complex societies are held together by the *interdependence* of the individuals, groups, and institutions within them.

Those early ideas may have overstated the differences in the processes that hold societies (of any type) together. For example, it is clear that interdependence is an important source of cohesion for groups and societies of any size. It is also clear that similarities among group members on a variety of characteristics contribute (either directly or indirectly) to integration (i.e., communality) within groups or societies. Current ideas about how societies composed of diverse (and unequal) peoples can create community are based in, and consistent with, long-standing sociological analyses. Theory and research on ethnic and gender relations illustrate those ideas.

Ethnic Differences and Social Integration

Durable inequalities organized around ethnic differences are the rule in ethnically (or racially) diverse societies. Such inequalities are also correlated with ethnic tensions and conflicts. Sociologists and political scientists offer a number of arguments to explain the relationship between ethnic inequality and social conflict and disruption (Hannan 1979; Hechter 1975; Lipset and Rokkan 1967; Olzak 1992). Others suggest how ethnic harmony can be created or restored in culturally diverse societies (see also Williams, Chapter 15). The *assimilationist* and *pluralist* models are especially germane to our discussion.

Social scientists use the term "assimilation" to describe both a process and its outcomes. Following Horowitz (1975), we define "assimilation" as a social process that results in the "erasing of group boundaries."[6] *Amalgamation* and *incorporation* are two distinct outcomes of assimilation processes (Horowitz 1975; Park and Burgess [1921] 1969). A nation or society that achieves amalgamation is one in which there exists a complete blending of dissimilar groups. The product of amalgamation may contain elements of each constituent group, but the amalgam is unlike any of the groups that entered the process. The "melting pot" ideal reflects the idea of amalga-

[6] See Milton M. Gordon (1964) for a thorough discussion of assimilation and the complexity of assimilation processes.

mation. On the other hand, societies that undergo incorporation are marked by a result that closely resembles (but may not be identical to) one of the constituent groups. The dominance of Anglo cultural forms in the United States is an example of incorporation. Neither differences in power nor invidious discrimination are necessary to produce incorporation, but discrimination and substantial differences in the relative power of assimilating groups can ensure it (see also Walker's arguments in Chapter 3).

The pluralist model describes societies in which distinct (racial or cultural) elements maintain their unique character but have equal civil, social, and political rights. As an example, distinct subcultural groups may share governmental institutions including national parliaments, universal taxing authorities, and common military services. However, each subcultural group may also maintain separate cultural, political, and economic institutions (e.g., ethnic religions, political parties, or occupational niches).

Gender Differences and Social Integration

The concepts and models used to describe ethnic differences can also be applied to the distinctive life course experiences of women and men. Consider, for example, occupational career paths, typically reflecting men's, not women's, experiences (Bem 1993; Moen 1998). The very notion of a "career," of moving through a series of related jobs over the life course, reflects a typically male biography.

As growing numbers of women (from every race, ethnic, age, and class category) began to enter, remain in, or reenter the work force, they were expected to become "like men," that is, to downplay family or other nonwork interests or obligations. Women were expected to follow an *assimilative* and, specifically, *incorporative* model of career development and progression. Sandra Lipsitz Bem (Chapter 4) raises questions about the social integration of both women and sexual minorities. She questions the incorporative form of assimilation and suggests alternative models. C. Wright Mills (1959) pointed out that a different arrangement existed in the past. Before the industrial revolution most people worked in either agriculture or other family businesses. Though there were divisions by age and gender, everyone in the household was engaged in productive work.

With industrialization, the new work career became synonymous with the male breadwinner template, although young women (and women of all ages in financial need) were also in the labor force. *Unpaid work*—domestic household labor, family caregiving, community volunteer participation—was rendered marginal to the "business" of society and, consequently, the business of mainstream social science. Such unpaid work has been disproportionately accomplished by women, perpetuating both women's marginal status and durable gender inequalities.

The heterogeneity embodied in women's life experiences (e.g., Moen, Dempster-McClain, and Williams 1989, 1992) and the distinctiveness of women's life paths compared with men's (e.g., Han and Moen 1999) demonstrate the difficulty of assimilating women into male templates. It also reframes the central question of this volume: shall we continue (or return to) an incorporative model of occupational careers or open ourselves to multiple patterns consistent with a pluralist model? The issue is how to integrate occupational, family, and community role pathways (for men as well as women) without perpetuating durable economic, status, and time inequalities based on gender.

Implications

The ongoing debates about managing diversity and "multiculturalism" can be described in assimilationist and pluralist terms. One side presumes that achieving social integration and harmony depends on eliminating as many differences as possible (i.e., creating similarity, see Parsons 1951; Schlesinger 1992). "Real" Americans are those who conform to some set of shared (but constrained) personal characteristics, beliefs, values, and behaviors. The alternative "valuing diversity" argument espouses pluralism. Its proponents presume that social harmony rests on recognizing and "privileging" the unique beliefs, values, and so on, of distinct cultural (or racial) groups.

Under the assimilationist model, social integration and a sense of community depend on minimizing differences. Individual inequalities (e.g., in income and social status) can be tolerated because they do not function as bases for social conflict among groups organized around nominal differences. On the other hand, the pluralist model permits—indeed requires by definition—group differences. Under this model, social integration depends on the elimination of *inequality* but not *difference*. But in practice, pluralism implies differences in beliefs, values, motivations, and behaviors that are typically reflected in concrete inequalities such as income or educational attainments. Consequently, the central issue that both assimilationists and pluralists must address is the persistent diversity of the American people and the inequalities that accompany it. It is this issue that occupies center stage in each of the following chapters.

Plan of the Volume

This book is divided into four parts. Part One, Diversity and Inequality, discusses the nature of durable inequalities, their origins, processes that increase their stability, and their connections to communal social relations. In Chapter 1, Charles Tilly defines durable inequalities and discusses the issue in broad organizational terms. He also analyzes the mechanisms that produce inequality and suggests some possible ways to change "durable" differences in opportunities and resources.

In Chapter 2, Melvin L. Kohn challenges Herrnstein and Murray's controversial ideas about genetic determinants of cognitive skills and their connections to durable inequalities. He presents a compelling alternative view that stresses social determinants of cognitive skills.

Henry A. Walker begins Chapter 3 by arguing that the connection between durable inequality and social stability is the fundamental issue that underlies current debates about ways of managing diversity. He argues that the choice between cultural assimilation and cultural pluralism is a false one and that decoupling diversity and inequality can be a major step in reducing the prejudices and tensions that permeate American society.

In Chapter 4, Sandra Lipsitz Bem questions the idea that the "new" American must reflect the beliefs, values, and attitudes of the "standard" (i.e., heterosexual, white male). Bem provides a thought-provoking examination of discrimination against women and sex and gender minorities, including lesbians and gay men. Bem's arguments question the value of the incorporation model of assimilation for these groups. She argues that the nation will never truly come to terms with diversity in a fair and inclusive way unless it recognizes that inequality based on discrimination frequently hides itself behind a facade of tolerant neutrality.

Part Two, The New Demography of Durable Inequality, focuses on the social and spatial demography of durable inequality. The key point of the chapters in this section is that, in systems characterized by durable inequalities based on race or ethnic differences, *social* location is often isomorphic with *geographical* location.

In Chapter 5, Charles Hirschman and C. Matthew Snipp describe recent patterns of socioeconomic attainments among seven race/ethnic groups in the United States and examine the extent to which members of the various groups have achieved economic integration.

Richard Alba, John Logan, Wenquan Zhang, and Brian J. Stults in Chapter 6 examine patterns of residence among several large, rapidly growing immigrant groups. For the first time in American history, immigrants are establishing first residences in the suburbs. These findings pose challenges to spatial-assimilation theory, which argues that suburbanization is evidence of social and economic progress along the path to full assimilation. The new trend means that, for the current generation of Americans, "strangers" are indeed moving next door (cf. Williams, Dean, and Suchman 1964).

In Chapter 7, William Julius Wilson examines the importance of spatial segregation to the creation and maintenance of durable inequality. Based on intensive ethnographic and survey research in Chicago, Wilson's work shows clearly the effects of the inner city's transformation from an area with plentiful employment opportunities to an economic wasteland with few jobs.

David L. Brown and Marlene A. Lee focus on metropolitan-nonmetropolitan differences in Chapter 8, describing disparities in employment and poverty. They argue that these spatial differences must be considered in policy discussions (such as welfare reform) if we are to reduce economic disparities in American society.

Part Three, Durable Inequality in American Institutions, examines contemporary trends and problems in a variety of institutions, including education, family, mass media, and religion. In Chapter 9, Ronald G. Ehrenberg, Donna S. Rothstein, and Robert B. Olsen focus on the relationship between the availability of historically black colleges and universities and rates of college admission and graduation among black students.

Chapters 10 and 11 focus on the role that military service plays in the social integration of diverse groups and in the creation of inequalities. Charles Moskos and John Sibley Butler describe the U.S. Army's successful efforts to achieve racial integration, with blacks amassing a record of achievement that is unmatched elsewhere. Based on their analysis of race relations in the army, they offer twelve concrete suggestions for reducing race inequality and improving race relations in civilian settings. Glen H. Elder, Jr., and Christopher Chan analyze the experiences of male veterans of World War II as a source of diversity in their life trajectories and corresponding inequality in their attainments.

The next three chapters look to the future in unusual ways. Their approaches differ with other scholarly writings on their respective topics, with other chapters in this book, and with each other. J. Milton Yinger in Chapter 12 defines religion and consensus and asks, "Is religion a source of consensus?"

Judith Treas in Chapter 13 shows that demographic and social developments have challenged the hegemony of the "traditional" American family, creating unprecedented diversity in living arrangements and family life. Current discussions about the legitimacy of alternative family forms mirror debates about characteristics of the ideal American family. Treas concludes that consensus regarding the nature of families does not require similarity and exclusion.

In Chapter 14, James Lowell Gibbs, Jr., describes the significance of visual images in shaping Americans' perceptions of one another. He reports data that show strong differences in the television viewing patterns of blacks and whites and analyzes the contributions of television and movies to valuing difference.

Part Four, the Afterword, contains two chapters that look backward in order to look forward. Chapter 15 showcases the half-century–old insights of Robin M. Williams, Jr., (1947), insights that are as germane today as they were in the 1940s. In Chapter 16, Peter I. Rose reviews Williams's classic work, *The Reduction of Intergroup Tensions*, drawing on it and Williams's later work to point to similarities between contemporary America and the America that existed following the Second World War. Both Rose and Williams underscore the global significance of the issues we have addressed in an American context. While American society has drawn strength from multiple, and sometimes overlapping, identities, when divisions harden, the possibilities of building and sustaining community become increasingly remote.

PART ONE

DIVERSITY AND INEQUALITY

CHAPTER ONE

Durable Inequality

Charles Tilly

Let us not ask "What causes human inequality in general?" but "How do categorical inequalities form, change, and disappear?" Because all social relations involve fleeting, fluctuating inequalities, let us concentrate on durable inequalities, those that last from one social interaction to the next, with special attention to those that persist over whole careers, lifetimes, and organizational histories.

Let us concentrate, furthermore, on distinctly bounded categories such as female/male, aristocrat/plebeian, citizen/foreigner, religious affiliation, ethnic origin, or race rather than continua such as rich/poor, tall/short, ugly/beautiful, and so on. Bounded categories deserve special attention because they provide clearer evidence for the operation of durable inequality, because their boundaries do crucial organizational work, and because categorical differences actually account for much of what ordinary observers take to be results of variation in individual talent or effort.

The central argument runs like this: Large, significant inequalities among human beings correspond mainly to categorical differences such as black-white, male-female, citizen-foreigner, or Muslim-Jew rather than to individual differences in attributes or propensities. Even where they use

This paper summarizes analyses presented at length in my *Durable Inequality* (Berkeley: University of California Press, 1998) and borrows extensively from early versions of that text. I am grateful to the Press for permission to publish the borrowed material.

ostensibly biological markers, such categories always depend on extensive social organization, belief, and enforcement. Durable inequality among categories arises because people who hold power in reward- and punishment-allocating organizations solve pressing organizational problems by means of categorical distinctions. Inadvertently or otherwise, those people set up systems of social closure, exclusion, and control. Multiple parties—not all of them powerful, some of them even victims of exploitation—then acquire stakes in those solutions. Variation in the form and durability of inequality therefore depends chiefly on the nature of the organization(s) involved, previous social locations of the categories, character of the organizational problems, and configurations of interested parties.

Because the argument is unfamiliar and complex, it may help to lay out its major elements and their causal connections even before defining crucial terms. The following list will serve as a preliminary map of the wilderness this chapter will explore:

1. My goal is to identify structural roots of inequality. First I define categorical inequality.
2. I then build a vocabulary of social structures (chains, hierarchies, triads, organizations, and categorical pairs).
3. Next, I analyze social transactions, comparing the degree of scripting with the amount of shared local knowledge each type of transaction requires.
4. Using these vocabularies, finally, I describe how and why organizations form, and how they institute categorical inequality. The mechanisms of exploitation and opportunity-hoarding install inequality, while the mechanisms of emulation and adaptation extend its influence.
5. I argue that these mechanisms—exploitation, opportunity-hoarding, emulation, and adaptation—favor organizations having a particular structure: the combination of paired categories with hierarchies. Widespread use of this particular structure accounts for most durable social inequality.
6. I give examples of how various organizations' use of categorical pairs have helped create durable inequalities.
7. I argue that inequality seeming to stem from people's individual differences actually results largely from organizations' institutionalization of categorical pairs.
8. It follows that reduction of racist attitudes will have little impact on durable inequality; the introduction of new organizational forms will have a larger impact.

Whatever else it accomplishes, my presentation should make clear what is at issue in such an organizational view of inequality-producing mechanisms. At a minimum, it challenges other analysts to clarify causal mechanisms implied by their own preferred explanations of durable inequality and to search for evidence that those causal mechanisms are actually operating.

Categorical Inequality

Although the word "organization" may call to mind firms, governments, schools, and similar formal, hierarchical structures, I mean the analysis to encompass all sorts of well-bounded clusters of social relations in which occupants of at least one position have the right to commit collective resources to activities reaching across the boundary. Organizations thus include corporate kin groups, households, religious sects, bands of mercenaries, and many local communities. Durable inequality arises in all of them, and all of them at times incorporate categorical distinctions originating in adjacent organizations.

Humans invented categorical inequality millennia ago and have applied it to a wide range of social situations. People establish systems of categorical inequality, however inadvertently, chiefly by means of two causal mechanisms:

First, where powerful, connected people command resources from which they draw significantly increased returns by coordinating the effort of outsiders whom they exclude from the full value added by that effort; call this mechanism *exploitation.*

Second, when members of a categorically bounded network acquire access to a resource that is valuable, renewable, subject to monopoly, supportive of network activities, and enhanced by the network's modus operandi; name this mechanism *opportunity-hoarding.*

The two mechanisms obviously parallel each other, but people who lack great power can pursue the second if encouraged, tolerated, or ignored by the powerful. Often the two parties gain complementary, if unequal, benefits from jointly excluding others.

Two further mechanisms cement such arrangements in place: *emulation,* the copying of established organizational models and/or transplantation of existing social relations from one setting to another, and *adaptation,* elaboration of daily routines such as mutual aid, political influence, courtship, and information gathering on the basis of categorically unequal structures. Exploitation and opportunity-hoarding favor the installation of categorical inequality, while emulation and adaptation generalize its influence.

A certain kind of inequality therefore becomes prevalent over a large population in two complementary ways. Either

1. The categorical pair in question—male-female, black-white, citizen-noncitizen, and so forth—operates in organizations that control major welfare-affecting resources, and its effects spread from there, or

2. it repeats in a great many similar organizations, regardless of their power.

In the first case, work-producing and coercion-wielding organizations—corporations and states, plantations and mercenary forces, textile mills and drug rings, depending on the context—take pride of place because they ordinarily control the largest concentrations of deployable resources within large populations. In some settings of ideological hegemony, nevertheless, religious organizations and their own categorical distinctions have similar effects on inequality around them.

In the second case, households, kin groups, and local communities hold crucial positions because within a given population they (1) form and change according to similar principles and (2) strongly influence biological and social reproduction. Gender and age distinctions, for example, do not ordinarily separate lineages from one another, but their repetition in many lineages lends them influence throughout the population. The basic inequality-generating mechanisms, nevertheless, operate in similar fashions over a wide variety of organizational settings.

The Structure of Social Relations

Categorical inequality represents a special case of categorical relations in general. It is a particular but spectacularly potent combination within a small set of network configurations that have reappeared millions of times at different scales, in different settings, throughout human history. No one has codified our knowledge of these configurations. Provisional nominees for the basic set include the *chain,* the *hierarchy,* the *triad,* the *organization,* and the *categorical pair:*

1. The chain consists of two or more similar and connected ties between social sites—persons, groups, identities, networks, or something else.
2. Hierarchies are those sorts of chains in which the connections are asymmetrical and the sites systematically unequal.
3. Triads consist of three sites having similar ties to each other.
4. Organizations are well-bounded sets of ties in which at least one site has the right to establish ties that bind members of internal ties across the boundary.
5. A categorical pair consists of a socially significant boundary and at least one tie between sites on either side of it.

(We might actually reduce the basic set to three, because a hierarchy is simply a special type of chain and, as we shall see, an organization is an over-

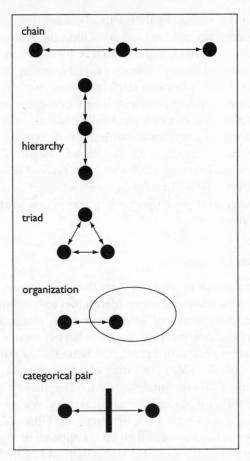

chain

hierarchy

triad

organization

categorical pair

Figure 1.1   Basic social configurations.

grown categorical pair; for present purposes, however, it helps to distinguish all five.) Figure 1.1 shows the five elementary forms.

I regard these network configurations as social inventions: perhaps developed incrementally by trial and error, no doubt reinvented independently many times, but when recognized more or less deliberately installed as means of coordinating social life. I may be wrong: An alternative line of thought, well represented by Fredrik Barth, regards all existing social structures not as fundamental elements of social life but as variable by-products of generative principles (Barth 1981). For Barth, the social structures we identify as kin groups, community networks, and the like resemble instantaneous distributions of vehicles on a stretch of superhighway: coherent, exhibiting recurrent regularities, but not entities in themselves because their structure derives entirely from the actions and interactions of individual drivers.

If Barth's view is correct, my elementary forms could be recurrently emergent outcomes of more elementary social relations. Triads, for example, could emerge simply because stable pairs tend to recruit third parties jointly. Hierarchies could, in principle, simply generalize patterns of asymmetrical interaction. If methodological individualists could specify and validate single-actor decision rules constituting sufficient conditions for the creation of chains, hierarchies, triads, paired categories, and organizations, they would make strong claims for their favored reductionism. Fortunately, it matters little for present purposes whether we are dealing with inventions or emergents; once they are in place, people use them for a wide variety of relational work.

Complex Configurations

Configurations multiply beyond their elementary forms: chains proliferate into long chains; two-step hierarchies into ten-step hierarchies; triads into dense networks of interconnection; categorical pairs into triplets; and so on. Anyone who works in a civil service, for example, becomes familiar not just with the relation between her rank and adjacent ranks but with a whole ladder consisting of asymmetrical connections.

Configurations also compound with each other; many hierarchies, as we shall see abundantly, incorporate categorical pairs, as when physicians are white males and nurses who work for them are Filipinas. An imaginary social structure compounding the elements appears in Figure 1.2, which connects hierarchies ABD and ABF, triads BDF and BEF, chain DFG, and categorical pair CD, then through command position A relates the entire organization—the bounded network—to external site X. In this imaginary case, site A enjoys the right to establish binding contracts between the whole and outside actors.

Whether or not these five network elements turn out to be the elementary particles of social life, they recur very widely, doing characteristically different forms of social work. Their recurrence poses a triple analytic challenge: to detect those characteristic differences among structures, to identify their causal regularities, and to investigate conditions for the structures' concatenation.

Strong and Weak Ties

First, consider characteristic differences among the structures. Chains, hierarchies, triads, organizations, and categorical pairs each have their own distinctive operating patterns and consequences. Mark Gra-

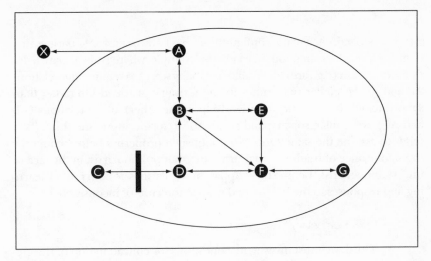

Figure 1.2 Combined configurations in an imaginary social structure (see text for description).

novetter's distinction (1985, 1995) of strong ties (those defined by substantial emotion, obligation, range, and durability) from weak ties (more fleeting, neutral, narrow, and discretionary) contrasts two of the basic structures. The distinction gains its importance from the general association of strong ties with small, dense network clumps containing many triads (three-party clusters) and the association of weak ties with long, single-stranded chains. On the average, strong ties sustain solidarity, trust, and commitment while circulating a good deal of redundant information. Weak ties break more easily, but also transmit distant information more efficiently.

Granovetter's famous application concerns job-finding, where weak ties play an exceptional role because they connect job seekers with a much wider range of opportunities, on the average, than do strong ones. Although subsequent research has shown that medium-weak ties, with their modicum of commitment, provide better-quality information than very weak ties, the broad distinction between effects of strong and weak ties has held up well to empirical scrutiny (Erickson 1996; see also Anderson 1974; Campbell, Marsden, and Hurlbert 1986; Campbell and Rosenfeld 1986; Corcoran, Datcher, and Duncan 1980; De Schweinitz 1932; Holzer 1987; Laumann 1973; Lin 1982, Lin and Dumin 1986; Marsden and Hurlbert 1988; Montgomery 1994; Murray, Rankin, and Magill 1981; Simon and Warner 1992). Weak ties occupy important places in all sorts of large-scale coordination. Without weak ties, for example, most people would acquire very little information about current politics, medical innovations, or investment opportunities.

Causal Regularities

Second, each of the configurations has its own causal regularities that demand individual attention. In triads, for example, where B and C have a distinctive relation (e.g., are close friends), stability seems to require that relations AB and AC be similar (e.g., subordination, rivalry, or friendship rather than subordination in one case and friendship in the other). If two relations (AB and AC) are similar, solitary, and symmetrical, furthermore, the third (BC) tends to assume the same form. No doubt such properties help account for the significance of triads in social structures that promote trust in the face of uncertainty and risk. Behind these apparent regularities lie both mutual learning and responses to the heightened transaction costs of inconsistency.

How Elementary Structures Combine

Third, we must investigate conditions for concatenation of the elementary structures: which ones fit together effectively under what circumstances, whether the presence of one sort of structure promotes the formation of the other, how many of a given kind an organization can contain without starting to collapse. As evidence concerning diminishing returns from large spans of control suggests, for example, very extensive hierarchies seem to negate their coordination advantages with rising transaction costs, and to invite subversion, shirking, or rebellion as well. No doubt other structural constraints limit the number of categorical pairs any organization of a given size can maintain, as well as viable combinations of categorical pairs with hierarchies. Categorical boundaries requiring mutual avoidance of parties on either side of the boundary except for ritualized encounters, for instance, most likely wreak havoc if installed in the upper reaches of extensive hierarchies.

Social Shims

Such a description of configurations, to be sure, freezes them into ice sculptures when in real life they more greatly resemble recurrent patterns seen in a waterfall. It summarizes different tendencies that we observers might notice in fast-moving transactions among social sites. In fact, the ties in question shift among configurations, as when actors in a chain invoke or abolish a categorical distinction among themselves (friendly neighbors, for example, forget about or suddenly react to racial barriers that lie between them) and members of a hierarchy temporarily behave as a fairly equal triad (lieutenant, sergeant, and private, for example, defend each other against the enemy's fire). Any generalizations we make about these configurations necessarily take the form "*In so far* as ties among sites form triads . . ."

Recall a crucial point about social processes, including those that produce durable inequality. Designed, prescribed, and inherited social structures never work quite as their participants imagine they should or will. People make incessant mistakes, interactions produce unanticipated consequences, and in many circumstances if everyone actually followed the ostensible rules either organizational disaster or an utter standstill would occur. A master cabinetmaker once came to install in my home a set of handsome bookcases he had built in his shop. With the shelves and hardware, his assistant brought in a large sack. I looked in the sack and saw several score small, thin wooden wedges. The conversation continued:

"What are those?"

"Shims."

"What for?"

"Well, it's clear you're not a cabinetmaker. We use shims because there's no such thing as a straight wall or a straight piece of wood. Shims straighten up the connections. Otherwise there'd be gaps all up and down the backs of the bookcases, and they might fall off the wall."

In human interaction, people constantly avert disasters and standstills by inserting social shims in the form of self-corrections, reassurances, clarifications, compensatory actions, and mutual aid. Social processes are worse than bookcases, however: because they keep moving, no social shim stays in place very long. Social structures stick together, more or less, precisely because improvisation never ceases.

Social Transactions

Figure 1.3 captures some of the variability involved. It represents two dimensions along which social transactions differ: the degree of common knowledge participants in the transactions deploy and the extent of scripting already available jointly to the parties for such transactions. Scripts range from such general configurations as triads and paired categories to the specific formulas people adopt to withdraw money from a bank. Just as pianists recognize and perform standard scales but also the intricate figures of a Beethoven sonata, interacting humans run from virtually universal routines to those activated by just one social situation.

Similarly, local knowledge extends from tacit understandings concerning connections among different locations in a city acquired by long-term residents to the memory of previous conversations that frames today's lunch between two old friends. Scripts provide models for participation in particular classes of social relations; shared local knowledge provides means of giving variable contents to those social relations. Among our

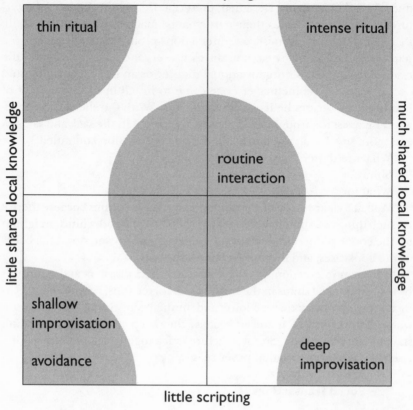

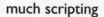

Figure 1.3 Scripting and local knowledge in social ties.

basic mechanisms, emulation relies chiefly on scripting, while adaptation relies heavily on accumulation of local knowledge.

Sociologists enamored of norms and values have sometimes considered scripts to lie at the center of all durable social processes, with socialization committing newcomers to scripts and sanctions minimizing deviation from scripts. Such a view involves astonishing confidence in the efficiency and effectiveness of scripting. Because local conditions vary and change incessantly and because social interaction repeatedly involves error, unanticipated consequences, repair, and readjustment, no organization whose members followed scripts to the best of their ability could actually survive; experienced bureaucrats and artisans, for example, know they can block any effective action in their organizations by following official rules meticulously. Scripts alone promote uniformity; knowledge alone promotes flexibility; their combination promotes flexibility within established limits.

Shallow Improvisation and Thin Ritual

With little scripting and local knowledge available, actors either avoid each other or follow *shallow improvisations* such as the maneuvers pedestrians on a crowded sidewalk adopt in order to pass each other with a minimum of bumping and blocking. Scripting can be extensive and common knowledge meager, as when a master of ceremonies directs participants to applaud, rise, sit, and exit; let us entitle this circumstance *thin ritual*. Here only weak ties bind participants. Thin ritual absorbs high transaction costs for the social results that it accomplishes; most people reserve it for very special occasions and escape it when they can.

Deep Improvisation

Where common knowledge is extensive and scripting slight, we enter the deep improvisation of professional jazz, intense sociability, soccer football, passionate sexual relations, and playful conversation. Extensive common knowledge, strong ties, and frequent improvisation reinforce each other. Participants in deep improvisation often draw on relevant scripts, as when a saxophonist inserts a fragment of "The Star-Spangled Banner" in the midst of a frenetic riff or old lovers laughingly enact the rituals of formal courtship. But in such instances the script becomes part of a private joke recast by local knowledge.

Intense Ritual

Intense ritual occupies the diagram's upper right corner—broad common knowledge plus extensive scripting—on the ground that in rich routines such as weddings, coming-of-age ceremonies, military reviews, and college commencements, the participants (however reluctantly) are affirming shared identities and mutual commitments by the temporary abandonment of improvisation or (more often) the doubling of public scripting with private improvisation in the form of nudges, winks, grimaces, and sotto voce comments. Anyone who imagines that intense ritual always expresses or engenders solidarity, however, should remember this: a funeral that revives old grievances and the impeccable but subtly aggressive performance by veteran dance partners who have grown to detest each other both illustrate the possible cohabitation of intense ritual with hostile interaction.

Routine Interaction

Routine interaction happens in the midsection, combining some scripting with significant local knowledge. As people carry on their social lives in firms, stores, schools, and neighborhoods, they deploy scripted routines such as greetings, payment procedures, apologies for rule violations, and expressions of personal concern, but they temper such scripts with locally applicable shared knowledge—including the shared knowledge encrusted within the scripts of a common language. Because scripts themselves repeatedly misfire, producing unanticipated consequences and minor disasters, people use local knowledge to repair social interactions as they go. Any representation of social life as consisting of norm following and deviance alone therefore misses the knowledge-using and knowledge-generating improvisation that makes effective social interaction possible.

Similarly, the common idea that workplaces ordinarily contain two competing sets of rules, practices, or social relations (the one "official" or "formal," the other "unofficial" or "informal") misses the point: it contrasts scripts with shared local knowledge, when the two necessarily intertwine (Stinchcombe 1990). Organizations typically herd social interaction toward the middle ground in the scripting/local knowledge space, providing enough scripts that relations have broadly predictable rhythms and consequences, but enough local knowledge that members can improvise effectively in the face of unexpected threats and opportunities.

How Social Relations Are Established

Like learning a language, establishment of new social relations often follows a zigzag pattern within the space: beginning with a rigidly followed but narrow script, accumulating local knowledge, improvising by means of that knowledge, making mistakes and discovering unanticipated consequences, correcting those mistakes and fixing the consequences until a precarious modus vivendi emerges, moving back to acquire new scripts, then broadening common knowledge until at times the newcomer participates in the thick, common-knowledge–assuming rituals of solidarity. By that time, any participant who follows the script rigidly—speaks with schoolbook grammar, observes every formality, works by rule—actually disrupts local social relations, unless she does so as a recognizable joke or as an understood way of controlling outsiders. Scripting and common knowledge operate dialectically, modifying each other so that each script bends under the weight of local knowledge but also limits the loci that share local knowledge, thus making the knowledge common.

By no means do all learning processes complete the arc from shallow improvisation through more extensive scripts to deep improvisation. Staying in an unfamiliar city among speakers of an unfamiliar language, I have often found myself acquiring rudimentary familiarity with a map, public transportation, and crucial phrases while working out a simple set of interaction routines for survival through the day. I find myself rehearsing the relevant scripts anxiously in anticipation of the next encounter, then getting by on that combination of a meager script with dangerously restricted local knowledge. Similarly, many an immigrant works up just enough involvement with the world outside her immigrant niche to avoid serious trouble when navigating that world. Again, reliance on scripts can be disruptive. The presence of just one important person who lacks familiarity with local language and practices can drive an entire work group or dinner party into the uncomfortable zone of stilted scripting and cramped improvisation. Because transaction costs absorb considerable resources and entail significant risks, acquisition of scripts and local knowledge generally occurs in discontinuous increments, and often stops somewhere near the lower left corner of our diagram.

How Social Structures Rely on Scripts and Common Knowledge

Both scripts and common knowledge vary from particular to general, from local to ubiquitous. Gender relations involve scripts that transcend any particular organization as well as shared understandings that people transfer unreflectively from one setting to another. One of the great secrets of categorical inequality is that it provides (for organizational work) the routines, understandings, and their justifications that organizational participants have acquired in other settings. Yet each durable social setting produces both (1) some unique scripts and common knowledge, however trivial, available only to its habitués, and (2) some local variations on the scripts and common knowledge attached to widely relevant categorical distinctions according to such principles as age, race, ethnicity, class, locality, and gender. Marge Kirk, concrete-truck driver, summed it up this way:

> It takes a lot of energy just to stand your ground—balancing male egos with your right to survive. I wanted a job, I wanted to be a good truck driver, I wanted to be able to pull my weight as a driver. So years have passed now and somehow I survived. The guys are beginning to see me as a real human, not just a broad with legs and boobs. And the dispatcher has passed to the point of seeing me as a driver, I think. (Schroedel 1985, 156–57)

Marge Kirk, a woman in an overwhelmingly male job, had worked her way up by means of incessant improvisation to a unique combination of scripts and local knowledge.

Our five configurations—chains, hierarchies, triads, organizations, and categorical pairs—provide widely available scripts. They rely on common knowledge—for example, shared understandings of how superiors and inferiors signal their relations to each other. They also generate common knowledge as people use them, for example, by relying on third parties in triads to patch up disagreements within any particular pair. Together, familiar scripts and accumulated common knowledge lower transaction costs of whatever activities an organization carries on. They thereby raise relative costs of shifting to some other structure of social relations. Managers of organizations ordinarily adopt the five configurations in various combinations as devices for managing social relations within the diagram's midsection, where some scripting and common knowledge combine.

How the configurations work, indeed, depends importantly on where in the two-dimensional space they fall. When goldsmiths who have common knowledge of their craft work together for the first time, they may use familiar scripts to establish hierarchies of reward and deference, but they can start to produce golden articles without extensive ritual. New cadets in military academies, however, ordinarily lack familiarity with both organizational structure and local lore; their superiors make up for those deficiencies by intensive scripting and drumming in of common knowledge. Only later do superiors let military recruits improvise within the limits set by well-known scripts.

Construction of Organizations

Activating the emulation mechanism, managers of organizations often accomplish their work by importing configurations—particular hierarchies, chains, triads, and categorical pairs—with which new organizational members already have considerable experience and therefore common knowledge. Organizations build in educational and class differences with their established patterns of deference, existing links among people from common ethnic origins, triads defined as "teams" recruited from other organizations, and categorical pairs such as physician/nurse or professional/layman. Such borrowing of categorical pairs, as we shall see in detail, plays a crucial part in durable patterns of inequality.

Structure-borrowing managers gain the advantage of low startup costs for new chunks of organization. But they also take on meanings, relational routines, and external connections whose features and consequences they cannot always control. Many a store manager has hired a few hard-working immigrants for a particular niche only to discover that part of his store has become a patronage network and he an unwitting patron. Many a new lawyer has learned that she will never make partner in her chosen firm because a hidden but powerful hierarchy separates graduates of elite law schools from the rest.

Each configuration, and each combination of configurations, no doubt conforms to its own regularities. I am pursuing the combination of paired categories with hierarchies on the hypothesis that exploitation, opportunity-hoarding, emulation, and adaptation converge to favor such a social arrangement and that its widespread insertion in organizations accounts for a major share of all durable inequality. Regularities peculiar to this pair of configurations include the generation of boundary-maintaining beliefs about differences between actors on either side of the boundary, diversion of some returns from exploitation to boundary maintenance, and many more to come.

Building Blocks of Organizations

A comprehensive relational sociology requires generalization of this analytic mode. Construction of organizations, for example, entails significant effort: delineation of an exclusive perimeter, creation of at least one effective center of authority within that perimeter, and establishment of controls over interactions spanning the perimeter. Ronald Coase spurred a revival of organizational analysis in economics by pointing out that without some significant gains from such bounding and installation of hierarchy, the very existence of firms posed an embarrassing theoretical problem for market-oriented economists (Coase 1992). Hierarchies, in Coase's formulation, reduce the transaction costs of complex interactions.

As Coase did not say, monopolization of resources underlies organizations. "All organizations," remarks Göran Ahrne, "seem to be founded around a set of collective resources, and access to these resources motivates people to join organizations and to stay with them" (Ahrne 1996, 112–13; see also Ahrne 1994). Ahrne leaves the impression that all clustered resources generate organizations, but that is not the case. The high seas teem with wonderful resources, but their (literal and figurative) fluidity has repeatedly frustrated human efforts to create bounded, exclusive organizations for exploitation of those resources; current struggles over fishing, struggles which threaten the economies of regions as far apart as Newfoundland and Senegal, stem from the easy entry of industrial fishing vessels into almost all the world's abundant seas (Linard 1996).

Organizers normally pursue the effort of creating a new, fully bounded organization successfully only if they can (1) capture valuable resources, (2) lower transaction costs and/or increase gains in deployment of those resources by means of bounded networks, and (3) form cross-boundary ties to sites providing them with sustaining opportunities and assets that will facilitate the realization of gains from the resources.

In these unusual circumstances, the creation of a complete perimeter, rather than the guarded frontier of categorical pairing, yields significant returns for resource holders. For a completely bounded organization to survive, those returns must include a margin for the sheer cost of monitoring and sustaining the boundary. Unlike the production of hierarchies, triads, chains, and even paired categories, no one is likely to create a new organization inadvertently. Most organizations, indeed, come into being modeled directly on other existing organizations—firms, associations, lineages, states, parties, households, churches, and similar well-established exemplars. Such borrowing lowers costs of creating new organizations, but it also reduces the structure's conformity to the tasks at hand. Improvisation and the accumulation of shared local knowledge then produce further adjustments to the local situation.

In such circumstances, direct parallels to the opportunity-hoarding, emulation, and adaptation that appear in categorical inequality promote formation of organizations. In fact, another way of thinking about organizations is as extreme forms of categorical inequality: frontier extended into a complete perimeter separating ins from outs, social relations across the perimeter restricted and coordinated, hierarchy concentrating control over social relations in one or a few locations.

Categorical Pairs in Practice

In themselves, paired categories do not necessarily feature great inequality. In firms using or selling complex technologies, for example, the line/staff distinction separates command hierarchies from positions providing technical services to members of that hierarchy but frequently affords ample rewards on the staff side. Managers sometimes encourage competition for better performance by fostering categorical distinctions among largely interchangeable units, as when a military commander pits companies A, B, and C against each other in competition for displays of solidarity, zeal, and effectiveness.

Consider brokers who make their livings by mediating between two organizations or populations, equal or not. Such brokers enhance their livelihoods by supporting categorical distinctions that keep cross-boundary transactions passing through them instead of knitting together complementary pairs across the boundary. Ethnic leaders often acquire just such interests in maintaining distinctions between dominant classes and their own constituencies; they become stronger advocates of bilingual education, distinctive cultural institutions, and installation of legal categories than many members of their own constituencies (e.g., Hofmeyr 1987).

Rural landlords likewise often set themselves up as interlocutors for their culturally distinct tenants, becoming defenders of that distinctness as they do so without in the least relinquishing their own membership in the cosmopolitan culture (e.g., Rutten 1994). Wherever powerful parties gain from the segregation and coordination of two networks, equal or not, paired categories provide an effective device for realization of that gain.

Consider some quick examples. Stalin knits together an effective political machine by recruiting ethnically identified regional leaders, training them in Moscow, making them regional party bosses, and giving their ethnic identifications priority within partly autonomous political jurisdictions. When the Soviet center later relaxes its grip, political entrepreneurs within regions mobilize followings around those ethnic identities, others mobilize against them, and ostensibly age-old ethnic conflicts flame into civil war.

In another example, the founder of a small manufacturing firm, following models already established in his trade, divides the firm's work into clusters of jobs he sees as distinct in character and qualifications, then recruits workers for those jobs within well-marked categories. As turnover occurs and the firm expands, established workers pass word of available jobs among friends and relatives only to collaborate with them once they join the workforce. Those new workers therefore prove more reliable and effective than others hired off the street, and all concerned come to associate job with category, so much so that owner and workers come to believe in the superior fitness of that category's members for the particular line of work.

Another case in point. Householders in an urban neighborhood build up a precarious system of trust on the basis of common backgrounds and shared relations to third parties, live with persons and property at risk to that system of trust, then react violently when newcomers whom they cannot easily integrate into the same networks threaten to occupy part of the territory. In the process, members of the two groups elaborate compelling stories about each others' perfidy and utter incompatibility.

In a final example, members of an immigrant stream peddle craft goods from their home region on big-city streets. Some of them set up businesses as suppliers, manufacturers, or retail merchants. New immigrants find work in the expanding trade, and not only an immigrant niche but an ethnically specific international connection provides exclusive opportunities for the next generation. In all these cases, organizational improvisations lead to durable categorical inequality. In all these cases, but with variable weight, exploitation and opportunity-hoarding favor installation of categorical inequality, while emulation and adaptation generalize its influence.

Durable Inequality and Reducing Intergroup Tension

When it comes to the determinants of durable inequality, are these special cases or the general rule? We have good reasons for thinking that categorical inequality in general results from varying intersections of exploitation, opportunity-hoarding, emulation, and adaptation. I will go farther, claiming that much of the inequality seeming to result from individual or group differences in ability actually stems from the same causes:

1. Authoritatively organized categorical differences in current performance (e.g., categorically differentiated cooperation or sabotage by fellow workers, subordinates, and supervisors);
2. Authoritatively organized categorical differences in rewards for performance (e.g., systematically lower pay for blacks than for whites doing similar work); and/or
3. Authoritatively organized differences in acquisition of capacities for performance (e.g., categorically segregated and unequal schools).

I also argue that similar social mechanisms generate inequality with respect to a wide range of advantages: wealth, income, esteem, protection, power, and more.

Nutrition turns out to provide quite a general model for categorical inequality, because in most settings feeding differs with categorical membership, but in many settings cumulative effects of feeding elsewhere help explain categorical differences in performance here. In direct parallel, information and social ties acquired now differ categorically, but previous categorical experience strongly affects information and social ties individuals and groups already have at their disposal, not to mention means they have of acquiring new information and social ties.

Also, categorically differentiated family experience strongly affects children's school performance and teachers' evaluations of that performance, evaluations which in turn channel children into categorically differentiated, career-shaping educational streams (Hout and Dohan 1996; Taubman 1991). To the extent that teachers, employers, public officials, and other authorities differentiate their responses to performances in any of these regards categorically, they contribute to durable, authoritatively organized categorical differences. Authorities do, in fact, frequently solve their own organizational problems—how to sort students, whom to hire, what rights to honor—in categorical ways.

Feelings of identity, on one side, and intergroup hostility, on the other, may well accompany, promote, or result from use of categorical differences to solve organizational problems. But the relative prevalence of such attitudes plays a secondary part in inequality's extent and form. Mistaken beliefs about another group reinforce exploitation, opportunity-hoarding, emulation, and adaptation but exercise little independent influence on their initiation. Or so I argue. It follows that reduction or intensification of racist, sexist, or xenophobic attitudes will have relatively little impact on durable inequality in these respects, while the introduction of certain new organizational forms—for example, the installation of different categories or changed relations between categories and rewards—will have large impacts.

If so, the identification of such organizational forms becomes a significant challenge for social scientists. It also follows that similar organizational problems generate parallel solutions in very different settings, in articulation with very different sets of categories. Hence it follows that matches of positions with categories and justifications for such matches vary much more than recurrent structural arrangements—as when similar clusters of jobs acquire contrasting racial, ethnic, or gender identifications in different labor markets. Causal mechanisms resemble each other greatly, while outcomes differ dramatically, thus inviting very different rationalizations or condemnations after the fact. Social scientists dealing with such durable forms of inequality must hack through dense ideological overgrowth to reach structural roots. I hope to have offered a sturdier, sharper machete.

CHAPTER TWO

Two Visions of the Relationship between Individual and Society: The Bell Curve versus Social Structure and Personality

Melvin L. Kohn

In October 1994, the American Enterprise Institute, with great fanfare and not a little expense, held a well-orchestrated conference of social scientists and journalists whom they deemed sympathetic to their decidedly conservative political philosophy, to herald the publication of a new book by Richard Herrnstein and Charles Murray, *The Bell Curve* (1994). All the conferees had been given advance copies of the book, while others—including book-review editors—found it difficult to obtain a copy until after the first wave of largely favorable reviews had been widely disseminated in the mass media (Clawson 1995). In due time—which is to say, a year or two later—the book was reviewed in many scholarly journals; almost all of *these* reviews were critical of the book's poor scholarship and shoddy methodology. Although it is doubtful that most of the public ever learned of the negative evaluation of the book by social scientists, with the passage of time interest in the book died down.

One could dismiss the book and the hoopla attending its publication as a historical oddity, a political phenomenon of only passing interest. And, yet, I think it would be foolhardy to do so. The immediate furor over the scientific merits and political purposes of *The Bell Curve* may have died down, but the thesis embodied in that book has not died and will not do so in the foreseeable future. On the contrary, it is a thesis that has come to prominent attention every quarter-century or so, and undoubtedly will come to prominent attention again. Every time it does, many people (journalists and congressmen included) think its arguments plausible. The point of view that *The Bell Curve* represents is an important perspective in political discourse in this society, and *The Bell Curve* appears to offer scientific buttressing to this point of view.

My principal objective in this chapter is to juxtapose the perspective enunciated by Herrnstein and Murray with alternative perspectives provided by sociology. Although several reviews of *The Bell Curve* take issue with the evidence that Herrnstein and Murray put forth to buttress their vision (see, in particular, Fischer et al. 1996; Goldberger and Manski 1995; Hauser 1995; Heckman 1995; Kohn 1996; and Taylor 1995), and some (in particular, Fischer et al. 1996; Hauser 1995; and Kohn 1996) take them to task for ignoring the evidence derived from perspectives other than their own, there has been little discussion of whether social science has provided *alternative* visions of the relationship of individual and society. I argue that social science has, indeed, provided alternative visions of this relationship, and that we even have a specialized field of sociology, the field of social structure and personality, devoted to explicating and testing one of these visions. It is not that social science has had nothing to say, but that Herrnstein and Murray have chosen to ignore what we have said.

The Perspective on Individual and Society Embodied in *The Bell Curve*

The Bell Curve embodies a vision of a "meritocratic," albeit increasingly stratified, society in which a largely genetically determined "intelligence" is coming more and more to determine the attainment of occupational and social position. More than that, it argues that low intelligence accounts for many of society's most distressing social problems. In making these arguments, *The Bell Curve* reinterprets all manner of complex social phenomena—stratification and mobility; race, class, and ethnicity; social problems; the family; you name it—in a consistently reductionist way. In fact, it is doubly reductionist, for it not only sees all these social phenomena as psychologically determined, it sees the central psychological variable—intellectual functioning—as biologically determined. In my review of the book (Kohn 1996), I appraised the assumptions that underlie Herrnstein and Murray's perspective, severely criticizing their methodological and conceptual failings. In particular, I criticized them for assuming that factor analyses depict the structure of *reality* rather than the structure of a set of items that one uses to index a *concept;* this assumption leads to their naive conclusion that "intelligence" is a "thing" rather than a concept. I also criticized them for treating tests of intellectual *performance* as if they somehow measured innate *ability,* and for attempting to assess the proportion of variance in intellectual functioning that can be attributed to heredity rather than recognizing that genetics plays its role as a determinant of intellectual functioning *in interaction with* the environment. And I took them to task for what I consider to be the most fundamental, and fundamentally flawed, assumption of all: that intellectual functioning is not responsive to social conditions. Perhaps paradoxically, I not only do not dispute the fact on which this assumption rests—namely, that measures of intellectual functioning are remarkably stable over time—I even claim that my own research provides more powerful evidence in support of that fact than anything they offer. My dispute with Herrnstein and Murray is over the *interpretation* of that fact, a difference of interpretation that gets to the heart of everything they do.

To Herrnstein and Murray, stability of intellectual functioning necessarily means that intellectual functioning is not responsive to social conditions, certainly not after early childhood. On that basis, Herrnstein and Murray, in all their analyses, treat intellectual functioning (which they erroneously call cognitive ability) as an independent variable in their analyses—the key explanatory variable for all sorts of social and social-psychological phenomena, never itself to be explained by any other social or psychological phenomena. To me, the stability of intellectual functioning is a profoundly important fact, though one whose implications cannot be simply assumed but must be investigated. I defer further consideration of the evidence until I present the perspective offered by my own specialized field of sociology, social structure and personality.

Intelligence and Class Structure

The Herrnstein-Murray approach to the relationship between individual and society is perhaps best exemplified in the book's subtitle, *Intelligence and Class Structure in American Life.* Take note, though, that the book does not deal with class *structure,* but with educational and occupational *attainment.* The distinction is essential. Herrnstein and Murray make no attempt to explain social structure, but only explain who ends up where in the social structure. Explanation is entirely at the level of individuals. I would have no objection to this—indeed, I will do the very same thing later in this essay—*if only* Herrnstein and Murray tailored their interpretations to the level of their analyses.

I can convey the flavor of their view of "class structure" by quoting some of what they say. In the second paragraph of Part 1 (on p. 25) they write:

"Social class remains the vehicle of social life, but intelligence now pulls the train." Not all sociologists would agree with the first part of that sentence, but I certainly would defend that proposition; the second part, though—that "intelligence now pulls the train"—is astonishing. My sense of astonishment grows as I read, sixty-six pages later, "The irony is that as America equalizes the circumstances of people's lives, the remaining differences in intelligence are increasingly determined by differences in people's genes." What can this possibly mean? How can anyone talk of America equalizing the circumstances of people's lives when every serious study shows ever-increasing disparities between the rich and the poor?

The most coherent statement of their position is given not in the book itself, but in a syllogism with which Herrnstein (1971) began a much earlier article in *The Atlantic Monthly*. The syllogism is printed in bold type at the very beginning of his article:

1. If differences in mental abilities are inherited, and
2. if success requires those abilities, and
3. if earnings and prestige depend on success,
4. then social standing will be based to some extent on inherited differences among people.

Hedged as it is with "if" statements, and further protected by the innocent-sounding term "to some extent," the syllogism—aside from the misleading term, ability—is incontrovertible. The real question is, *to what extent* is social standing the result of inherited differences in intelligence? Herrnstein and Murray would have us believe that inherited differences in intellectual performance are of very great importance for "social standing." They reach this conclusion by transforming the "if" statements into probability statements, and then vastly over-estimating all of the probabilities. But, such a four-step process represents the *product* of four probabilities. All four probabilities have to be very strong if the entire process is to have a more than trivial effect. If even a single one of these probabilities is low, or if two or three of them are only moderate, then the total process results in very little effect at all. It's not that the syllogism is wrong, but that the probabilities are much lower than Herrnstein and Murray would admit—except in their appendices. The whole process doesn't amount to very much. There are other determinants of socioeconomic achievement that are far more important than IQ.

Herrnstein and Murray are so fixated on the importance of IQ as a determinant of achieved class position that they ignore virtually everything else that is known about social class in the contemporary United States. Their view does not admit the existence of racial discrimination, of unemployment, of jobs migrating to the Third World, of tax reductions for the rich and the dismantling of our never-very-advanced welfare state. Theirs is a far rosier view of a society that has nearly achieved equal opportunity for all, a meritocracy of ability, as they term it—as if there were something meritorious in having inherited a high IQ. In such a society, economic success is determined by intellectual ability—not by motivation, hard work, or "personality" in the common meaning of that term, but solely by cognitive ability, which in their view is largely inherited.

And what evidence do they offer to support this view of the world? They offer table after table, graph after graph—and virtually none of it is directly pertinent to the issues. They offer anecdotal evidence, for example, about admissions to Harvard University. They offer all sorts of evidence about correlations between IQ and social class, which proves nothing. In all their discussion of educational and occupational attainment, they never face up to the reality that there are structural constraints on such attainment. And, of course, they never entertain the possibility that IQ may not always be the independent variable in their implicit causal models, that people's IQs may be positively or negatively affected by their educational and occupational experiences. It's all very logical, given their assumptions and the blinders that they wear.

Social Problems

Another major part of *The Bell Curve* (Part 2) discusses the relationship between IQ and several social phenomena, most of them social problems: poverty; dropping out of school; unemployment, idleness, and injury; family and parent-child relations; welfare dependency; crime; and a lack of what they call civility and citizenship. As in their treatment of class structure, the focus of analysis is never the extent or the causes of the social phenomenon; they are not concerned, for example, about *why* the United States has as much poverty or crime as it does, but only about *who* is poor or is convicted of a serious crime. Their theme is that people of low IQ account for the lion's share of the problems. In evidence thereof, they attempt to show that IQ dwarfs socioeconomic status as a determinant of who manifests each of the problematic behaviors.

As Herrnstein and Murray explain, their procedure for the study of the role of IQ in the production of social problems is to use the National Longitudinal Survey of the Labor Market Experience of Youth (NLSY) as their source of data, and to use the Armed Forces Qualification Test (AFQT), which is included in the NLSY, as their measure of IQ. I have no quarrel with either choice (but see Fischer et al. 1996, who question their use of the AFQT as a measure of IQ). I am astonished, though, at their decision to limit their analyses to non-Latino whites, arguing (on p. 125) that doing so enables them to make "yet another central point: Cognitive ability affects social behavior without regard to race or ethnicity." They apparently do not realize that all that they have accomplished has been to make it impossible to generalize any of their findings to Latinos or blacks, as they most certainly do in their policy recommendations.

The crux of their method is to use multiple-regression analysis, with one or another type of problematic behavior as the dependent variable, IQ as one of the independent variables, and other possibly confounding variables—notably and centrally, socioeconomic status—as other independent variables in the equation. The question is always whether IQ continues to have a statistically significant effect on the particular dependent variable when socioeconomic status (and a very few other variables) are in this way statistically controlled. They only mention in passing, as if it were the only possible thing to do, that the socioeconomic status they measure is *parental* socioeconomic status, not achieved socioeconomic status—which is, of course, entirely consonant with their assumption that the social environment could affect individual psychological functioning, if at all, only during early childhood.

Because Herrnstein and Murray seem to know nothing of the research literature on social structure and personality, it never occurs to them to consider any more complex causal models—to consider, for example, the possibilities that IQ might not only affect but also be affected by social conditions; that the behaviors in question might be affected by other aspects of personality—motivation, for example; or, for that matter, that IQ might itself be affected by other aspects of personality; or, finally but to my mind crucially, that the *parental* socioeconomic status of late adolescents and adults might not be as pertinent for their analyses as people's own achieved status. Given their premises, their methodology makes sense. Once one questions their premises, it becomes clear that their mode of analysis loads the dice in favor of their hypothesis. The surprising thing about their analyses is not that their hypotheses are confirmed, but that they are so weakly confirmed. This is evident in table after table, but especially in their long appendices, to which they relegate many of their most important findings.

I should add that their analyses are based on unspeakably crude indices of all the social variables they consider—apparently, only IQ is important enough to be worth measuring well.

Race and Ethnicity

Although much of the public discussion of *The Bell Curve* has focused on its treatment of race, the book is really about class, not race. As

I have already noted, the central empirical analyses are limited to non-Hispanic whites; and the pervasive implication that there might be genetic limitations to the intelligence of nonwhites is made by innuendo and is carefully hedged. Only two chapters in this massive book deal directly with race. One (Chapter 13) equivocates at length about whether "ethnic" differences (here treated as meaning black-white, Latino-white, Jewish-Gentile, and Oriental-Occidental differences) might be genetic in origin. The other (Chapter 14) is a rather pathetic discussion of whether ethnic differences (now defined as black-white-Latino differences) in educational and occupational attainment, marriage rates, unemployment, being on welfare, and all sorts of other things might result from differences in IQ. And that's about all. Still, race pervades the book, and especially its policy pronouncements. The book talks about class, but implies race.

Sociological Alternatives

What does sociology offer as an alternative to Herrnstein and Murray's simplistic conception of the relationship between individual and society? The accumulated knowledge of at least three specialized fields of sociology stands in juxtaposition, even opposition, to Herrnstein and Murray's thesis.

One pivotal body of knowledge is the corpus of research on social problems, research that belies Herrnstein and Murray's narrow formulation of what should be considered in any realistic appraisal of the social factors conducive to poverty, crime, welfare dependency, or any of the other social problems that are discussed in *The Bell Curve*. Parental socioeconomic status, even if it were well measured, is so small a part of what should be taken into account as to be a ludicrous over-simplification of the part played by the social environment in the production of social problems.

Second, and even more telling—think again of the subtitle of the book, *Intelligence and Class Structure in American Life*—there is an immense research literature on social stratification and mobility that stands in opposition to the Herrnstein-Murray thesis of an increasingly meritocratic society in which "intelligence" is the key to occupational attainment. Several of the reviews of *The Bell Curve* (in particular, Fischer et al. 1996; Goldberger and Manski 1995; Hauser 1995; Heckman 1995; Korenman and Winship 1996; and Taylor 1995) discuss this research literature, some of them noting that a few key studies (notably Jencks et al. 1972; Jencks et al. 1979) have included measures of intellectual functioning in their assessments of social mobility and found intellectual functioning to be much less important than Herrnstein and Murray would have us believe. The main thrust of the reviews by sociologists and economists is that Herrnstein and Murray seriously underestimated the effects of parental socioeconomic status by sloppy measurement and failure to take unreliability of measurement into account. They even more seriously underestimated the broader effects of the social environment by not looking at many other pertinent factors, even those available in the data-set with which they worked—deliberately not examining education (on the dubious rationale that educational attainment is largely a consequence of IQ) and not even considering such obvious candidates for inclusion in their analyses as gender. All this would have been known to anyone familiar with the research literature on stratification and mobility.

Two major reassessments—those by Korenman and Winship (1996) and by Fischer and his colleagues at Berkeley (1996, Chapter 4 and Appendix 2)—not only criticize what Herrnstein and Murray have done, but reanalyze the very data that Herrnstein and Murray used. Their analyses are much more sophisticated methodologically than are Herrnstein and Murray's, particularly in taking account of unreliability of the measurement of socioeconomic status and in correcting Herrnstein and Murray's failure to make use of even the limited range of social variables included in the data-set with which they worked. Both reanalyses confirm that Herrnstein and Murray have seriously underestimated the importance of parental socioeconomic status, and have drastically underestimated the importance of social factors generally, in their conclusion that intelligence is more important than socioenvironmental factors in accounting for socioeconomic achievement. Moreover, as both research teams acknowledge, even their reassessments treat IQ (as measured at ages fifteen to twenty-three) as if it had not been affected by social experience, even by educational experience. Assuming unidirectionality of effect exaggerates the magnitude of that effect. Herrnstein and Murray do not acknowledge this issue to be problematic, for they cannot conceive of reciprocal effects; but the issue is very real indeed.

The foregoing domains of sociological research contest the Herrnstein and Murray thesis, but they do not confront Herrnstein and Murray with a systematic alternative conceptualization of the relationship between individual and society. The third pertinent body of sociological research, that offered by the field of social structure and personality, attempts to do precisely that. In presenting this perspective, I take the liberty of using my own work as illustrative, and supplement it with references to other pertinent research.

The Perspective Offered by the Field of Social Structure and Personality

Social Structure

Our basic premise is that any serious effort to deal with social structure must try to conceptualize social structure and its several dimensions rigorously, must try to index these dimensions precisely, and must make every effort to differentiate between the social-structural conditions people experienced as children and those they experience as adults. We attempt, with varying degrees of success, not to reify social structure or any of its components. Just as intelligence is a concept and not a "thing," so too is social structure. But concepts are to be taken seriously, for they are our way of depicting reality.

The definition of social structure that I employ comes from that font of sociological wisdom, Robin M. Williams, Jr.'s *American Society:* "Human beings in society do exhibit complexes of action, thought, and emotion (1) shared by many individuals, (2) repeated in many successive situations, and (3) definitely related to *other* patterns in the same social aggregate. This is essentially all that is here meant by 'structure': an appreciable degree of regularity and relationship. There is thus nothing obscure or mystical about the concept, and the question of how definite and enduring the structure is in any particular case is left open for empirical study" (1951, 20–21).

My primary interest is the structure of society as a whole, particularly the fundamental lines of organization and cleavage characteristic of that society. Like Herrnstein and Murray, I focus my discussion on class and stratification. Where I part company with Herrnstein and Murray is with their sloppy conceptualization of what they call class structure, their primitive indices, and their facile assumption that only the class position of one's parental family matters for personality and behavior in later years.

I would differentiate between social class and social stratification. Even Williams did not make such a distinction when he published *American Society* in 1951, nor did I for many years thereafter. But, as we have learned from the sociologists of Eastern Europe when those countries were socialist (for example, Wesolowski 1979), and from the keen analytic work of Erik Wright (1978), it is conceptually useful to make such a distinction. Social classes are groups defined in terms of their relationship to ownership and control over the means of production and of their control over the labor power of others. Social classes are distinct groups ("nominal" categories), not a continuum, nor even a set of categories that can be ranked as higher or lower along some *single* underlying dimension. Social stratification, by contrast, is conceived as a single continuum, an ordinal ranking of stratification positions. Admittedly, the empirical overlap between class and stratification is considerable, yet there is analytic utility in making the distinction. When Herrnstein and Murray talk about "class" structure, they really mean social stratification.

Indices of class structure and class position must be based on some conceptualization of relationships to ownership and control of the means of production and control over the labor power of others. My own preferred conceptualization is a variant of Erik Wright's original (1978) schema, in which—for American society at the present time—I distinguish six social classes, differentiated on the basis of ownership, supervisory position, and, among nonsupervisory employees, the distinction between manual and nonmanual work (Kohn and Schoenbach 1983). Our research has shown that class position, thus indexed, is significantly and meaningfully related to intellectual flexibility, to values for oneself and one's children, and to one's orientations to self and society (Kohn and Schoenbach 1983). Using indices tailored to the particular times and circumstances of other countries, we have also shown significant and meaningful relationships of social class with intellectual flexibility, values, and orientations for Japan (Kohn et al. 1990), a non-Western capitalist society, and for Poland when it was socialist (Kohn et al. 1990; Kohn and Slomczynski 1990).

Whether or not social stratification is as fundamental a dimension of social structure as is social class, it is even more powerful than class in its effects on individual personality and behavior. Just how powerful we find its effects to be depends, in part, on how well we measure social stratification. Herrnstein and Murray simply average mother's education, father's education, family income, and the occupational status of that member of the household who has the highest such status. This is surely one of the least thoughtful procedures one could use and one that is almost designed to underestimate the full effects of social stratification. Certainly, so important a concept deserves more sophisticated treatment.

The fundamental premise of the concept social stratification was expressed well by Williams in *American Society* in 1951 (78–90): we should think of social stratification as a *single* hierarchical ranking of individuals. Alternatively, one can think of social stratification as a single hierarchical ranking of families (Kohn and Slomczynski 1990, Chapter 7). Following Williams, we ordinarily think of such a ranking in terms of power, privilege, and prestige. Lacking direct indices of these, we use occupational status, educational attainment, and income as our indicators of social stratification. The crucial point is not the particular indicators, important though they be, but Williams's insight that, whatever indicators we use, we are attempting to index a *single* dimension. Nowadays, we can do this with ease using factor analysis, or—better yet—confirmatory factor analysis, which attempts to infer the underlying dimension from the covariance of the indicators.

Using such an index of social stratification, we consistently find that stratification, like class but even more powerfully than class, has profound effects on intellectual functioning, values, and orientations to self and society (Kohn and Schoenbach 1983; Kohn et al. 1990; Kohn and Slomczynski 1990). I would add that one's achieved stratification position is much more pertinent than the stratification position of the family in which one was raised (Kohn [1969] 1997). The latter is important, as a huge corpus of work in status attainment demonstrates, mainly because socioeconomic origins greatly affect socioeconomic attainment (see Blau and Duncan 1967 and innumerable subsequent studies in many countries).

The Processes by Which Social Structure Affects Personality and Behavior

Herrnstein and Murray think of social-structural position mainly as something to be statistically controlled, so that they can demonstrate that intelligence still has a potent effect on individual behavior. Those of us who are engaged in research on social structure and personality think of social structure not as something to be statistically *controlled,* but as something whose effects on personality are to be *explicated.*

The central interpretive task in understanding the relationships between social structure and personality is to systematically link two levels of analytic discourse—the large-scale social and the individual. Our way of drawing these linkages is to ask how position in the larger social structure affects the immediately impinging conditions of people's lives, and how people's conditions of life affect, and are affected by, their values, their orientations, and their thinking processes (Kohn 1963, 1989, [1969] 1997; House 1981). In my collaborators' and my analyses of the psychological effects of class and stratification, the immediately impinging conditions of life that prove to be most important are mainly job conditions, particularly those job conditions that facilitate, or limit, the exercise of self-direction in one's work—namely, the substantive complexity of that work, how closely it is supervised, and how routinized it is. To have a more advantaged class position or a higher stratification position means having much more opportunity to be self-directed in one's work, which in turn has major consequences for intellectual flexibility, values, and orientations to self and society.

Reciprocity of Effects

My formulation assumes something that Herrnstein and Murray deny at every juncture: that social conditions can affect intellectual functioning. I not only claim that my assumption is more tenable than theirs, but also that the empirical evidence supports mine and refutes theirs. The most directly pertinent evidence comes from Carmi Schooler's and my analysis of the reciprocal effects of the substantive complexity of men's work and their intellectual functioning (Kohn and Schooler 1978; 1983, Chapter 5).

The analysis is based on interviews with a representative sample of U.S. men employed in civilian occupations in 1964, a representative subsample of whom were reinterviewed ten years later. The 687 men who were interviewed both times provide the data for the analysis.

We defined the substantive complexity of work as the degree to which the work, in its very substance, requires thought and independent judgment. We used several indicators of substantive complexity of work: our evaluations of the complexity of the work the respondent does in dealing with things, with data or ideas, and with people (based on his description of the work he performs in each of these three realms); our evaluation of the highest level of complexity at which he ordinarily works, regardless of the realm in which he does this work; and the amount of time he spends working in each of the three realms—seven indicators in all.

In measuring intellectual flexibility, we deliberately did not use IQ tests, for the simple reason that in studying adults, we saw no reason to use measures that are especially attuned to scholastic performance. Instead, we inferred intellectual flexibility from the respondents' actual intellectual performance in the course of a long and demanding interview. We sampled a variety of indicators—including the men's answers to seemingly simple but highly revealing cognitive problems, their handling of projective tests designed to assess their competence at seeing the relationships between the whole and its constituent parts, their propensity to "agree" when asked agree-disagree questions, and the assessment of their "intelligence" made by the interviewer following a long session that required a great deal of thought and reflection. None of these indicators is assumed to be completely valid; but we do assume that all the indicators reflect, in some substantial degree, people's flexibility in attempting to cope with the intellectual demands of a complex situation. We tested this assumption with confirmatory factor analysis, relying on the fundamental premise of such analyses—that the underlying factor is inferred from the covariance of the indicators. It does not matter that one or another, or even several, of the indicators may be "biased," so long as the indicators do not all share the same bias.

Admittedly, our measure is based on only a few indicators, a mere seven. But the confirmatory factor analysis shows the measurement model to fit the covariance of the indicators very well indeed. Moreover, we have compelling evidence that intellectual flexibility, as we measure it, is far from epiphenomenal: The correlation between men's intellectual flexibility at the time of the baseline interview and ten years later is an astonishing 0.93. *This* finding accords very well with Herrnstein and Murray's assertion that measures of intellectual functioning are stable. But, where they would undoubtedly jump to the inference that a 0.93 over-time correlation means that intellectual flexibility is almost entirely the product of genetics and perhaps also of very early life experience, linear structural-equations modeling shows the relationship between the substantive complexity of work and intellectual flexibility to be decisively reciprocal: The substantive complexity of work is not only *affected by* intellectual flexibility *but also affects* intellectual flexibility. In fact, the effect of the substantive complexity of work on intellectual flexibility is fully one-fourth as great as the stability of this exceptionally stable facet of personality. Social conditions explain not only the small amount of change but also a substantial portion of the stability that we find in people's levels of intellectual flexibility. Intellectual flexibility is highly responsive to social conditions well into adulthood.

We then broadened the analysis in two ways. We examined not only the substantive complexity of work but all three job conditions that are conducive to or limit the exercise of self-direction in work. And we examined not only intellectual flexibility but also other fundamental dimensions of personality. Our longitudinal analyses of employed U.S. men consistently show that the job conditions determinative of occupational self-direction affect, and in many instances are also affected by, intellectual flexibility, values, and orientations to self and society (Kohn and Schooler 1983, Chapter 6). Moreover, simulated longitudinal analyses of cross-sectional data show consistent patterns of reciprocal effects for employed U.S. women (J. Miller et al. 1979; Kohn and Schooler 1983, Chapter 9), for Polish men and women (Kohn and Slomczynski 1990), and for Japanese men (Naoi and Schooler 1985; Kohn et al. 1990). These analyses do not always show an effect of personality on occupational self-direction, but—contrary to Herrnstein and Murray's underlying premise—they *invariably* show an effect of job conditions on personality.

Herrnstein and Murray treat "intelligence" or "cognitive ability" as the *independent* variable in nearly all their analyses, always allowing IQ to affect other variables, rarely if ever allowing IQ to be affected by any other variable. But, if there is one general conclusion that I would draw from the study of social structure and personality, it is that the relationships between social structure and personality are *quintessentially reciprocal*. It neither makes sense to treat social structure as having unidirectional effects on personality (as some sociologists still do) nor to treat intellectual functioning or any other dimension of personality as having unidirectional effects on people's positions in the social structure—as Herrnstein and Murray consistently do.

Cognitive Functioning as One—Not the Only—Facet of Personality

Herrnstein and Murray are so enthralled with "intelligence" as to be oblivious to other facets of personality. From the perspective of research on social structure and personality, intellectual functioning must be viewed as but one facet, not the whole, of personality. Although this may seem self-evident, its implications are not at all self-evident.

One implication is that we should never look at intellectual functioning—or any other major facet of personality—in isolation, failing to notice that social-structural conditions have decidedly similar relationships with cognitive functioning as they do with many other facets of psychological functioning as well. To be valid, interpretations of what is known about any *one* of these psychological phenomena must apply as well to all the other psychological phenomena.

If, to take my favorite example, substantively complex work increases intellectual flexibility, and also increases one's valuation of self-direction for oneself and one's children, and is also conducive to holding an orientation that sees the world as meaningful and predictable, then any valid explanation of these phenomena must be general. It is not sufficient to explain the relationship between work complexity and intellectual flexibility, or between work complexity and parental valuation of self-direction, as if either of these were the only phenomenon to be explained. Moreover, and even more important, a full explanation of these relationships cannot just take the substantive complexity of work as a given. Complexity of work is itself a function of one's location in the class and stratification systems of the society.

A second implication of the recognition that intellectual functioning must be seen not as standing alone, but as a component part of personality, is that it leads us to question whether intelligence has quite the driving role that Herrnstein and Murray ascribe to it. I sympathize with their holding this view, for in a paper I published many years ago, I hypothesized: "It is . . . entirely possible that the process by which substantive complexity [of work] affects values and orientations may be mediated, at least in part, through intellectual flexibility. Increased intellectual flexibility may increase one's valuation of self-direction and one's tolerance of different beliefs; decreased intellectual flexibility may result in greater valuation of conformity to external authority and increased authoritarian conservatism" (Kohn 1980, 205). It's a lovely hypothesis, one in which I still take a rather perverse sort of pride. Its only fault is that it fails the crucial empirical test.

This empirical test, which uses the data of Schooler's and my longitudinal study of U.S. men, is a linear structural-equations model in which we attempted to assess the reciprocal effects of job conditions and three facets of personality—intellectual flexibility, self-directedness of orientation, and a sense of well-being or of distress (Kohn and Schooler 1983, Chapter 6). The model (p. 149, Table 6.4) depicts a dynamic system in which job conditions affect all three dimensions of personality, all three dimensions of personality affect job conditions, and the three dimensions of personality affect one another. Of central importance to our present concerns, we do *not* find that intellectual flexibility plays an intervening role in the effect of job conditions on either self-directedness of orientation (as hypothesized) or distress. On the contrary, substantively complex work stimulates a more self-directed orientation, which in turn is conducive to greater intellectual flexibility. It's a matter of motivation. Intellectual flexibility is increased when people's conditions of life motivate them to think for themselves.

The Life Course

To this point, I have focused entirely on employed adults, mainly adults in mid-career, leaving aside the question of whether my conclusions apply more generally. I believe that they do, and I would like to cite several important nuggets of evidence.

First, and particularly relevant to issues regarding cognitive functioning, Joanne Miller, Kazimierz Slomczynski, and I (1985) studied the effects of the substantive complexity of work, closeness of supervision, and routinization on "intellective process," by which we meant intellectual flexibility and open-mindedness, the opposite pole of authoritarian conservatism. We did separate analyses for the youngest, intermediate, and oldest cohorts of employed men. Our analyses unequivocally show as great an effect of these job conditions, particularly of the substantive complexity of work, on intellectual flexibility and on open-mindedness for the oldest cohorts of both U.S. and Polish employed men as for the youngest and middle cohorts. These findings argue strongly for the continuing effects of job conditions on intellective process, regardless of the age of the worker and—by extrapolation—regardless of stage of career or of life course.

Even these analyses start with men already into their careers. Jeylan Mortimer and her collaborators have confirmed our essential findings for men at the very beginning of their careers (Mortimer, Lorence, and Kumka 1986). And, in their most recent work, Mortimer and her colleagues have confirmed such processes even for high school students in their part-time employment (Mortimer et al. 1996).

Second, Karen Miller, Carmi Schooler, and I (1985, 1986) have extended the concept of occupational self-direction to schoolwork. We hypothesized that students' exercise of self-direction in schoolwork would have psychological consequences quite similar to those of adults' exercise of self-direction in paid employment. To test this hypothesis, we included a battery of questions about schoolwork in interviews of the offspring of the men in the 1974 U.S. follow-up study, most of these offspring being high-school or college students at that time. With these data, we developed a measurement model of educational self-direction, a direct analogy to the models of occupational self-direction we had earlier developed for employed men and women.

Our findings about the reciprocal effects of students' educational self-direction and personality were remarkably consonant with our findings about employed adults' occupational self-direction and personality. Educational self-direction substantially affects both cognitive and noncognitive aspects of students' personalities—even with the pertinent dimension of both parents' personalities statistically controlled (Herrnstein and Murray, take note). We even found—just as Schooler and I had found for employed adults—that the effect of educational self-direction on intellectual flexibility is only partially direct; fully half of the effect is indirect through self-directedness of orientation. Greater educational self-direction increases students' self-directedness of orientation, and greater self-directedness of orientation increases intellectual flexibility. It is again a matter of motivation.

Social Change

Our studies of the United States, Poland, and Japan and the many replications that buttress their conclusions (see the review in Kohn and Slomczynski 1990, Chapter 9) had all been done under conditions of apparent social stability. Even the Polish survey of 1978 had been conducted two years before the advent of *Solidarnosc* and before there were any decided signs of impending change. The massive changes that began in Eastern Europe and the former Soviet Union in the late 1980s inevitably raised the important theoretical question of whether our interpretation of the relationship between social structure and personality applies also during times of radical social change.

I follow Williams in conceiving of social change as change in the structure of the society, not merely as an eventful or dramatic period in the life of that society: "Change occurs when there is a shift in pattern, when new relationships emerge . . ." (1970, 620–21). By *radical social change,* I refer not to the pace of change but to the nature of the change—the transformation of one political and economic system into a quite different system.

The very idea of there being a relationship between social structure and personality implies a dynamic interchange. What we learn about this interchange during times of social stability is a static slice of a dynamic process. Whether what we thereby learn is typical of the more general process or is specific to times of social stability is questionable. Every link in the causal chain from social-structural position to job conditions to personality might well be weakened or even broken by the process of radical social change.

To test this possibility, my collaborators and I carried out surveys in 1992–93 with representative samples of adult men and women living in the urban areas of Poland and Ukraine (Kohn et al. 1997). We found that, insofar as the relationships between social structure and personality had been similar in socialist Poland to what they were in the capitalist United States and Japan, nothing had changed in the transition to post-socialist society. For Poland and for Ukraine under conditions of radical social change, men and women of more advantaged social position are more self-directed in their orientations, and more intellectually flexible, than are men and women of less advantaged position. The reason is the same as in all our studies done under conditions of apparent social stability: because people of more advantaged social position have greater opportunity to be self-directed in their work, and occupational self-direction is conducive to a more self-directed orientation and to greater intellectual flexibility.

There had, however, been one major difference in our findings for socialist Poland and the capitalist countries—namely, in the relationship between social structure and a sense of well-being or distress. For the United States, managers were likely to have a strong sense of well-being and manual workers were likely to be distressed. For socialist Poland, managers were much more likely to be distresssed and manual workers to have a strong sense of well-being. Radical social change has resulted in nearly a complete reversal from what the pattern had been under socialism: Manual workers in Poland are now the most distressed social class and managers the least distressed. For the manual workers of a country to be transformed in just a few years from the least distressed to the most distressed social class, and for managers to move from being decidedly distressed to having a strong sense of well-being, means that the psychological effects of the transformation have been not only dramatic, but astonishingly rapid.

Radical social change has thus affected the relationships of social structure and personality primarily in that social structures in process of transformation come to exhibit the patterns characteristic of the type of society they are in process of becoming. By late 1992, Poland already exhibited the capitalist pattern. As of late 1992 and early 1993, Ukraine *seemed* to be following a similar trajectory, although at a slower pace and perhaps from a farther-back starting point. Note, though, that radical social change has resulted *not* in the weakening of the relationships between social structure and personality, but in making for even greater cross-national consistency in these relationships.

Conclusion

There *is* an alternative perspective to Herrnstein and Murray's, one much better established by the weight of evidence, but also—perhaps unfortunately—one that is harder to communicate to policy makers and the public. Herrnstein and Murray have a simple story to tell; we who work in the field of social structure and personality have a much more complex story to tell. And that is the heart of the difference, and perhaps the message that is most important to communicate. There is no single facet of personality, not intelligence nor any other, that "drives" the relationship between individual and society. On the contrary, people's social-structural positions both affect and are affected by many aspects of personality, intellectual flexibility among them. But—contrary to Herrnstein and Murray—cognitive functioning, important though it is, is not the centerpiece of the edifice. We look for linkages between social-structural position and personality in the experiences directly attendant on social-structural position, principal among them the conditions of work that people experience—whether that "work" be in paid employment, in schoolwork, or in any other realm of activity. Social structure continues to affect personality throughout the life course, from childhood, through first job, and on through one's entire career—and, presumably, into retirement. The effects of social structure on personality (and, presumably also, of personality on position in the social structure) obtain not only during times of apparent social stability, but even during times of radical social change.

It is a complex process, which should not be surprising, given that complexity lies at the very heart of our explanation of how and why social-structural position affects and is affected by personality. Reductionism does a great injustice to the complexity of life and to our understanding of that complexity.

CHAPTER THREE

Two Faces of Diversity: Recreating the Stranger Next Door?

Henry A. Walker

Diversity. The condition or quality of being diverse, different or varied; difference, unlikeness.
—*The Compact Edition of the Oxford English Dictionary*

The American nation wrestles with a perplexing question: Can it maintain its impressive heterogeneity and remain united? The question invites a paraphrase of the prophecy that Wicker (1968) offered a generation ago, "[Are we] on the verge of becoming (many) nations?" There exist signs that national fragmentation is already under way. Today, many U.S. citizens use the ethnic composition of juries to decide whether trials are fair or their verdicts just. In earlier times, a declaration of justice meant that the verdict fit the facts. On the political front, legal scholars have proposed, and legislative bodies have enacted, steps to ensure that a "fair proportion" of legislators are members of particular races or ethnic groups (Guinier 1994).[1]

---

[1] Although similar policies were labeled "racist" in an earlier historical period, they do not lack public support. A recent survey found that one-third (32.2%) of white respondents and 42.3% of black respondents agreed that people are best represented by co-ethnics (Davis and Smith 1994). When asked about representation in the U.S. Congress, the number of whites who held such views fell dramatically to 5.8%. However, one-fourth of blacks (25.9%) expected better representation from black elected officials.

The question is not whether we will have heterogeneity. Harvard law professor Charles Ogletree makes clear "[that] we simply cannot avoid [diversity]" (1996, 68). We *are* a nation of many nations. We have been so since the days of the founders. The fundamental issue is whether, and how, we can effectively manage our diversity.

Adherents of two political and ideological perspectives occupy center stage in the current debate. They paint two faces of diversity. Each side describes a nation at risk of increased racial intolerance and dissension, and of cultural and political schism. They are at odds over national strategies for managing heterogeneity and avoiding calamity. Each describes a unique path to racial harmony and national stability. The strategies they offer are hotly debated but rarely analyzed. I use insights from sociological and social psychological theory to explore the implications of the two approaches to managing heterogeneity. I show that neither approach provides a satisfactory solution and conclude by describing a third approach that appears promising. I begin with a brief overview of the problem.

Two Faces of Diversity

Americans have always raised questions about the relationship between race and ethnic diversity and national stability. America is a nation of immigrants and the roots of our racial and cultural heterogeneity lie in our immigrant history. The national origins of settlers have changed often, and each wave of new immigrants has been questioned about its place in American society. The founders wrestled with questions about African slaves and their descendants. Immigrants from Ireland and eastern Asia generated concern in the middle and late nineteenth century. Central European Jews and settlers from southern and eastern Europe fueled domestic concerns earlier in this century.[2]

Immigration patterns and national immigration policy favored northwestern and central Europeans for the better part of two centuries. Immigration reforms enacted in the 1960s dramatically changed that pattern. Since then, most immigrants have come from Asia and Latin America. Immigration reform coincided with skyrocketing increases in domestic taxes and the cost of living and the globalization of industrial production. An increasing share of the world's unskilled and semiskilled jobs have moved to less-developed countries, and American workers have come to believe that Asia and Latin America are importing jobs—their jobs—and

---

[2] Some immigration was major only in its social psychological effects. As an example, Chinese and Japanese immigrants were never more than a small minority of the U.S. population at the height of the "Yellow Peril." Approximately .5% of the U.S. population was of Chinese origin when Congress passed the Chinese Exclusion Act (1882).

exporting people who survive on U.S. tax dollars. Global markets have pushed American workers into tighter competition for jobs, social welfare benefits, and political power. Increasingly, their competitors are drawn from younger, rapidly growing, and highly visible immigrant groups.

The new immigrants have added more color to the national palette but Americans have mixed views on what that means. Some argue that the nation must have a steady flow of immigrants to maintain its vitality and stature as a world leader. Others claim that the new immigrants have brought *more* trouble. They argue that the growing movement to maintain the purity of immigrant cultures (Sowell 1994) threatens to tear the country apart. The cries of these latter day Jeremias suggest an essential irony of the label "Rainbow Nation": Rainbows *separate* the visible spectrum into its component hues.

Heterogeneity and Inequality

Industrialization mixes races and ethnic groups (Hannan 1979; Hechter 1975; Lipset and Rokkan 1967) but the diversity this creates is not the problem. The combination of diversity and inequality drives the current debate. People in modern societies compete for an array of jobs, political power, and status. Ethnic differences in resources and motivations ensure the creation of *durable inequalities* (Bonacich 1972). Durable inequalities exist when people's nominal characteristics like race, gender, or ethnic heritage are correlated with their standing on ranked inequalities like education or income. (See Tilly, Chapter 1.)

As the term suggests, reducing or eliminating durable inequality is difficult. Durable inequalities promote or reinforce ethnic prejudices that maintain ethnic identities and reinforce ethnic boundaries. Strong ethnic identities and rigid ethnic boundaries inhibit the transfer of collective identification from race or ethnic heritage to functional categories like occupation or class or to national identities (Gellner 1969; Hannan 1979; Hechter 1975; Lipset and Rokkan 1967). As a result, durable inequalities and ethnic competition generate tensions and conflicts that can divide and destroy nations (Park 1950).[3]

In U.S. society, blacks, Hispanics, and American Indians have less schooling, poorer jobs, and lower incomes than the white majority. Non-white ethnics experience less mobility than white ethnics (i.e., they are less able to realize the American Dream). Finally, nonwhites generally hold

---

[3] The present concern is not simply an academic exercise. The wreckage of multiethnic states lines the byways of recent history. The Soviet Union, Yugoslavia, and Czechoslovakia are recent additions to the list of states that have collapsed under the weight of ethnic conflict. As I write, Sri Lanka, Bosnia, and several other multiethnic states are torn by ethnic strife.

stronger racial or ethnic identities than their white ethnic counterparts (Alba 1990; Waters 1990; Omi and Winant 1994).

Conflicting Visions: Encouraging Assimilation versus Celebrating Diversity

There exist two dominant strategies for managing heterogeneity and eliminating ethnic conflict, and they reflect conflicting visions of the relationship between heterogeneity, inequality, and conflict. Advocates of the first strategy claim that cultural and racial differences must be eliminated or reduced substantially to reduce durable inequality. They support policies that promote assimilation to transform diverse peoples, with different languages and clashing beliefs and values, into a unified American society. In their view, cultural assimilation in particular weakens ethnic identities and boundaries and aids the development of functional (e.g., occupational or class) or national identities (see Schlesinger 1992). Attenuation of ethnic identities reduces ethnic tensions and conflicts and promotes national stability. On the other hand, they assert that any policy that reinforces cultural differences strengthens ethnic inequalities and invites cultural and national suicide. The strategy is entirely consistent with Park's (1950) claim that *assimilation* is the only stable racial accommodation.[4]

A second strategy rests on the idea that the attribution of unequal value to difference is the engine that turns benign differences into durable inequalities, intergroup tension, and conflict. Its advocates claim that ethnic inequality is a product of unrestrained ethnocentrism. Race and ethnic prejudice and discrimination ensure the unequal distribution of society's valued resources.[5] Conflict is a natural reaction of subordinate groups to the unequal and inequitable treatment they receive from a dominant group.

Representatives of this camp argue that members of dominant groups must embrace those who are different and evaluate the cultural systems they bring with them *on their own terms.* They must recognize that those from other

---

[4] Total assimilation produces either *incorporation* or *amalgamation* (Gordon 1964; Horowitz 1975), but groups must complete seven subprocesses—including cultural assimilation—to achieve it. The cultural characteristics of a single group predominate in the incorporative form of cultural assimilation. Amalgamation produces a hybrid blend of cultural forms. In either case, the elimination of race or ethnic differences is the pertinent result. Finally, research suggests that groups complete cultural assimilation more easily than any other subprocess, but ethnic boundaries often retain their rigidity despite substantial cultural assimilation (Gordon 1964).

[5] There are several variants of this argument. They range from "standard" Marxist treatments that attribute inequality to the class hegemony of a racially homogeneous elite (Cox 1948) to the classlike domination of a superordinate ethnic or racial group (Blauner 1972).

races or ethnic groups have experiences, skills, and abilities that, although different, are of equal value to those possessed by their own group (Takaki 1993). The position implies that giving equal status to disparate cultural practices reduces inequalities on other valued social dimensions and paves the way to racial harmony.[6] Race and ethnic harmony depend on accepting, valuing, and *celebrating diversity*. On the other hand, failure to take such action creates more hostility, engenders more intense identity politics, and invites internecine conflicts that can disembowel a nation.

Social Science Theory and Race Conflict

Social scientists contribute frequently to public discussions about strategies for managing diversity. Only rarely do they apply social science theories to these issues. Social science analyses cannot tell us which strategies we should use to manage heterogeneity. Whether we choose one or the other depends on subjective criteria (e.g., our values and objectives). On the other hand, policy decisions trigger social processes. The *objective* outcomes of those processes are fully amenable to social science analyses.

Race and Status-Organizing Processes

Race and ethnicity describe human groups. As descriptors, they are no more (and no less) important than a classification scheme based on the size of great toes. Their importance as powerful social forces rests on their acquisition of *status value*. Racial and ethnic categories have evaluative significance; individuals use race and cultural markers to estimate a person's social standing. To the extent that people use ideas about race or ethnic heritage to organize social life, the study of race relations is a special case of the more general class of status-organizing processes.

Status-organizing processes are a long-standing topic of social research (Bales 1950; Ridgeway and Walker 1995). Several theories describe features of the phenomenon, but *status characteristic theory* (Berger, Cohen, and Zelditch 1966; Berger et al. 1977) is the best known and most extensively researched. Other theories, including *identity theory* (Alexander and Wiley 1981; Stryker 1981) and *affect control theory* (Heise 1979; Smith-Lovin and

---

[6] The argument suffers from two problems. First, it treats group differences in the distribution of characteristics as evidence of the similarity of individual group members on the same characteristics. Second, the argument neglects the possibility that qualitative differences may have ramifications for rankings on other dimensions. For example, cultural differences in information or motivations have important implications for economic or political behavior. Treating cultural differences as *though* they are equally important or equally useful is not likely to enhance the social standing of "disadvantaged" ethnic groups. (See Sowell 1994 for an extended discussion of this issue.)

Heise 1988), focus on the importance of various *identity elements*, including race, and their significance for social interaction. I use ideas from these theoretical traditions and from theories of legitimacy processes to discuss two proposals for managing diversity.[7] I assume that both address a single question: Under what conditions do race and other ascribed characteristics lose their status significance and cease to be an organizing focus for conflict?

Race Conflict as Social Interaction

I begin by assuming that, at the most elementary level, conflict is simply one form of social interaction. Human actors possess multiple identities (Stryker 1981). They evaluate situations and make judgments about which identity in their repertoires will generate the outcomes most favorable to them (Alexander and Wiley 1981). Because interaction requires them to take the actions of others into account, actors must also identify and evaluate the identities of their co-actors (Couch 1992; Mead 1934, 1938; Miller, Hintz, and Couch 1975).

Some analysts claim that actors make evaluations of roles and identities in process (cf. Blumer 1969). However, others argue that actors bring evaluations of identities and identity elements to interaction. For example, affect control theorists (Heise 1979; Smith-Lovin and Heise 1988) claim that actors share *fundamental sentiments* (i.e., general evaluations of role identities). Fundamental sentiments influence interaction in powerful ways. Actors seem to manage their behavior to reduce the discrepancy between fundamental and *transient* sentiments (i.e., evaluations that emerge in process). Working from an identity theory perspective, Burke and his associates report similar findings (Burke and Tully 1977; Burke and Reitzes 1981; Mutran and George 1982). Finally, status characteristic theorists assume that individuals enter interaction with evaluations of, and performance expectations for, those who possess states of *diffuse status characteristics* like race or gender. Diffuse characteristics are those whose states (female and male are states of gender) carry social evaluations. For example, females are accorded lower social evaluations than males in most societies. Additionally, the states of diffuse characteristics are associated with states of other specific characteristics (e.g., musical ability, aggression) and with *general expectation states*. General expectation states carry the same relative rank as the affiliated state of a characteristic. Unless there exists evidence to the contrary, women are generally expected to possess less of any valued char-

---

[7] Barbara Ilardi and Anne McMahon motivated me to think about the general—rather than individual—character of status-organizing processes. I borrow extensively from our work that focuses on the institutional enactment of affirmative-action practices and procedures (McMahon, Ilardi, and Walker 1994).

acteristic than men (Berger et al. 1977). Status characteristics theory describes the way that interacting parties use information about the states of characteristics they possess to organize interaction.

I treat fundamental sentiments and status expectations as expressions of beliefs about the relationship between situational elements: qualities, possessions, and performances (Parsons 1951). *Qualities* are characteristics or attributes of persons, attributes such as race or gender (e.g., status characteristics). *Possessions* are transferable objects that actors can own or control. Possessions include common objects like homes, sports cars, and books but may include social roles (e.g., family roles or occupations). *Performances* are the behaviors enacted by individuals. Actors rank or evaluate qualities and develop expectations about their relation to other qualities, possessions, and performances.

A Theory of Legitimated Relevance Structures

I argue elsewhere (Walker 1992) that the social force of fundamental sentiments and of expectations about the relationship between qualities and other situational elements is linked to their legitimacy. Legitimacy is both evaluative and constitutive of social organization (Weber 1968). On the *evaluative* dimension, legitimacy refers to any individual's sense that actual or expected relations between qualities, possessions, and performances are desirable and proper. This property is called *propriety* (Dornbusch and Scott 1975; Walker and Zelditch 1993). On the *constitutive* dimension, actual or expected legitimate relations describe normative conceptions of reality (i.e., what is expected or ought to be). Constitutive legitimacy exists when a set of rules or standards governs the actions of group members. For example, an organization's bylaws describe positions within the organization, the qualifications or characteristics of desirable role occupants, and expected role performances. Legitimacy theorists call this property of social organization *validity* (Dornbusch and Scott 1975; Weber 1968). Validity can influence individual actors' attributions of propriety to norms of conduct (Walker and Zelditch 1993).

Legitimate standards are bolstered by the support of peers or of high status actors and institutions. Social orders are *endorsed* when they are supported by our peers (Dornbusch and Scott 1975; Walker and Zelditch 1993). Social orders that receive support from high status actors are *authorized* (Dornbusch and Scott 1975; Walker and Zelditch 1993).

Legitimated Relevance Structures and Managing Heterogeneity

Beliefs about the relationship between qualities, possessions, and performances vary across groups, societies, and cultural systems. Once they are established and acquire legitimacy, belief systems become part of a group's constitutive frame. New group members are not required to recreate them. They are transmitted from knowledgeable actors to those who are less knowledgeable.

I use the idea of a *legitimated relevance structure* (L-structure) to represent systems of legitimized beliefs. I argue that legitimation establishes *relevance* bonds between situational elements. The relationship between two qualities possesses relevance if those who possess states of one element are expected to possess particular states of the second. Consider the collective (i.e., societal) expectation that females are less aggressive than males. The idea expresses a relevance relation between gender and aggression.

The weight of tradition, the actions of legitimizing agents (e.g., charismatic figures), and rational-legal principles legitimate belief systems (Weber 1968). Actors use L-structures as guides to beliefs and actions. In the discussion that follows, I use the graphic representation developed by status characteristic theorists (Berger et al. 1977) to describe a series of L-structures.

The Legitimacy of Prejudice

I offer the L-structure in Figure 3.1 as a description of U.S. race relations. *D* represents the diffuse characteristic, race, which has two ranked states, black and white.[8] States of D carry signs to show that blacks have lower social rank than whites in American society. Each race is connected by relevance relations to socially evaluated or ranked states of several *specific characteristics* (Cs). Finally, each race is linked by a relevance relation to a *general expectation* (Γs) that carries the same relative evaluation as the race.

In simple terms, Figure 3.1 describes race prejudice. Prejudices are expectations about the relationship between some personal characteristic (Ds), like race, and standing on other socially valued qualities (Cs). More formally, call D_x, C_x and Γ_x *status elements* (E_x). Prejudice exists if for any two status elements, E_{xi} and E_{xj}, it is the case that E_{xi} is relevant to E_{xj}.

Figure 3.1 illustrates several features of prejudice. First, the states of valued qualities (Cs) that are relevant to race do not carry consistent evaluations. Some expectations or prejudgments are negative but others are positive (Brown 1995). In the example, whites are presumed to possess higher intellect but *less* dancing ability than blacks. Second, many characteristics are not relevant to race at all (i.e., their race-based status is unevaluated). Finally, prejudices also imply general beliefs or expectations (Γs) about persons who are

---

[8] I retain the symbolism of status characteristics theory (Berger, Cohen, and Zelditch 1966) because it is familiar to many readers. I limit the number of states of the quality, D, for ease of presentation. There is no logical limit on the number of states for a given D.

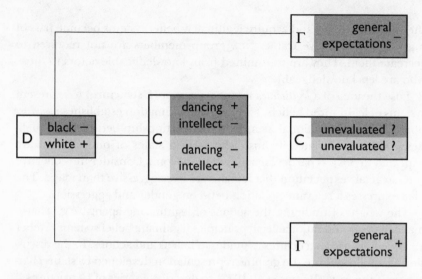

Figure 3.1 L-structure of specific and general prejudices. (C = specific performance characteristics; D = diffuse characteristics; Γ = general expectations.)

distinguished by race or ethnic heritage. As an example, people generally expect that Anglo-Americans are superior to Mexican Americans. I argue, consistent with status characteristic theory, that people use Γs to form expectations about the link between race and unevaluated Cs.

Prejudices are not limited to judgments about simple roles or identities, like laborers or thieves. They involve, as well, judgments about complex roles that require multiple skills and abilities.[9] As an example, Americans expect athletic ability and intelligence of traditional or "drop-back" quarterbacks but intelligence is given more weight than athletic ability. Figure 3.2 captures the complexity of prejudice. The L-structure describes one consequence of giving greater importance to intellect than to athleticism in forming expectations about the quarterback's role. Historically, Americans have expected greater competence at quarterback from white than black men.[10]

[9] I do not intend to deny the essential complexity of *all* social roles. The point concerns collective perceptions of the numbers and types of characteristics that are important to role performances. The idea that individual qualities combine with expectations associated with the roles they fill is consistent with the research of affect control theorists (Heise 1979; Smith-Lovin and Heise 1988). That line of work shows that attributions made of specific roles vary with the characteristics of role occupants.

[10] I restrict the description to men to suggest that gendered expectations are also crucial for this role. We do not expect any women, no matter what their race, to fill this role. Our expectations concerning gender or race competence change, however, when the role under scrutiny is that of synchronized swimmer or option quarterback.

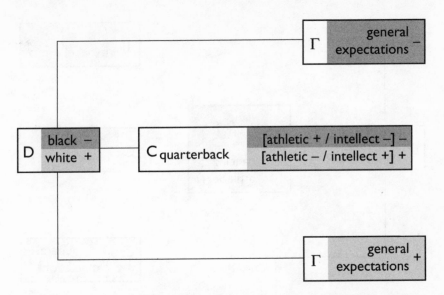

Figure 3.2 L-structure of complex prejudice. (C = specific performance characteristics; D = diffuse characteristics; Γ = general expectations.)

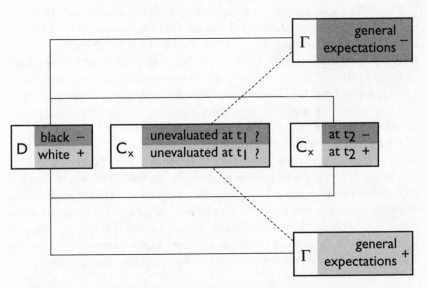

Figure 3.3 L-structure describing spread of prejudice. (C = specific performance characteristics; C_x = unevaluated characteristics; D = diffuse characteristics; Γ = general expectations; t_1 = time 1; t_2 = time 2.)

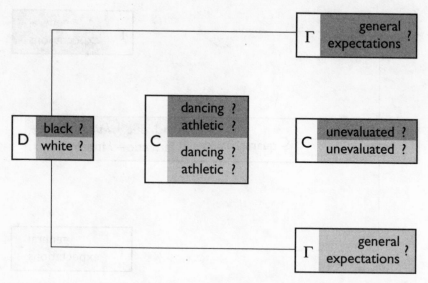

Figure 3.4 L-structure without race prejudice. (C = specific performance characteristics; D = diffuse characteristics; Γ = general expectations.)

Figure 3.3 shows how general expectations (Γ) shape expectations about the relationship between race and unevaluated characteristics (C_x). If C_x is not relevant to race at time t_1, actors use race-based general expectations to infer a person's standing on C_x at t_2. The inferred judgments (dashed lines represent inferred relations) carry the same evaluations as the relevant Γ. The example shows that blacks are expected to hold lower rank than whites on C_x at t_2. Stated concretely, prejudices spread to new situations and to new or previously unevaluated skills, abilities, or performances.

Figure 3.3 completes a description of what specialists in race relations have known for several generations (Allport 1954; Hughes and Hughes 1952). Prejudices are based on group—not individual—qualities. Prejudices connect race statuses to unequal expectations for many characteristics and actions. They also spread to new people and situations. In turn, unequal expectations shape interaction and the distribution of valued social goods (e.g., jobs, college admissions, or positions on athletic teams). In the next section, I use this framework to discuss competing strategies for managing diversity.

L-Structures and Managing Heterogeneity

Figure 3.4 represents a situation in which race is not relevant to other qualities, performances, or possessions.[11] It is the goal toward which

---

[11] Figure 3.4 represents an ideal type. It does not describe either historical or contemporary American society.

both strategies for managing diversity are presumably directed. I use question marks to represent unevaluated states of qualities and expectations. The absence of lines or paths connecting the states of D to either Cs or Γs emphasizes the point: Race is neither associated with nor dissociated from states of other status bearing elements (Cs). The principal analytical question is whether and how strategies that encourage assimilation or the celebration of diversity fuel the transition from a L-structure like that in Figure 3.1 to a structure like that in Figure 3.4.

Assimilation Strategy

Consider multiracial and multiethnic societies like the United States in which the president and other powerful leaders are committed to an assimilation strategy. The president argues forcefully that ethnic identities must be weakened substantially and that durable inequality must be eliminated to create racial harmony. She affirms her administration's commitment by setting up policies that focus on identifying and eradicating cultural differences between blacks and whites (e.g., language, religion, motivations). Additionally, she establishes programs that instill the same cultural characteristics in members of both groups. If successful, the program would eliminate race differences on cultural characteristics. Simultaneously, her administration takes a zero-tolerance policy on race discrimination. The U.S. Department of Justice identifies, prosecutes, and punishes persons and institutions convicted of using race or ethnic heritage to create unfair advantages.

Policies of this sort might create homogeneity of cultural characteristics. However, eliminating group differences on cultural characteristics has almost no impact on the relationship between race or ethnic heritage and either specific or general expectations associated with race. The states of cultural characteristics that the policies are designed to eliminate do not lose their status value. Their status values continue to influence evaluations made of any person who exhibits them. Figure 3.5 illustrates the implications of the processes I describe.

Language is the focal characteristic in Figure 3.5. Assume that X is the primary language of black Americans and that X carries lower status evaluations than English. What is the effect of complete linguistic assimilation (i.e., all white and black Americans speak only English)? Cultural assimilation does nothing to change the fundamental connection between race and general expectations such as those described in Figure 3.1. The language policy legitimizes English as a more desirable or suitable language than X and reinforces the idea that X is the language of an "inferior" people. Under this scenario, race prejudice persists because race remains a *master status characteristic* (Hughes and Hughes 1952). Discrimination based on race prejudice sustains durable inequalities. Finally, persistent durable

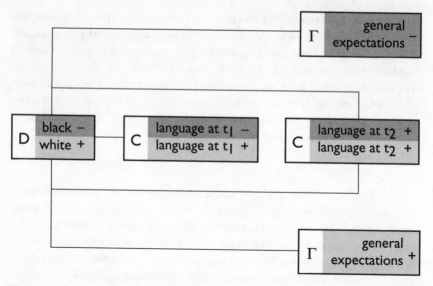

Figure 3.5 L-structure that describes cultural assimilation. (C = specific performance characteristics; D = diffuse characteristics; Γ = general expectations.)

inequality can engender greater racial animosity in culturally homogeneous societies than in culturally diverse environments.[12]

Diversity Strategy

Consider next a president who carries out a strategy that celebrates diversity. She is convinced that race and ethnic prejudices produce inequality. She argues that the key to eliminating durable inequalities, and the ethnic tensions they generate, lies in creating a system of cultural pluralism that reduces differences in the status value of cultural characteristics. Her administration establishes programs that encourage ethnic groups to maintain their distinct cultures. Citizens are inspired to believe that "[cultural diversity] is one factor in assessing an individual as someone who has the potential to contribute something distinctive and important" (Rudenstine 1996).[13] In short, her policies advance the belief that

---

[12] This can be particularly troublesome for racially distinct groups that have undergone the incorporative form of cultural assimilation. As an example, black Americans have taken on many of the cultural characteristics of white, Anglo-Saxon Protestants. The persistent subordinate status of blacks undermines the rationale for further cultural assimilation and serves as one source of black hostility toward the white majority.

[13] I use this quotation from Harvard's president in 1999 as an exemplar of ideas associated with the strategy.

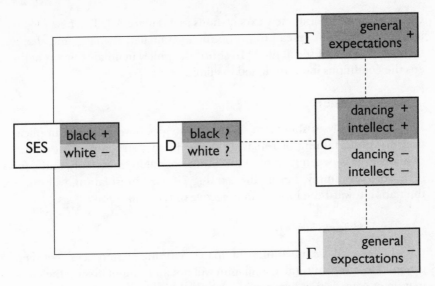

Figure 3.6 L-structure that describes the generation of race prejudice. (C = specific performance characteristics; D = diffuse characteristics; Γ = general expectations; SES = socioeconomic status.)

group characteristics are important to individual success. Figure 3.6 represents the theoretical implications of this strategy.

Figure 3.6 describes a situation free of race prejudice (i.e., race has no status value). The two races differ on socioeconomic status, a scarce resource.[14] Several theories (Bonacich 1972; Jasso 1991; Ridgeway 1991) argue that race will acquire status value under these circumstances, with blacks having higher status than whites. I argue that the president's proclamation triggers the assignment of status value to race. The assertion legitimizes the idea that blacks and whites, "[make] contributions [performances] [that are] distinctive and important." Note that the statement does not identify the performance domains or the performance characteristics (Cs) to which race is relevant. Furthermore, the president does not claim that one race or ethnic group is superior to any other. Yet, the authority of the presidency (and of any other authoritative figures who express support for the president's position) legitimizes these expectations. They activate L-structures like that in

[14] These initial conditions are identical to the starting conditions for several theories that describe how nominal or ascribed characteristics acquire status value. Each argument presumes that the initial inequalities occur in the *absence* of prejudice or discrimination. Bonacich (1972) was one of the earliest to address this issue, but her arguments were embedded in a broader analysis of ethnic antagonism. More recently, Ridgeway (1991) and Jasso (1991) have offered more systematic theories of the process.

Figure 3.1 and generate new expectations as in Figure 3.3. The newly legitimized expectations spread to previously unevaluated domains and shape the organization of social life.[15] In short, the policy maintains or strengthens the conditions it was designed to eliminate.

Discussion

My analyses show that the two strategies have different implications for undermining or replacing the legitimacy structures that define relationships between race or cultural heterogeneity, inequality, and conflict. They also imply that neither strategy, if used in isolation, will move the nation toward the long-term objective of racial harmony.

Assimilation Strategy

Cultural assimilation eliminates cultural differences between groups. However, cultural assimilation will not and cannot ensure the elimination of competition between races and ethnic groups. As a result, it cannot guarantee conflict-free relations. Beyond cultural assimilation, ethnic groups must undergo a series of complex *processes* before they can accomplish total assimilation (Gordon 1964). Members of ethnic groups may become culturally identical as they undergo the incorporative form of assimilation (Horowitz 1975) but continue to identify themselves as members of distinct ethnic groups. (See discussions of "white" ethnics in Alba 1990; Waters 1990.) Under the best circumstances, cultural assimilation may only make the identification of ethnic outsiders more difficult. More important, without substantial progress through the other six stages of assimilation, cultural assimilation can fuel, rather than reduce, hostility and conflict.

Diversity Strategy

My analyses suggest that a strategy of celebrating diversity will be no more successful than policies that focus on cultural assimilation. Theories of status organization (Berger et al. 1977) imply that status-based inequalities are reinforced when group characteristics are singled out as potential or actual bases for distributing scarce resources. The effect is magnified when policies emphasize vague or ambiguous criteria (see Rudenstine's distinctive somethings cited above) rather than identifiable skills or abilities. Furthermore, celebrating diversity works at cross-purposes with policies designed to reduce prejudice. Prejudice reduction *can* reduce

---

[15] This example illustrates the creation of a L-structure that describes race-based status differences. The argument applies to existing L-structures as well; the actions I describe strengthen existing L-structures.

race-based discrimination. Public policies that connect ascribed characteristics to either performances or rewards enhance prejudices. They activate L-structures that shape individuals' expectations about the relationship between race and the distribution of socially valued rewards. In turn, legitimized prejudice motivates actions that create unequal distributions of opportunities and outcomes.

Treating cultural differences as if they had the same value or status leads to the same end. As an example, American ethnic groups differ with respect to their economic motivations and aspirations. Occupational aspirations play a role in determining a job seeker's eventual location in the occupational structure. If cultural differences in motivations affect occupational aspirations, they cannot be treated as if they were ineffectual. Ethnic differences in occupational distributions will persist if ethnic groups differ on dimensions (like motivations) that influence occupational placement. As I show above, ethnic inequalities on a single valued characteristic can generate processes that create or maintain ethnic inequality on other status dimensions (Jasso 1991; Ridgeway 1991).

A Third Strategy: Decoupling Race from Situational Elements

If neither cultural assimilation nor celebrating diversity is likely to create racial harmony, is there any strategy that might have a better chance of success? A legitimacy analysis suggests a possibility. Any number of policy makers have argued that harmony depends on prejudice reduction. Such policies must change fundamental sentiments or delegitimate L-structures that link characteristics like race to other characteristics, performances, and possessions.

Elizabeth G. Cohen's path-breaking work on interaction disability (Cohen 1972; Cohen and Roper 1972) shows that equating persons on specific performance characteristics (Cs) can reduce or eliminate the performance-differentiating consequences of race and gender prejudice.[16] Cohen's strategy might be effective because it decouples ascribed characteristics from other characteristics (e.g., skills and abilities) and performances. Her interventions attack legitimized belief systems (L-structures) that equate race or ethnic sameness with homogeneity of characteristics and actions. Her work shows that persons from *different* ethnic groups can possess the same valued qualities. The decoupling process can be enhanced

---

[16] Cohen used laboratory interventions to equate actors on specific characteristics. She did not determine whether the effects of those interventions transferred to other situations. However, other researchers (Markovsky, Smith, and Berger 1984; Robinson and Preston 1976; Wagner, Ford, and Ford 1986) show that the interventions transfer to new situations *and* to other interaction partners.

if cultural assimilation reduces the number of dimensions on which members of the affected groups differ.

Cohen's technique differs substantially from the strategies reviewed above. The assimilation strategy attempts to create equality and harmony between races and ethnic groups by eliminating the tangible differences that establish their group character. The position is entirely consistent with the outcomes described by assimilation theory (Park 1950). However, policies that select—and policies must always select—which characteristics to privilege or to cast into oblivion ensure continued prejudice and discrimination.[17] The strategy reaffirms relevance relationships between race or ethnic heritage and a variety of secondary social characteristics.

By way of contrast, proponents of a diversity strategy claim that differences in the status given to racial or cultural characteristics drive the development of durable inequality. As a solution, they recommend policies that treat cultural differences *as though* they are equivalent. They seem to assume that those who accept the equivalence of tangible characteristics will accept the equivalence of the groups with which the characteristics are associated. This strategy also reaffirms the connection between social groups and the characteristics that group members are expected to possess. The idea of group characteristics dies slowly. While the distributions of skills, abilities, and other valued qualities may vary across groups, there exists as much diversity within groups as between them. Cohen's strategy exposes the *irrelevance* of race or ethnic heritage to cultural characteristics that matter. She points out that valued (and disvalued) qualities, possessions, and performances are distributed among the members of all social groups. Over the long term, her strategy erodes the general expectations associated with ascribed characteristics.

Some may question the suitability of Cohen's strategy for treating societal problems. Although Cohen began her work in the isolation of a laboratory, her ideas are based on sound theoretical reasoning. She and her colleagues have used sociological theory to devise successful intervention strategies for school districts across the nation. Finally, note that the U.S. Army has used similar techniques to reduce tension and ethnic stratification within its ranks (see Moskos and Butler's Chapter 10 in this volume; Moskos and Butler 1996). The army's successes are noteworthy because of the size and scope of the organization.

These last observations raise interesting possibilities. Any program or policy that disrupts the linkages between states of ascribed characteristics,

[17] As an example, English has become the national language and the dominant language in international commerce and science. Yet, recent attempts to designate it the *official* national language have met with opposition from a number of ethnic groups.

other valued characteristics, and general expectations ought to weaken interaction patterns that bolster inequalities based on ascribed characteristics. In turn, reducing durable inequalities ought to reduce ethnic hostility. The process does not require cultural homogeneity. In fact, a particular form of cultural pluralism would appear to reduce both inequality and hostility. I refer to societies that recognize and encourage the cultural amalgamation or "borrowing" that describes the history of human progress (Sowell 1994). In such societies, no group retains "possession" of particular cultural forms, and their leaders do not claim that race and cultural heritage serve as qualifications for the distribution of scarce societal resources. Under such circumstances, members of pluralistic societies might live in harmony with, and befriend, the strangers next door.

CHAPTER FOUR

Gender, Sexuality, and Inequality: When Many Become One, Who Is the One and What Happens to the Others?

Sandra Lipsitz Bem

he concept of *e pluribus unum* has for so long been treated as a source of pride for our nation, as a theory and a practice of how Americans have historically absorbed and honored their diversity, that even Walker, Moen, and Dempster-McClain gesture toward it in the introduction to this volume as a symbol of our country's distinctive pluralism.

I, however, treat the concept quite differently. More specifically, I use it as a symbolic jumping-off point for my argument that our country will never truly come to terms with diversity in a fair and inclusive way, nor will we ever stop turning every nondominant group's difference into disadvantage, until we recognize that discrimination frequently hides itself behind a facade of neutrality. And ironically enough, we can begin to see at least some of this hidden discrimination if we ask two questions that follow logically from the superficially neutral concept of *e pluribus unum*. (At least they follow logically now that we no longer believe in the melting pot theory of becoming one people.) I pose these two questions in my title: When many become one, who is the one, and what happens to all the oth-

This chapter is adapted with permission from Sandra L. Bem, *The Lenses of Gender: Transforming the Debate on Sexual Inequality* (New Haven, CT: Yale University Press, 1993).

ers? Although these questions could be asked with respect to many types of discrimination (including that based on race, religion, class, national origin, and language), I discuss them, first, with respect to discrimination against women and, then, with respect to discrimination against sex and gender minorities, especially lesbians and gay men.

Androcentrism: Out of Two, One—and the One Is Male

> By marriage, the husband and wife are one person in law: that is, the very being or legal existence of the woman is suspended during the marriage, or at least is incorporated and consolidated into that of the husband; under whose wing, protection, and cover, she performs everything. (Blackstone 1979, 1:430)

This eighteenth-century example, known as the doctrine of coverture, gives us one version of an answer to our questions: When a man and a woman become one, the one they become is the man, and the woman no longer exists. Granted that this example is both extreme and outdated in its particularity, nevertheless, I will argue in this chapter that, even today, our social institutions are so thoroughly saturated with androcentrism (i.e., they still so thoroughly presume that the one is a man) that rather than being truly inclusive of the differences between women and men, they instead transform those differences into a massive female disadvantage. And they do this in most instances not by discriminating against women overtly but by disguising what is really just a male standard or norm as gender neutrality.

Early Views of Androcentrism

The first feminist to name the concept of androcentrism was Charlotte Perkins Gilman, who wrote in *The Man-Made World or Our Androcentric Culture* in 1911 that

> all our human scheme of things rests on the same tacit assumption; man being held the human type; woman a sort of accompaniment and subordinate assistant, merely essential to the making of people. She has held always the place of a preposition in relation to man. She has always been considered above him or below him, before him, behind him, beside him, a wholly relative existence—"Sydney's sister," "Pembroke's mother"—but never by any chance Sydney or Pembroke herself. . . . It is no easy matter to deny or reverse a universal assumption. . . . What we see immediately around us, what we are born into and grow up with, . . . we assume to be the order of nature. . . . Nevertheless, . . . what we have all this time called "human nature" . . . was in great part only male nature. . . . Our androcentric culture is so shown to have been, and still to be, a masculine culture in excess, and therefore undesirable. (20–22)

Without actually using the term itself, Simone de Beauvoir brilliantly elaborated on the concept of androcentrism, and integrated it more completely into a theory of sexual inequality, in *The Second Sex* (1952), which was originally published in France in 1949. According to de Beauvoir, the historical relationship of men and women is not best represented as a relationship between dominant and subordinate, or between high and low status, or even between positive and negative. No, in all male-dominated cultures,

> man represents both the positive and the neutral, as is indicated by the common use of *man* to designate human beings in general; whereas woman represents only the negative, defined by limiting criteria, without reciprocity. . . . It amounts to this: just as for the ancients there was an absolute vertical with reference to which the oblique was defined, so there is an absolute human type, the masculine. Woman has ovaries, a uterus; these peculiarities imprison her in her subjectivity, circumscribe her within the limits of her own nature. It is often said that she thinks with her glands. Man superbly ignores the fact that his anatomy also includes glands, such as the testicles, and that they secrete hormones. He thinks of his body as a direct and normal connection with the world, which he believes he apprehends objectively, whereas he regards the body of woman as a hindrance, a prison, weighed down by everything peculiar to it. . . . Thus humanity is male and man defines woman not in herself but as relative to him; she is not regarded as an autonomous being. . . . She is defined and differentiated with reference to man and not he with reference to her; she is the incidental, the inessential as opposed to the essential. He is the Subject, he is the Absolute—she is the Other. (xv–xvi)

These quotations make androcentrism fairly clear, but I want to analyze it further and then provide some concrete examples to illustrate it. As I see it, androcentrism is the privileging of males, male experience, and the male perspective. One can describe this privileging in a variety of ways. For example, one can say it's the treating of males as the main characters in the drama of human life around whom all action revolves and through whose eyes all reality is to be interpreted, and the treating of females as the peripheral or marginal characters in the drama of human life whose purpose for being is defined only in relation to the main—or male—character. This goes along with Gilman's idea that women are always defined in relation to men. On the other hand, one can also say that androcentrism is the treating of the male as if he were some kind of universal, objective, or neutral representative of the human species, in contrast to the female, who is some kind of a special case—something different, deviant, extra, or other. This goes along with de Beauvoir's idea that man is the human and woman is the other.

Some examples will help to clarify the concept of androcentrism even further. In language, there's the generic use of "he" to mean "he or she"; this treats "he" as universal, human, genderless, and "she" as specifically female. In the Old Testament story of Adam and Eve, there is the fact that not only is Adam created first (in God's image) but Eve is created (out of Adam) to be his helper. Even worse, only Adam is explicitly given the power to name every creature on earth from his own perspective. And then, of course, there is Freud's theory of penis envy, a theory which treats the male body as so obviously being the human norm—and the female body as so obviously being an inferior departure from that norm—that the mere sight of the other sex's genitals not only fills the three-year-old boy with "a horror of the mutilated creature he has just seen," it also leads the three-year-old girl to "make her judgment and her decision in a flash; she has seen it and knows that she is without it and wants to have it" (Freud 1925, 190–91).

Three Androcentric Legal Rulings

Let me shift now to some examples of androcentrism that are both more modern and more pertinent to everyday life. I begin with the U.S. Supreme Court's rulings related to pregnancy—in particular, the Court's rulings on whether employers can exclude pregnancy from the package of disability insurance benefits that they provide to their employees. The situation is this: An employer says its insurance benefits will cover every medical condition that keeps an employee away from work, *except* pregnancy and giving birth. Is this exclusion all right? The U.S. Supreme Court says yes. Question: Why it is all right to exclude pregnancy if discrimination against women is now illegal? Because, says the Court, although such an exclusion may appear on the surface to discriminate against women, in actuality, it is gender-neutral.

The Court has tried to argue this claim of gender neutrality in a number of different ways. Most important, however, the Court wrote in *General Electric Co. v. Gilbert* (1976) that "pregnancy-related disabilities constitute an *additional* risk, unique to women, and the failure to compensate them for this risk does not destroy the presumed parity of the benefits . . . [that accrue] to men and women alike."

The problem here should be clear. Just like Sigmund Freud himself, the Court is androcentrically defining the male body as the standard human body; hence it is seeing nothing unusual or inappropriate about giving that standard human body the full insurance coverage that it would need for each and every condition that might befall it. Consistent with this androcentric perspective, the Court is also defining equal protection as the granting to women of every conceivable benefit that this standard human body might require—which, of course, does not include disability coverage for pregnancy.

Had the Court had even the slightest sensitivity to the meaning of androcentrism, there are at least two truly gender-neutral standards that it would have surely considered instead. In set-theory terms, these are (1) the *intersection* of male and female bodies, which would have narrowly covered only those conditions that befall both men and women alike; and (2) the *union* of male and female bodies, which would have broadly covered all those conditions that befall both men and women separately. In fact, however, the Court was so blind to the meaning of androcentrism that it saw nothing amiss when, in the name of equal protection, it granted a whole package of special benefits to men and men alone.

The androcentric privileging of male experience does not always involve the male body. As often as not, it involves the male biography. Consider, for example, the case of *Personnel Administrator of Massachusetts v. Feeney* (1979). In this case the U.S. Supreme Court ruled that although women were "overwhelmingly" disadvantaged by a state law mandating a lifetime preference for qualified veterans over qualified nonveterans in the filling of civil service positions, such a law was not unconstitutional. Why? Because "the statute has always been neutral as to gender," and so the distinction "is, as it seems to be, quite simply between veterans and nonveterans, not between men and women." As far as the Court's equal protection analysis is concerned, it is thus an irrelevant aspect of history that so many fewer women than men have been allowed to enter the privileged position of being veterans.

Consider finally our culture's legal definition of self-defense, which holds that a defendant can be found innocent of homicide only if he or she perceived imminent danger of great bodily harm or death and responded to that danger with only as much force as was necessary to defend against it. Although that definition had always seemed to have nothing whatsoever to do with gender and hence to be perfectly gender-neutral, it no longer seemed quite so gender-neutral once feminist legal scholars began to study it. They pointed out how much better it fit with a scenario involving two men in an isolated episode of sudden violence than with a scenario involving a woman being battered, first in relatively minor ways and then with escalating intensity over the years, by a man who is not only bigger and stronger than she is, but from whom she cannot readily get police protection because he is her husband. The "aha" experience here is the realization that if this woman's situation had been anywhere near the center of the policy makers' consciousness on the day when they were first drafting our culture's supposedly neutral definition of self-defense, they might not have placed so much emphasis on the defendant's being in imminent danger at the particular instant when the ultimate act of self-defense is finally made.

Of course, it is not only in the context of insurance or veteran's benefits or even self-defense that the male difference from women is "affirmatively compensated" (MacKinnon 1987, 36) by American society whereas the female difference from men is treated as an intrinsic barrier to sexual equality. To quote Catharine MacKinnon more fully:

[V]irtually every quality that distinguishes men from women is . . . affirmatively compensated in this society. Men's physiology defines most sports, their needs define auto and health insurance coverage, their socially designed biographies define workplace expectations and successful career patterns, their perspectives and concerns define quality in scholarship, their experiences and obsessions define merit, their objectification of life defines art, their military service defines citizenship, their presence defines family, their inability to get along with each other—their wars and rulerships—defines history, their image defines god, and their genitals define sex. For each of their differences from women, what amounts to an affirmative action plan is [thus] in effect, otherwise known as the structure and values of American society. (36)

Androcentrism in the Workplace

Of all the androcentric institutions on MacKinnon's list that are typically thought of as gender-neutral, there is perhaps no institution more directly responsible for denying women their rightful share of America's economic and political resources than the structure of the American work world. That work world may seem to many Americans to be as gender-neutral as it needs to be now that explicit discrimination against women has finally been made illegal. In fact, however, it is so thoroughly organized around a worker who is not only presumed to be male rather than female, but who is also presumed to have a wife at home to take care of all of the needs of his household—including the care of his children—that it "naturally" and automatically ends up transforming what is intrinsically just a male/female difference into a massive female disadvantage.

Imagine how differently our social world would be organized if all of the workers in our workforce were women rather than men, and hence most of the workers in our workforce—including those at the highest levels of government and industry—were also either pregnant or responsible for childcare during at least a certain portion of their adult lives. Given such a workforce, "working" would so obviously need to coordinate with both birthing and parenting that institutions facilitating that coordination would be built into the very structure of the social world. There would thus be not only such things as paid pregnancy leave, paid days off for sick children, and paid childcare, but also a match—rather than a mismatch—between the hours of the work day and the hours of the school day. There would probably also be a completely different definition of a prototypical work life, with the norm being not a continuous forty hours or more per week from adulthood to old age, but a transition from less than forty hours per week when the children are young to forty hours or more per week when the children are older.

The lesson of this alternative reality should be clear. It is not women's biological and historical role as mothers that is limiting their access to America's economic and political resources. It is a social world so androcentric in its organization that it provides but one institutionalized mechanism for coordinating work in the paid labor force with the responsibilities of being a parent: having a wife at home to take care of one's children.

To people who do not yet appreciate either what androcentrism is or how it operates institutionally, the suggestion that we need to change our social institutions so that they are more accommodating to women or more inclusive of women's experience seems completely wrong-headed. As they would surely describe it, it seems like a move away from gender neutrality and hence in the absolutely wrong direction of where America ought to be going.

But in fact, America's institutions have been so thoroughly organized for so long from an androcentric perspective—that is, they have for so long been taking care of men's special needs automatically while women's special needs have been either treated as special cases or simply left unmet—that *the only way for them to even begin to approximate gender neutrality is for our society to finally begin giving women as complete a package of special benefits as it has always given to men and men alone.*

Consider an analogy that plays on another of my own nonprivileged attributes, not my femaleness this time, but my shortness. (I happen to be only four feet nine inches tall). Imagine, if you will, a whole community of short people just like me. Given the argument sometimes made in our society that short people are unable to be firefighters because they are neither tall enough nor strong enough to do the job, the question arises: Would all the houses in this community eventually burn down? Well yes, if we short people had to use the heavy ladders and hoses designed by and for tall people. But no, if we (being as smart as short people are) could instead construct lighter ladders and hoses usable by both tall and short people. The moral here should be obvious: It isn't short biology that's the problem for short people; it's short biology being forced to function in a tall-centered social structure.

At first glance, *e pluribus unum* may sound unimpeachable as a national motto. But the "unum" who ends up serving as the model or template for our social institutions is not some equal opportunity amalgam of the many.

It is, in the context of men and women living in an androcentric society, the man. And this unfortunately forces the woman to function in a social world whose institutions do not fit her very well because they were designed with somebody else in mind. As familiar, comfortable, gender-neutral, and natural as our society's institutions may thus appear to be now that explicit discrimination against women has finally been made illegal, in fact, our institutions are still so thoroughly saturated with androcentrism that even those that do not discriminate against women explicitly—like the definition of self-defense—must be treated as inherently suspect.

Gender Polarization: Out of Many, Two and Only Two—and the Two Are Male/Masculine/Heterosexual and Female/Feminine/Heterosexual

In determining the meaning of any Act of Congress, . . . the word "marriage" means only a legal union between one man and one woman as husband and wife, and the word "spouse" refers only to a person of the opposite sex who is a husband or a wife (Defense of Marriage Act, Senate Bill S1999, July 29, 1996). After being charged with violating the Georgia statute criminalizing sodomy by committing that act with another adult male in the bedroom of his home, respondent Hardwick brought suit . . . , challenging the constitutionality of the statute insofar as it criminalized consensual sodomy . . . Held: The Georgia Statute is constitutional . . . Georgia Code Ann. [sec.]16-6-2 (1984) provides, in pertinent part, as follows: "(a) A person [heterosexual or homosexual] commits the offense of sodomy when he performs or submits to any sexual act involving the sex organs of one person and the mouth or anus of another . . . ." John and Mary Doe [a heterosexual couple] were also plaintiffs in the action. They alleged that they wished to engage in sexual activity proscribed by [sec.]16-6-2 in the privacy of their home, and that they had been "chilled and deterred" from engaging in such activity by both the existence of the statute and Hardwick's arrest. . . . The District Court held, however, that because they had neither sustained, nor were in immediate danger of sustaining, any direct injury from the enforcement of the statute, they did not have proper standing to maintain the action. . . . The only claim properly before the Court, therefore, is Hardwick's challenge . . . as applied to consensual homosexual sodomy. We express no opinion on the constitutionality of the Georgia statute as applied to other acts of sodomy. (*Bowers v. Hardwick* 1986, 186, 188)

As these quotations suggest, when we move from discrimination against women to discrimination against gender and sexuality minorities, including lesbians and gay men, the motto for our society moves a bit too, from *e pluribus unum* to *e pluribus duo*. The principle, however, remains the same. People come in at least eighteen varieties of sex/gender/desire: two sexes (male/female) times three genders (masculine/feminine/androgynous) times three sexualities (heterosexual/homosexual/bisexual). Yet our society treats two—and only two—of these varieties as the human standard or norm. And not only that, it also treats the privileging of these as biologically natural and hence neutral. Put somewhat differently, our society treats as a given that there is some kind of natural link between what sex you are and what kind of gender and sexuality you have. Hence the only two clusters of sex/gender/desire that are seen as natural and normal are, as noted above, male/masculine/attracted to women and female/feminine/attracted to men.

In fact, however, no natural link exists between sex, gender, and sexuality. Instead there is a set of cultural processes that create the appearance of such a natural link. I call these cultural processes *gender polarization*.

There are many different levels of gender polarization. Assuming the existence of two and only two sexes (which we will later have reason to question), gender polarization at the simplest level is just the cultural exaggeration of whatever sex differences exist naturally—by removing facial, leg, and body hair from women, for example, and by building up muscle mass in men. But it isn't only the exaggeration of what already exists. It is also the cultural construction of differences from scratch to make the sexes even more different from one another than they would otherwise be—by creating distinctive male and female hairstyles, for example, and male and female clothing styles. These gender markers take on particular cultural significance during childhood when there is nothing other than the genitalia (which are usually covered) to identify sex.

More important for our purposes here, however, gender polarization is also the cultural construction of mutually exclusive behavioral scripts for males and females, with the corollary that any person or behavior that deviates from these scripts is defined as problematic—as unnatural or immoral from a religious perspective or as biologically anomalous or psychologically pathological from a scientific perspective. Stated more abstractly (and thereby covering all the examples described thus far and others as well), gender polarization is the organizing of virtually all of social life around the male-female distinction. It is the superimposing of the male-female distinction on so many aspects of the social world that a cultural connection is thereby forged between sex and virtually every other aspect of human experience, including not just modes of dress and social roles but even ways of expressing emotion and experiencing sexual desire.

Like androcentrism, gender polarization reproduces itself in generation after generation because its assumptions are embedded in cultural discourses and social institutions, including science, religion, law, education, and the mass media, to name but a few. My focus in this chapter, however, is on science. More specifically, I describe how, since the middle of the nineteenth century, even the supposedly neutral and objective fields of medicine, psychology, and psychiatry have together given scientific and medical legitimacy not only to the gender-polarizing cultural requirement that the sex of the body match the gender of the psyche but also to the cultural privileging of exclusive heterosexuality.

Nineteenth-Century Science: Sexual Inversion

The mid- to late nineteenth century was a time of great social disruption in the United States, with much of this disruption (though certainly not all) centering on two different kinds of threats to the society's sex and gender order. The first threat involved feminist demands for women's rights, including both the right to vote and the right to higher education. The second threat involved a dramatic shift in both the meaning and the social organization of sexual behavior, with not only a thriving business emerging in prostitution and a growing rate of out-of-wedlock pregnancy, but also the beginnings in urban areas of a predominantly male homosexual subculture.

Although there are many different things that can be emphasized about the significance of these sexual developments, what I want to emphasize here is that because they occurred at approximately the same time as the feminist demand for equal rights, they helped to create the feeling that the whole sex and gender system of the nineteenth century was coming apart at the seams. It was not just the rights of women that were at issue after all. It was the very political, social, psychological, and even sexual meaning of being male or female.

In the context of this massive disruption to the sex and gender order, it is not surprising that social scientists and physicians began to focus an extraordinary amount of their attention on both the nature of men and women and the meaning of sexuality. For the conservative social reformers, what this involved was the mounting of a political battle against anything and everything that facilitated nonprocreative sexuality, including not only prostitution and homosexuality but also masturbation, abortion, and birth control. For the social scientists and the physicians, what it involved was a veritable explosion of theorizing both about the biological origins of male-female difference (which I do not talk about here) and about the biological and pathological nature of gender deviation.

Odd as it may seem in the twentieth century, this explosion of theorizing about gender deviation was not yet focused on homosexuality *per se*, but on what was then seen as the biological and psychological pathology of anyone who deviated from the culture's traditional gender scripts, including not only those we would today call homosexuals, bisexuals, and lesbians, but feminists as well. One of the reasons both feminists and sexual minorities could be pathologized with the very same condition or disease is that nineteenth-century culture had not yet conceptualized sexual orientation as a distinct and separate aspect of a person's psyche. Any departure from the culture's gender-polarizing scripts was thus seen as but another instance of what psychiatrists, physicians, and sexologists were just then beginning to define as "sexual inversion." This new category of pathology, it must be emphasized, was conceptualized "not as homosexuality, but as . . . a complete exchange of gender identity of which erotic behavior was but one small part" (D'Emilio and Freedman 1988, 226).

Consistent with this totalizing emphasis on gender identity rather than on sex-of-partner preference, whenever it was discovered about a particular married couple that, rather than being a man and a woman, they were actually two women—one of whom dressed and "passed" as a man—the doctors of the day all but ignored the "wife." She, they thought, was just the passive—and gender-normal—victim of her inverted "husband" (Greenberg 1988, 382).

In time, of course, both the culture and the medical and scientific communities did begin to conceptualize a person's sexual orientation as a distinct aspect of a person's psyche, at which point the sexual inversion discourse split into two branches. The first branch, which I here discuss at some length, stigmatized *sexual* deviations from the culture's male and female scripts as pathological, this branch being the whole tradition of research, theory, and therapy with homosexuals. In contrast, the second branch, which will not be discussed here, stigmatized *nonsexual* deviations from the culture's male and female scripts as pathological. At least three separate traditions within psychology and psychiatry have been a part of this second nonsexual branch, all three of which are discussed at length in *The Lenses of Gender* (Bem 1993). These three traditions have been concerned, respectively, with the assessment of masculinity-femininity, the treatment and prevention of masculinity-femininity "disorders," especially "transsexualism" and "gender-identity disorder" in childhood, and the development of masculinity-femininity in "normal" children.

Twentieth-Century Science: Freud and Homosexuality

The twentieth-century's tradition of research on homosexuality as a sexual orientation begins—as does so much else in psychology and psychiatry—with the psychoanalytic theory of Sigmund Freud. Although, in the hands of Freud's followers, psychoanalytic theory was ultimately to become the century's most powerful instrument for privileging hetero-sexuality by pathologizing homosexuality, Freud's own analysis of homo-sexuality actually contained the seeds of a scientific challenge to the privileging of heterosexuality. Two specific details of Freud's theory are especially relevant.

First, the "sexual instinct" that children bring into the world is "at first without an object" (Freud 1905, 99). Put somewhat differently, it is initially so "auto-erotic" and so "polymorphously perverse" that it can readily attach itself to any object or activity that gives the infant physical pleasure (98–100). (This is often described, somewhat inaccurately, as original bisexuality.) Second, the sexual instinct ultimately "finds a sexual object" only after a lengthy process of psychosexual development (73). Given the polymor-phous perversity of the initial instinct, moreover, that psychosexual process necessarily involves both the progressive focusing of the individual on just one subset of all possible sexual objects and the progressive exclusion—or repression into the unconscious—of all other sexual objects.

What both of these two details share in common is the underlying assumption that "the sexual instinct and the sexual object are merely sol-dered together" during the course of the child's psychosexual develop-ment. As Freud was himself aware, this "loosen[ing of] the bond that exists in our thoughts between instinct and object" (Freud 1905, 14) not only has the very radical effect of transforming heterosexuality from a natural phe-nomenon requiring no explanation at all to a phenomenon requiring just as much explanation as homosexuality, it also has the effect of placing homosexuality outside the bounds of therapeutic intervention.

The reason for Freud's seeing such little possibility of a therapeutic cure for homosexuality is quite straightforward. "One must remember," he wrote, "that normal sexuality also depends upon a restriction in the choice of object; in general, to undertake to convert a fully developed homosex-ual into a heterosexual is not much more promising than to do the reverse" (Freud 1920, 207). The reason for his pessimistic prognosis was simple: The task to be carried out does "not consist in resolving a neurotic conflict but in converting one variety of the genital organization of sexuality into the other." This is "never an easy matter" (206).

None of this is to say, however, that Freud ever treated homosexuality and heterosexuality as equivalent. He did not. And the reason he did not was that he always privileged reproductive sexuality as the "final normal shape of psychosexual development" (Freud 1905, 73). This made homo-sexuality not an illness or a pathology but "a variety of the sexual function produced by a certain arrest of sexual development" (from Freud's letter to an American mother, quoted in Bayer 1981, 27). This theoretical conclusion contains much heterosexism, of course, but as we shall see, it is not nearly so heterosexist as what was to come later.

Freud's Psychoanalytic Successors

Beginning in about 1930, Freud's psychoanalytic successors made two fundamental changes to psychoanalytic theory, changes whose cumulative effect was to destroy not only the radicalism inherent in Freud's analysis of heterosexuality but also the social tolerance inherent in Freud's analysis of homosexuality. The first change was to undo Freud's assumption of original bisexuality; this in turn undid the psychoanalytic symmetry that had existed between heterosexuality and homosexuality. Put somewhat differently, whereas latent homosexuality had earlier been assumed to exist within every heterosexual just as latent heterosexuality was assumed to exist within every homosexual, now heterosexuality was seen as an original state requiring no special explanation, and homosexuality was seen as the result of a traumatized heterosexuality that lay dormant—but open to therapeutic actualization—in every homosexual. The second change was to situate the homosexual's arrest of development during an earlier period of childhood than Freud had originally situated it—in particular, during the oral period rather than the oedipal period. This shift backward in time had the effect of pathologizing the homosexual much more than had been the case in Freud's own writing. And thus it came to pass that in 1952, homosexuality was included without controversy in the first official listing of mental disorders published by the American Psychiatric Association.

During this same period, the psychoanalytic literature on homosexuality also took on an extraordinarily hostile and abusive tone which was not even acknowledged by psychoanalysts until the 1980s, when an article published in the *American Journal of Psychoanalytic Therapy* (Kwawer 1980) finally suggested that the psychoanalytic discourse on homosexuality may have been distorted over the years by the psychoanalysts' own unconscious anxieties.

This failure on the part of psychoanalysis to keep its own homophobia under control had dire consequences in the post–World War II years, when homosexuality became "incorporat[ed] . . . into the demonology of the McCarthy era" (D'Emilio 1983, 48). The federal government thereby banned homosexuals from all government service and also authorized a national witch hunt by the FBI in concert with local vice squads. Although the responsibility for this homophobic frenzy cannot be placed entirely in the hands of the psychiatric or even the psychoanalytic establishment, it is reasonable to suppose that if these two august groups had not themselves produced a discourse with such a rigid commitment to the pathologizing of homosexuality, the federal government might not itself have been able to so easily justify a policy of systematically denying gay men and lesbians their political and civil rights.

Depathologizing Homosexuality

Much has changed since the 1950s, of course, not the least of which is that homosexuality *per se* is no longer included in the American Psychiatric Association's official list of mental disorders. This depathologizing of homosexuality must be seen both as a product of the politics of the gay rights movement and as a part of a whole new intellectual tradition related to human sexuality in both the humanities and the social sciences. This new tradition conceptualizes human sexuality not as having any primordially natural form, but as being a biohistorical construction whose form can be as differently shaped from one time and place to another as, for example, eating, which is also a biohistorical construction. So humans everywhere will have sex, just as humans everywhere will eat, but what rules they will establish about how and with whom they will have sex, what institutions they will set up to enforce those "how" and "who" rules, and even what they will define as sexual or sexually desirable in the first place will have no universal—or ahistorical—form.

From this perspective, nothing is sacred or even biologically special about the requirement of exclusive heterosexuality in the mutually exclusive scripts for males and females in contemporary America; that exclusiveness is simply a historical fact about how sexuality happens to be organized in this particular time and place. Moreover, it is a historical fact that has been helped along by a whole variety of cultural discourses and social institutions, including the allied disciplines of medicine, psychology, and psychiatry, whose gender-polarizing theories since the middle of the nineteenth century have defined only exclusive heterosexuality as natural and normal—and everything else as pathological. In other words, when gender polarization became superimposed on the diversity of sexual desires, diversity that is a part of our natural human capacity, two and only two types of human beings were defined as natural and normal: men attracted to women and women attracted to men. Everything else was pathologized—and not just pathologized but criminalized as well.

Depathologizing All Those Who Violate
Gender Polarization: Diversity as Natural

Since the end of the nineteenth century, most discussions about nonmasculine males, nonfeminine females, and nonheterosexual males and females have focused on the twin questions of cause and cure. The underlying assumption has always been the same: something has misfired in the biology or the experience of these individuals and needs to be fixed.

In addition to the problematic assumption of pathology, the question, "What went wrong?" contains an even deeper problematic assumption: that homogeneity within each sex is natural and diversity unnatural. This deeper assumption is apparent even in discussions that do not explicitly pathologize anyone but merely assume that the psychic outcome of these gender and sexuality minorities requires causal explanation whereas the psychic outcome of the majority does not. Again the assumption here is that something is natural about all the "matches" between sex, gender, and sexuality and something unnatural about all the "mismatches."

As I see it, however, there are too many "mismatches" in too many times and places for them to be anything other than completely natural. Moreover, what these so-called mismatches show is that the nature of human gender and sexuality is not predetermined in either the individual or the culture by either nature or nurture; rather, at both the individual and the cultural levels, they are the outcome of an interaction between biology and history. And because of that interaction, the potential for diversity is enormous, across different cultures and across different males and females within the same culture.

Once again the best analogy is with food preferences. Human beings are born with a general desire to eat and a general capacity to desire whatever specific foods are defined as edible in a particular time and place. At the cultural level, this openness to experience interacts with differences in the availability of different foods and with a whole variety of other historical factors to produce the enormous diversity of food preferences that exists from culture to culture. At the individual level, this same openness interacts with individual differences in personal experience and with any individual differences that may exist in the biology of taste to produce the enormous diversity of food preferences that also exist from person to person within the same culture.

This biohistorical model of human food preferences reverses the usual assumption about what kind of relation to expect between the sex of the body and the nature of one's gender and sexuality. Specifically, it suggests not gender polarization between males and females but richness and diversity across different cultures, as well as among males and females within the same culture.

With this one critical assumption reversed, the psychological question that so often comes up in discussions of nonmasculine males, nonfeminine females, and nonheterosexual males and females—"What went wrong?" or even "Why do they exist?"—makes no sense. Nothing went wrong, and they exist, in one form or another, for the same reason that their more conventional counterparts exist. Because in the domain of gender and sexuality, just as in the domain of eating, diversity is natural.

For many years, Cornell anthropologist Kathryn March has begun her guest lecture in my undergraduate course on the social construction of gender and sexuality with the following analogy: *Sex is to gender as light is to color.* Her idea here is a simple one. Both sex and light are natural physical continua, whereas gender and color are historically and culturally constructed categories that arbitrarily divide sex and light into named clusters invested with cultural meaning. Thus, in neither domain is there anything sacred— or biologically special—about the particular categories constructed by any given culture.

I have always loved this analogy because it allows me to make an ironic reversal. With respect to color categories, anthropologists have found that some cultures have only two categories and others only three, whereas we in the United States have the full 256 of the big Crayola coloring box. Wow, I always say to my class, isn't it wonderful to be so richly blessed with so many possibilities rather than to be so impoverished as to have only light and dark or light and dark and red? But isn't it also ironic, I then add, that in the domain of sex/gender/desire, it's the other cultures who have that Crayola coloring box of multitudinous possibilities, and it is we who are impoverished, with two and only two (plus everyone we "otherize," of course) from birth to death?

And this impoverishment applies even to what is surely seen as the single most natural biological given in the whole domain of sex, gender, and sexuality: the existence of two and only two sexes. But as it turns out, even this is a product of gender polarization because at least 4 percent of all babies born in our society are *intersexuals,* who become males and females only through a difficult process known as surgical and hormonal "correction." Even at this most basic level, in other words, out of the many come two and only two, with all of the others "corrected" out of existence. And this despite the fact that in all of the research on intersexuals between 1930 and 1960, when surgical and hormonal correction was not yet standard practice, intersexuals appear to have managed their lives sufficiently well that there was "not a psychotic or a suicide in the lot" (Fausto-Sterling 1993, 24).

Conclusion

We are a diverse society with not only multiple sexes, genders, and sexualities, but multiple races, classes, ethnicities, religions, languages, and countries of origin as well. In the context of all this diversity, we clearly need to construct one *something* out of the many—perhaps a method for dealing more inclusively with the conflict that such diversity necessarily produces. But let us not be too quick to condemn the "fragmentation" and "conflict" that our society is experiencing in these multicultural times because, until recently, there has been altogether too much silencing of all the voices save the one (or the two and only two) that have been falsely represented as the many.

PART TWO

THE NEW DEMOGRAPHY
OF DURABLE INEQUALITY

CHAPTER FIVE

The State of the American Dream: Race and Ethnic Socioeconomic Inequality in the United States, 1970–90

Charles Hirschman and C. Matthew Snipp

merica is a nation of immigrants, but not all immigrant groups have experienced the same reception and opportunities or have been accorded the same influence. American ideals and cultural values were largely shaped by the Anglo heritage of the founding settlers. For most of the nation's history, those ideals have continued to define the American experience for subsequent waves of arrivals. The millions of new immigrants were expected—as were native American Indians and African slaves—to assimilate into American society and to conform to Anglo-American ideals and values. They were also expected to discard their ethnic heritage as quickly as possible. Economic incentives, including hope for their own and their children's upward mobility, motivated the immigrants' acceptance of cultural change and adaptation.

Despite the massive immigration during the late nineteenth and early twentieth centuries, the image of American society as an extension of Eng-

The authors wish to acknowledge the support provided to the second author by the Vilas Trust of the University of Wisconsin, support that was used for the processing and analysis of the data presented herein. Some of the data presented in this paper also appear in an unpublished manuscript, "Assimilation in American Society: Occupational Achievement and Earnings for Ethnic Minorities in the United States, 1970 to 1990," by the same authors.

lish society persisted throughout the first six decades of the twentieth century. As we near the end of the twentieth century and envision the future of American society, the patterns in the first half of the century—the exchange of cultural conformity for a chance at upward mobility, the American Dream—seem obsolete. There appears to be less societal pressure on new immigrants to surrender their culture, language, and traditions. In fact, group identities, including race, ethnicity, and gender, now frame claims to political power and political participation. Sensing this shift in political roles, other groups, such as American Indians, have made a concerted effort to assert the importance of their ethnic ancestry. Many traditionalists see these trends as divisive forces, while others view the emphasis on cultural diversity as the defining character of contemporary American society.

It is important to assess the state of the American Dream as the twentieth century ends—to chart where we have been and to anticipate where we are going. In this chapter, we analyze patterns and trends in social and economic inequality among the major racial and ethnic groups in American society. We track occupational and earnings attainment among men from seven major racial and ethnic groups between 1970 and 1990. The years from 1970 to 1990 represent an especially important period in American history, given the government activism of the preceding decade. In the 1960s, federal and local governments enacted civil rights laws, created affirmative action procedures, and developed equal employment opportunity programs. For the first time in American history, public policy prohibited discrimination against Americans who did not fit Anglo standards of appearance, beliefs, and behavior. From the vantage point of the present, we look back over history to see if there has been progress in the uplifting of groups that historically have been outside the economic mainstream.

We find that there has indeed been progress in the reduction of socioeconomic inequality across race and ethnic groups over the twenty years from 1970 to 1990. With the exception of Japanese Americans, however, there remain wide socioeconomic gaps between minority populations and the majority. In 1989, African Americans, Latinos, and American Indians had an income gap from the majority population that was still around $10,000 for working men—only slightly less than the gap in 1969.

Inequality in American Society

Race and ethnic differences in occupational and economic attainment raise three key issues. First is a concern about *social justice*. Ethnic (and race) differences in life chances are at odds with values that are deeply ingrained in American society: (1) that every American should have an equal opportunity to compete for the wealth of the nation; and (2) the distribution of resources should be determined by a fair and open process influenced primarily by personal merit and achievement. The fact that some groups, despite hard work and ingenuity, receive less than others raises questions about these values.

A second issue concerns the *rigidity of stratification* in America. In open societies, economic well-being is determined by effort and ability in a competition among equal actors (Lenski 1966). In rigidly stratified and closed societies, economic resources and personal well-being are disproportionately determined by ascribed characteristics (such as race or family background). The measurement of changes in the structure and determinants of inequality reveals whether American society is becoming more or less open.

Finally, the persistence of inequality is linked to the ideal of *assimilation*. The stratification literature in sociology (and especially studies of status attainment) has traditionally viewed a reduction in economic differentials as an important gauge of socioeconomic assimilation (Hirschman 1983). For example, recent data from the General Social Survey show that black-white differences persist although their magnitude has declined (Grusky and DiPrete 1990). The presence of black-white differences in education, income, occupational status, or other measures of economic well-being are prima facie evidence that socioeconomic assimilation has not occurred.

The Origins and Development of Assimilation Theory

Park and Burgess(1969, 360) defined assimilation as "a process of interpenetration and fusion in which persons and groups . . . are incorporated . . . into a common cultural life." In subsequent work, Park's *race cycle theory* described a cycle of race relations in which culturally distinct groups came into contact and eventually fused into a common culture and society. The cycle included four distinct phases: "contact, competition, accommodation, and assimilation" (Park 1950, 150).

Park and his colleagues at the University of Chicago conducted studies in the 1920s when the city of Chicago was teeming with recent European immigrants. The process of assimilation Park described captured the experience of the European newcomers. Since Park, sociologists have tended to think about assimilation as an evolutionary process taking place in more or less discrete periods or phases.

Milton Gordon's book *Assimilation in American Life* (1964) represents the next major milestone in assimilation theory. Gordon described seven different types of assimilation: cultural (acculturation), structural, marital (amalgamation), identificational, attitude receptional (absence of prejudice), behavioral receptional (absence of discrimination), and civic (absence of value and power conflict). Gordon also posited that while these different types of assimilation were connected to one another, one did not necessarily follow from the other. He noted, for example, that African Americans (in the 1950s and early 1960s) had undergone cultural assimilation but had not experienced large-scale entrance into cliques, clubs, and institutions of the host society, that is, structural assimilation.

In the years since the publication of Gordon's book, assimilation theorists have proposed a variety of schemes to describe the incorporation of ethnic minorities into the dominant society. For example, Greeley (1974) suggested that assimilation is neither linear nor unidirectional. And Yinger (1985) contended that the subprocesses Gordon (1964) had identified could be found working independently of one another. These theories display an appreciation for the complexity of assimilation and imply that complete assimilation of some groups (e.g., blacks) is not likely in the foreseeable future.

Over the years, the ideal of assimilation and the race cycle theory have endured a hail of criticism. Some of these criticisms were anticipated, even prior to the development of assimilation theory. Horace Kallen (1924) argued that immigrants should not be expected to surrender their culture and identity as a condition for participation in American society. Critics, in the 1960s, argued that ethnicity plays a central role in the lives of even the most acculturated groups (Glazer and Moynihan 1970). For many groups in American society, ethnicity is largely a symbolic construction and has a relatively minor role in their lives (Gans 1979; Waters 1990). Alba (1985), for example, wrote about the "twilight of ethnicity" among Americans of Italian descent. More recently, the phenomenon of ethnic resurgence has challenged the race cycle theory and the idea that assimilation is inevitable. There has been a remarkable revival of ethnic awareness, even among groups whose cultural identities were once considered destined for extinction, such as American Indians (Cornell 1988; Nagel 1996).

Why does ethnicity seem to matter for some groups and not for others? Gordon's theory suggests that prejudice and discrimination are critical. Acculturation is not sufficient for full participation in American society as long as "gatekeepers" continue to restrict access to neighborhoods, primary group associations, and opportunities for economic mobility. One prominent hypothesis is that "race"—physiological differences in skin color and other outward features—defines the essential difference between minority groups that are allowed to assimilate and those that are not (Cox 1948; Jordan 1974). Other perspectives suggest that racism (the differential treatment of persons of different "races") is contingent on historical conditions and that American society holds the potential to assimilate persons of different races as well as of different ethnic groups (Myrdal 1944; Wilson 1978).

There is a large body of empirical research on various dimensions of assimilation, including studies of socioeconomic assimilation, segregation in schools and housing, inter-marriage, and prejudice (Hirschman 1983). Socioeconomic assimilation (as measured by occupational and earnings attainment) is widely considered an indicator of secondary-group structural assimilation (Gordon 1964; Lieberson 1980). Although it is not possible to present a comprehensive review of the empirical studies of ethnic assimilation in American society, there are some important themes in the literature on socioeconomic assimilation that inform and guide our study.

Our analysis compares Anglo and other "white" Americans with African Americans; American Indians; Chinese, Filipino, and Japanese Americans; and Americans of Hispanic origin. European immigrants and their descendants have generally enjoyed considerable upward mobility throughout the twentieth century (Greeley 1978; Lieberson 1980). This is not to say that none were affected by bigotry and discrimination. On the contrary, there is a long history of ethnic antagonism in this country (e.g., anti-Semitic and anti-Catholic sentiment; see Baltzell 1964; Higham 1970). Nevertheless, the large socioeconomic differences that existed among these European ethnics in 1900 had virtually disappeared by the 1960s (Duncan and Duncan 1968; Neidert and Farley 1985; Lieberson and Waters 1988).

Compared with immigrants from Europe, American Indians, African Americans, and nonwhite immigrants from Asia and Latin America have not fared as well. The American Indian population is small and has experienced discrimination, forced isolation, and intense pressure from the federal government to assimilate into American society. Despite these efforts, many (perhaps most) American Indians remain outside the mainstream (i.e., the modern, largely urban) U.S. economy (Hoxie 1984; Fixico 1986; Gundlach and Roberts 1978; Snipp 1989; Snipp and Sandefur 1989). Racial discrimination and segregation have been major barriers to the advancement of blacks in American society (Duncan 1969; Featherman and Hauser 1976; Farley and Allen 1987; Massey and Denton 1993).

Hispanic and Asian groups warrant separate consideration, as they have experienced explosive population growth since the immigration reforms of 1965 and 1986 (Chiswick and Sullivan 1995). The Latino population (particularly Mexican Americans) is an old and established American ethnic group. During the 1960s and 1970s they also comprised the largest and fastest-growing immigrant group. It is difficult to make generalizations about the assimilation of Latinos because of their ethnic heterogeneity and the disparate circumstances of their immigration, internal migration, and settlement patterns (Bean and Tienda 1987). Even within a small group like Cuban Americans, there are substantial differences with respect to the circumstances of their immigration and the extent to which they have become assimilated (Portes and Bach 1985).

Although there is considerable diversity in the Latino population, there are also commonalties such as language. However, compared with Latinos, the so-called Asian and Pacific Islander population has spectacular diversity. Except for the continent of origin, there are few visible similarities. Many of these groups are exceedingly small in number, making it difficult to obtain reliable data on their socioeconomic characteristics. However, in the 1980s, Asian and Pacific Islanders were the fastest growing segment of the American population (Barringer, Gardner, and Levin 1993).

Asians, especially those of Japanese and Chinese descent, pose an anomaly for assimilationist thinking about racial and ethnic inequality. Despite long histories of discrimination and persecution, Americans of Japanese and Chinese descent have, in fact, attained even *higher* levels of social and economic well-being than the white population. Only part of this success can be linked to their high levels of schooling and concentration in urban areas (Hirschman and Wong 1984; Nee and Sanders 1985). Some observers who attribute their success to hard work and ingenuity describe Asians as "model minorities." But the evidence of the successful assimilation of all groups of Asians is mixed. Some recent Asian immigrants, especially those who were forced to flee in the aftermath of the Vietnam War, have had a much more difficult experience. Whether these disadvantages will persist into the future is an open question.

Finally, there is compelling evidence to suggest that there is growing socioeconomic diversity *within* each of these groups—African Americans, Latinos, American Indians, and Asians. For example, studies have shown that in recent years, some segments of the African American population have enjoyed greater opportunities and attained a middle-class lifestyle, while many more are left behind in inner city ghettos (Landry 1987; Wilson 1987; Farley and Allen 1987). The increasing socioeconomic inequality within minority group populations is a crucial issue (but is not addressed directly in our subsequent analysis).

In this research, we measure the socioeconomic differences between groups and estimate how much of the interethnic gap can be "explained" by antecedent characteristics. Interethnic inequality is measured as the differences between the mean occupational and earnings attainment of each minority group (African Americans, American Indians, Chinese, Japanese, Filipinos, and Latinos) and those of non-Hispanic whites (Hirschman 1980).

Data and Methods

Data

We use data from the Public Use Microdata Sample (PUMS) files of the decennial censuses of 1970, 1980, and 1990. These data permit us to examine recent trends in the socioeconomic achievements of seven racial and ethnic minorities. Census data have virtues and liabilities. Large samples are a primary virtue. They allow us to study relatively small populations that are usually not represented in national surveys. Our analyses include comparisons of the socioeconomic characteristics of whites, African Americans, Latinos, Japanese, Chinese, Filipinos, and American Indians. The primary liability of census data is the paucity of background variables that might explain relative levels and trends in race and ethnic inequality.

We restrict the sample to men between the ages of twenty-five to sixty-four who were working at the time of the census and received positive earnings the previous year. This sample does not completely represent these ethnic populations or even all adult men in these ethnic groups. But important theoretical and practical considerations led us to restrict the analysis to this subset of the population.

First, women's roles, and particularly their participation in the economy, have changed dramatically since 1970. The question of gender stratification is intertwined with changes in racial and ethnic stratification in such complex ways that a full study of the topic would exceed the scope of this chapter. Second, the age range was dictated by the fact that we are most interested in persons who are *economically active.* Many persons younger than twenty-five years old are either still in school or just entering the workforce. Persons age sixty-five and older are likely to be retired or very close to retirement. Third, we selected men who were employed in order to facilitate comparisons with earlier studies of race and ethnic assimilation (Duncan 1969; Hirschman and Wong 1984). These restrictions limit our results to a select segment of the population, but other work leads us to believe that our estimates of ethnic differences will be conservative. In our prior study, we found that the restricted sample (only those in the labor force and with earnings last year) excluded 15 percent of white men in the working years, but excluded 25 percent of black men (Hirschman and Wong 1984, 589). Ethnic differences reported below would in all likelihood be larger if we included persons who were not active members of the workforce.

Variables

Our study focuses on ethnic differences in two indicators of economic well-being: occupational status and earnings, and changes in these indicators

Table 5.1. Definition and measurement of demographic and socioeconomic characteristics

Ethnicity	Self-reported racial identification. Hispanic is self-identified in a separate item in the 1980 and 1990 censuses and based on a composite measure in the 1970 census. Whites are non-Hispanic whites; black Hispanics are coded black.
Age	Age at last birthday: 25–34; 35–44; 45–64.
Birthplace/length of U.S. residence	A composite measure based on country of birth and place of residence five years ago. Coded as native born; foreign born, in U.S. five years ago; foreign born, not in U.S. five years ago.
Place of residence	State or region of residence April 1, 1970, 1980, 1990. Coded for California; New York; Hawaii; South, metropolitan area; South, nonmetropolitan area; rest of U.S., metropolitan; rest of U.S., nonmetropolitan.
Years of schooling	Number of years of formal schooling completed. Coded as 0–8; 9–11; 12; 13–15; 16 or more.
Occupational SEI	Duncan's Socioeconomic Index, updated for 1980 and 1990.
Sector	Composite variable based on class of worker and industry classification. Coded as self-employed; government employed; retail trade, not self-employed; other periphery, not self-employed, not government employed, not in retail trade; other core, not self-employed, not government employed.
Weeks worked last year	Number of weeks worked in 1969, 1979, and 1989. Coded as less than fifty weeks, fifty or more weeks.
Hours worked last week	Hours worked during the week before the census (April 1). Coded as less than forty, forty, more than forty.
Earnings	Total income received from wages and salaries, self-employment income from farm and nonfarm sources. Earners with zero or negative incomes were excluded from each sample.

from 1970 to 1990. We estimate a series of regression models that include age, education, residence, immigration status, and other variables as covariates. A complete list and description of these variables is presented in Table 5.1. Our measure of occupational status is the Duncan Socioeconomic Index (SEI), which has been updated to reflect changes in the occupational structures reflected in the 1980 and 1990 censuses (Duncan 1961; Hauser and Warren 1997). Earnings are defined as wage and salary income as well as income received from farm or nonfarm self-employment. We use the consumer price index to adjust for inflation and express income in constant 1989 dollars.

Many of our independent variables are conventionally scaled, such as education, which is measured in years of completed schooling. However, there are several others which merit clarification. We use self-reported responses to the "race" question on the census form to create ethnic categories. We added an additional category for Hispanic. In 1970, this item was a composite based on Spanish surname, Puerto Rican birthplace or parentage, and Spanish language. For 1980 and 1990, the Hispanic category was based on a self-identification question on Spanish or Hispanic origin. The white category is the residual and properly refers to non-Hispanic whites. We combined the variables for place of birth and "place of residence 5 years ago" to construct a measure of immigrant status. Foreign-born persons who were not living in the United States five years before the decennial census (1965, 1975, and 1985) are presumed to be recent immigrants. Place of residence is measured with a classification that uses information on region, state, and metropolitan location. This coding was used previously by Hirschman and Wong (1984) in an attempt to identify geographical locations of ethnic concentrations and of greater and lesser economic opportunity.

The economic sector variable identifies those who are self-employed— a common means of economic adaptation for immigrants—and those in retail trade (a low-wage sector). The balance are classified according to a widely used classification for core and periphery industries (Tolbert, Horan, and Beck 1980). The measures for residence and sector are admittedly crude approximations, but we contend that they reflect differential access to opportunities in the American stratification system.

Any empirical analysis requires compromises based on the quality of data and measurement. We acknowledge that the Hispanic category covers a broad array of ethnic heritages, but inconsistent measurement across the three censuses and small numbers in particular groups do not permit disaggregation. An equally thorny problem concerns the difficulty of separating out the impact of immigration and ethnicity. Major fractions of the Hispanic and Asian populations are foreign born whereas almost all blacks, American Indians, and a majority of whites are native born. One solution would be to limit our analysis to native-born ethnic populations, but this would exclude significant shares (sometime a majority) of some ethnic groups.

Analytical Strategy

We present descriptive data in Table 5.2. Equations in Tables 5.3 and 5.4 model the economic well-being of ethnic minorities, estimating three sets of ethnic effects: (1) gross, (2) total, and (3) direct and indirect effects. The *gross effect* is the level of ethnic inequality between whites and ethnic minorities on either Duncan SEI points or 1990 dollars. The *total effect* is the level of ethnic inequality net of age and birthplace. The remaining effects are based on a detailed decomposition of the total effect of ethnicity on attainment. *Direct effects* measure the level of ethnic inequality on occupational attainment and earnings after the effects of the remaining covariates (e.g., residence, education, and industrial sector) are removed. *Indirect effects* are the effects of ethnicity on occupational attainment and earnings that are mediated through the covariates in our models. We cal-

Table 5.2. Indicators of socioeconomic attainment among men aged twenty-five to sixty-four by ethnicity: 1970, 1980, and 1990

	Mean SEI			Mean Annual Earnings*			N		
	1970	1980	1990	1970	1980	1990	1970	1980	1990
White	36.5	39.4	40.1	$35,125	$35,278	$35,523	3,139	3,063	3,013
Black	24.0	28.3	30.2	$20,436	$23,061	$23,172	2,726	2,540	2,482
Am. Ind.	27.4	31.9	31.2	$22,149	$25,925	$21,511	939	2,272	2,585
Japanese	38.4	44.7	47.4	$35,429	$37,205	$42,750	1,130	1,647	3,037
Chinese	42.9	46.7	46.1	$32,243	$31,424	$32,017	911	1,859	2,977
Filipino	33.7	39.1	38.2	$25,044	$30,463	$28,945	611	1,379	3,029
Hispanic	28.6	29.7	32.7	$27,304	$23,797	$25,760	1,394	2,231	2,841

	Standard Deviation (SEI)			Coefficient of Variation (SEI)			Standard Deviation (earnings)			Coefficient of Variation (earnings)		
	1970	1980	1990	1970	1980	1990	1970	1980	1990	1970	1980	1990
White	20.0	20.5	20.9	0.55	0.52	0.52	23,726	23,042	31,477	0.68	0.65	0.89
Black	13.9	16.4	17.7	0.58	0.58	0.59	12,500	14,898	18,127	0.61	0.65	0.78
Am. Ind.	16.4	18.3	17.6	0.60	0.57	0.56	16,054	19,334	17,293	0.72	0.75	0.80
Japanese	21.9	21.3	20.9	0.57	0.48	0.44	22,189	23,245	33,909	0.63	0.62	0.79
Chinese	24.1	23.5	23.2	0.56	0.50	0.50	22,959	24,307	30,035	0.71	0.77	0.94
Filipino	23.2	22.7	21.2	0.69	0.58	0.55	17,473	23,807	26,332	0.70	0.78	0.91
Hispanic	17.5	17.5	18.8	0.61	0.59	0.57	19,561	17,163	23,803	0.72	0.72	0.92

	Ratio of SEI to White Mean			White Minority Gap (SEI)			Ratio of Mean Earnings to White Mean			White Minority Gap (earnings in thousands of dollars)		
	1970	1980	1990	1970	1980	1990	1970	1980	1990	1970	1980	1990
White	100	100	100	—	—	—	100	100	100	—	—	—
Black	66	72	75	−12.5	−11.1	−9.9	58	65	65	−$14.7	−$12.2	−$12.4
Am. Ind.	75	81	78	−9.1	−7.5	−8.9	63	73	61	−$13.0	−$9.4	−$14.0
Japanese	105	113	118	1.9	5.3	7.3	101	105	120	$0.3	$1.9	$7.2
Chinese	118	119	115	6.4	7.3	6.0	92	89	90	−$2.9	−$3.9	−$3.5
Filipino	92	99	95	−2.8	−0.3	−1.9	71	86	81	−$10.1	−$4.8	−$6.6
Hispanic	78	75	82	−7.9	−9.7	−7.4	78	67	73	−$7.8	−$11.5	−$9.8

Am. Ind. = American Indian; SEI = socioeconomic index.
*Adjusted to constant 1989 dollars.
Sources: Public Use Microdata Sample (PUMS) files of the 1970, 1980, and 1990 Census of Population, U.S. Bureau of the Census.

culate indirect effects by estimating successive regression equations and subtracting the ethnic coefficients with the intervening variable from the ethnic coefficients in the preceding equation without the intervening variable (Alwin and Hauser 1975).

Results: Ethnic Differences in Socioeconomic Attainments

Table 5.2[1] shows the means and standard deviations for SEI and earnings for each ethnic group for the years 1970, 1980, and 1990. The SEI and earnings of Japanese workers and the SEI of the Chinese exceed those of the white sample. On the other hand, the earnings and occupational status of Hispanics, blacks, American Indians, and, to a lesser degree, Filipinos are well below the earnings and occupational status of whites.

The results are remarkably stable. The rankings of groups on SEI and earnings are virtually *unchanged* between 1970 and 1990. The average SEI of all groups increased between 1970 and 1990. Most of the gains were in the four- to six-point range except for Japanese workers who gained nine points. There was little net change in the earnings hierarchy. However, the pattern is more mixed than that for occupational status. In constant dollars, white earnings were stagnant from 1970 to 1990. Blacks, on the other hand, enjoyed modest gains in each decade since 1970. The same is true for Japanese workers. Other groups experienced modest gains in one decade and declines in another. This instability might be the result of compositional differences due to immigration, changing racial self-identification (in the case of American Indians), or reporting errors in the earnings data.

Models of Ethnic Stratification, 1970–90

The patterns in Table 5.2 reveal the relative status (and change in status) of ethnic minorities in American society. They do not take into account ethnic differences in education, place of residence, or other attributes that may affect socioeconomic attainment entirely apart from any consideration of ethnic relations. For example, some ethnic groups may have higher earnings because they are more heavily concentrated in higher paying urban labor markets, not because they receive different rewards for their work. We use regression analysis to decompose the ethnic effects on occupational and earnings achievements.

---

[1] To present descriptive statistics, we selected a representative sample of whites and blacks in the public use files and included all PUMS observations of the smaller populations such as American Indians and Asian Americans.

The coefficients in Table 5.3 show the gross, total, direct, and indirect effects of ethnicity on occupational SEI for the years of 1970, 1980, and 1990. The first panel shows the *gross* differences in SEI for each ethnic group compared to white men. In spite of the overall upgrading of average occupational status (reported in Table 5.2), there has been remarkably little change in ethnic inequality over the twenty years observed here. The average employed black man was thirteen SEI points behind the average employed white man in 1970 and ten points behind in 1990. The situation of American Indian and Hispanic men was similar to that of black men, although both groups were generally two to three SEI points closer to the status of white men. All three of these established minority groups held substantially lower-status occupations than white men. In contrast, Asian American men were in occupations that were, on average, as good as or better than those of white men. Whereas Filipino men held slightly lower status jobs in 1990, Chinese and Japanese American men worked at higher-status positions than did white men.

The second panel shows ethnic differences net of the effects of age and immigrant status. The total effects are almost identical to the gross effects.

Table 5.3. Effects of ethnicity on occupational attainment of men aged twenty-five to sixty-four in the labor force 1970, 1980, and 1990 (average SEI points)

		Black	American Indian	Japanese	Chinese	Filipino	Hispanic
Gross	1970	−13	−9	2	6	−3	−8
	1980	−11	−8	5	7	0	−10
	1990	−10	−9	7	6	−2	−7
Total	1970	−13	−10	2	5	−4	−9
	1980	−11	−8	6	8	0	−10
	1990	−10	−9	8	7	−1	−7
Indirect via:							
Residence	1970	0	−1	−2	−1	−3	−1
	1980	1	−1	−3	−1	−2	−1
	1990	0	−1	−6	−4	−5	−1
Schooling	1970	−7	−6	6	5	2	−6
	1980	−6	−4	7	6	5	−7
	1990	−5	−5	10	7	7	−5
Sector	1970	1	0	0	0	0	0
	1980	0	0	0	0	0	0
	1990	0	0	0	0	0	0
Direct	1970	−7	−3	−2	1	−3	−2
	1980	−6	−3	2	3	−3	−2
	1990	−5	−3	4	4	−3	−1

SEI = socioeconomic index.

Because there are important ethnic differences in immigrant status (Asians and Hispanics are more likely to be foreign born), one could conclude that there is little occupational handicap for immigrants.

The third panel presents indirect effects (through which ethnic differences are mediated) in residence, schooling, and industrial sector. The parameter estimates are dependent on the order in which the variables are entered in successive equations. Although the temporal sequence of these variables cannot be specified with any assurance, we have estimated three equations by adding each variable in a sequential and cumulative order. First, place of current of residence is added to the model with ethnicity, age, and immigrant status as independent variables. In turn, the same exercise is repeated for years of schooling and sector—adding the variable to the prior equation and measuring the change in the ethnic coefficients. The final equation shows the "direct effects" of ethnicity that remain after all these other considerations are held constant.

Current place of residence has an unexpected role as a mediator of ethnic advantage/disadvantage in occupational attainment. There is a slight disadvantage for American Indians and Hispanics because they live in geographical areas with a lower average SEI. The effect on the black-white differential is negligible. Residence appears to be a more serious handicap for Asian Americans, especially in 1990. Japanese, Filipino, and Chinese Americans have an average occupation that is four to six SEI points lower in 1990 than they would have if their geographical distribution was the same as for the population as a whole.

Educational composition plays two quite different roles for the six ethnic minorities in our samples. For the three disadvantaged minorities (blacks, American Indians, and Hispanics), having less education is the single most important reason for their lower occupational attainment. The absolute levels of occupational disadvantage associated with education are four to seven SEI points, and this accounts for about half or more of their total SEI ethnic-disadvantaged status in 1990.

In contrast, Asian Americans have much higher average levels of education than the general population, and all other things being equal, this boosts their occupational attainments. Indeed the occupational advantage associated with above-average levels of schooling for Asians has risen a bit over the two decades, and there was about a seven-point SEI advantage for Chinese and Filipinos and a ten-point SEI advantage for Japanese Americans in 1990.

In spite of the great attention given to "sector" or industry in the sociological literature, this variable plays no role in mediating ethnic differences in occupational attainment for any of the ethnic groups across the three time periods represented here.

The last panel in Table 5.3 shows the direct effects of ethnicity on occupational attainment after all the relevant variables from the census files are included in the equations. The coefficients are modest, at least relative to gross (or total) differences in occupational attainment. In 1990, holding all measured variables constant, the average employed black man held an occupation five SEI points lower than the average white man; American Indian and Filipino men were three points lower; and Hispanics were one point lower. The comparable direct effect of being Japanese or Chinese was four SEI points above the white level.

Some interpret the net or direct effect as a measure of ethnic discrimination, but all we can really say is that the relationship is unexplained. Discrimination (e.g., negative and positive preferences within certain labor markets) may play a role, but other unmeasured factors, including family background and social networks, may also account for some of the differences. Moreover, discrimination may also be operating indirectly through the intervening variables (e.g., in funding for inner city or reservation schools, funding that affects the quantity and quality of schooling).

Earnings Attainment

Table 5.4 presents comparable results for earnings attainment. The twenty years from 1970 to 1990 was a period of stagnant wages and rising inequality in the American economy (Karoly 1993; Levy 1995). How did the state of the economy play out in terms of wage differences among various subgroups of workers? The first panel of Table 5.4 shows that ethnic differentials in male earnings were largely unchanged over the same period. The black-white differential actually dropped a bit (from $14,700 in 1969 to $12,200 in 1979) and remained at $12,400 by 1989. American Indian earnings fluctuated over the period, but their disadvantage relative to whites of almost $13,000 in 1969 grew to $14,000 by 1989. Unlike all other ethnic groups, Japanese men reached parity with the earnings of whites in 1969 and had pulled ahead (by $7,000) in 1989. Chinese, Filipino, and Hispanic men earned less than whites in 1969 and continued to do so in 1989, although the size of the differences peaked in 1979.

Holding constant age composition and immigrant status reveals the total effects of ethnicity on earnings in the second panel of Table 5.4. By and large, the pattern of ethnic advantage and disadvantage is similar to the gross effects. Black and American Indian men are the most disadvantaged—about $12,000 to $13,000 below the average for white men. Hispanic men are only slightly better off with a $9,300 earnings gap in 1989. Next are Filipinos and Chinese with deficits of $7,100 and $3,500 below white men. Japanese Americans earned $7,600 more than white men in 1989.

Table 5.4. Effects of ethnicity on the earnings attainment of men aged twenty-five to sixty-four in the labor force 1969, 1979, and 1989

		Black	American Indian	Japanese	Chinese	Filipino	Hispanic
Gross	1969	−$14,691	−$12,965	$301	−$2,885	−$10,083	−$7,820
	1979	−$12,216	−$9,351	$1,930	−$3,852	−$4,815	−$11,481
	1989	−$12,351	−$14,012	$7,227	−$3,507	−$6,578	−$9,763
Total	1969	−$14,664	−$12,772	$547	−$1,858	−$8,232	−$7,398
	1979	−$11,934	−$9,017	$2,524	−$2,582	−$3,339	−$10,665
	1989	−$12,062	−$13,326	$7,634	−$3,502	−$7,138	−$9,329
Indirect via:							
Residence	1969	−$115	−$1,307	$2,466	$1,682	$2,017	−$1,307
	1979	$67	−$488	−$266	$12	$5	$174
	1989	−$465	−$843	−$3,911	−$2,451	−$3,398	−$561
Schooling	1969	−$4,084	−$3,476	$3,138	$2,689	$166	−$4,165
	1979	−$3,360	−$2,571	$3,758	$3,020	$2,726	−$4,516
	1989	−$3,276	−$3,777	$6,822	$5,092	$4,742	−$3,518
Sector	1969	−$1,000	−$1,118	$456	$220	−$1,118	−$730
	1979	−$1,081	−$849	−$145	−$921	−$541	−$629
	1989	−$1,355	−$912	−$327	−$1,023	−$1,178	−$539
Occupation	1969	−$2,023	−$1,030	−$571	$348	−$959	−$763
	1979	−$1,638	−$835	$601	$953	−$798	−$673
	1989	−$1,635	−$992	$1,405	$1,361	−$877	−$421
Weeks and	1969	−$980	−$1,118	$20	−$318	−$652	−$763
Hours	1979	−$1,353	−$1,344	−$46	−$514	−$1,071	−$721
Worked	1989	−$1,618	−$2,011	$162	−$594	−$1,114	−$747
Direct	1969	−$9,036	−$5,793	−$2,723	−$10,151	−$7,329	−$8,506
	1979	−$6,342	−$8,183	$5,951	−$10,055	−$8,183	−$6,051
	1989	−$3,713	−$4,791	$3,484	−$5,887	−$5,313	−$3,543

We decompose the total effects of each ethnic group on earnings (actually the ethnic-white earnings gap) in the third panel. Place of residence plays an unexpected role for Asian Americans. In 1969, the geographical concentration of Japanese, Chinese, and Filipinos in Hawaii and California was a distinct economic advantage—about $1,700 to $2,500—in comparison to whites. By 1989, these locations were a liability, with Asians suffering a $2,500 to $3,900 deficit because of their concentrations in these same areas. The geographic distribution of black, American Indian, and Hispanic men was a modest liability of several hundred dollars.

As with occupational attainment, education is the single most important variable mediating ethnic differentials in earnings. In 1989, about 25 to 33 percent of the economic gap between black, American Indian, and Hispanic men and white men can be explained by the lower educational attainment of these minority groups; the difference is about $3,500 dollars. In contrast, the higher education (compared to white men) of Japanese, Chinese, and Filipino men is the major reason for their higher earnings ($4,700 for Filipino men, $5,100 for Chinese men, and $6,800 for Japanese men).

Holding constant all of the measured background variables, including education, minorities were usually found in occupations and sectors that paid substantially less than those occupied by white men. The sum of the indirect effects of ethnicity on earnings via both occupation and sector was about $3,000 for black men, $2,000 for American Indians, and $1,000 for Hispanic men. The job sorting process for Filipino men reveals an economic disadvantage comparable to American Indian men. On the other hand, Chinese and Japanese do relatively well in finding well-paying occupations. However, all groups, with the exception of Japanese men, have a problem finding jobs that employ them for enough hours per week and weeks per year to close the gap with white men. For black and American Indian men, the problems of unemployment and underemployment cost them about $2,000 relative to white men. The economic penalty for the other groups is less, ranging from $600 to $1,100.

The final panel of Table 5.4 shows the direct effects of ethnicity after controlling for all of the covariates included in prior models. The magnitude of the deficits due to direct effects is substantial: in the range of $5,000 to $10,000 for all ethnic groups (except Japanese) in 1969. There have been changes, mainly in reducing the size of the deficit, for the twenty-year period measured here. However, by 1989, all minority groups (with the exception of Japanese) still experienced very substantial direct deficits relative to whites—in the range of $3,500 to $5,900.

Rather than speculate on the reasons for the residual net effects, it may be more instructive to consider the overall magnitude and patterns of ethnic inequality. There are three ethnic "patterns" of earnings inequality. The first is represented by blacks, American Indians, and Hispanics. These groups suffer substantial inequality relative to whites (about $10,000 per year) and there has been little moderation over time. About 25 to 33 percent of the gap is due to lower educational levels, but the remainder is due to differences on labor market factors: occupation, industry, weeks and hours worked, and other unmeasured factors. The second type or pattern is illustrated by Chinese and Filipinos. The size of the deficit for these groups is about half the size of that for blacks, Hispanics, and American Indians. The sources of the Chinese and Filipino disadvantage are current residence, labor market positions, and unmeasured factors. Their potential disadvantage is reduced by their higher levels of schooling. In fact, their educational advantage over whites generates (all else being equal) about a $5,000 gain. Without this educational "boost," their economic situations would be similar to the level of blacks, American Indians, and Hispanics. Finally, the third pattern is represented by the Japanese. Japanese have higher incomes than whites in 1979 and 1989. In large part, this is due to their higher educational attainment, but they also experience an "advantage" that is not measured by the variables in the model.

Conclusions

There was much talk in the 1990s about *reverse* discrimination, the problems of white men who are unable to find jobs or obtain promotions because of preferences given to minorities. These perceptions seem quite at odds with the findings of this chapter, findings which show only modest changes in race and ethnic stratification among male workers over the two decades from 1970 to 1990.

However, we show that the patterns of race and ethnic inequality are complex. Looking first at occupational attainment, black, American Indian, and Hispanic men suffer about a ten-point SEI occupational deficit relative to whites, while Asian American men are equal to or above white men in their occupational positions.

For the groups that are behind whites, the "problem" is primarily educational deficits. If black, American Indian, and Hispanic men had educational attainments equal to whites, the results here suggest that they would only experience modest occupational disadvantages. There would still be a five-point SEI deficit for black men, but this would be half of their current handicap. The reason for the higher occupational attainment of Asian American men is simply their educational level. If the Asian American men had the same education as white men, there would be only modest ethnic occupational differences.

Turning to differences in income, earnings inequality is a much deeper problem for racial and ethnic minorities in America. All minorities, with the exception of Japanese, earn less than whites. For blacks, American Indians, and Hispanics, the financial shortfall relative to whites is huge—about $10,000 per male worker for the period under study—and there has been little sign of progress. Chinese and Filipino men are also behind, but the gap is somewhat less.

These results—the persistence of race and ethnic differentials in late twentieth-century America—challenge conventional theories about the declining role of ascribed factors in the American stratification system. There are three "big" hypotheses in the stratification literature that need to be reviewed in light of these findings. The first is the "inheritance of poverty" thesis—some groups are disadvantaged because of their social origins. Without any measures of the characteristics of the families of origin, census data do not permit a direct test of this hypothesis. Although not the most important factor, some studies have demonstrated that family-of-origin characteristics are a partial explanation of black-white socioeconomic inequality (Duncan 1969). It is plausible that differential social origins play an important role in the generation of socioeconomic differentials for other ethnic groups.

The second hypothesis is the relative role of qualifications versus discrimination in accounting for socioeconomic attainment. If the economy worked according to meritocratic precepts, then measures such as education and other personal attributes that make workers more productive would be the major determinants of socioeconomic success. Of course, the economy is not an impersonal machine; it is human beings who in fact recruit and promote workers. This leaves open the possibility that employers and supervisors hire and reward workers on the basis of invidious distinctions, not only according to their qualifications. By measuring the impact of education on occupation and earnings, it is possible to get an approximate reading on the role of "qualifications" versus other factors.

Our results show that education plays a critical role in *reproducing inequality* across race and ethnic lines. In other words, one path to economic attainment is educational attainment. But most ethnic inequality is unexplained by education and other measures of the relative quality of workers. Does this mean that discrimination is operating? Perhaps. In slack labor markets, employers can select among many qualified applicants. It would be surprising if gatekeepers ignored ethnic characteristics as irrelevant to hiring decisions. The traditional image of discrimination is one of a color bar—where racial minorities are simply excluded. The modern style is to avoid hiring certain minority groups because "they" are more prone to be unreliable, cause discipline problems, or not fit in with other workers.

A third hypothesis in the stratification literature that should be reviewed is that ethnic inequality is generated by the structure of employing organizations. In addition to large public institutions and private corporations, there are tens of thousands of small businesses whose ownership and management is closely tied to geographical, kinship, and ethnic boundaries. The ethnic enclave is not simply a geographical concentration of enterprises, but loosely structured informal relationships among businesses for whom ethnicity signals the presumption of trust. These informal ties serve to organize the recruitment of labor throughout many industries and firms in the economy, meaning that some minority groups are found in particular sectors and not others. Although census data are not particularly appropriate for examining this kind of hypothesis, our results suggest that the informal economy may be an important dimension behind the high levels of racial and ethnic inequality in the American labor market.

The economy of the latter half of the 1990s has been characterized by rising opportunity, with a record low unemployment rate. Will this reduce the kinds of persistent racial and ethnic inequalities we have documented for the 1970s and 1980s? Perhaps. Tight labor markets make it more costly for employers to make invidious distinctions among workers. But the slow pace of change during the 1970s and 1980s suggests that racial inequality is woven deeply into the fabric of American society.

CHAPTER SIX

Strangers Next Door: Immigrant Groups and Suburbs in Los Angeles and New York

Richard Alba, John Logan, Wenquan Zhang, and Brian J. Stults

Starting in the 1960s, we have seen the renewal of large-scale immigration to the United States. Half or more of many of the new immigrant groups (e.g., Asian Indians and Cubans) are located already in the suburbs (Waldinger 1989; Alba and Logan 1991). This rapid suburbanization presents a distinct contrast to the model established by European immigrant groups earlier in this century. According to this model (known as the spatial assimilation model), members of immigrant groups first established urban enclaves. They subsequently migrated as individuals and families to suburbs, typically after achieving some degree of social mobility and spending a generation or more in cities (e.g., Burgess 1925; Wirth [1928] 1965; Massey 1985). If, however, immigrant groups are now settling in suburbs when they first arrive in the United States or soon afterwards, and establishing ethnic enclaves there, we have to ask whether suburbanization has the same meaning for new immigrant groups that it has had for older ones.

Is the nature of suburbs changing? Have strangers moved in next door? In this chapter we examine suburbanization patterns in the two metropolitan regions that are receiving the most new immigrants: Los Angeles and New York. We first look at percentages of racial/ethnic groups in the suburbs versus the city. We discover that immigrant minorities now account for sizable percentages of the suburban population—suburbia is no longer a refuge where whites can escape the diversity of the cities.

Next we ask which members of immigrant minorities reside in the suburbs—are they affluent? Educated? Married? One surprising result is that lack of English is no longer a high barrier to entering the suburbs, especially for Asians in Los Angeles. This strengthens the notion that a new pattern, unanticipated by spatial-assimilation theory, is emerging.

To help understand this new pattern, we ask whether suburbanization carries the same exposure to the majority group that it did in the past. We analyze segregation in the city and suburbs using two standard segregation indices. One index supports the idea that the suburbs still expose minorities to the majority group. The other is less clear and demands a closer look at specific geography.

Last, to find out in what kinds of suburbs different immigrant minorities tend to concentrate, we look at maps showing the areas of suburban concentration of Asians and Latinos in New York and Los Angeles. No single pattern emerges; we conclude that much of the meaning of suburbanization is specific to the group and to the metropolitan context.

The Spatial-Assimilation Model

That suburbanization is a key step in the process of assimilation has been well established for past immigrant groups. Observations originating with the Chicago School have been formalized by Douglas Massey (1985) into a series of propositions that constitute the model of spatial assimilation, and these have generally been supported empirically. "Spatial assimilation" is equated with entry of immigrant minorities into communities where the ethnic majority predominates; it is thus the inverse of ethnic segregation. Massey built into the model elements from the ecological model of ethnic succession, hypothesizing in particular that ethnic enclaves are "located in older, central city neighborhoods" and that they develop through processes including chain migration, ethnic succession, and ethnic institution building. While collective processes drive enclave development, individual-level ones, specifically acculturation and socioeconomic mobility, propel spatial assimilation. The key mechanism in the model explains that members of ethnic minorities, seeking to improve their residential situation after achieving a measure of acculturation and economic success, frequently forsake ethnic urban enclaves for more ethnically intermixed suburbs; thereby, they ensure further assimilation, especially "structural assimilation," to use Gordon's (1964) term, of their children.

It has long been recognized that African Americans and perhaps some other nonwhite minorities are exceptions to the spatial-assimilation model (Massey and Denton 1993). There are now a number of reasons to question its contemporary validity for new immigrant groups. The model largely reflects the experiences of low-wage immigrant groups moving to employment opportunities in urban industries. Historically, these experiences correspond roughly with the period from the mid-nineteenth to the mid-twentieth centuries. The contemporary situation differs from the earlier one in several critical respects. To begin with, the contemporary immigration stream is considerably more diverse: it encompasses a wide spectrum of human capital, ranging from groups such as Filipinos and Indians, many of whom come in search of employment in medical professions and engineering, to Mexicans, the group that probably best fits the classical profile of a low-wage labor migration (Portes and Rumbaut 1996). Further, the residential distribution of Americans has changed fundamentally between the past immigration era and the contemporary one: suburbs were a relatively inconsequential segment of the housing market in the early twentieth century, but they now accommodate a plurality of Americans (Jackson 1985). Insofar as immigrants make housing choices that resemble those of other Americans, they will obviously turn up in suburbs in substantial numbers. Moreover, employment opportunities have increasingly gravitated towards suburbs (Logan and Golden 1986), and this provides another reason for immigrants to go there. Lastly, suburbia itself has become increasingly diverse, as some suburbs have become major locations for employment and thus commuting destinations rather than just the residence of workers who commute to larger cities. As a consequence, the term now covers a huge range of residential situations, including niches where recent, labor-seeking immigrants can locate themselves.

Suburbanization in Two Immigrant Metropolises

In an analysis of 1990 census data for the nation (Alba et al. 1999), we have found that the members of most of the racial/ethnic groups growing rapidly through immigration (to be called "immigrant minorities" below) are now more likely to reside in suburbs than in central cities. Moreover, the suburbanization levels of these groups either increased or held steady during the 1980s, even though this decade witnessed the heaviest immigration since the pre–World War I era. We note also that the census data presented here and elsewhere in the paper are based on racial/ethnic categories that are not limited to the foreign born, but also contain some U.S.-born individuals, who are usually members of the second generation. The term "immigrant minority" is still justified, however, because the households of the groups are overwhelmingly headed by the

Table 6.1. Central city/suburban distributions of racial/ethnic groups in Los Angeles and New York, 1990

	Los Angeles CMSA			New York CMSA		
	Suburbs (%)	Cities (%)	Population Size	Suburbs (%)	Cities (%)	Population Size
Total Population	62.2	37.8	14,531,529	51.9	48.1	17,125,727
Non-Latino Whites	68.8	31.2	7,257,232	67.5	32.5	10,683,538
Non-Latino Blacks	46.6	53.4	1,170,986	25.2	74.8	2,919,089
Hispanics	55.9	44.1	4,714,405	23.8	76.2	2,635,097
Asians	61.5	38.5	1,297,622	35.2	64.8	845,218
Mexicans	58.7	41.3	3,736,443	35.7	64.3	95,477
Puerto Ricans	64.5	35.5	65,048	17.2	82.8	1,196,125
Cubans	63.3	36.7	60,302	50.0	50.0	156,281
Dominicans	55.9	44.1	3,356	11.1	88.9	403,930
Salvadorans	26.8	73.2	274,788	52.7	47.3	62,995
Other Spanish	49.8	50.2	574,468	32.1	67.9	720,289
Chinese	71.2	28.8	307,781	22.9	77.1	317,110
Japanese	65.8	34.2	176,880	61.0	39.0	47,478
Filipinos	54.7	45.3	295,114	42.3	57.7	104,579
Koreans	55.7	44.3	194,198	36.9	63.1	117,606
Asian Indians	65.7	34.3	68,620	46.6	53.4	187,344
Vietnamese	66.6	33.4	145,464	32.4	67.6	14,576
Other Asians	47.0	53.0	109,565	29.1	70.9	56,525
West Indians	40.4	59.6	34,975	20.8	79.2	515,337

CMSA = consolidated metropolitan statistical area.

foreign born and, in some groups, by individuals who immigrated during the 1980s, in the decade before the census (see Alba et al. 1999).

Table 6.1 shows how these national patterns play out in the two metropolitan regions receiving the largest numbers of new immigrants, those surrounding Los Angeles and New York.[1] (For more extended analyses of Los Angeles than we can present here, see Allen and Turner 1997; Waldinger and Bozorgmehr 1996. Perhaps because of its much richer urbanness, New York so far lacks a recent analysis that takes in city and suburbs; on New York City, see Waldinger 1996. On the geography of immigration in general, see Farley 1996.) These two regions differ in significant respects that could bear

[1] The metropolitan regions we analyze here are defined in the broadest possible sense and correspond, with one exception, to what are deemed Consolidated Metropolitan Statistical Areas (CMSAs) by the Census Bureau; CMSAs are aggregations of the more familiar PMSAs, or Primary Metropolitan Statistical Areas. In the case of the New York region, we have dropped the small Connecticut portion that appears in the Census Bureau definition; but otherwise, the boundaries of the regions are as defined in 1990.

on minority suburbanization. One difference is their overall level of sub-urbanization: a higher percentage of the Los Angeles population (62 per-cent) than of the New York population (52 percent) resides outside of the central cities. Obviously, the greater the proportion of the total population in suburbia, the greater is the likelihood that any randomly selected indi-vidual, majority or minority, resides there. In addition, the suburbs in the New York region are more socioeconomically selective than are those in Los Angeles. In other words, the average incomes of urbanites and suburban-ites differ more in New York than in Los Angeles, and thus it generally requires more income to get to the suburbs in New York than it does in Los Angeles. (In 1990, the median household incomes of the average suburban and urban tracts in New York differed by more than $20,000—$50,645 ver-sus $30,077. The difference was less than half as great in Los Angeles—$41,637 versus $32,437.) Socioeconomic selectivity tends to retard the suburbanization of some minorities, who must pay considerably more than members of the majority to enter suburbia (Alba and Logan 1991).

Substantial Numbers of Immigrant Minorities in the Suburbs

Nevertheless, the data in Table 6.1 demonstrate that substantial numbers of immigrant minorities are now found in suburbs in both regions. This seems to be especially true in Los Angeles and for Asian groups. In fact, by 1990, a number of Asian immigrant minorities in Los Angeles had sub-urbanization levels on a par with that of the non-Latino white majority. Thus, while 69 percent of non-Latino whites were then located in suburbs, 71 per-cent of Chinese and 66–67 percent of Japanese, Asian Indians, and Viet-namese were residing there. All these groups, as well as other Asian groups in the Los Angeles region, saw their suburbanization percentages increase during the 1980s, despite this decade's very high immigration, which, based on the spatial-assimilation model, would be expected to deflate suburban-ization levels because of the flow of recently arrived immigrants into urban enclaves. To take but one example, the Chinese (the largest Asian group in the region) increased their level of suburbanization by 16 percentage points, up from 55 percent in 1980. At the same time their number in the region nearly tripled (from 115,000 to 308,000).

In New York, there is a stronger disparity between non-Latino whites and immigrant minorities, including those from Asia. It is nevertheless also true that Asians there are generally closer to the suburbanization level of whites than are other immigrant minorities and that Asian suburbaniza-tion levels are rising, albeit here only modestly, in the face of continuing immigration into the region. Of all the Asian groups in and around New York City, the Japanese come closest to whites—in 1990, 61 percent of the group resided outside of cities, compared to 68 percent of the majority. (That the Japanese in the New York area are an immigrant minority is debatable because of the presence of many managers in Japanese firms on temporary assignment in the United States; these individuals and their families are concentrated in the suburbs just north of New York City, and thus the Japanese settlement pattern is probably more characteristic of affluent sojourners than of immigrants.) Other Asian groups, such as the Indians (47 percent in suburbs) and Filipinos (42 percent), lag further behind. In a striking contrast to the situation in Los Angeles, the Chinese are furthest behind whites in New York, with only 23 percent of the group in suburbs. Undoubtedly, the significance of Manhattan's Chinatown and of its recently emerged satellite communities in other parts of New York City (e.g., in the Flushing area of Queens) as areas of settlement for new immigrants is an important part of the explanation for this difference between the regions (Zhou 1992). Nevertheless, the number of Chinese in New York suburbs more than doubled between 1980 and 1990.

In one respect, the Latino groups present a more stable picture than do the Asians. Certainly, their distributions between suburb and city have changed less impressively than those of some Asian groups. Yet for Latino groups, too, one has to acknowledge a rapidly expanding presence in suburbs. Consider by way of example the Mexicans in Los Angeles, by far the largest Latino group. They had virtually the same percentage in suburbs (59 percent) in 1990 as in 1980; however, behind this picture of stability was still major growth in suburban populations, as a result of continuing immigration. Thus, the absolute number of Mexican suburbanites rose by two-thirds during the 1980s, in tandem with the substantial increase in size of the total Los Angeles Mexican population. By 1990, in fact, Mexicans accounted for one of every four Los Angeles suburbanites, up from one of every five in 1980. A similar pattern holds also when we look at the New York region, as a result of the increasing numbers of Latinos from groups other than the major three (Cubans, Mexicans, and Puerto Ricans). The total number of Latinos in suburbs grew by 60 percent, though it must be acknowledged that they accounted for a much smaller fraction of the total suburban population—just 7 percent—than was the case in Los Angeles.

Comparison with Nonimmigrant Minorities

The increasing presence of immigrant minorities in suburbs takes on added significance when compared against the suburbanization levels of nonimmigrant minorities (mainly non-Hispanic blacks, but also Puerto Ricans in New York). These nonimmigrant minorities have (both relatively and absolutely) low levels of suburbanization. In New York, just one-fourth of African Americans and just one-sixth of Puerto Ricans are suburbanized; the proportion for African Americans is considerably higher in Los Angeles—nearly half—but still lags behind those of all the immigrant groups save one. These 1990 suburbanization levels represent, moreover, just slight increases above the 1980 levels. Because nonimmigrant minorities are not increasing in number very rapidly, in contrast to the rapid growth of immigrant minorities, it follows that the absolute numbers of their suburbanites remained rather stable between 1980 and 1990, in further contrast to trends among immigrant minorities. For instance, the number of black suburbanites in Los Angeles increased by only 20 percent between 1980 and 1990.

Not all immigrant minorities are present in large numbers in suburbs: a few have suburbanization levels resembling those of nonimmigrant minorities. In New York, these are Afro-Caribbeans (or West Indians) and Dominicans; in Los Angeles, Salvadorans. A combination of recent arrival and perhaps undocumented status, poverty, and racial distinctiveness accounts in varying proportions for these exceptional cases. The suburbanization level of the Afro-Caribbean group is very similar to that of African Americans, suggesting that skin color overrides immigrant status in their case. The Dominican and Salvadoran levels of suburban residence (11 percent and 27 percent, respectively) are the lowest to be found among all the groups in their respective metropolitan regions. For both, recency of arrival and level of poverty distinguish them from other immigrant minorities, including other Latino ones. Frequency of undocumented status probably plays a role, too. For instance, in contrast to Puerto Ricans, also a group where poverty-level income and dark skin are common, Dominicans are more recently arrived and more likely to be undocumented. (Because Puerto Ricans are U.S. citizens, the documented/undocumented distinction has no meaning for them.)

National Trends

Overall, nevertheless, the patterns in Los Angeles and New York bear out the findings from national data, even if they do not duplicate them precisely. The presence of immigrant minorities in the suburbs of those metropolitan regions that receive large streams of contemporary immigrants is quite substantial and growing. Asian groups are the most likely on average to reside in suburbs; and their suburbanization levels are, for the most part, increasing, in some cases quite impressively. But Latino immigrant minorities also have relatively robust levels of suburbanization (with the notable exceptions of the Dominicans of New York and the Salvadorans of Los Angeles). Because of continued immigration, the rapid increase of Asian and Latino groups implies significant absolute growth in their suburban numbers, even if the percentages of suburban residents remain fairly constant. This analysis does not tell us whether households move to the suburbs upon arrival in the United States or after a period spent in urban ethnic enclaves; undoubtedly, it is some of both. But what should be clear is that suburbia is no longer a refuge where most members of the majority group can count on escaping the diversity of cities, for immigrant minorities account for sizable percentages of the suburban population. In Los Angeles, more than one of every three suburbanites is a member of such a minority; in New York, it is almost one of every five.

Who Lives in Suburbs?

Having established that immigrant minorities are found in large numbers in the suburbs of regions such as Los Angeles and New York, one has to ask which members of these groups have become suburbanites. In principle, even in the face of a rapid expansion of the immigrant presence in suburbs, suburbanization could continue to play the role that spatial-assimilation theory assigns it. For this to be true, the large-scale entry into suburbia of immigrant minorities has to be explicable in terms of other changes occurring to them, socioeconomic mobility and cultural assimilation above all. In such a scenario, suburbanization would be selective of minority-group individuals and households that resemble in many respects the majority-group members who already reside there; consequently, these new suburbanites would have, for the most part, assimilated into the mainstream or be on the verge of doing so. Their arrival in the suburbs would thus signify more that the engines of assimilation and social mobility are working full steam than that suburbs themselves are being diversified.

A Previous National Analysis

To address this issue, we examine the determinants of suburban residence in Los Angeles and New York. We ask whether these determinants conform to the expectations of spatial assimilation, and we accomplish this with analytical models that allow the determinants to vary from one group to another and from one metropolitan context to another. Specifically, our models are based upon logistic regression analyses that parallel those we have created using national samples (Alba and Logan 1991; Alba et al. 1999). In these national analyses, we have already addressed the selectivity of suburbanization for immigrant minorities. We have found that in both 1980 and 1990, household and family characteristics (such as the presence of a married couple in the household) have large influences on the likelihood of suburban residence, as do socioeconomic variables. The latter variables, household income and the education of the householder (or spouse, as determined by random selection), demonstrate that suburbanization is socioeconomically selective for immigrant (and nonimmigrant) minorities. These relationships are the ones anticipated by the spatial-assimilation model. There is, however, one quite critical change between 1980 and 1990: namely, the import of assimilation—more precisely, linguistic acculturation—has declined, especially for Asian groups. In 1980 at the national level, linguistic assimilation played a large role in determining which members of most groups wound up in suburbs: in general, the greater the individual's proficiency in English, the greater was his or her likelihood of residing in a suburb. By 1990, this role had declined, or for some groups even disappeared. A change of this sort is not consistent with spatial assimilation.

The Current Analysis

The current analysis looks at how this important shift is reflected in 1990 in the two most prominent regions where immigrants settle. The results are displayed in Table 6.2, where we present predicted probabilities of suburban residence, rather than the original logistic regression characteristics, to explore the implications of the analysis.[2] These probabilities are calculated for hypothetical individuals whose characteristics are varied in systematic ways from a standard bundle. The first column in the table (P1) presents the predicted probability of suburban residence for an individual who has rather typical characteristics for a young suburbanite ($50,000 in 1989 household income, a bachelor's degree, English speaking only, thirty years of age, and married). The second column (P2) also presents a predicted probability but now of an individual whose socioeconomic characteristics have worsened by roughly a standard deviation on income and education (to $20,000 in household income and only a high school diploma), while everything else remains the same. The third column (P3) changes only the language characteristic (now the hypothetical individual does not speak English well), while again holding the other characteristics to their values in column 1. Thus, columns 2 and 3 represent tests of the effects of socioeconomic status and linguistic acculturation, respectively, by group and by metropolitan context. All the probabilities are calculated from models estimated from 1990 census data.

[2] In Tables 6.2 and 6.3, we are forced to drop the smaller immigrant minorities, such as the Vietnamese of New York ($N = 14,576$ in Table 6.1), because they do not provide enough cases in the Public Use sample (the basis for Table 6.2) and the small size would distort the values of the D index in Table 6.3.

Table 6.2. Predicted probabilities of suburbanization

	P1	P2	P3
Los Angeles CMSA			
Non-Latino Whites	.677	.712	.547
Non-Latino Blacks	.559	.478	.593
Chinese	.656	.578	.735
Japanese	.677	.633	.660
Koreans	.632	.550	.532
Filipinos	.638	.566	.578
Asian Indians	.603	.531	.769
Vietnamese	.721	.678	.665
Mexicans	.732	.668	.574
Cubans	.591	.546	.697
Salvadorans	.569	.381	.432
New York CMSA			
Non-Latino Whites	.656	.669	.284
Non-Latino Blacks	.345	.254	.224
West Indians	.253	.176	.352
Chinese	.384	.230	.155
Koreans	.426	.307	.273
Filipinos	.447	.363	.386
Asian Indians	.334	.195	.413
Mexicans	.557	.474	.370
Puerto Ricans	.502	.350	.241
Cubans	.514	.372	.295
Dominicans	.261	.148	.193

CMSA = consolidated metropolitan statistical area; P1 = $50,000 income, bachelor's degree, thirty years of age, married household, and speaks only English; P2 = Same as P1 but with $20,000 income and a high school graduate; P3 = Same as P1 but speaks English poorly.

To note some of the obvious patterns in the table before coming to the question of the role of language, there is much more racial and ethnic inequality in suburbanization in New York than in Los Angeles. When all groups are given the same profile of "advantaged" characteristics in column 1 ("advantaged" in the sense that they correspond to those of a fairly typical suburbanite), the degree of variation among the groups is much less in Los Angeles than in New York, and, as we noted earlier, the likelihood of suburbanization is generally higher. In Los Angeles, only non-Latino blacks, Cubans, and Salvadorans remain notably behind the predicted suburbanization probability for the majority group; and a few immigrant minorities, such as Mexicans, have even pulled modestly ahead. But in New York, all the immigrant minorities remain behind whites, and typically by a large margin. In New York, in other words, even equalizing groups in terms of the characteristics most relevant to suburban residence would not eliminate the inequality in suburbanization, which clearly has an independent racial/ethnic dimension.

Despite this marked difference between the contexts, socioeconomic effects are to be found virtually everywhere. The one exception—and it is one we have noted in our national analyses, too (see Alba and Logan 1991)—is in the majority group. Non-Latino whites tend to live in suburbs, regardless of their income and education levels; and consequently, in their case, P1 and P2 are approximately the same in both regions. But for other groups, the tendency of suburban residence to become less likely with lower socioeconomic status is apparent in the comparison of P1 to P2. For example, lowering household income by $30,000 and education by four years reduces the predicted probability that a Chinese New Yorker will reside in a suburb from .38 to .23. There is also a tendency in the table for the difference between P1 and P2 to be a bit smaller in Los Angeles than in New York. Note that the equivalent lowering of socioeconomic variables reduces the suburbanization probability of a Chinese Angeleno from .66 to .58. This is consistent with the generally lower income stratification between city and suburb in Los Angeles compared with New York.

Linguistic assimilation also affects the probability of suburbanization for many groups and, like socioeconomic status, tends to have larger effects in New York. This is apparent even in the majority group: raising the English-language ability of a non-Latino white New Yorker from poor English to only English (at home) prompts a large rise in the expected probability of suburban residence, from .28 (in P3) to .66 (in P1); the equivalent shift in Los Angeles produces a much more modest change, from .55 to .68. In a few cases, effects that are substantial in New York disappear altogether (or even appear to be reversed) in Los Angeles. This occurs for the Chinese, most notably: in New York, linguistic assimilation raises the probability of suburban residence in the table from .16 to .38, while in Los Angeles, individuals who do not speak English well have a slightly higher predicted probability of living in suburbia. The New York pattern is the one that would be expected in metropolitan regions with urban Chinatowns, where many fresh immigrants, whose proficiency in English is minimal, tend to settle. The Los Angeles pattern suggests, at a minimum, that suburban Chinatowns balance any urban ones.

What one can see from this analysis is that the shift we have detected in national patterns, from a clear correspondence between linguistic assimilation and suburbanization in 1980 and presumably in earlier periods to a weak one by 1990, is better represented by Los Angeles. In New York, the older pattern is still rather prevalent. To be sure, linguistic assimilation has not been equally important for all groups, even in the past. This is because some groups come with extensive knowledge of English, acquired in their home countries, and thus language is not a barrier to their suburbanization. This is the case for the Filipinos and Asian Indians, who do not show any language disadvantage in New York. But the shift for other groups holds intriguing implications, for it means that limited competence in English is not a large impediment to entry into suburbia; suburbanization is no longer very selective of the linguistically assimilated. Because limited competence in English should mean little ability to carry out everyday activities outside of ethnic networks, it would appear that forms of co-ethnic assistance must now exist in suburbs, not just in urban enclaves.

The finding of a diminished role of linguistic assimilation (which, incidentally, is particularly marked among Asian groups) thus strengthens the notion that a new pattern, unanticipated by spatial-assimilation theory, is appearing. As suburbanization of immigrant minorities has proceeded, suburban concentrations of these groups have emerged, epitomized by Monterey Park outside of Los Angeles (Horton 1995). These concentrations allow households headed by individuals who do not speak English well to enter suburbia without detriment to their ability to function (e.g., shop or participate in recreational activities), for they can find sufficient numbers of co-ethnics and also an ethnic infrastructure in their vicinity. In some cases, these are households that have only recently immigrated to the United States; in others, they come from urban ethnic enclaves. That immigrants from most of the Asian groups enter with relatively high levels of human and economic capital has, without doubt, facilitated the emergence of the new pattern. It in turn suggests that we look at the linkage between suburbanization and ethnic segregation.

Segregation in City and Suburb

The major rationale for the key role assigned to suburbanization in the spatial-assimilation model lies in its presumed consequences, which include a decline of residential segregation and an increase in contact with the racial/ethnic majority. Arrival in the suburbs is conceived within the model as a function of individual-level mobility out of urban ethnic enclaves and into more intermixed settings. Past research has supported the hypothesis that suburbanization and residential integration are linked for most groups (Massey and Denton 1987).

Analysis of Segregation Indices P* and D·

Hence, we turn now to an analysis of segregation indices, which have been calculated across census tracts in the Los Angeles and New York

Table 6.3. Segregation indices for Los Angeles and New York, 1990

Los Angeles CMSA	D			P*		
	Suburbs	Cities	Difference	Suburbs	Cities	Difference
Non-Latino Blacks	0.647	0.710	0.063	0.309	0.180	0.129
Mexicans	0.559	0.627	0.068	0.339	0.230	0.109
Cubans	0.604	0.558	−0.046	0.445	0.424	0.021
Salvadorans	0.718	0.746	0.028	0.277	0.187	0.090
Chinese	0.618	0.554	−0.064	0.444	0.366	0.078
Japanese	0.512	0.471	−0.041	0.544	0.459	0.085
Filipinos	0.517	0.558	0.041	0.481	0.363	0.118
Koreans	0.572	0.598	0.026	0.561	0.366	0.195
Asian Indians	0.542	0.534	−0.008	0.585	0.537	0.048
Vietnamese	0.674	0.643	−0.031	0.477	0.360	0.117

New York CMSA	D			P*		
	Suburbs	Cities	Difference	Suburbs	Cities	Difference
Non-Latino Blacks	0.730	0.821	0.091	0.387	0.112	0.275
West Indians	0.733	0.817	0.084	0.444	0.137	0.307
Mexicans	0.662	0.686	0.024	0.586	0.321	0.265
Puerto Ricans	0.515	0.684	0.169	0.623	0.221	0.402
Cubans	0.674	0.604	−0.070	0.518	0.388	0.130
Dominicans	0.789	0.796	0.007	0.443	0.161	0.282
Chinese	0.493	0.579	0.086	0.828	0.448	0.380
Filipinos	0.586	0.630	0.044	0.766	0.470	0.296
Koreans	0.606	0.646	0.040	0.815	0.502	0.313
Asian Indians	0.528	0.640	0.112	0.762	0.406	0.356

CMSA = consolidated metropolitan statistical area; D = index of dissimilarity; P* = index of exposure to the majority group.
Note: Differences are calculated for each index so that positive values are supportive of the spatial-assimilation model and negative values contradict it.

metropolitan regions and are presented in Table 6.3. Two indices are shown for each specific racial/ethnic group and by the two different types of metropolitan space (city versus suburb): the index of dissimilarity (D) is the better known segregation index and is a measure of evenness of distribution (in comparison to non-Hispanic whites); the index of exposure to the majority group (xP^*y) indicates the degree of co-residence with the majority group, i.e, the proportion of non-Latino whites in the population of the tract of the average minority-group member. Note also that the difference columns in the table are calculated so that positive differences indicate support for the spatial-assimilation hypothesis.

In one respect, the results are entirely consistent with that hypothesis, as conventionally stated: in every case, the value of xP*y is greater in suburbia than in central cities, indicating that suburban minorities reside on average in neighborhoods containing more majority-group members than do minorities in central cities (see also Massey and Denton 1988). The differences between suburbs and central cities are often substantial. In many cases, residing in suburbia appears to mean that the average minority lives in a neighborhood where non-Hispanic whites predominate. However, once again, there is a contrast between Los Angeles and New York: the xP*y differences between suburbs and central cities are larger for New York, and the association of suburban residence with a neighborhood that is more than 50 percent non-Latino white is more clear-cut, at least for immigrant minorities. In New York, Afro-Caribbeans and Dominicans are the only such minorities to reside on average in suburbs where non-Hispanic whites are less than a majority; in Los Angeles, this is true for most minorities.

But the values of the index of dissimilarity, the more standard measure of residential segregation, display less consistency with the spatial-assimilation hypothesis. According to it, the index should be smaller in the suburban parts of metropolitan regions than in their urban cores; in other words, the suburban residential distribution of an immigrant minority should more closely resemble that of whites. With African Americans and Puerto Ricans excluded, the values of the index are in favor of the hypothesis— eleven cases support it, while six go against it. But just as telling are that the differences in the index tend to be small, even when they favor the hypothesis, and that the suburban values are large by the conventional benchmarks: they are above .5 in virtually every case, and many are near or above .6, a value generally taken as indicative of a high level of segregation (Massey and Denton 1987). The support for the spatial assimilation hypothesis is quite equivocal.

Nevertheless, evenness of residential distribution is just one criterion for assessing the degree of segregation. An uneven distribution does not in and of itself indicate in particular the existence of enclaves that are densely populated by a group. Unevenness can arise, for instance, when a group settles at relatively low densities over a wide area centered around one or a few suburban communities. Such unevenness could be described as indicating a degree of concentration or clustering, rather than segregation. This type of pattern is a plausible one for new immigrant groups in suburbs. The analysis by Horton (1995) of Asians in Monterey Park indicates a fairly high degree of residential interspersion of Asians with other groups, including whites. Hence, the pattern it represents is consistent with the high levels of residential exposure to the non-Hispanic white majority, levels that we find in the P* Index. This example suggests that we look more closely at the geography of immigrant minorities in suburbia, to identify residential clusters and to examine the kinds of suburbs that these clusters involve, the kinds where immigrant minorities settle.

The Geography of Immigrant-Group Settlement

We have mapped the suburban concentrations of major immigrant populations in Los Angeles and New York.[3] To avoid excessive complexity, we have produced maps (Figures 6.1–6.4) for selected aggregations of groups—specifically, for Asians and non–Puerto Rican Latinos in New York and for Asians and Mexicans in Los Angeles. Except for this last, the maps show all suburban tracts in which these groups represent 10 percent or more of the population; because Mexicans are a large part of the Los Angeles population, we opted for a threshold of 35 percent in a tract (i.e., about one-third) in their case (see Alba et al. 1997). The central cities are shown as hatched areas, and labels are provided for the major suburban concentrations of groups (often, however, the concentrations spill beyond the boundaries of a single place and have been named according to the places that represent their largest portions of their central core). Tables 6.4 and 6.5 show selected characteristics of these concentrations.

The maps and the types of suburbs that figure in immigrant-minority concentrations appear very different from one group to another and from one metropolitan context to another. One dimension of this difference is captured by comparing Asians with other immigrant minorities.

Asians in Affluent Suburbs in New York

In both regions, Asian groups tend to be concentrated in more affluent suburbs than the ones other immigrant minorities enter; however, the overall racial/ethnic composition of Asian suburbs varies substantially between Los Angeles and New York. Fairly typical for New York is the concentration in northern Bergen County, where Koreans represent the main Asian group. The median income of the area, nearly $67,000 in 1990, marks it as a relatively affluent suburb. And, as is usually the case for Asian suburbs in New York, Asians themselves represent only 15 percent of the population, a modest percentage, in other words. Even at its peak value (in Edison/Piscataway, New Jersey, where Asian Indians represent the largest Asian group) the Asian percentage of the population is just 20 percent. Generally, in the Asian suburbs around the New York region, non-Latino

---

[3] The maps have been produced with the Mapinfo program. For a far more elaborate set of maps of the Los Angeles area, see the highly informative book by Allen and Turner (1997).

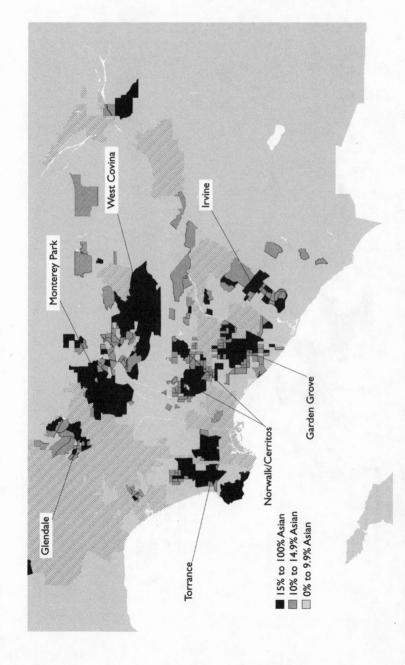

Figure 6.1 Los Angeles areas of suburban concentration: Asians.

Glendale

Monterey Park

West Covina

Irvine

Torrance

Norwalk/Cerritos

Garden Grove

■ 15% to 100% Asian
■ 10% to 14.9% Asian
□ 0% to 9.9% Asian

Immigrant Groups and Suburbs **123**

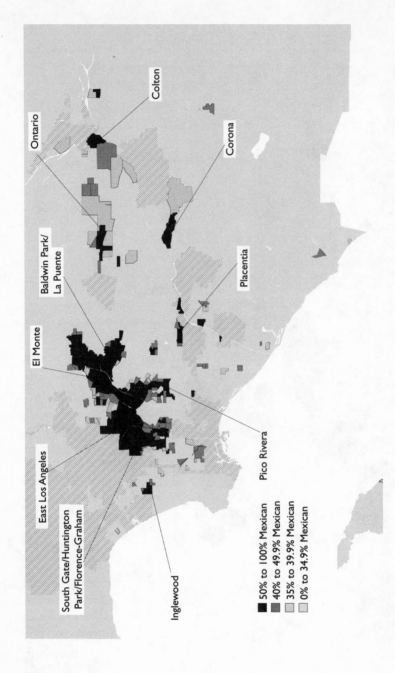

Colton

Ontario

Corona

Baldwin Park/
La Puente

Placentia

El Monte

Pico Rivera

East Los Angeles

South Gate/Huntington
Park/Florence-Graham

Inglewood

■ 50% to 100% Mexican
■ 40% to 49.9% Mexican
□ 35% to 39.9% Mexican
□ 0% to 34.9% Mexican

Figure 6.2 Los Angeles areas of suburban concentration: Mexicans.

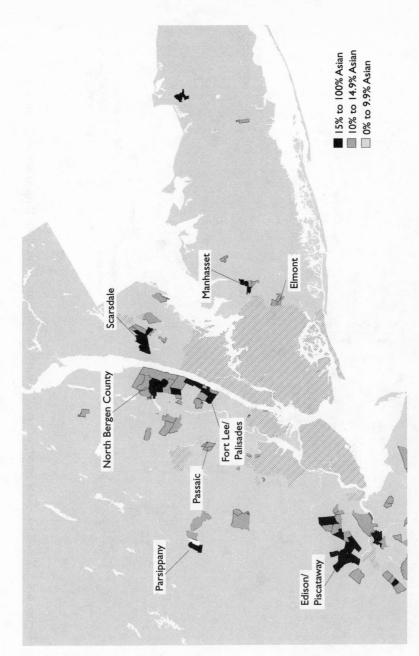

Figure 6.3 New York–New Jersey areas of suburban concentration: Asians.

15% to 100% Asian
10% to 14.9% Asian
0% to 9.9% Asian

Scarsdale

Manhasset

Elmont

North Bergen County

Fort Lee/
Palisades

Passaic

Parsippany

Edison/
Piscataway

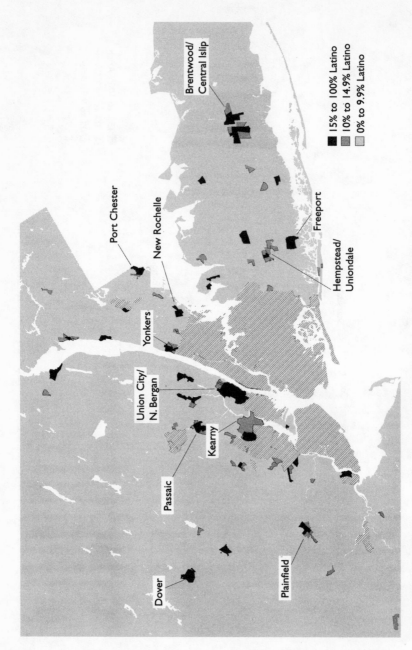

Figure 6.4 New York–New Jersey areas of suburban concentration: Non–Puerto Rican Latinos.

15% to 100% Latino
10% to 14.9% Latino
0% to 9.9% Latino

Brentwood/
Central Islip

Port Chester

New Rochelle

Freeport

Hempstead/
Uniondale

Yonkers

Union City/
N. Bergan

Passaic

Kearny

Dover

Plainfield

Table 6.4. Characteristics of suburban areas of immigrant concentration in Los Angeles

	Group N	Group Percentage of Population	Non-Latino White Percentage	Area Household Income (median)
Asians				
Monterey Park	149,155	31.3	33.1	$37,284
Torrance	86,541	23.0	48.2	$46,723
West Covina	82,560	22.1	36.1	$52,651
Garden Grove	72,472	18.6	59.4	$43,442
Norwalk/Cerritos	70,234	19.9	50.2	$50,220
Irvine	25,621	16.6	74.2	$58,487
Glendale	25,075	15.0	64.2	$40,473
Mexicans				
South Gate/Huntington Park/Florence-Graham	308,335	64.3	8.7	$24,523
East Los Angeles	198,169	77.3	8.5	$24,818
Baldwin Park/La Puente	151,213	59.5	19.8	$34,892
Pico Rivera	140,755	58.9	28.0	$35,226
El Monte	121,257	58.5	15.3	$28,683
Indio	53,228	77.6	16.3	$23,372
Ontario	53,034	45.1	40.3	$30,362
Inglewood	35,613	54.6	7.3	$26,933
Colton	26,105	43.9	40.7	$25,989
Santa Paula	23,325	41.1	45.7	$28,633
Corona	14,887	52.3	38.2	$29,455
Placentia	13,728	53.2	31.9	$32,148
Suburban Average	—	—	55.3	$41,637

whites are the predominant group in the population. In northern Bergen County, they make up 80 percent, for example. In short, in the New York region, suburbanization has brought Asians into areas that tend to be average or above average in affluence and to have non-Hispanic whites as the dominant population group.

Asians in Multiethnic Suburbs in Los Angeles

In Los Angeles, the Asian suburbs are not as affluent on average as in New York, but they are still more affluent than the suburbs where Latino groups reside. But the more marked departure from the New York pattern lies in the racial/ethnic character of these suburbs. Consider the suburban concentration centered around Monterey Park, the largest Asian area in the region. Containing nearly 150,000 Asians, with Chinese the most numerous group, it is clearly much larger—about ten times larger, in fact—than any of the Asian areas in the New York suburbs. The concentration of Asians in the population—about one-third—is also notably higher. Moreover, whites do not predominate in the remainder of the population, as they do in New

Table 6.5. Characteristics of suburban areas of immigrant concentration in New York

	Group N	Group Percentage of Population	Non-Latino White Percentage	Area Household Income (median)
Asians				
Edison/Piscataway	15,236	20.0	65.3	$53,895
Fort Lee/Palisades	11,458	18.3	71.7	$46,851
North Bergen County	9,251	14.8	79.6	$66,707
Scarsdale	4,871	15.6	80.3	$94,206
Passaic	3,656	12.8	40.8	$30,702
Manhasset	2,401	14.4	81.2	$70,766
Parsippany	2,371	15.2	77.8	$55,501
Elmont	2,288	11.1	56.3	$48,801
Non–Puerto Rican Latinos				
Union City/North Bergen	82,822	51.7	34.8	$29,091
Passaic	18,097	29.7	30.6	$26,804
Yonkers	12,276	21.1	35.0	$23,646
Brentwood/Central Islip	9,303	17.2	44.8	$45,667
Hempstead/Uniondale	8,292	18.7	30.1	$38,479
Kearny	8,029	20.6	69.9	$35,501
Port Chester	5,956	29.4	51.6	$33,269
Freeport	5,768	24.3	40.7	$37,433
Plainfield	5,350	17.9	28.9	$33,520
New Rochelle	3,532	19.5	55.1	$27,845
Dover	3,368	22.3	52.7	$38,958
Suburban Average	—	—	80.9	$50,645

York. They, too, are about one-third of the population, so that another one-third is made up of other groups, mainly Latino in this case. While Monterey Park represents a perhaps extreme example of this pattern, it is also found in some other Asian suburbs, such as Torrance and West Covina. There are also, to be sure, suburbs that approach the New York model, suburbs such as Irvine, where Asians are just 17 percent of the population and non-Hispanic whites are 74 percent. Nevertheless, in Los Angeles, some Asians enter a type of multiracial/multiethnic suburb, one of at least average affluence, that has yet to emerge in New York.

Latinos in Less Affluent Suburbs in New York

The heavily Latino areas also share a socioeconomic character in Los Angeles and in New York, one that sets them apart from the Asian areas. In both regions, the suburbs that Latinos enter tend to be below average, and sometimes well below average, in affluence. The leading Latino suburb in the New York region is the Union City/North Bergen concentration (oddly, this North Bergen is located in Hudson, not Bergen, County and is thus distinct from the similarly named Asian concentration). This concentration has grown up around a Cuban settlement that dates to the early refugee waves and the resettlement policy of the federal government devised to disperse them. Latinos constitute a majority of the population in this cluster, which is quite large and contains altogether some 83,000 people and which is also relatively working class, with a median income of just $29,000 in 1990. Moreover, Union City and North Bergen are classic inner suburbs, located just outside of Jersey City, New Jersey, and near other old industrial cities, such as Bayonne, Elizabeth, Hoboken, and Newark.

These features of the Union City/North Bergen concentration are detectable in most of the other Latino concentrations around New York, such as those in Passaic (a former central city), Kearny, New Rochelle, and Yonkers. In general, Latinos make up a higher proportion of the total population in their suburban areas of concentration than do Asians in theirs. And the heavily Latino suburbs are considerably less affluent than the Asian ones: in fact, the highest median income of a Latino suburb is below all but one of the median incomes of the Asian suburbs. Finally, the Latino suburbs are frequently home to other minority populations, including Puerto Ricans and African Americans. Illustrative is the Hempstead/Uniondale area, where Salvadorans and other Latinos have been entering suburbs that also have large African American populations. Given that a lengthy stream of research findings demonstrates that suburbs with many African Americans are different from other suburbs—in urbanness, crime, poverty, and other ways (e.g., Alba, Logan, and Bellair 1994)—a conclusion that the processes directing Latino immigrant minorities to suburbs are different from those for Asians seems eminently plausible.

Latinos in Ethnic Enclaves in Suburban Los Angeles

In the Los Angeles region, the heavily Latino suburbs are highly consolidated, and much of the suburban Mexican population is located in a thick band of tracts that runs from South Gate/Huntington Park/Florence-Graham in the southwest to Baldwin Park/La Puente in the northeast. (We could have treated these suburban areas as a single cluster, but we chose instead to break it up along some natural dividing lines, to avoid having a single suburban concentration with some 800,000 Mexicans.) In these areas, Mexicans, along with other Latinos, account for the large majority of the population. Indeed, insofar as non-Mexican Latinos have areas of concentration in suburbs (they have only a few), these tend to be in areas where Mexicans predominate, such as the South Gate/Huntington Park area. Non-Latino whites are a minority element in the populations of Latino suburbs, and in some cases they represent just tiny minorities, under 10 percent of residents. Thus, in the Los Angeles region, to a degree that is not true in New York, the suburbs where Latinos are concentrated represent true ethnic enclaves, where Latinos, especially Mexicans, predominate and other groups are numerically in the minority. These enclaves have developed around long-standing areas of Latino settlement, such as East Los Angeles, areas that date to the earlier part of this century and are partly linked to the role of Mexicans in the region's agriculture (Ortiz 1996; Sanchez 1993). In short, the extra-urban residence of Mexicans in the Los Angeles region is not a new phenomenon.

No Single Pattern Emerges

What seems immediately apparent in this excursion into the geography of immigrant minorities in suburbs is that no single pattern exists; the meaning of suburbanization is specific to the group and to the metropolitan context. The closest we have come to the kind of pattern that one would anticipate from the spatial-assimilation model is for the Asians in New York, where Asians enter middle-class or upper-middle-class suburbs with large numbers of non-Latino white residents; but even here, the model must be qualified because the Asians themselves are not as culturally assimilated as it presumes, as we showed earlier. But the pattern of Latino suburban concentration is quite different in New York and, to a significant extent, resembles that of a nonimmigrant minority, African Americans; both tend to be concentrated in and around inner suburbs that have lower-than-average affluence and some of the problems of inner cities. Things are different once again in Los Angeles, for Asians are present in some middle-class multiracial/multiethnic suburbs, a type of suburb that has not emerged on a significant scale in New York; and Latinos have established the kind of extensive ethnic enclaves in suburbia that the spatial-assimilation model associates with cities. These enclaves have cores that have been linked throughout this century to a disproportionate Mexican presence; indeed, these are some of the areas covered by the term "barrio."

Conclusion

The settlement of immigrant minorities in suburbs is for the first time in American history as influential in shaping their pattern of incorporation into the larger society as their settlement in cities (or, in an earlier era, in rural areas and small towns). This new pattern poses a challenge for the conceptual models we have acquired from the experiences of past immigrant groups, primarily those of the mass immigration era of the early twentieth century. The premier model of this type is that of spatial-assimilation theory.

Our analysis has demonstrated that spatial assimilation's application to contemporary immigrant minorities is problematic. To start with, the strong association between linguistic assimilation and suburbanization presumed by the theory apparently no longer accords with immigrant settlement patterns. Even in the very recent past, suburbs tended to select members of the immigrant and second generations who spoke English well or even had abandoned their mother tongue in daily life (Alba and Logan 1991; Alba et al. 1997). There is now a lower barrier for recent arrivals, even if they speak English with difficulty, to enter suburbs. Undoubtedly, as the percentages of contemporary immigrant groups in suburbs have grown, it has become easier for new arrivals to go there, because the networks and infrastructure necessary to meet their needs exist. Indeed, the phenomenon of chain migration, whereby immigrants go where kin and other co-ethnics have preceded them, implies this, once the kernels of immigrant suburban settlement are established.

The fact that new immigrants who do not speak English well are arriving in suburbs in large numbers implies in turn some degree of residential concentration. In this aspect of current settlement patterns lies the greatest challenge to spatial-assimilation theory. By the evidence of segregation indices and our geographical analysis, this does not usually mean the emergence of ethnic enclaves in suburbs (the suburban equivalents to, say, urban Chinatowns, where a group is so densely settled that its culture and institutions are dominant). Of the four maps we analyzed in the previous section, only that of the Mexicans in Los Angeles appears to fit the requirements for a suburban enclave (because non-Mexican Latinos concentrate in parts of the Mexican areas, they also could be described as settling in suburban enclaves). Yet only the Asians in the New York region appear to settle in suburbs in a way anticipated by the spatial-assimilation model. The two remaining maps, for the non–Puerto Rican Latinos in New York and the Asians in Los Angeles, suggest the emergence of multiracial, multiethnic suburbs, though in the New York region these communities have some urban characteristics and some disadvantages that most suburbs lack, such as concentrations of poor minorities. While the extensive suburban barrio of Los Angeles sets up one kind of challenge to spatial-assimilation theory, the middle-class multiracial, multiethnic suburb that is exemplified by Monterey Park may pose the greater challenge. Socioeconomic mobility is probably linked to spatial mobility away from the suburban barrio on the part of Mexican Americans seeking to upgrade their residential situations, but the equivalent linkage is not as likely to Asians from Monterey Park. Even in New York, one has to acknowledge that the density of the immigrant minorities seems great enough in many cases to allow for the emergence of a significant infrastructure in support of the group's ethnicity, as a visit to Fort Lee, New Jersey, or Scarsdale, New York, would indicate.

This analysis also clearly indicates that the precise impact of suburbanization is group and context specific and should not be theorized as a uniform process. The impact of the metropolitan context is impossible to overlook, and indeed Los Angeles and New York, the two greatest contemporary meccas for immigrants in the United States, seem to be placed at opposite ends of the metropolitan spectrum. Los Angeles is the suburban metropolis par excellence, where even many neighborhoods in central cities have a suburban character and the social and physical boundary between city and suburb is thus not sharply demarcated (Allen and Turner 1997). New York, by contrast, has the more conventional division between urban and suburban spaces, although the correspondence is not perfect. The region has several suburban communities with an urban character, such as Union City, New Jersey, and Hempstead, on Long Island. Both communities have many Latino immigrants.

The way immigrant groups enter and settle in these metropolitan regions thus varies not only by the characteristics of the groups but also by the character of the regions. In tracking this interaction between group and region, we think it again important to underscore the significance of the kind of suburb represented by Monterey Park (the community at the core of the suburban Asian concentration we have identified). So far, it appears to be still rather unusual. In fact, Monterey Park has, by a good margin, the highest Asian population density of any sizable suburb in the United States (Horton 1995). Should a number of other middle-class, multiracial, multiethnic suburbs emerge, the consequences for ethnic incorporation could be profound.

And the consequences will not be limited to the ethnic minorities. A blind spot of the spatial-assimilation model, as of assimilation theory in general, is that it considers only the impacts of the receiving society on racial/ethnic minorities and fails to include the impacts in the other direction, of minorities on the larger society. In this context, the impacts of immigrant minorities on suburbia itself are worthy of consideration. Suburbs were once regarded as largely homogeneous communities, offering places of retreat for middle-class, native-born families desiring to escape from urban problems, including the racial/ethnic diversity of cities (Jackson 1985). But, increasingly, diversity is coming to suburbs, at least to those in metropolitan regions that are attracting substantial portions of the contemporary immigrant stream. As we have shown in a previous analysis for New York (Alba et al. 1995), the number of all-white tracts, and in particular of tracts where the white majority has no contact with immigrant minorities, fell off rather dramatically between 1970 and 1990, as the volume of immigration swelled. Thus, the strangers have indeed moved next door. Could a more cosmopolitan suburbia be the ultimate result?

CHAPTER SEVEN

Jobless Poverty: A New Form of Social Dislocation in the Inner-City Ghetto

William Julius Wilson

In September 1996 my book, *When Work Disappears: The World of the New Urban Poor,* was published. In this chapter, I integrate some of the main arguments and conclusions presented in that book with social policy research in order to address current issues of welfare reform.

When Work Disappears describes a new type of poverty in our nation's metropolises: poor, segregated neighborhoods in which a majority of adults are either unemployed or have dropped out of the labor force altogether. What is the effect of these "jobless ghettos" on individuals, families, and neighborhoods? What accounts for their existence? I suggest several factors and conclude with policy recommendations: a mix of public and private sector projects is more effective than relying on a strategy of employer subsidies.

The Research Studies

When Work Disappears was based mainly on three research studies conducted in Chicago between 1986 and 1993. The first of these three studies included a variety of data: a random survey of nearly 2,500 poor and nonpoor African American, Latino, and white residents in Chicago's poor neighborhoods; a more focused survey of 175 participants who were reinterviewed and answered open-ended questions; a survey of 179 employers selected to reflect distribution of employment across industry and firm size in the Chicago metropolitan areas; and comprehensive ethnographic research, including participant-observation research and life-history interviews by ten research assistants in a representative sample of inner-city neighborhoods.

The first of the two remaining projects also included extensive data: a survey of a representative sample of 546 black mothers and up to two of their adolescent children (aged eleven to sixteen—or 887 adolescents) in working-class, middle-class, and high-poverty neighborhoods; a survey of a representative sample of 500 respondents from two high-joblessness neighborhoods on the South Side of Chicago; and six focus-group discussions involving the residents and former residents of these neighborhoods.

Jobless Ghettos

The jobless poverty of today stands in sharp contrast to previous periods. In 1950, a substantial portion of the urban black population was poor but they were working. Urban poverty was quite extensive but people held jobs. However, as we entered the 1990s most adults in many inner-city ghetto neighborhoods were not working. For example, in 1950 a significant majority of adults held jobs in a typical week in the three neighborhoods that represent the historic core of the Black Belt in Chicago—Douglas, Grand Boulevard, and Washington Park. But by 1990, only four in ten in Douglas worked in a typical week, one in three in Washington Park, and one in four in Grand Boulevard.[1] In 1950, 69 percent of all males aged fourteen and older who lived in these three neighborhoods worked in a typical week, and in 1960, 64 percent of this group were so employed. However, by 1990 only 37 percent of all males aged sixteen and over held jobs in a typical week in these three neighborhoods.

The disappearance of work has had negative effects not only on individuals and families, but on the social life of neighborhoods as well. Inner-city joblessness is a severe problem that is often overlooked or obscured when the focus is mainly on poverty and its consequences. Despite increases in the concentration of poverty since 1970, inner cities have always featured high levels of poverty. But the levels of inner-city joblessness reached during the first half of the 1990s were unprecedented.

---

[1] The figures on adult employment are based on calculations from data provided by the 1990 U.S. Bureau of the Census (1993) and the *Local Community Fact Book for Chicago—1950* (1953) and the *Local Community Fact Book for Chicago—1960* (1963). The adult employment rates represent the number of employed individuals (aged fourteen and older in 1950 and sixteen and older in 1990) among the total number of adults in a given area. Those who are not employed include both the individuals who are members of the labor force but are not working and those who have dropped out or are not part of the labor force.

I should note that when I speak of "joblessness" I am not solely referring to official unemployment. The unemployment rate represents only the percentage of workers in the *official* labor force—that is, those who are *actively* looking for work. It does not include those who are outside of or have dropped out the labor market, including the nearly six million males aged twenty-five to sixty who appeared in the census statistics but were not recorded in the labor market statistics in 1990 (Thurow 1990).

These uncounted males in the labor market are disproportionately represented in the inner-city ghettos. Accordingly, in *When Work Disappears*, I use a more appropriate measure of joblessness, a measure that takes into account both official unemployment and non–labor-force participation. That measure is the employment-to-population ratio, which corresponds to the percentage of adults aged sixteen and older who are working. Using the employment-to-population ratio we find, for example, that in 1990 only one in three adults aged sixteen and older held a job in the ghetto poverty areas of Chicago, areas representing roughly 425,000 men, women, and children. And in the ghetto tracts of the nation's one hundred largest cities, for every ten adults who did not hold a job in a typical week in 1990 there were only six employed persons (Kasarda 1993).

The consequences of high neighborhood joblessness are more devastating than those of high neighborhood poverty. A neighborhood in which people are poor but employed is much different than a neighborhood in which people are poor and jobless. *When Work Disappears* shows that many of today's problems in the inner-city ghetto neighborhoods—crime, family dissolution, welfare, low levels of social organization, and so on—are fundamentally a consequence of the disappearance of work.

It should be clear that when I speak of the disappearance of work, I am referring to the declining involvement in or lack of attachment to the formal labor market. It could be argued that, in the general sense of the term, "joblessness" does not necessarily mean "nonwork." In other words, to be officially unemployed or officially outside the labor market does not mean that one is totally removed from all forms of work activity. Many people who are officially jobless are nonetheless involved in informal kinds of work activity, ranging from unpaid housework to work that draws income from the informal or illegal economies.

Housework is work, baby-sitting is work, even drug dealing is work. However, what contrasts work in the formal economy with work activity in the informal and illegal economies is that work in the formal economy is characterized by, indeed calls for, greater regularity and consistency in schedules and hours. Work schedules and hours are formalized. The demands for discipline are greater. It is true that some work activities outside the formal economy also call for discipline and regular schedules. Several studies reveal that the social organization of the drug industry is driven by discipline and a work ethic, however perverse.[2] However, as a general rule, work in the informal and illegal economies is far less governed by norms or expectations that place a premium on discipline and regularity. For all these reasons, when I speak of the disappearance of work, I mean work in the formal economy, work that provides a framework for daily behavior because of the discipline, regularity, and stability that it imposes.

Effect of Joblessness on Routine and Discipline

In the absence of regular employment, a person lacks not only a place in which to work and the receipt of regular income but also a coherent organization of the present—that is, a system of concrete expectations and goals. Regular employment provides the anchor for the spatial and temporal aspects of daily life. It determines where you are going to be and when you are going to be there. In the absence of regular employment, life, including family life, becomes less coherent. Persistent unemployment and irregular employment hinder rational planning in daily life, a necessary condition of adaptation to an industrial economy (Bourdieu 1965).

Thus, a youngster who grows up in a family with a steady breadwinner and in a neighborhood in which most of the adults are employed will tend to develop some of the disciplined habits associated with stable or steady employment—habits that are reflected in the behavior of his or her parents and of other neighborhood adults. These might include attachment to a routine, a recognition of the hierarchy found in most work situations, a sense of personal efficacy attained through the routine management of financial affairs, endorsement of a system of personal and material rewards associated with dependability and responsibility, and so on. Accordingly, when this youngster enters the labor market, he or she has a distinct advantage over the youngsters who grow up in households without a steady breadwinner and in neighborhoods that are not organized around work—in other words, a milieu in which one is more exposed to the less disciplined habits associated with casual or infrequent work.

With the sharp recent rise of solo-parent families, black children who live in inner-city households are less likely to be socialized in a work environment for two main reasons. Their mothers, saddled with child-care responsibilities, can prevent a slide deeper into poverty by accepting welfare. Their fathers, removed from family responsibilities and obligations,

---

[2] See, for example, Bourgois (1995) and Venkatesh (1996).

are more likely to become idle as a response to restricted employment opportunities, which further weakens their influence in the household and attenuates their contact with the family. In short, the social and cultural responses to joblessness are reflected in the organization of family life and patterns of family formation; there they have implications for laborforce attachment as well.

Given the current policy debates that assign blame to the personal shortcomings of the jobless, we need to understand their behavior as responses and adaptations to chronic subordination, including behaviors that have evolved into cultural patterns. The social actions of the jobless—including their behavior, habits, skills, styles, orientations, attitudes—ought not to be analyzed as if they are unrelated to the broader structure of their opportunities and constraints that have evolved over time. This is not to argue that individuals and groups lack the freedom to make their own choices, engage in certain conduct, and develop certain styles and orientations; but I maintain that their decisions and actions occur within a context of constraints and opportunities that are drastically different from those in middle-class society.

Explanations of the Growth of Jobless Ghettos

What accounts for the growing proportion of jobless adults in inner-city communities? An easy explanation would be racial segregation. However, a race-specific argument is not sufficient to explain recent changes in such neighborhoods. After all, these historical Black Belt neighborhoods were *just as segregated by skin color in 1950* as they are today, yet the level of employment was much higher then. One has to account for the ways in which racial segregation interacts with other changes in society to produce the recent escalating rates of joblessness. Several factors stand out: the decreasing demand for low-skilled labor, the suburbanization of jobs, the social deterioration of ghetto neighborhoods, and negative employer attitudes. I discuss each of these factors next.

Decreasing Demand for Low-Skilled Labor

The disappearance of work in many inner-city neighborhoods is in part related to the nationwide decline in the fortunes of low-skilled workers. The sharp decline in the relative demand for unskilled labor has had a more adverse effect on blacks than on whites because a substantially larger proportion of African Americans are unskilled. Although the number of skilled blacks (including managers, professionals, and technicians) has increased sharply in the last several years, the proportion of those who are unskilled remains large, because the black population, burdened by cumulative experiences of racial restrictions, was overwhelmingly unskilled just several decades ago (Schwartzman 1997).[3]

The factors involved in the decreased relative demand for unskilled labor include changes in skilled-based technology, the rapid growth in college enrollment that increased the supply and reduced the relative cost of skilled labor, and the growing internationalization of economic activity, including trade liberalization policies, which reduced the price of imports and raised the output of export industries (Schwartzman 1997). The increased output of export industries aids skilled workers, simply because they are heavily represented in export industries. But increasing imports, especially those from developing countries that compete with labor-intensive industries (for example, apparel, textile, toy, footwear, and some manufacturing industries), hurts unskilled labor (Schwartzman 1997).

Accordingly, inner-city blacks are experiencing a more extreme form of the economic marginality that has affected most unskilled workers in Americans since 1980. Unfortunately, there is a tendency among policy makers, black leaders, and scholars alike to separate the economic problems of the ghetto from the national and international trends affecting American families and neighborhoods. If the economic problems of the ghetto are defined solely in racial terms they can be isolated and viewed as only requiring race-based solutions as proposed by those on the left, or as only requiring narrow political solutions with subtle racial connotations (such as welfare reform), as strongly proposed by those on the right.

Overemphasis on Racial Factors

Race continues to be a factor that aggravates inner-city black employment problems as we shall soon see. But the tendency to overemphasize the racial factors obscures other more fundamental forces that have sharply increased inner-city black joblessness. As the late black economist Vivian Henderson put it several years ago, "[I]t is as if racism having put blacks in their economic place steps aside to watch changes in the economy destroy that place" (Henderson 1975, 54). To repeat, the concentrated joblessness of the inner-city poor represents the most dramatic form of the growing economic dislocations among the unskilled stemming in large measure from changes in the organization of the economy, including the global economy.

---

[3] The economist David Schwartzman defines "unskilled workers to include operators, fabricators, and laborers, and those in service occupations, including private household workers, those working in protective service occupations, food service, and cleaning and building service." On the basis of this definition he estimates that 80 percent of all black workers and 38 percent of all white workers were unskilled in 1950. By 1990, 46 percent of black workers and 27 percent of white workers were employed in unskilled occupations (Schwartzman 1997).

Suburbanization of Jobs

But inner-city workers face an additional problem: the growing suburbanization of jobs. Most ghetto residents cannot afford an automobile and therefore have to rely on public transit systems that make the connection between inner-city neighborhoods and suburban job locations difficult and time consuming.

Although studies based on data collected before 1970 showed no consistent or convincing effects on black employment as a consequence of this spatial mismatch, the employment of inner-city blacks relative to suburban blacks has clearly deteriorated since then. Recent research (conducted mainly by urban labor economists) strongly shows that the decentralization of employment is continuing and that employment in manufacturing, most of which is already suburbanized, has decreased in central cities, particularly in the Northeast and Midwest (Holzer 1996).

Blacks living in central cities have less access to employment (as measured by the ratio of jobs to people and the average travel time to and from work) than do central-city whites. Moreover, unlike most other groups of workers across the urban-suburban divide, less-educated central-city blacks receive lower wages than suburban blacks who have similar levels of education. And the decline in earnings of central-city blacks is related to the decentralization of employment—that is, the movement of jobs from the cities to the suburbs—in metropolitan areas (Holzer 1996).

Social Deterioration of Ghetto Neighborhoods

Changes in the class, racial, and demographic composition of inner-city neighborhoods have also contributed to the high percentage of jobless adults in these neighborhoods. Because of the steady out-migration of more advantaged families, the proportion of nonpoor families and prime-age working adults has decreased sharply in the typical inner-city ghetto since 1970 (Wilson 1987). In the face of increasing and prolonged joblessness, the declining proportion of nonpoor families and the overall depopulation has made it increasingly difficult to sustain basic neighborhood institutions or to achieve adequate levels of social organization. The declining presence of working- and middle-class blacks has also deprived ghetto neighborhoods of key structural and cultural resources. Structural resources include residents with income high enough to sustain neighborhood services, and cultural resources include conventional role models for neighborhood children.

On the basis of our research in Chicago, it appears that what many high jobless neighborhoods have in common is a relatively high degree of social integration (high levels of local neighboring while being relatively isolated from contacts in the broader mainstream society) and low levels of informal social control (feelings that they have little control over their imme-diate environment, including the environment's negative influences on their children). In such areas, not only are children at risk because of the lack of informal social controls, they are also disadvantaged because the social interaction among neighbors tends to be confined to those whose skills, styles, orientations, and habits are not as conducive to promoting positive social outcomes (academic success, pro-social behavior, employ-ment in the formal labor market, etc.) as those in more stable neighbor-hoods. Although the close interaction among neighbors in such areas may be useful in devising strategies, disseminating information, and develop-ing styles of behavior that are helpful in a ghetto milieu (teaching children to avoid eye-to-eye contact with strangers and to develop a tough demeanor in the public sphere for self-protection), they may be less effective in pro-moting the welfare of children in society at large.

Despite being socially integrated, the residents in Chicago's ghetto neighborhoods shared a feeling that they had little informal social control over the children in their environment. A primary reason is the absence of a strong organizational capacity or an institutional resource base that would provide an extra layer of social organization in their neighborhoods. It is easier for parents to control the behavior of the children in their neigh-borhoods when a strong institutional resource base exists and when the links between community institutions such as churches, schools, political organizations, businesses, and civic clubs are strong or secure. The higher the density and stability of formal organizations, the less illicit activities such as drug trafficking, crime, prostitution, and the formation of gangs can take root in the neighborhood.

Few Community Institutions

A weak institutional resource base is what distinguishes high job-less inner-city neighborhoods from stable middle-class and working-class areas. As one resident of a high jobless neighborhood on the South Side of Chicago put it, "Our children, you know, seems to be more at risk than any other children there is, because there's no library for them to go to. There's not a center they can go to, there's no field house that they can go into. There's nothing. There's nothing at all." Parents in high jobless neighborhoods have a much more difficult task controlling the behavior of their adolescents and preventing them from getting involved in activ-ities detrimental to pro-social development. Given the lack of organiza-tional capacity and a weak institutional base, some parents choose to protect their children by isolating them from activities in the neighbor-hood, including avoiding contact and interaction with neighborhood families. Wherever possible, and often with great difficulty when one considers the problems of transportation and limited financial resources, they attempt to establish contacts and cultivate relations with individuals, families, and institutions, such as church groups, schools, and community recreation programs, outside their neighborhood. A note of caution is necessary, though. It is just as indefensible to treat inner-city residents as super heroes who overcome racist oppression as it is to view them as helpless victims. We should, however, appreciate the range of choices, including choices representing cultural influences, that are available to inner-city residents who live under constraints that most people in the larger society do not experience.

Effect of Joblessness on Marriage and Family

It is within the context of labor-force attachment that the public policy discussion on welfare reform and family values should be couched. The research that we have conducted in Chicago suggests that as employment prospects recede, the foundation for stable relationships becomes weaker over time. More permanent relationships such as marriage give way to temporary liaisons that result in broken unions, out-of-wedlock pregnancies, and, to a lesser extent, separation and divorce. The changing norms concerning marriage in the larger society reinforce the movement toward temporary liaisons in the inner city, and therefore economic considerations in marital decisions take on even greater weight. Many inner-city residents have negative outlooks toward marriage, outlooks that are developed in and influenced by an environment featuring persistent joblessness.

The disrupting effect of joblessness on marriage and family causes poor inner-city blacks to be even more disconnected from the job market and discouraged about their role in the labor force. The economic marginality of the ghetto poor is cruelly reinforced, therefore, by conditions in the neighborhoods in which they live.

Negative Employer Attitudes

In the eyes of employers in metropolitan Chicago, the social conditions in the ghetto render inner-city blacks less desirable as workers, and therefore many are reluctant to hire them. One of the three studies that provided the empirical foundation for *When Work Disappears* included a representative sample of employers in the greater Chicago area who provided entry-level jobs. An overwhelming majority of these employers, both white and black, expressed negative views about inner-city ghetto workers, and many stated that they were reluctant to hire them. For example, a president of an inner-city manufacturing firm expressed a concern about employing residents from certain inner-city neighborhoods:

> If somebody gave me their address, uh, Cabrini Green I might unavoidably have some concerns. *Interviewer:* What would your concerns be? *Respondent:* That the poor guy probably would be frequently unable to get to work and . . . I probably would watch him more carefully even if it wasn't fair, than I would with somebody else. I know what I should do though is recognize that here's a guy that is trying to get out of his situation and probably will work harder than somebody else who's already out of there and he might be the best one around here. But I, I think I would have to struggle accepting that premise at the beginning. (Wilson 1996, field notes)

In addition to qualms about the neighborhood milieu of inner-city residents, the employers frequently mentioned concerns about applicants' language skills and educational training. An employer from a computer software firm in Chicago expressed the view "that in many businesses the ability to meet the public is paramount and you do not talk street talk to the buying public. Almost all your black welfare people talk street talk. And who's going to sit them down and change their speech patterns?" (Wilson 1996, field notes) A Chicago real estate broker made a similar point:

> A lot of times I will interview applicants who are black, who are sort of lower class. . . . They'll come to me and I cannot hire them because their language skills are so poor. Their speaking voice for one thing is poor . . . they have no verbal facility with the language . . . and these . . . you know, they just don't know how to speak and they'll say "salesmens" instead of "salesmen" and that's a problem. . . . They don't know punctuation, they don't know how to use correct grammar, and they cannot spell. And I can't hire them. And I feel bad about that and I think they're being very disadvantaged by the Chicago Public School system. (Wilson 1996, field notes)

Another respondent defended his method of screening out most job applicants on the telephone on the basis of their use of "grammar and English":

> I have every right to say that that's a requirement for this job. I don't care if you're pink, black, green, yellow or orange, I demand someone who speaks well. You want to tell me that I'm a bigot, fine, call me a bigot. I know blacks, you don't even know they're black. (Wilson 1996, field notes)

Finally, an inner-city banker claimed that many blacks in the ghetto "simply cannot read. When you're talking our type of business, that disqualifies them immediately, we don't have a job here that doesn't require that somebody have minimum reading and writing skills" (Wilson 1996, field notes).

How should we interpret the negative attitudes and actions of employers? To what extent do they represent an aversion to blacks *per se* and to what degree do they reflect judgments based on the job-related skills and training of inner-city blacks in a changing labor market? I should point out that the statements made by the African American employers concerning the qualifications of inner-city black workers did not differ significantly from those of the white employers. Whereas 74 percent of all the white employers who responded to the open-ended questions expressed negative views of the job-related traits of inner-city blacks, 80 percent of the black employers did so as well.

This raises a question about the meaning and significance of race in certain situations—in other words, how race intersects with other factors. A key hypothesis in this connection is that given the recent shifts in the economy, employers are looking for workers with a broad range of abilities: "hard" skills (literacy, numerical ability, basic mechanical ability, and other testable attributes) and "soft" skills (personalities suitable to the work environment, good grooming, group-oriented work behaviors, etc.). While hard skills are the product of education and training—benefits that are apparently in short supply in inner-city schools—soft skills are strongly tied to culture, and are therefore shaped by the harsh environment of the inner-city ghetto. For example, our research revealed that many parents in the inner-city ghetto neighborhoods of Chicago wanted their children not to make eye-to-eye contact with strangers and to develop a tough demeanor when interacting with people on the streets. While such behaviors are helpful for survival in the ghetto, they hinder successful interaction in mainstream society.

Statistical Discrimination

If employers are indeed reacting to the difference in skills between white and black applicants, it becomes increasingly difficult to discuss the motives of employers: are they rejecting inner-city black applicants out of overt racial discrimination or on the basis of qualifications?

Nonetheless, many of the selective recruitment practices do represent what economists call "statistical discrimination": employers make assumptions about the inner-city black workers *in general* and reach decisions based on those assumptions before they have had a chance to review systematically the qualifications of an individual applicant. The net effect is that many black inner-city applicants are never given the chance to prove their qualifications on an individual level because they are systematically screened out by the selective recruitment process.

Statistical discrimination, although representing elements of class bias against poor workers in the inner city, is clearly a matter of race both directly and indirectly. Directly, the selective recruitment patterns effectively screen out far more black workers from the inner city than Hispanic or white workers from the same types of backgrounds. But indirectly, race is also a factor, even in those decisions to deny employment to inner-city black workers on the basis of objective and thorough evaluations of their qualifications. The hard and soft skills among inner-city blacks that do not match the current needs of the labor market are products of racially segregated communities, communities that have historically featured widespread social constraints and restricted opportunities.

Thus the job prospects of inner-city workers have diminished not only because of the decreasing relative demand for low-skilled labor in the United States economy, the suburbanization of jobs, and the social deterioration of ghetto neighborhoods, but also because of negative employer attitudes. This combination of factors presents a real challenge to policy makers. Indeed, considering the narrow range of social policy options in the "balance-the-budget" political climate, how can we immediately alleviate the inner-city jobs problem—a problem which will undoubtedly grow when the new welfare reform bill takes full effect and creates a situation that will be even more harmful to inner-city children and adolescents?

Public Policy Dilemmas

What are the implications of these studies on public policy? A key issue is public-sector employment. If firms in the private sector cannot hire or refuse to hire low-skilled adults who are willing to take minimum-wage jobs, then policy makers should consider a policy of public-sector employment-of-last-resort. Indeed, until current changes in the labor market are reversed or until the skills of the next generation of workers can be upgraded before they enter the labor market, many workers, especially those who are not in the official labor force, will not be able to find jobs unless the government becomes an employer-of-last-resort (Danziger and Gottschalk 1995). This argument applies especially to low-skilled inner-city black workers. It is bad enough that they face the problem of shifts in labor-market demand shared by all low-skilled workers; it is even worse that they confront negative employer perceptions about their work-related skills and attitudes.

For all these reasons, the passage of the 1996 welfare reform bill, which did not include a program of job creation, could have very negative social consequences in the inner city. Unless something is done to enhance the employment opportunities of inner-city welfare recipients who reach the time limit for the receipt of welfare, they will flood a pool already filled with low-skilled, jobless workers.

Labor Market Trends

New research into urban labor markets by the economist Harry Holzer (1996) of Michigan State University reveals the magnitude of the problem. Surveying 3,000 employers in Atlanta, Boston, Detroit, and Los Angeles, Holzer found that only 5 to 10 percent of the jobs in central-city areas for workers who are *non-college graduates* require very few work credentials or cognitive skills. This means that most inner-city workers today not only need to have the basic skills of reading, writing, and performing arithmetic calculations, but need to know how to operate a computer as well. Also, most employers require a high school degree, particular kinds of previous work experience, and job references. Because of the large over-supply of low-skilled workers relative to the number of low-skilled jobs, many low-educated and poorly trained individuals have difficulty finding jobs even when the local labor market is strong (Holzer 1996; Center on Budget and Policy Priorities 1996a).

The problem is that in recent years tight labor markets have been of relatively short duration, frequently followed by a recession which either wiped out previous gains for many workers or did not allow others to fully recover from a previous period of economic stagnation. It would take sustained tight labor markets over many years to draw back those discouraged inner-city workers who have dropped out of the labor market altogether, some for very long periods of time. We are currently in one of the longest economic recoveries in the last half century, a recovery that has lasted more than six years and generated 14 million net new jobs and the lowest official unemployment rate in three decades. This sustained recovery is beginning to have some positive effects on the hard-core unemployed. The ranks of those out of work for more than six months declined by almost 150,000 over a two-month period in early 1997. How long this current period of economic recovery will last is anybody's guess. Given our recent economic history, we should not be surprised if it soon comes to an end and we are faced with a new recession.

Concerned about these issues, I sent President Clinton a memorandum shortly before the Democratic Convention in August 1996. Mr. Clinton has long realized the crucial relationship between welfare reform and job creation. His initial welfare plan emphasized job creation. However, the welfare bill that he signed included no such provision. I pointed out that to remedy the most glaring defects of the bill, it is essential to have a mechanism for state and local governments to respond to widespread joblessness in the inner cities. When I wrote this memorandum, I was aware that the president was giving some thought to the idea of tax credits and wage subsidies to encourage businesses to hire welfare recipients. I pointed out that while giving subsidies and tax credits to private employers to hire welfare recipients and other disadvantaged individuals may help, research suggests that subsidies and credits are hardly sufficient by themselves to accomplish this goal.

The Failure of Employer Subsidies

The track record of private employers is not especially encouraging. Past efforts to subsidize employers to hire welfare recipients and other disadvantaged individuals have generally failed to work on a large scale. For example, during the late 1960s and early 1970s, the federal government funded such a program by the National Alliance of Business. Employers received a $3,200 subsidy for each disadvantaged worker, including welfare recipients, that they hired (an amount that would be much higher in inflation-adjusted terms today). That effort resulted in a very low take-up rate among employers (Center on Budget and Policy Priorities 1996a). Why? Simply because not enough employers have been willing to hire people whom they view as troublesome or "damaged goods." Indeed, a study by the economist Gary Burtless (1985) revealed that the low-income individuals who were supposed to be aided were *less* likely to be hired as a result of a targeted wage subsidy. Employers evidently thought that if the government was willing to subsidize the hiring of these individuals so heavily, they must have serious work-related problems.

Studies also show that when employers do receive a subsidy for hiring such individuals—whether though a tax credit or a direct subsidy—the subsidy often rewards an employer for a hire he or she would have made anyway. When that occurs, it costs the government money but the number of jobs for this population does not increase (Center on Budget and Policy Priorities 1996a). Thus, studies conducted over the past two decades suggest that a single approach involving tax credits or wage subsidies will fail to move a significant number of welfare recipients into employment.

Example of a Successful Project

On the other hand, empirical research supports the idea that a program that involves a mix of employer subsidy, training and education, and public-sector job creation can have significant positive effects in moving disadvantaged workers, including welfare recipients, into jobs (see Harvard economist Lawrence Katz 1996). For example, the Youth Incentive Entitlement Pilot Project, a demonstration in selected communities conducted from late 1978 to early 1981, guaranteed part-time school-year jobs and full-time summer jobs to disadvantaged youth aged sixteen to nineteen at the minimum wage if they stayed in school (Farkas et al. 1982, 1984). The project not only created jobs in the public and nonprofit sectors, it also offered 100 percent wage subsidies to private sector for-profit firms to entice them to hire disadvantaged in-school youth. Representing a saturation job creation program for in-school youth from impoverished neighborhoods, it attempted to involve both public and private sector employers. Indeed, private, for-profit employers, especially those representing retail trade, provided 29 percent of the jobs in the program.

The project substantially increased the employment rate and earnings of those in the treatment programs compared with those in four "comparable" areas that were selected as control sites (Farkas et al. 1982, 1984). The program sites were Baltimore, Denver, Cincinnati, and Mississippi (eight rural counties); the comparison sites were Cleveland, Phoenix, Louisville, and Mississippi (six neighboring rural counties). As Judith Gueron pointed out, "to assure, to the maximum extent possible, that differences in the behavior of youths reflected program effects rather than site differences, the comparison areas were chosen to match program sites over a wide variety of dimensions" (1984, 12).

The employment rates of minorities in the program were raised to the level of whites in the same areas. Black male employment increased from two-thirds of the white male rate, to parity with the employment level of white males. "Black female employment increased even more, from two-thirds of the white rate to one-third above it" (Farkas et al. 1984, xvi). For the fifteen- to sixteen-year-old cohort, the employment rate during the school year "increased by 115 percent over what it would have been in the absence of the program"(Farkas et al. 1984, xvi). During the different years of operation of the project, earnings during the school year were estimated to have increased by 46 to 161 percent. Summer earnings jumped by approximately 50 percent. Because the program only funded jobs at the minimum wage, most of the gains in earnings were due to increases in employment rates and hours worked per week instead of higher wages. The youth employment in the private sector increased by an average of 18 percent during the operation of the program (Katz 1996).

Although the private-sector employer take-up rate was low, efforts by intermediaries (i.e., community-based agencies) to place youths in jobs combined with substantial wage subsidies substantially expanded private-sector employment for disadvantaged youth who are normally difficult to employ. In other words, the probable reasons for the relatively large private sector component "were the full (100%) wage subsidy and the fact that the youth were on the payroll of the CETA prime sponsor, not the private sector employer. Thus, the youth were really public sector employees out-stationed at private sector work sites." Accordingly, subsidies "seem to work better when a third party acts as an intermediary than when people try to market themselves. . . . But even then, only 20 percent of employers contacted were interested in taking on a disadvantaged youth."[4]

My Recommendations

In my memorandum to the president I therefore urged caution in not placing too many of his "eggs" in the private-sector job placement basket. I pointed out that we will need a mix of both private- and public-sector initiatives to enhance employment. In inner cities, where the number of very low-skilled individuals vastly exceeds the number of low-skilled jobs even before welfare reform adds tens of thousands more people to the low-skilled labor pool, a healthy dose of public-sector job creation will be needed. Public jobs can help people whom private employers initially will not touch to learn acceptable work habits and build an employment record, from which they may be able to graduate to private-sector positions.

To make my point very clear, I pointed out to Mr. Clinton that I am not suggesting that he call for a new federal public works program because I understand the difficulties in getting such a program approved in today's political climate. I am only recommending that he enable governors and mayors to use a mix of private-sector and public-sector approaches as they see fit, based on local conditions. I pointed out that he could not be criticized for a "big government" approach if he allows state and local officials, so many of whom are now Republicans, to make this choice. Indeed, Governor Thompson's welfare plan in Wisconsin includes significant public-sector employment along with private-sector employment.

The president responded to my memorandum by indicating that several of my recommendations were already under consideration by his administration. He later proposed to Congress two initiatives, which were subsequently included in the budget and tax bills that were signed into law: a $3 billion welfare-to-work jobs challenge to help cities and states create employment opportunities for the hardest to hire welfare recipients by the year 2000, and an enhanced and targeted "work opportunity tax credit" that increases financial incentives for the private sector to create jobs for long-term welfare recipients. Although the second initiative emphasizes tax credits, the former allows for the creation and administration of community service work. Nonetheless, when I went back and reread the

[4] Judith Gueron, President of Manpower Demonstration Research Corporation, private communication, 1996.

description of the budget for fiscal year 1998, it was clear that the emphasis in the first initiative was on the use of these funds "to provide subsidies and other incentives to private businesses."

The conclusion I draw from the current evidence is that as the president and the Congress of the United States take future steps to address the jobs problem for welfare recipients and other disadvantaged workers, they ought not to rely heavily on a strategy of employer subsidies—either tax credits or wage subsidies. Instead they ought to consider a mixed strategy that places a major emphasis on job creation in the public and nonprofit private sectors (Katz 1996).

The Need for Action

At the same time that the new welfare law has generated a greater need for work opportunities, high jobless urban and rural areas will experience more difficulty in placing individuals in private-sector jobs. To create work opportunities for welfare recipients, these areas will therefore have to "rely more heavily upon job creation strategies in the public and private non-profit sectors" (Center on Budget and Policy Priorities 1996a, 4). Although the placement of disadvantaged workers in private-sector jobs can help contain the overall costs in some communities (including many jobless ghetto areas and depressed rural areas) a mainly private-sector initiative will not be sufficient to generate enough jobs to accommodate the large oversupply of low-skilled individuals.

West Virginia, a state that has been plagued with a severe shortage of work opportunities, has provided community service jobs to recipients of welfare for several years. In Wisconsin, Governor Thompson's welfare reform plan envisions community service jobs for many parents in the more depressed areas of the state, and the New Hope program in Milwaukee provides community service jobs for those unable to find employment in the private sector (Center on Budget and Policy Priorities 1996a). It is especially important that this mixed strategy include a plan to make *adequate* monies available to localities or communities with high jobless and welfare dependency rates. Three billion dollars for this purpose is hardly sufficient.

Obviously, as more people become employed and gain work experience, they will have a better chance of finding jobs in the private sector when jobs become available. The attitudes of employers toward inner-city workers could change, in part because they would be dealing with job applicants who have steady work experience and who could furnish references from their previous supervisors. Children are more likely to be socialized in a work-oriented environment and to develop the job readiness skills that are seen as important even for entry-level jobs.

Thus, given the recent welfare reform legislation, *adequate* strategies to enhance the employment opportunities of inner-city residents should be contemplated, strategies that would be adequately financed and designed to address the employment problems of low-skilled workers not only in periods of tight labor markets, but, even more important, in periods when the labor market is slack. With the sharp reduction in the federal deficit and the talk about an economic surplus in the near future, now is an ideal time to urge the president and to press Congress to develop such strategies. If steps are not taken soon to enhance the job prospects of hundreds of thousands of inner-city residents, including welfare recipients who reach their time limit for receipt of welfare, we could be facing major social dislocations in many urban areas, especially if the current economic recovery ends in the near future.

CHAPTER EIGHT

Persisting Inequality between Metropolitan and Nonmetropolitan America: Implications for Theory and Policy

David L. Brown and Marlene A. Lee

Contemporary America is an overwhelmingly metropolitan society, but 54 million persons—over one in five Americans—continue to live in small towns and rural areas. Moreover, this spatial diversity is associated with substantial and persistent socioeconomic inequality. We observe, however, that spatial differences and particularly metropolitan-nonmetropolitan differences are relatively neglected in social theory. To the extent that social theory contributes to shaping social policy, we contend that aspatial social theory may contribute to maintaining, and in some instances exacerbating, inequality.

In this chapter our goals are to illustrate the case for incorporating metropolitan-nonmetropolitan space into sociological theories of national development and to provide a foundation for public policy. Toward these

This work was supported by the Cornell University Agricultural Experiment Station (USDA Hatch Grant NYC-159402; Thomas A. Hirschl and David L. Brown, Co–Primary Investigators). We want to acknowledge the helpful comments of Peggy R. Cook, Nina Glasgow, Mark Nord, Frank Young, and two anonymous reviewers. Nancy Pierce prepared the manuscript, and Stefan Rayer prepared the figures.

ends we describe persisting socioeconomic differences between metropolitan and nonmetropolitan America and discuss some implications of these differences for restructuring the nation's welfare system.

Space and Social Theory

The social meaning of space is imprecise, or as Gottdiener (1987) has observed, a catchall for a myriad of properties existing at all levels of society. Some clarification of the term can be gained by differentiating between space as a *particular* setting in which social relations occur and space as a *relational concept*, e.g., position with respect to other areas of similar or different scale (Lobao 1996). We favor the "relational" concept of space, with a focus on metropolitan-nonmetropolitan interdependence. This differentiates us from some other scholars in this volume, scholars whose primary focus is on differential location within a city and/or a metropolitan area. Our overall contention is that in the United States, as in other countries, a person's place of residence in a nation's settlement structure can shape social and economic outcomes, and can have a profound impact on their life chances.

The incorporation of space into general sociological theory has received renewed interest in recent years. This new focus on the social meaning of space follows several decades in which "aspatial covering laws were assumed to work everywhere" (Lobao 1996, 80). Not only were generalizations assumed to be "space invariant," but most varieties of development theory predicted that regional and metropolitan-nonmetropolitan diversity and inequality would diminish as nations developed. Hence, spatial differentiation was generally considered to be of temporary and trivial importance and was subordinated to temporal and historical concerns. However, as will be shown later in this paper, development has been geographically uneven in the United States. While considerable leveling has occurred, structural differentiation between regions and between metropolitan and nonmetropolitan areas is still an important social fact in contemporary America. Where individuals live and work shapes their life chances. Accordingly, space, in addition to time and history, should be considered in sociological analyses.

Untangling Cause and Effect

While a growing number of scholars—social scientists, sociologists, and geographers in particular—agree that space should be incorporated into social theory and research, there is little agreement on the manner in which space enters into social behavior. Is space merely a container for, or reflection of, social relations? Or does space have a causal role in social processes? Some critics have labeled this latter position, that space is a causal force in social relations, "spatial fetishism." The essence of their critique is captured in Storper and Walker's observation: "The prevailing assumption [of these critics but not of Storper and Walker] in social science is that society and economy have geographic outcomes, but not geographic foundations" (1989, 226).

Few could disagree that spatial localities are sites for social behavior, or "environmental containers for human life" (Soja 1989, 79). This general notion is consistent with several sociological concepts: Parsons's (1951) identification of immediate environments in which social interaction occurs; Goffman's (1959) concept of "regions," for instance, settings that are bounded by barriers to perception; and Giddens's (1979) concept of "locale," the constraints that shape the routines of daily life. However, such observations amount to little more than an assertion that norms and values determine how we interpret location and how this interpretation of space gives meaning to the social behavior that occurs within the locale. It is a long way from this position—which essentially claims that space is socially constructed or that spatial processes are derivative of social process (Sheppard 1996)—to one in which space plays a fundamental causative role in social relations. Moreover, even among scholars who agree that space is a causal force, there is disagreement over whether spatial arrangements are an elemental cause of social behavior or whether space acts in a more contingent manner.

Gottdiener's (1987) position is illustrative of scholarship contending that space is a basic causal force in social relations. His position is that social organization takes place spatially, and spatial units represent unique configurations in the social process. Relationships between spatial units (such as neighborhoods) are fundamental determinants of social outcomes. The causal power of space exists because space is more than physical, administrative, or socially constructed boundaries. It is a set of forces acting together in a unique manner. Hence, Gottdiener concludes, "One cannot discuss either spatial configuration or social production separately; they are about each other"(1987, 410).

We are more comfortable with the alternative position that space has an important, but contingent, causative role in social relations.[1] This view is best exemplified by Andrew Sayer, who contends that general social and economic processes can be considered independently of their spatial manifestations, but that spatial variation in actual outcomes can be understood only by taking into account how contingent characteristics of localities modify these processes (1993; cited in Sheppard 1996). Sayer is not particularly clear on what constitutes contingent characteristics of place. For

[1] Soja's (1989) "Socio-spatial dialectic" is the middle ground in this debate. He argues that the social relations of production are both space forming and space contingent.

us, however, such characteristics include both site factors and situation. In other words, spatial configuration includes both the internal social structure of particular types of places and the interplace relationships that occur in the system of settlement.[2]

In stating that space has a contingent causative role in social relations, we are taking a multilevel approach and asserting that local social structure contextualizes social behavior. We do not question the existence of basic sociological relationships, but we observe that these relationships are modulated by variability in social contexts. For example, attachment to the labor force reduces the likelihood of poverty, but the strength of this relationship varies across local labor markets depending on their industrial and occupational structures. In other words, it's not that work doesn't matter everywhere, but that it provides more protection against poverty in some contexts than in others because of the differential availability of well-paying jobs.

Previous Research

Our perspective is not new to sociological thinking, but because it is somewhat abstract it might be useful to discuss some insights that have been gained from this perspective in previous sociological research. Hirschl and Rank (1999), for example, use Fisher's theory of the impact of differential density on lifestyles, social and political attitudes, and acceptance of stigmatized behavior. They explain why welfare participation among eligibles is inversely related to the level of urbanization. They explain the greater likelihood of urban participation by arguing that residents of concentrated high-density and high-poverty areas are enmeshed in rich networks of information exchange that increase their likelihood of knowing about the welfare system and understanding how to participate in it.

David James's study of the dismantling of the racial state in the United States during the 1960s is another good example of research that posits intervening local structures as contingencies in the operation of society-wide processes. James observes that "theories that focus on the national state cannot explain the enormous variation in local implementation of national policies" (1998, 191). His research demonstrates that differences in racial enfranchisement were closely related to interlocal variation in class and political structures.

A recent study of uneven spatial development in the U.S. South is particularly relevant to the present paper. In this work, Tomaskovic-Devey and Roscigno (1997) investigate intra-regional variation in the "Sunbelt economic boom." They show that more successful areas are characterized by

---

[2] Sheppard (1996, 1340–41) defines relational attributes as "action at a distance of objects having causal impact even when they are located a considerable distance away."

the coexistence of heterogeneous elite structures with less racially polarized class politics. Persistently poor areas, in contrast, have a significantly higher concentration of landowning and a higher percentage of black residents.

Our basic position then is that development has been geographically uneven in the United States, and while considerable leveling has occurred, spatial differentiation is still an important social fact in contemporary American society. Although social and economic processes may be considered independently of their spatial manifestations, the persistence of spatial inequalities suggests that it is critical to take into account how characteristics of locality modify social and economic processes. Failure to consider how the internal social structure of particular types of places and interplace relationships in a social system affect social and economic outcomes may contribute to maintaining or exacerbating spatial inequality.

Metropolitan-Nonmetropolitan Differences Are Persistent and Important

Modernization theory in sociology and economics predicts that economic development is inversely related to regional and/or rural-urban inequality. This view is rooted in the belief that improved internal factor mobility (including transportation, communication, and information technologies) should tend to eliminate geographic dualism or spatial polarization. More specifically, the modernization position is that interregional linkages will emerge as an economy develops, and these linkages will facilitate the spread of development from wealthier to poorer regions. This is consistent with the classic "trickle down" position in which a rising tide will raise all boats. Williamson's (1965) "24 nation study" is generally cited as evidence that national development diminishes spatial inequality. Similarly, sociological human ecology, with its focus on the interaction of population, organization, environment, and technology in territorially based social systems, also predicts regional and/or rural-urban convergence as the costs of distance are diminished by advances in technology (Hawley 1971).

In contrast, other scholars (such as Myrdal 1957 and Hirschmann 1958) question whether capitalist market mechanisms inevitably produce spread effects. They believe that economic advantages tend to accumulate in places of initial advantage with very little growth being passed on to peripheral areas.[3] Neomarxist scholars also reject the inverse relationship between development and spatial inequality. Mandal, for example, believes that "the

[3] Similarly, many scholars have argued that population concentration and development are inextricably linked because cities are more efficient locations in which to conduct business than their rural counterparts (Tilly 1974). However, urban growth and/or urbanization do not necessarily imply that the rural hinterland is disadvantaged in the process. For example, Schultz (1953) contends that the city helps to increase the productivity of rural labor and capital.

unequal development between regions and nations is the very essence of capitalism" (1976, 43). He contends that unequal development is essential for the survival and reproduction of capitalism itself. Or as Neil Smith states, "The mobility of capital brings about the development of areas with a high rate of profit, and the underdevelopment of those areas with a low rate of profit" (1990, 148). In other words, the effect of capital is to differentiate space.

Socioeconomic Differences

With these contrasting views in mind, what do the data show regarding metropolitan-nonmetropolitan inequality in the United States today? The following figures overwhelmingly demonstrate that metropolitan-nonmetropolitan inequality in socioeconomic status persists in contemporary America.

Figure 8.1 compares metropolitan and nonmetropolitan poverty rates since 1959. These data show dramatic declines in both the nonmetropolitan poverty rate and in the gap between metropolitan and nonmetropolitan rates during this period. This narrowing of the metropolitan-nonmetropolitan gap in poverty rates to about a 2 percent difference might suggest that nonmetropolitan persons are now almost as well off as their metropolitan counterparts. However, further analysis demonstrates persisting metropolitan-nonmetropolitan disparity. As shown in Figure 8.2, nonmetropolitan real household income was only about three-fourths that of metropolitan areas in 1995, with a real dollar gap of almost eight thousand dollars.[4] Moreover, the data show that this gap has been relatively constant over the past quarter century. Mark Nord (1996b) has shown that this paradox between a diminishing poverty gap and a persisting household income gap can be explained by the fact that nonmetropolitan areas contain a much larger proportion of households with incomes barely above the poverty line. As shown in Figure 8.3, nonmetropolitan families are disproportionately represented in the "near poverty" category, with 42 percent being either poor or near poor by official definitions. In comparison only 32 percent of metropolitan families are poor or near poor.[5]

Disaggregating metropolitan poverty rates into core and suburban counties indicates that the nonmetropolitan rate is much more similar to

[4] No official estimates of metropolitan-nonmetropolitan cost-of-living differences have ever been computed. The most recent attempt was by Hoch, Hewitt, and Virgin (1984), who concluded that a little more than half of the metropolitan-nonmetropolitan differential may be offset by cost and quality-of-life differences. In other words, the nominal difference is narrowed but not eliminated.

[5] The switch in nomenclature from households to families reflects the fact that the Census Bureau's Consumer Income Series is for households, while the *Current Population Survey* reports poverty data for individuals and families.

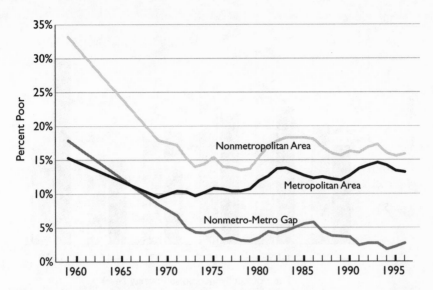

Figure 8.1 Poverty rate by residence, 1959–96. Metropolitan area delineations changed at approximately the middle of each decade. Statistics for 1994–96 are based on the most recent metro delineation. There were no data available for 1960–68, 1970, and 1984. Prepared by U.S. Department of Agriculture—Economic Research Service using data from the U.S. Bureau of the Census Consumer Income Series P-60, 1959–97.

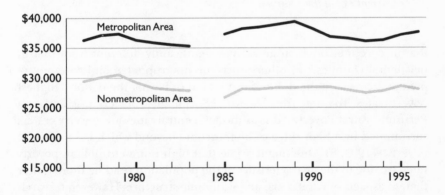

Figure 8.2 Median household income 1977–96 (in 1996 dollars). Metro delineations changed in 1984 and 1994. Metro and nonmetro median household income estimates were not published for 1984. The 1994 change produced only a negligible discontinuity. Prepared by U.S. Department of Agriculture—Economic Research Service using data from the U.S. Bureau of the Census Consumer Income Series P-60, 1976–96.

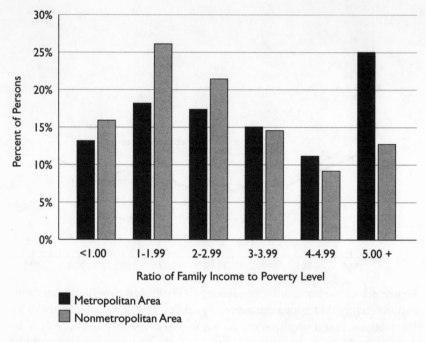

Figure 8.3 Distribution of persons by ratio of family income to poverty level, 1996. Prepared by U.S. Department of Agriculture—Economic Research Service based on data from the U.S. Bureau of the Census *March 1997 Current Population Survey.*

that in core metropolitan areas, and significantly different from that in peripheral counties.[6] In other words, nonmetropolitan and core metropolitan areas share the dubious distinction of having the nation's highest poverty rates. To quote from the Rural Sociological Society Task Force on Persistent Rural Poverty, "It is as though central cities are poverty craters surrounded by a high ridge of high income beyond which lies a plain of poverty" (1993, 8). One might argue that high nonmetropolitan poverty rates are due to the characteristics of the population residing there rather than to aspects of rural social and economic structure. However, research by Brown and Hirschl (1995) demonstrates that the higher likelihood of nonmetropolitan poverty is not solely the result of nonmetropolitan versus metropolitan differences in population composition.

[6] Socioeconomic diversity within the nonmetropolitan category is also important. For example, Tompkins County, the home of Cornell University, has low poverty, virtually full employment, and an abundance of opportunities, while its nonmetropolitan neighbors (Cayuga, Cortland, Schuyler, and Seneca counties) are all seriously disadvantaged.

Poverty is not spread evenly across nonmetropolitan America. Rather, nonmetropolitan poverty is concentrated in particular regions and among particular racial and ethnic populations in those regions. More than half of all nonmetropolitan poor persons live in the South where the poverty rate of almost 20 percent (in 1990) far exceeds that in the non-metropolitan parts of other regions. Moreover, in most instances higher nonmetropolitan poverty rates reflect the inadequate income of the racial and ethnic groups concentrated in each region (Beale 1996). Blacks account for the occurrence of high nonmetropolitan poverty in the Mississippi Delta, across the coastal plain and in the upland South. Hispanics predominate in the southern Great Plains and in the lower Rio Grande Valley, while the few persistent poverty areas located in the Upper Plains reflect the location of Native American settlements. White poverty only predominates in southern Appalachia and in the Ozark-Ouachita Uplands.

Nonmetropolitan workers are disadvantaged in the labor market compared with their metropolitan counterparts, and nonmetropolitan minorities are even more likely to be represented among low-wage workers, part-time workers, and the jobless. Low levels of education play a role in the lower earnings of nonmetropolitan minorities (McGranahan and Kassel 1996), but the low availability of full-time, full-year jobs and the types of industries in which minorities are concentrated also contribute to their high likelihood of being poor. For nonmetropolitan Hispanics in particular, the high levels of part-time work (among those who prefer full-time work) may be due to their concentration in agricultural industries.

The Rural Sociological Society Task Force on Persistent Rural Poverty (1993) reviewed a variety of theoretical explanations for the persistence of concentrated poverty in nonmetropolitan America. Common to all of these explanations is a rural opportunity structure that is inherently unstable and that contains relatively few well-paying jobs, jobs with benefits, and/or jobs that provide even minimal prospects for career mobility. Figures 8.4 and 8.5 contain data on metropolitan and nonmetropolitan earnings per job by industry. These data show several trends: nonmetropolitan workers make about three-fourths of the earnings of their metropolitan counterparts; there has been no decline in the metropolitan pay premium since 1980; and earnings per nonmetropolitan job are lower in every industrial sector. Research also shows that the metropolitan pay advantage holds after controlling for educational attainment and other demographic characteristics of the workers.

The overall conclusion to be drawn from this section is that while metropolitan-nonmetropolitan inequality in socioeconomic status declined in the Unites States during the first half of the century, substantial disparity persists

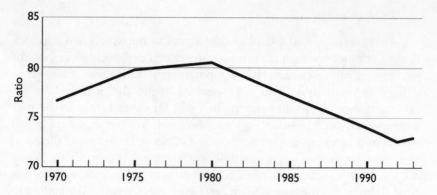

Figure 8.4 Nonmetro to metro ratio of real earnings per nonfarm job, 1970–93. Data for 1984–91 revised by Bureau of Economic Analysis. All years' earnings converted to 1993 using the implicit price deflator for personal consumption expenditures. Adapted from U.S. Department of Agriculture. *Rural Conditions and Trends* 1996;7:Appendix Table 3.

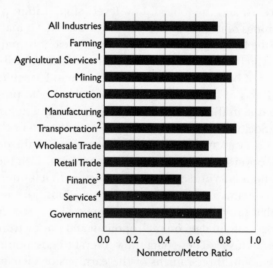

Figure 8.5 Earnings per job by industry, 1995. [1]Includes forestry and fishing. [2]Includes communications and public utilities. [3]Includes insurance and real estate. [4]Includes health, legal, educational, recreational, business, repair, and personal services. Adapted from U.S. Department of Agriculture. *Rural Conditions and Trends* 1996;8:Appendix Table 8.

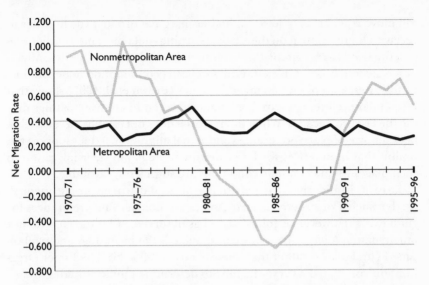

Figure 8.6 Average annual net migration rate/100, metropolitan-nonmetropolitan United States, 1970–96. Metropolitan-nonmetropolitan designation as of 1993. 1970–96 data adapted from Fuguitt and Beale 1996.

in 1995. Most of the families are poor because relatively few well-paying, high-skill jobs are to be found in nonmetropolitan labor markets (Jensen and Tienda 1989; O'Hare 1988). Low-wage extractive jobs gave way to low-wage manufacturing jobs, which are giving way to low-wage jobs in tourism and personal services (Fuguitt, Brown, and Beale 1989). Moreover, this concentration of disadvantage perpetuates itself because nonmetropolitan tax bases are insufficient to maintain or improve the social and physical infrastructure necessary to attract and retain well-paying jobs and educated, high-skill workers.

Why Are Metropolitan-Nonmetropolitan Differences Important?

Why should one care about nonmetropolitan areas in an over-whelmingly metropolitan society? Perhaps most importantly, one in five Americans continues to live and work in such areas. Moreover, recent trends in population redistribution indicate that the rate of metropolitanization in America has slowed perceptively since around 1970. In fact, the relative rates of population growth and net migration have favored nonmetropolitan areas in two of the last three decades (Figure 8.6) (Fuguitt and Beale 1996; Johnson and Beale 1994). These trends are inconsistent with conventional migration theory which contends that workers will move from areas of lower to higher marginal productivity in order to receive a higher return on their labor. Earnings data presented earlier suggest the need to reexamine this hypothesis in modern-day America. Migration is steered by a complex interplay of both economic and noneconomic factors. Research by Fuguitt and colleagues (Brown et al. 1997) shows that residential preferences have consistently favored low-density settings during the last two decades. While this research does not establish a causal link between size-of-place preferences and actual migration, it does support the notion that preferences for lower density settings will steer migration to such places when economic conditions are sufficiently favorable.

It seems ironic, given the persistence of rural-urban economic inequality, that such a large percentage of Americans holds strong preferences for rural living. However, as John Logan has observed, "[T]hese facts do not much matter. A large share of what we value is the mythology and symbolism of rural places, rather than their reality" (1996, 26). The Roper Organization conducted a survey in 1992 to determine public attitudes toward rural people and communities and showed that anywhere from 60 to 73 percent of respondents regarded rural communities as having friendlier people, better "personal values," a stronger sense of family, a better quality of life, better community spirit, and greater honesty in business dealings. These data also showed that respondents clearly differentiate between what they perceive as positive attributes of rural residents and negative valuations of rural community services and infrastructure (Beale 1995; see also Willits, Bealer, and Timbers 1990).

Space and Public Policy

Because geographic disparity is typically considered to be a temporary stage in capitalist development, leveling geographic differences is seldom considered to be an important policy goal. In fact, many policy analysts view geographically targeted policies as wasteful and running counter to a nation's long-term pattern of development. Public policies are strategic views of the need for and impact of public intervention to achieve societal goals. Although one should not exaggerate the point, social scientific theory and research play an important role in the formulation of social and economic policies. Context-invariant theories, e.g., theories in which covering laws work the same everywhere, typically result in "one size fits all"– type policies. Moreover, because aspatial theories fail to consider how contingent characteristics of localities might effect social behavior, such theories provide little guidance for anticipating possible geographic differences in the outcomes of public policies. They provide little or no justification for targeting assistance to areas of greater need or opportunity, nor do they shed much light on how universalistic policies such as Social Security or Medicare might actually level socioeconomic inequality across different residential contexts.

Some implications of neglecting space in public policy can be illustrated by considering the recent welfare reform legislation enacted by the U.S. Congress. This legislation came after years of debate regarding the root causes of poverty, individual versus public responsibilities, and the essential nature of the federal system. Ironically, despite clear evidence that poverty is concentrated in central cities and in rural areas, and that characteristics of the poor such as labor-force attachment, family structure, and welfare utilization vary in different residential settings, geographic dimensions of poverty were seldom discussed in the welfare debate. The basic assumption seemed to be that the causes of poverty operate in the same way everywhere, and that all states and localities possess equal capacity to deal with the problem.

Our metropolitan-nonmetropolitan spatial perspective leads us to expect that welfare reform will differentially disadvantage low income, and particularly "near poor," nonmetropolitan families. This argument derives from our overall contention that the causes of poverty are contingent on local social structure and that various aspects of rural structure will exacerbate these causal forces and result in a disproportionate number of nonmetropolitan families experiencing increased economic distress. More specifically, our argument focuses on three issues: the geographic concentration of the low-income nonmetropolitan population in states with low capacity and/or will to provide assistance; the relatively low absorptive capacity of rural labor markets; and the more limited capacity of rural and small town public institutions and infrastructures.

States Unwilling or Unable to Assist

States with high nonmetropolitan poverty generally have low per-capita income, high overall poverty rates, and low Aid to Families with Dependent Children (AFDC) benefit levels (Figure 8.7). Mark Nord has investigated the association between benefit levels and the geography of poverty, and concludes, "[B]lock granting of welfare programs, eliminating national standards, and increasing state discretion are likely to increase the disadvantage of the rural poor" (1996a, 6). He did not suggest that this results from an "urban bias" in the political process, but rather because low-benefit states have a high number of needy families, limited fiscal capacity, and arguably weaker support for welfare. Accordingly, he concludes that nonmetropolitan disadvantage could only be overcome by a progressive federal block grant that allocates money with respect to states' need and

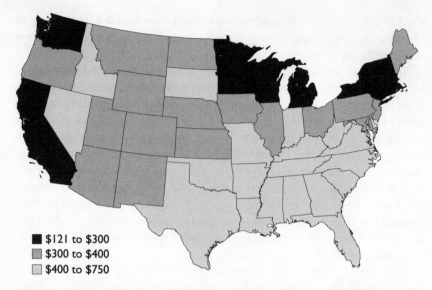

Figure 8.7 Average monthly Aid to Families with Dependent Children benefit per family, 1994. Prepared by U.S. Department of Agriculture—Economic Research Service based on *Social Security Bulletin Annual Statistical Supplement 1996*, p. 358.

ability to pay. The Brookings Institution (Reischauer and Weaver 1995) has observed that reallocating federal funds among states will be extremely difficult, and may significantly reduce the total amount of resources targeted to poverty alleviation. Current high–AFDC-benefit states may see their payments significantly reduced while low-benefit states can expect dramatic increases in funds under a needs-based formula. It is unlikely that the current high-benefit states will replace lost federal dollars with their own sources of revenue, and it is quite possible that some low-benefit states will withdraw their own funds from welfare programs and replace them with the federal windfall.

Low-income nonmetropolitan persons will probably also suffer disproportionately from cuts in the Food Stamp Program. This federally funded program provides services directly to the poor. The two maps displayed in Figure 8.8, one of per capita food stamp expenditures and one of poverty rates, are essentially mirror images of each other. They show that this program with its uniform national standard consistently targets expenditures to high-poverty-rate areas in the nonmetropolitan South and Southwest. Moreover, because such a high percentage of poor nonmetropolitan families includes at least one worker, cuts in the Food Stamp Program will fall

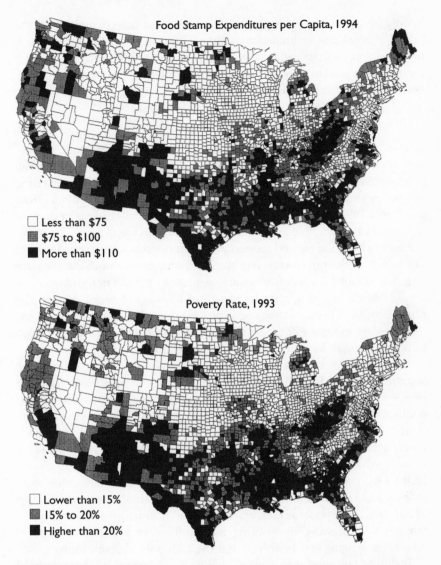

Food Stamp Expenditures per Capita, 1994

☐ Less than $75
▨ $75 to $100
■ More than $110

Poverty Rate, 1993

☐ Lower than 15%
▨ 15% to 20%
■ Higher than 20%

Figure 8.8 The Food Stamp Program, with its consistent national standard, is very effectively targeted to high-poverty counties. Prepared by U.S. Department of Agriculture—Economic Research Service based on U.S. Bureau of the Census *Consolidated Federal Funds Data File, 1994*; U.S. Bureau of the Census *Small Area Income and Poverty Estimates; 1993 State and County Income and Poverty Estimates* (revised 1998).

heavily on the rural working poor. The Center on Budget and Policy Priorities (1996b) has estimated that almost 20 percent of food stamp cuts over the next six years will be absorbed by working poor households. They estimate that working poor households will lose over five hundred dollars per year in food stamps by the year 2002.

Inadequate Rural Labor Markets

The welfare-to-work transition that is the cornerstone of the nation's new welfare policy is predicated on the belief that the economy can produce enough jobs to employ a majority of persons presently receiving welfare assistance. Leif Jensen and Yoshima Chitose (1997) used data from the March 1994 *Current Population Survey* and empirically estimated that the ratio of workfare-eligible job seekers to available jobs was nineteen to one in nonmetropolitan areas and sixteen to one in metropolitan areas. In other words, both residential sectors lack sufficient capacity to absorb the workfare population, but job opportunities are particularly tight in nonmetropolitan areas.[7] Moreover, the higher incidence of low-wage, low-skill jobs in the nonmetropolitan economy suggests that persons who make the transition from welfare to work will have a relatively low probability of securing a job with high enough income to raise them out of poverty.

Poor nonmetropolitan families already have strong labor-force attachment—two-thirds have at least one worker, and one-fourth have two or more working adults. Accordingly, ending cash assistance to able-bodied adults will do nothing but diminish these families' already meager standards of living and economic security. Underemployment and low-quality jobs are the major problems in nonmetropolitan labor markets, not a lack of work effort. This is not to say that education and skill upgrading combined with economic development would not benefit low-income nonmetropolitan persons. However, it should be recognized that in the absence of improved job opportunities, many poor and near-poor nonmetropolitan families who are already working hard will suffer a significant loss of income, and many may be forced to move from valued communities.

It should be noted that rural economic development is a controversial proposition that is not advocated by all policy makers. Equity advocates recommend development assistance to stimulate economic growth, stem out-migration, and retain capital in depressed regions. Efficiency advocates, in contrast, view this type of assistance as wasteful, counterproductive, and run-

[7] When AFDC recipients who are attending school (or who have absent spouses and their own children under six) are included in the workforce-eligible adult population, the ratio of job seekers to available jobs rises to 33:1 in nonmetropolitan areas and 34:1 in metropolitan areas.

ning counter to the nation's ongoing process of development. Efficiency-driven policies encourage resource redistribution and easing adjustment costs, actions that are seen as consistent with and supportive of national-level trends and changes. There is no room for place-sentimentality in the efficiency framework. Inefficient places are considered to be a brake on national growth and overall national prosperity (Brown 1998).

Inadequate Small-Town Infrastructures

Finally, nonmetropolitan governments are not likely to be able to offer the same complement of services and infrastructures that metropolitan areas can mount in support of the welfare-to-work transition. Weaker fiscal, technical, and managerial capacity is likely to result in barriers to participation among the low-income nonmetropolitan population. Job training, child care, and other employment services are not likely to be available in every town; and in many states, not in every county. Lack of local access will be exacerbated by the absence of public transportation in most nonmetropolitan communities. Participation in training activities, job searches, and commuting are all made more costly and complicated by a lack of transportation. The rewards from employment, net of transportation costs, may be minimal for low-income nonmetropolitan households who have few alternatives to the private automobile.

Conclusions

Spatial inequality is persistent in developed societies and deserves more attention in both social theory and social policy. Our argument is not that the causal forces in society are different in different types of places, but that the attributes that define particular types of areas—and differentiate them from other residential categories—modify the effects of these causal forces on social behavior. For example, we do not dispute that weak labor-force attachment is a basic cause of poverty, but we observe that this factor has less effect in nonmetropolitan areas where high proportions of low-income persons already work, and where local economies are characterized by a heavy dependence on low-wage, low-skill jobs. In other words, the impact of work effort is modulated by local opportunity structure. Our essential argument is that *where one lives matters*. Multilevel approaches that recognize the importance of local context are increasingly popular in the social sciences. Such work will further specify the role of space in social relations, and will establish a stronger foundation for incorporating space in social policy.

PART THREE

DURABLE INEQUALITY IN AMERICAN INSTITUTIONS

CHAPTER NINE

Do Historically Black Colleges and Universities Enhance the College Attendance of African American Youths?

Ronald G. Ehrenberg, Donna S. Rothstein, and Robert B. Olsen

ecently, Historically Black Colleges and Universities (HBCUs) have become the center of intense policy debates. Do HBCUs enhance the college attendance of African American youths? Previous research has been inconclusive. Among other improvements, our study adjusts for the relative availability of HBCU enrollment opportunities in each state. We find that African Americans are more likely to choose HBCUs over other colleges if more HBCU openings are available. However, more HBCU openings don't increase overall African American enrollment. As we have shown elsewhere, attendance at an HBCU does enhance African American students' college graduation rates.

Historically Black Colleges and Universities

The Rise and Decline of HBCUs

Throughout most of the late nineteenth and early twentieth century, the majority of African American citizens lived and were educated in

Our research was funded by grants from the Andrew W. Mellon and William H. Donner Foundations and we are grateful to these organizations for their support. The views expressed here are solely those of the authors.

the South. They were formally excluded from southern, segregated, white institutions of higher education and found higher educational opportunities only in the HBCUs. Some HBCUs (for example, Morehouse, Spelman, and Fisk) were private institutions that were initially established by church-related organizations. Others (for example, Florida A & M, Grambling, and Morgan State) were public institutions established in the southern states after the Civil War to provide separate education for African American youths. The southern states established public HBCUs in order to meet the requirements of the second (1890) Morrill Act without allowing African Americans to attend the same institutions as whites. As part of providing funding for land-grant institutions, the act required that the states provide educational opportunities for all of their citizens.

As the African American population began to move to the North in response to urban industrial employment opportunities, the relative importance of the HBCUs for the education of African American college-age students began to decline. The famous 1954 *Brown v. Board of Education* U.S. Supreme Court decision, which outlawed separate but equal public schools, actually had very little impact on many of the southern states, and formally segregated higher educational systems remained. When integrated at all, the white institutions often did so only as a result of suits pursued by the National Association for the Advancement of Colored People (NAACP).[1] It was not until the passage of the 1964 Civil Rights Act, Title VI of which prohibited the allocation of federal funds to segregated public educational institutions, that any real progress toward integration was made. However, this progress was very slow, and in a 1973 U.S. Supreme Court decision, *Adams v. Richardson,* the southern states were formally and finally ordered to dismantle their dual higher educational systems.

As recently as 1964, over half of all bachelor's degrees granted to African Americans were granted by HBCUs. By 1973, with the continued African American migration to the North and the beginnings of integrated higher education in the South, the HBCU share of African American bachelor's degrees had fallen to between one-fourth and one-third, the range in which it remains today. Over 90 percent of the HBCU institutions are four-year institutions and over 95 percent of the students enrolled in HBCUs attend four-year institutions. While more HBCUs are private than public, the former are often quite small and about three-fourths of the students at HBCUs are enrolled in public institutions. Approximately 20 percent of all African American college students are now enrolled in the HBCUs (Hoffman, Snyder, and Sonnenberg 1992). This latter share is less than the HBCU share of African American bachelor's degrees for two reasons: African American

[1] Many of these are vividly described in Rowan (1993).

enrollments in non-HBCU two-year institutions and higher graduation rates for African American students who attend four-year HBCUs than for those who attend other four-year colleges (Ehrenberg and Rothstein 1994).

Policy Debates Surrounding HBCUs

Despite the declining relative importance of the HBCUs in the production of African American bachelor's degrees, they have become the subject of intense public policy debate in recent years. Court cases have been filed in a number of southern states, cases that assert that African American students continue to be underrepresented at traditionally white public institutions, that discriminatory admissions criteria are used by these institutions to exclude African American students (e.g., basing admissions only on test scores and not also on grades), and that per student funding levels, program availability, and library facilities are substantially poorer at the public HBCUs than at other public institutions in the state. In one 1992 case, *United States v. Fordice,* the U.S. Supreme Court ruled that Mississippi had not done enough to eliminate racial segregation in its state-run higher educational institutions. Rather than mandating a remedy, however, the Court sent the case back to the Federal District Court for action.

In March of 1995, Federal District Court judge Neal B. Biggers responded to the state proposal by ruling that Mississippi could not close public HBCUs near historically white colleges or universities (or close historically white colleges or universities near HBCUs) as a way of eliminating racial segregation in college enrollments. Rather, he ordered the state to spend more money to establish new graduate programs at two HBCUs (Jackson and Alcorn State) to enhance their attractiveness to white students, as well as to establish endowments at these two institutions to provide scholarship funds to attract white students (Smothers 1995). In addition, he ordered the three public HBCUs in the state to raise their admission standards to levels comparable to those at other public institutions in the state and ordered the state to finance remedial programs that would assist students who did not meet the higher standards to achieve admission to the public institutions. The adoption of the tougher admission standards were subsequently deferred until the 1996–97 academic year (Healy 1995a).

The increase in admission standards at HBCUs in Mississippi and proposals for similar changes in other southern states have led to substantial concern in the African American community (Healy 1995b, 1996a). While proponents of the higher admission standards argue that they will lead to enhanced education in terms of courses taken, grades, and test scores, critics fear that they will lead to drastic declines in enrollments in HBCUs and to a decline in higher educational opportunities for African American youths in general, especially disadvantaged youths. That is, they assert that the presence of HBCUs in southern states enhances African American students' college enrollment probabilities and that the higher admission standards will weaken HBCUs and thus diminish African American students' college enrollment rates. African American freshman enrollments did decline by 9 percent in Mississippi public universities in 1996 and 1997; many attributed this to the new higher admissions standards (Healy 1996b).[2]

Prior Research and Background Data

Have HBCUs enhanced the probability that African American high school graduates will enroll in postsecondary education? Proponents of strengthening HBCUs argue that they have. They point to evidence that historically, after controlling for other factors, the proportion of African Americans enrolled in college was higher in states in which HBCUs were present than it was in other states (Brazziel and Brazziel 1980).

Such comparisons—even with contemporary data—are not particularly useful, however, because they do not disentangle the effects of HBCUs *per se* from the effects of other variables that differ across states and influence college-going behavior. These may include the quality of the high school educations received by African Americans, their high school graduation rates, their families' incomes, and their parents' education levels and aspirations. For example, suppose that high school graduates from families in which parents have gone to college are more likely to go to college than graduates from families in which parents have less education. Suppose also that the proportion of African American parents with college educations is higher in states with HBCUs. It may be the variation in parents' education levels, not whether an HBCU is present in the state, that "causes" the observed interstate variation.[3]

A Previous Study by Constantine

To avoid this problem, Constantine (1995) used data from the *National Longitudinal Study of the High School Class of 1972* (henceforth NLS72) to model the college enrollment decisions of African American

---

[2] This decline in African American enrollments led to an appeal to the U.S. Supreme Court in late 1997 that the Court revisit their *Fordice* decision. However, the Court declined to revisit the case (Lederman 1998).

[3] Of course, one may argue that higher African American parental education levels in states with HBCUs are due to the impact that HBCUs had on college enrollment rates in a previous generation. This interpretation is entirely consistent with our point. At issue is whether the presence of HBCUs today enhances African American college enrollment rates today, not what their effects were in the past.

high school graduates. NLS72 is a national probability sample of approximately 22,000 students who graduated from high school in 1972, over 3,000 of whom were African Americans.[4] These individuals were surveyed five more times, in 1973, 1974, 1976, 1979, and 1986. The last survey included only about two-thirds of the original sample (primarily for financial reasons) and college graduates were disproportionately surveyed in this follow-up. Constantine analyzed the data for 1,192 respondents for whom she also had observations on earnings in 1986.

She divided respondents' postsecondary educational decision into three groups: attend a four-year HBCU; attend another four-year college; or don't attend any four-year college. She included decisions made within the first three years after high school graduation. She estimated a multinomial logit model in which the outcome chosen was specified to depend on the individual's ability, other individual characteristics, family characteristics, characteristics of the student's high school, and a number of state-specific variables, including whether the state had at least one public HBCU.

Constantine's results suggest that the presence of public HBCUs in a state had three effects: it increased the probability that a student would enroll in a four-year HBCU by about .12; it had virtually no effect on the probability that a student would enroll in another four-year college; and it decreased the probability that a student would not enroll in a four-year college. Because the latter category includes both enrollees in two-year colleges and noncollege enrollees, she concluded that the presence of public HBCUs draws into four-year HBCUs those students who would have otherwise attended a two-year institution or not attended any college. If it were the latter, one could conclude that the presence of HBCUs increased the sum African American enrollments in two- and four-year colleges in the 1970s. However, because Constantine grouped two-year college enrollees and non-enrollees together, she could not draw this conclusion.

Moreover, to say that there is a public HBCU in a state tells one little about the opportunities HBCUs provide relative to the number of African American high school graduates who may desire to attend them. Consider the following hypothetical example: Suppose that there are two states and that each has five thousand African American high school graduates a year and a single public HBCU. Suppose further that the HBCU in the first state has a capacity of one thousand first-year students, while that in the second is much smaller and has a capacity of one hundred first-year students. Intuition suggests that, other things being equal, African American college enrollments will be higher in the first state. Put another way, it is not the presence of

[4] See Research Triangle Institute (1981) for a description of NLS72.

Table 9.1. Full-time equivalent undergraduate enrollments at Historically Black Colleges and Universities in a state relative to four times the number of African American high school seniors in the state (SLOTS)

	SLOTS72[a]	SLOTS80[a]
Alabama	.167	.084
Arkansas	.128	.079
Delaware	.414	.223
District of Columbia	.314	.204
Florida	.096	.043
Georgia	.143	.048
Kentucky	.086	.079
Louisiana	.203	.142
Maryland	.181	.104
Mississippi	.198	.149
Missouri	.106	.077
North Carolina	.200	.137
Ohio	.048	.024
Oklahoma	.091	.082
Pennsylvania	.046	.032
South Carolina	.091	.043
Tennessee	.180	.093
Texas	.146	.077
Virginia	.215	.130
West Virginia	.505	.886
Mean[b]	.153	.094
Standard Deviation[b]	.069	.111

[a]SLOTS72 is based on 1972 *Higher Education General Information Survey* (HEGIS) (enrollment) and U.S. Bureau of the Census *1970 Census of Population* (number of seniors) data; SLOTS80 is based on 1980 HEGIS and U.S. Bureau of the Census *1980 Census of Population* data.
[b]Mean and standard deviations are across individuals in the *National Longitudinal Study of the High School Class of 1972* (NLS72) and *High School and Beyond Survey* (HSB) samples, not across states.

HBCUs in a state *per se*, but rather their size relative to the number of African American high school graduates that should influence the probability that an African American high school graduate goes on to college.

Adjusting for HBCU "SLOTS"

Does significant variation in the relative availability of enrollment opportunities in HBCUs actually occur across states in which HBCUs are present? Table 9.1 presents data, by state, on the ratio of the number of full-time equivalent undergraduate enrollments in all HBCUs in the state to four times the number of African American high school seniors in the state (SLOTS) for both 1972 and 1980. The denominator is multiplied by four so that the resulting ratio approximates the fraction of African American high school seniors for whom there is space in HBCUs in the state. While some HBCUs operated at less than full capacity during these years, capacity (as opposed to enrollment) data are not available. Total HBCU enrollments are used rather than public enrollments because private HBCUs follow a low-tuition policy to maintain their accessibility to low-income students.[5] In practice, this distinction does not matter. Using public enrollments in the numerator yielded similar results in the econometric estimation that follows in the next section. Finally, the number of high school seniors rather than the number of high school graduates is used in the denominator because the availability of positions in HBCUs may affect the effort put forth by high school seniors to complete high school.

The data in Table 9.1 suggests that the scale of HBCUs relative to the number of African American high school seniors varied widely across states that had HBCUs in both 1972 and 1980. In 1972, the ratio, henceforth SLOTS, ranged from under .05 in Pennsylvania and Ohio to over .5 in West Virginia. The mean value of SLOTS faced by African American high school seniors present in the NLS72 data was .153. By 1980, the mean value of SLOTS faced by seniors in the *High School and Beyond* survey (henceforth HSB), a national probability sample of students who graduated from high school in the early 1980s and is comparable to NLS72, fell to .094, with the value of SLOTS ranging from .02 in Ohio to more than .8 in West Virginia.

The West Virginia number is not an error. By 1980 African American students made up less than 15 percent of the enrolled students at the two HBCUs in West Virginia, West Virginia State and Bluefield State (Hill 1984).[6] However, because educational opportunities were available for African Americans at these HBCUs, we believe that the value of SLOTS for African Americans in West Virginia accurately represents their opportunity to attend an HBCU.[7]

Analytical Approach

The discussion above and the data on the variation in SLOTS suggest that rather than focusing on differences in African American college enrollment decisions between states that have and those that do not have

---

[5] For example, in 1992 and 1993 average tuition and fees were $5,008 at the 41 private United Negro College Fund schools, less than half the national average for private schools (Fordyce 1993).

[6] For example, between 1970 and 1980 alone, African American high school enrollment in West Virginia fell from 6,113 to 5,260, a decline of 14 percent (U.S. Bureau of the Census 1973, Table 51; U.S. Bureau of the Census 1983, Table 76). The evolution of these schools into predominantly white institutions predates the 1970s.

[7] An alternative is to simply exclude the small number of African American students in West Virginia from the samples we use for the analysis. The two methods yielded similar results.

HBCUs, we should instead focus on how college enrollment decisions differ across states in which HBCUs are present, with an emphasis on the role of the relative availability of slots for first-year students in HBCUs. That is, we should ask how differences in SLOTS across states influence college enrollment decisions.

We do this in a manner analogous to Constantine's by estimating multinomial logit models of the college enrollment decision of African Americans. However, our analyses differ from hers in a number of important ways. First, we use data from both the NLS72 and HSB to see whether the effects of HBCUs on enrollments have varied over time.

Second, we estimate models with four possible outcomes rather than the three-outcome model that Constantine used. High school seniors are assumed to choose between enrolling in a four-year HBCU, enrolling in another four-year college, enrolling in a two-year college that offers degree programs, or not enrolling in a college. This enables us to ascertain if HBCUs did affect the aggregate (two-year plus four-year) African American college enrollment rate in 1972 and 1980.

Third, and perhaps most crucially, we restrict our attention to students who graduated from high school in states in which HBCUs are present. We focus on how the value of SLOTS influences the students' choice of college and college-going behavior. Again, SLOTS is the ratio of full-time equivalent undergraduate enrollments in HBCUs in the state relative to four times the number of African American high school seniors in the state, a measure of the relative availability of positions in HBCUs. We are careful to indicate, however, how results differ when we include individuals in the sample who graduated from high school in states without HBCUs, and we assign them a value of zero for SLOTS.

Finally, unlike Constantine, we do not restrict our analyses of NLS72 to the subset of students who were present in the 1986 follow-up and for whom wage data were available. As indicated above, her sample was a nonrandom subsample of the original sample. In particular, four-year college graduates were disproportionately represented in the 1986 follow-up and this "choice-based" sampling may lead to inconsistent estimates.[8] Rather, for both NLS72 and HSB we analyze the decisions of all individuals who were present in the sample three years after their high school graduation. When we use HSB, we also analyze the decisions of people six years after

---

[8] When the probability of being in a sample is related to the outcome under study (that is, "choice-based sampling") inconsistent estimates may occur. See Manski and Lerman (1977). The problem arises in Constantine's sample because to be a four-year college graduate one had to have been enrolled in a four-year college. Because four-year college graduates were disproportionately included in her sample, so were four-year college enrollees.

high school graduation to see if including delayed college entrants alters any of our conclusions.

Empirical Findings

Using both NLS72 and HSB, we estimated multinomial models of African American high school graduates' decisions to enroll in four-year HBCUs, enroll in other four-year colleges, enroll in a two-year college, or not enroll in college within their first three years after high school graduation. An individual who had ever enrolled in a four-year HBCU during the period was classified as enrolled in an HBCU. An individual who had ever enrolled in a four-year college, but had not enrolled in a four-year HBCU, was classified as enrolled in an other four-year college. An individual who had ever enrolled in a two-year college during the period, but was never enrolled in a four-year college during the period, was classified as enrolled in a two-year college. An individual's choice of college sector was specified to be a function of his or her individual characteristics, family characteristics (such as parents' education and income), high school characteristics, distance to the nearest two- and four-year colleges, and the SLOTS variable in his or her state. Complete tables of coefficient estimates and definitions of all of the explanatory variables are available from the first author.

A Preference for HBCUs

Our empirical findings are similar for the two data sets. Students from states with large SLOTS values are more likely to attend HBCUs and less likely to attend other four-year or two-year colleges than students from states with small SLOTS values. Put another way, African American high school graduates are more likely to attend HBCUs rather than other colleges when positions in HBCUs are available to them.

Table 9.2 summarizes simulations we conducted to give a sense of the magnitudes of these effects. These simulations use the NLS72 estimates and values of the data for each individual. In panel A, we focus on all of the African American high school graduates from states in which an HBCU was present in the sample. Row 1 indicates that within three years of high school graduation, 19.3 percent of them enrolled in four-year HBCUs, 16.6 percent enrolled in other four-year colleges, and 12.9 percent enrolled in two-year colleges. Row 2 shows the predicted enrollment percentages in each category obtained using the estimated coefficients and the values of the explanatory variables for each individual. The predictions of the model are virtually identical to what actually occurred and were used as the baseline in what follows.

Row 3 indicates the predictions of the model if we increase the value of SLOTS in each individual's state by one standard deviation of its variation

Table 9.2. Simulated effects of increasing the ratio of full-time equivalent enrollments at Historically Black Colleges and Universities (HBCUs) in a state relative to the number of African American seniors in the state by one standard deviation: *National Longitudinal Study of the Class of 1972*

	Enrolled in Four-Year HCBU (%)	Enrolled in Other Four-Year (%)	Enrolled in Two-Year (%)	Other[a] (%)
		Panel A All African Americans		
I Actual	19.3	16.6	12.9	51.2
2 Predicted by Model	19.2	16.7	12.9	51.2
3 Predicted If HBCU Slots Increase	28.6	8.8	10.8	51.7
4 Change (row 3 minus row 2)[b]	9.4	−7.8	−2.0	0.5
		Panel B Bottom-Quartile Test Score		
I Actual	7.8	5.0	13.2	73.9
2 Predicted by Model	10.1	4.8	13.8	71.3
3 Predicted If HBCU Slots Increase	14.7	2.4	11.4	71.6
4 Change (row 3 minus row 2)	4.5	−2.4	−2.3	0.2
		Panel C Bottom-Quartile Family Income		
I Actual	17.4	14.8	11.6	56.2
2 Predicted by Model	17.6	11.7	12.6	58.0
3 Predicted If HBCU Slots Increase	25.8	5.8	10.4	57.9
4 Change (row 3 minus row 2)	8.1	−5.9	−2.1	−0.1

[a]Column totals do not always add to 100 in rows 1, 2, and 3 and to zero in rows 4 due to rounding errors.
[b]Authors' computations from multinomial logit model estimates (which are available from the first author) and the values of the explanatory variables for each individual.

across individuals (or .069). That is, it indicates how increasing the availability of positions in HBCUs in the state relative to the number of African American high school seniors would influence the seniors' enrollment probabilities. Because the mean value of SLOTS across individuals in the sample was .153, this represents a substantial increase. Row 4, which is simply the difference between rows 3 and 2, indicates the predicted change that would occur.

Quite strikingly, we predict the probability of a student attending an HBCU to increase by 9.4 percent, an almost 50 percent increase in enrollments at HBCUs. However, none of this increase would come from students who were currently not enrolled in college. Rather, it reflects a large shift, 7.8 percent, of students from other four-year colleges and a smaller shift, 2.0 percent, of students from two-year colleges. Put another way, we predict that increasing the number of HBCU slots does *not* increase the aggregate African American enrollment rate.[9]

It is well known that students who initially enroll in two-year colleges are much less likely to graduate eventually from a four-year institution than students who initially enroll in four-year institutions.[10] Moreover, our own previous research provides strong evidence that HBCUs enhance graduation rates of African American four-year college students (Ehrenberg and Rothstein 1994). Hence, although these results suggest that HBCUs do not enhance the probability that an African American enrolls in college, they do enhance enrollees' chances of graduating from a four-year college.

Adjusting for Economic and Educational Disadvantages

Supporters of HBCUs often argue that HBCUs are particularly important to economically and educationally disadvantaged African American youth. Their relatively low tuitions, both in the public and private sectors, are believed to make it possible for economically disadvantaged youth to gain access to higher education. Their provision of remedial education and a supportive environment, along with their willingness to take a chance and admit students who perform poorly on standardized admission tests, is believed to enhance the college enrollment rates of educationally disadvantaged students.

Is there evidence to support these arguments in our data? Panels B and C of Table 9.2 repeat the simulations performed in panel A, but restrict the samples used in the simulation to individuals who came from the bottom quartiles of the test score and family income distributions, respectively, for African American youth in NLS72.[11] The "actual" rows are now the proportions of African American high school students in each group who choose each outcome. Not surprisingly, low test scores substantially reduce the aggregate college enrollment rate and the probability of being enrolled in any four-year college (compare row A1 with row B1). However, being in the bottom quartile of the family income distribution reduces college enrollment by a much smaller amount (compare row A1 with row C1).

Simulations of the effects of increasing SLOTS on the enrollment behavior of these subsets of individuals (rows B4 and C4) provide very sim-

[9] The aggregate college enrollment rate for the group is simply the sum of the three enrollment percentages, or equivalently one hundred minus the "other" percentage.

[10] See Clotfelter et al. (1991), Table 2.18, for example.

[11] The test scores are a weighted sum of scaled test scores on three sections (mathematics plus one-half the sum of reading and vocabulary) given to NLS72 respondents.

Table 9.3. Simulated effects of increasing the ratio of full-time equivalent enrollments at Historically Black Colleges and Universities (HBCUs) in a state relative to the number of African American seniors in the state by one standard deviation: 1980 *High School and Beyond* Senior Cohort

	Enrolled in Four-Year HCBU (%)	Enrolled in Other Four-Year (%)	Enrolled in Two-Year (%)	Other[a] (%)
Panel A				
All African Americans				
1 Actual	18.5	20.5	16.2	44.8
2 Predicted by Model	18.5	20.6	16.2	44.8
3 Predicted If HBCU Slots Increase	23.8	16.3	14.3	45.6
4 Change (row 3 minus row 2)[b]	5.3	−4.3	−1.9	0.8
Panel B				
Bottom-Quartile Test Score				
1 Actual	14.4	10.8	19.3	55.5
2 Predicted by Model	13.8	12.3	18.7	55.2
3 Predicted If HBCU Slots Increase	17.8	9.4	16.6	56.3
4 Change (row 3 minus row 2)	4.0	−2.9	−2.1	1.1
Panel C				
Bottom-Quartile Family Income				
1 Actual	19.4	13.8	16.6	50.2
2 Predicted by Model	18.4	13.0	15.3	53.4
3 Predicted If HBCU Slots Increase	23.4	9.8	13.2	53.6
4 Change (row 3 minus row 2)	5.0	−3.2	−2.1	−0.2

[a]Column totals do not always add to 100 in rows 1, 2, and 3 and to zero in rows 4 due to rounding errors.
[b]Authors' computations from multinomial logit model estimates (which are available from the first author) and the values of the explanatory variables for each individual.

ilar results to those described in panel A. Increasing SLOTS has virtually no impact on the overall college enrollment rate for each group. Rather, an increased availability of positions in HBCUs again simply shifts enrolled students from two-year and other four-year to four-year HBCU schools. These results suggest that HBCUs do not yield extra benefits, in terms of their effects on initial enrollment probabilities, to economically and educationally disadvantaged youth above and beyond what they yield to other African American youths.

Do the results we found for 1972 using NLS72 data continue to hold in later years? Table 9.3 presents the results of similar simulations for African

American high school seniors in 1980. These simulations use individual data from HSB and the estimated multinomial logit model for 1980. Comparing rows A1 of Tables 9.2 and 9.3, one observes that the actual African American high school senior college enrollment rate (within three years of high school graduation and in states with HBCUs) increased between 1972 and 1980 from about 48.8 to 55.2 percent in the data. However, the enrollment rate at four-year HBCUs fell from 19.3 to 18.5 percent.

Focusing next on the predicted changes in the enrollment rates presented in row A4, if we increase SLOTS by one standard deviation (which in 1980 was .109) we observe the same qualitative results as in the 1972 data. Enrollments in four-year HBCUs are predicted to increase, but all of this increase comes from predicted declines in other four-year college enrollments and two-year college enrollments. Put another way, the simulation predicts no increase in the aggregate college enrollment rate. Finally, panels B and C, which repeat the simulations for educationally and economically disadvantaged students, again reiterate the 1972 findings, namely, that the impact of increased availability of HBCU slots relative to the number of African American high school seniors is about the same for educationally and economically disadvantaged seniors as it is for other African American high school seniors.

Using Other Specifications and Samples

We conducted a number of additional simulations to see how sensitive our 1980 HSB findings are to alternative specifications and samples. Table 9.4 is based on enrollment decisions made during the first six years rather than the first three years after high school. Not surprisingly, a higher percentage of African American high school seniors in HSB had enrolled in some form of college within six years after high school graduation (62.5 percent) than had done so within three years (55.2 percent). However, the simulation results shown in the table (which are based on a multinomial logit model estimated using the six-year data) are very similar to those reported previously. The effects of slots in HBCUs on college enrollment decisions does not vary between early (first three years after high school) and later (years four through six) enrollees.

Table 9.5 reports simulations performed separately for African American males and females. Rows A1 and B1 of the table suggest that the overall college enrollment rate was higher for the females than for the males in 1980 and that females were also slightly more likely to attend HBCUs that year. As the table notes indicate, the underlying model that was estimated allowed an individual's gender to affect directly the enrollment choice decision and it also allowed the effects of SLOTS to vary with gen-

Table 9.4. Simulated effects of increasing the ratio of full-time equivalent enrollments at Historically Black Colleges and Universities (HBCUs) in a state relative to the number of African American seniors in the state by one standard deviation: 1980 *High School and Beyond* Senior Cohort, six years post–high school

	Enrolled in Four-Year HCBU (%)	Enrolled in Other Four-Year (%)	Enrolled in Two-Year (%)	Other[a] (%)
	Panel A All African Americans			
1 Actual	20.6	23.4	18.5	37.5
2 Predicted by Model	20.7	23.2	18.5	37.6
3 Predicted If HBCU Slots Increase	26.8	18.0	15.7	39.5
4 Change (row 3 minus row 2)[b]	6.1	−5.2	−2.8	1.9
	Panel B Bottom-Quartile Test Score			
1 Actual	15.5	14.1	21.8	48.6
2 Predicted by Model	14.8	15.9	21.9	47.5
3 Predicted If HBCU Slots Increase	19.3	12.1	18.6	50.0
4 Change (row 3 minus row 2)	4.5	−3.8	−3.3	2.5
	Panel C Bottom-Quartile Family Income			
1 Actual	20.6	14.6	19.4	45.5
2 Predicted by Model	20.8	13.6	18.1	47.5
3 Predicted If HBCU Slots Increase	26.4	9.9	14.9	48.8
4 Change (row 3 minus row 2)	5.6	−3.7	−3.2	1.3

[a]Column totals do not always add to 100 in rows 1, 2, and 3 and to zero in rows 4 due to rounding errors.
[b]Authors' computations from multinomial logit model estimates (which are available from the first author) and the values of the explanatory variables for each individual.

der. However, the simulations do not yield large differences in results. In both cases, an increase in SLOTS does increase enrollments in four-year HBCUs, but it also decreases enrollments in other two-year and four-year colleges and produces no overall increase in enrollments.

A third simulation addresses possible concerns that our underlying enrollment-choice model included SLOTS but did not control for enrollment opportunities in other four-year colleges in the state. We computed the ratio of full-time equivalent undergraduate enrollments in other four-year colleges in a state divided by four times the total number of high school seniors in the state, reestimated the multinomial logit model

Table 9.5. Simulated effects of increasing the ratio of full-time equivalent enrollments at Historically Black Colleges and Universities (HBCUs) in a state relative to the number of African American seniors in the state by one standard deviation: 1980 *High School and Beyond* Senior Cohort, by gender

	Enrolled in Four-Year HCBU (%)	Enrolled in Other Four-Year (%)	Enrolled in Two-Year (%)	Other[a] (%)
		Panel A		
		African American Males		
1 Actual	17.9	20.7	15.3	46.2
2 Predicted by Model	17.9	20.6	15.3	46.2
3 Predicted If HBCU Slots Increase	25.2	13.9	13.0	47.8
4 Change (row 3 minus row 2)[b]	7.3	−6.7	−2.3	1.6
		Panel B		
		African American Females		
1 Actual	18.9	20.5	16.9	43.8
2 Predicted by Model	18.9	20.4	16.9	43.8
3 Predicted If HBCU Slots Increase	24.5	16.5	14.7	44.3
4 Change (row 3 minus row 2)	5.6	−3.9	−2.2	0.5

[a]Column totals do not always add to 100 in rows 1, 2, and 3 and to zero in rows 4 due to rounding errors.
[b]Authors' computations from multinomial logit model estimates (which are available from the first author) and the values of the explanatory variables for each individual.

including this additional variable, and then conducted simulations using these new estimates. These simulations again suggest that an increase in SLOTS does lead to an increase in enrollments at four-year HBCUs, but in this model the increase appears to be fully offset by a decrease in other four-year college enrollments. Again there is no increase in the overall enrollment rate and no additional effect on the college enrollment behavior of students with lower test scores or lower family incomes.

Finally, we estimated the enrollment-choice model using the HSB data for African American high school seniors in all states, not simply those in states with HBCUs, assigning a value of zero to SLOTS in states without HBCUs. We then again simulated what the effect of increasing SLOTS would be on the college enrollment decisions of African American youths. One reason for conducting these final simulations is that some people believe that the effects of HBCUs can best be estimated by making comparisons between HBCU and non-HBCU states, as well as by making comparisons across the HBCU states. As indicated above, we do not subscribe to this viewpoint.

Table 9.6. Simulated effects of increasing the ratio of full-time equivalent enrollments at Historically Black Colleges and Universities (HBCUs) in a state relative to the number of African American seniors in the state by one standard deviation: 1980 *High School and Beyond* Senior Cohort, all states

	Enrolled in Four-Year HCBU (%)	Enrolled in Other Four-Year (%)	Enrolled in Two-Year (%)	Other[a] (%)
Panel A **All African Americans**				
1 Actual	14.1	26.2	17.8	41.9
2 Predicted by Model	14.1	26.3	17.7	41.9
3 Predicted If HBCU Slots Increase	19.9	20.9	16.1	43.0
4 Change (row 3 minus row 2)[b]	5.8	−5.4	−1.6	1.1
Panel B **Bottom-Quartile Test Score**				
1 Actual	11.3	16.1	20.3	52.3
2 Predicted by Model	10.6	17.0	20.4	52.0
3 Predicted If HBCU Slots Increase	15.0	13.1	18.4	53.5
4 Change (row 3 minus row 2)	4.4	−3.9	−2.0	1.5
Panel C **Bottom-Quartile Family Income**				
1 Actual	15.2	20.4	16.6	47.8
2 Predicted by Model	14.3	18.9	17.2	49.6
3 Predicted If HBCU Slots Increase	20.0	14.5	15.3	50.2
4 Change (row 3 minus row 2)	5.7	−4.4	−1.9	0.6

[a]Column totals do not always add to 100 in rows 1, 2, and 3 and to zero in rows 4 due to rounding errors.
[b]Authors' computations from multinomial logit model estimates (which are available from the first author) and the values of the explanatory variables for each individual (save that SLOTS is set equal to zero for individuals in states without any HBCUs and individuals from all states are included in the estimation).

The results are reported in Table 9.6. A comparison of rows A1 in Tables 9.3 and 9.6 indicates that the overall college enrollment rate of 58.1 percent in this all-state sample was higher than the overall enrollment rate of 55.2 percent in the HBCU state sample. Both the four-year college enrollment rate (the sum of four-year HBCU and four-year other) and the two-year college enrollment rate were also slightly higher in the overall sample. A comparison of row A1 with row A2, which contains the predictions using the actual values of the explanatory variables for each individual, indicates that the model predicts well within the sample.

The conceptual experiment that we conduct to simulate the effects of increasing SLOTS in this model is again to increase SLOTS faced by each individual by its standard deviation in the sample of high school graduates from HBCU states, holding all other variables constant. That is, we predict how the enrollment probabilities would change for each individual if we increased SLOTS in the state. For high school graduates from non-HBCU states, this is equivalent to creating HBCUs in their states.

The results appear in row A4 of Table 9.6 and are very similar to those found in the corresponding row of Table 9.3. We predict that an increase in SLOTS again increases enrollment at four-year HBCUs. However, this increase again comes almost entirely at the expense of lower enrollments at other four-year and two-year colleges. We report results from simulations for students with lower test scores or lower family incomes in panels B and C of Table 9.6, and they tell the same story.

Concluding Remarks

The evidence we have presented in this paper, using data from both NLS72 and HSB, suggests that the availability of slots at HBCUs for African American high school graduates does influence their college enrollment behavior. Other factors held constant, we predict that an increase in the number of full-time equivalent undergraduate enrollments at four-year HBCUs in a state relative to four times the number of African American high school seniors in the state will increase the probability that an African American high school graduate enrolls in a four-year HBCU. However, this does *not* increase the probability that more students will be enrolled in college in general, because all of the increased enrollment at HBCUs appears to come from students who otherwise would have been enrolled in two-year or other four-year colleges. Put another way, HBCUs appear to influence *where* African Americans go to college, not *whether* they go to college.

It is well known that students who initially enroll in two-year colleges are much less likely to receive four-year college degrees than students who initially enroll in four-year colleges. Moreover (as we have shown previously), other factors held constant, African American four-year college students who enroll in HBCUs have higher graduation probabilities than those who enroll in other four-year colleges (Ehrenberg and Rothstein 1994). Hence, the availability of slots at HBCUs does enhance the probability that African American high school graduates will receive college degrees. However, the evidence on whether this enhanced educational success is matched by enhanced labor-market success is mixed (Constantine 1995; Ehrenberg and Rothstein 1994).

Proponents of HBCUs often argue that they play a unique role in the education of educationally and economically disadvantaged students. We found no evidence, however, that the availability of slots in HBCUs affects the college enrollment choices of educationally and economically disadvantaged youths differently than it does other African American youths.

The bottom line of our discussion is that a reduction in enrollment in African American youths at HBCUs because of higher state-imposed admission standards may, in the short run, simply lead these students to enroll instead in two-year colleges rather than not enrolling in college at all. However, unless new remedial programs are developed that enable students to qualify directly for other four-year colleges, African American youths' four-year college enrollment rates are likely to decline. Furthermore, the net effect of such enrollment shifts will likely be to decrease the proportion of African American youths who receive four-year college degrees. It is an open question whether, in the longer run, improvements in high school curriculum induced by the higher college admission standards will lead to higher college enrollment and graduate rates for African American youths in these states.

The renewed interest in the role of HBCUs in southern states comes at the same time that courts are deciding whether to restrict the use of race in admissions decisions. A federal appeals court decision in the *Hopwood* case (which dealt with the University of Texas law school), as well as a vote by the University of California Regents followed by a public referendum in California, have barred the use of race in admissions decisions in public universities in California, Texas, and several other states. A recent suit against the University of Michigan seeks to achieve the same result in that state. Clearly, serious analyses are required to determine whether such restrictions influence where underrepresented minorities go to college, their college graduation rates, and whether they attend college at all.[12]

---

[12] Underrepresented minority enrollments plunged at both the Berkeley and Texas law schools in the first year after these restrictions went into effect, but analyses have yet to be undertaken as to whether aggregate minority enrollments in all law schools in these states also fell.

C H A P T E R   T E N

Overcoming Race: Army Lessons for American Society

Charles Moskos and John Sibley Butler

Black failure is the dominant paradigm in the way race is talked about in America. That commentators attribute this failure to a diverse array of causes—white racism, black family breakdown, macroeconomic changes, cultural differences, public policy, and so on—does not change the relentlessly negative picture of black America that is the premise for most racial discussion in these waning years of the twentieth century.

The U.S. Army contradicts this prevailing race paradigm.[1] The army enjoys a level of racial integration and a broad record of black achievement that are unmatched elsewhere. It is a world in which the African American

---

[1] This chapter is an updated and summarized version of Moskos and Butler (1996). We would like to acknowledge the support of the U.S. Army Research Institute for the Behavioral and Social Sciences (ARI) for the research reported in this chapter. The authors alone are responsible for the conclusions and findings reported herein.

ARI is the lineal descendant of the Research Branch, Information and Education Division, U.S. Army, established by George C. Marshall in World War II. This was the entity that sponsored the research published in *The American Soldier*, Vols. 1 and 2 (Stouffer, Suchman, et al. 1949; Stouffer, Lumsdaine, et al. 1949). Robin M. Williams, Jr., a co-author of *The American Soldier* was a senior analyst for the War Department, European Theater of Operations, during World War II (see Williams 1946, 1989).

heritage is part and parcel of the institutional culture. It is the only place in American life where whites are routinely bossed around by blacks.

In this chapter, we examine the success of race relations in the army. We then give concrete examples of some of the ways in which the army's experience can be transferred to the civilian sector.

The Success of Race Relations in the Army

In contrast to the self-imposed racial segregation found in college dining halls, a visitor to an army dining facility is likely to see blacks and whites commingling and socializing by choice. Give or take a surly remark here, a bruised sensibility there, the races get on remarkably well. A rule of thumb is that the more military the environment, the more complete the integration. Interracial comity is stronger in the field than in garrison, stronger on duty than off, stronger on post than in the world beyond the base. Remarkably, in the grueling conditions of recent deployments—Desert Shield and Desert Storm in the Persian Gulf, Somalia, Haiti, Bosnia—not one interracial incident was severe enough to come to the attention of the military police—not one.

Even off duty and off post, one sees far more interracial mingling of soldiers than in civilian life. Most striking, the racial integration of military life has some carryover into the civilian sphere. A study of residential segregation, based on the 1990 census, revealed that the most racially integrated communities in America were towns with large military installations (Farley and Frey 1994). These included Fayetteville (Fort Bragg) and Jacksonville (Camp Lejeune), in North Carolina; Killeen (Fort Hood), Texas; and Lawton (Fort Sill), Oklahoma. This contrasts with the reports of demographers and social analysts of increasing self-segregation of whites both in regional geography and private residential communities.[2]

In noting the success of race relations in the army, we do not intend to turn a blind eye to real and serious problems that continue to exist. Certainly, the army is not a racial utopia. Black and white soldiers are susceptible to the same kinds of interracial suspicion and resentment that exist outside the army. Though it stands in sharp and favorable contrast to nonmilitary institutions, the army is not immune to the demons that haunt race relations in America.[3]

---

[2] "Many Seek Security in Private Communities," *The New York Times*, September 3, 1995, 1. For a fuller treatment of the persisting, if not growing, separation of the races, see Massey and Denton 1993.

[3] A 1994 report of the House Armed Services Committee reiterated the disparate readings blacks and whites have on race relations, and, while reporting an absence of overt racism in the military, found continuing "subtle forms of racism" that affected minority career advancement and disciplinary actions as well as perception of reverse discrimination by whites.

A particularly alarming incident occurred in December 1995 when two white soldiers stationed at Fort Bragg murdered a black couple on the streets of Fayetteville, North Carolina. The killings were clearly racially motivated and investigators found Nazi flags and racist literature in the mobile home of one of the soldiers. The principal culprit was found guilty in March 1997 and given two concurrent life sentences ("Ex-G.I. Gets Life Term in Racial Killings," *The New York Times*, March 7, 1997, A8).

Whatever its racial tensions, the army stands out as an organization in which blacks succeed and often surpass their white counterparts. Consider the following. A 1995 report found that for those working in the federal civil service, blacks were 2.4 times more likely to be fired than whites ("Race Disparities in Federal Civil Service," *The Washington Post*, April 10, 1995, 1). This is a rather surprising statistic considering the federal government's strong commitment to establishing a favorable environment for racial minorities. A comparison with the army is informative. "Involuntary separation" is the army analog to being fired. Black soldiers are 20 percent less likely to be involuntary separated than white soldiers.

How do whites and blacks perceive the racial climate in the military? As in virtually all areas of American life, blacks in the army see race relations less favorably than do whites, although the differences in perception are much smaller than they are in civilian life. According to opinion surveys conducted by the authors during the course of this study, black soldiers are twice as likely (64 percent) to discern racial discrimination in the military than are whites (34 percent). Whites are not only less likely to see racial discrimination in the army, when they do, they see it as reverse discrimination. Even so, blacks are three times more likely (whites five times) to say that race relations are better in the army than in civilian life. Black career soldiers are also somewhat more likely (83 percent) than white career soldiers (73 percent) to express satisfaction with their army career (Westat, Inc. 1986). Also revealing, a survey of army veterans reported that almost twice as many blacks (69 percent) than whites (37 percent) wished they had stayed in the army (Laurence 1994).

Any discussion of race in the military must be placed in context. The most common topics of concern and conversation among and between the races have nothing to do with race but deal with the work of the army and with the good and the bad of military life. Friction in the army is found not so much between whites and blacks as between lower-ranking soldiers and sergeants, enlisted men and officers, line units and staff units, and so on.

Proportion of Blacks in the Army

Among the military services, we focus on the army because it the largest and by far the one with the highest proportion of blacks. In 1998,

Table 10.1. Blacks as percentage of total personnel by grade and service (1998)

Grade*	Army (%)	Navy (%)	Air Force (%)	Marine Corps (%)
Commissioned Officers				
0–7 and above (generals)	8.3	2.8	3.6	3.7
0–6 (colonel)	6.5	2.8	3.3	4.0
0–5 (lieutenant colonel)	9.9	3.4	6.6	4.3
0–4 (major)	12.5	4.8	6.1	4.4
0–3 (captain)	12.2	6.5	5.8	5.2
0–2 (1st lieutenant)	10.5	8.9	6.1	8.2
0–1 (2nd lieutenant)	10.2	7.7	7.3	9.3
Total Commissioned Officers	11.0	5.9	6.0	6.0
Warrant Officers	15.0	14.6	n/a	13.9
Total Officers	11.6	6.2	6.0	6.9
Enlisted Personnel				
E-9 (sergeant major)	32.6	7.4	19.2	26.0
E-8 (master sergeant)	36.5	9.7	17.9	29.5
E-7 (sergeant 1st class)	37.6	12.7	20.0	26.8
E-6 (staff sergeant)	38.3	17.1	20.0	26.8
E-5 (sergeant)	31.6	21.7	18.6	18.1
E-4 (corporal/specialist)	25.5	20.7	15.0	13.3
E-3 (private 1st class)	25.1	22.9	15.9	13.5
E-2 (private)	23.8	20.2	17.8	14.2
E-1 (private recruit)	23.7	21.5	20.2	14.8
Total Enlisted	29.6	19.7	17.6	16.8
Total Personnel	26.7	17.7	15.3	15.8

*Army titles given in parentheses have equivalent pay grades in other services.
Source: U.S. Department of Defense. *Semi-Annual Occupational Profile.* Packer Air Force Base, FL: Defense Equal Opportunity Management Institute, Research Division, 1998.

the 128,000 blacks in the army constituted about half of all blacks in military uniform. As shown in Table 10.1, African Americans made up close to 27 percent of all army personnel on active duty. This is about double the proportion found in the U.S. Navy, U.S. Air Force, or U.S. Marine Corps. By rank, the number of blacks in the army breaks down as 24 percent of the lower enlisted levels, 35 percent of noncommissioned officers (NCOs), and 11 percent of commissioned officers. Relative to the other military services, the army stands out in absolute and proportional numbers of blacks at all levels, especially in the senior NCO and officer levels. Especially noteworthy is that 8 percent of all army generals are black, a figure three times greater than the proportion of flag rank officers in the other services.

Black female soldiers require special mention. Females account for 15 percent of all army personnel. African Americans account for a disproportionate 20 percent of all women officers. Most remarkable, blacks constitute 47 percent of all enlisted women, which makes them the largest racial group among female soldiers. It is also noteworthy that black female soldiers have a first-term attrition rate (i.e., not completing the enlistment obligation) about half that of white female soldiers.

Is the Disproportional Number of Blacks Opportunity or Victimization?

The large number of blacks in the army has caused a "peacetime benefits versus wartime burdens" dilemma. In times of war, the disproportionate numbers of blacks are seen as inflicting high casualties on America's most victimized group. In times of peace, these numbers are viewed as an opportunity for African Americans. These benefits go beyond simple employment: an analysis of mortality rates shows that black soldiers die at only half the rate of their age counterparts in civilian society. The most striking difference, by cause, is the markedly lower homicide death rate for black army men. The homicide rate for blacks is an astounding twelve times higher in civilian life than in the army (Rothberg et al. 1990).

For many years, it has been earnestly claimed by critics of heavy black representation in the army that African Americans have been used by their country as cannon fodder. For obvious reasons, this argument had incredible emotional resonance during the Vietnam War. We have conducted a thorough analysis of Vietnam casualty rates and can report definitively that this charge is untrue. Black fatalities amounted to 12.1 percent of all Americans killed in Southeast Asia—a figure proportional to the number of blacks in the U.S. population, and slightly lower than the number of blacks in the army at the close of the war in Southeast Asia.

We introduce racial data on the combat deaths of American soldiers in the seven overseas deployments since the end of the Vietnam War: Mayaguez, Lebanon, Grenada, Panama, the Gulf War, Somalia, and Saudi Arabia. (No deaths by hostile action had occurred in Bosnia at the time of this writing.) As shown in Table 10.2, blacks account for 14.8 percent of combat deaths in these operations. This figure is slightly higher than the civilian black population of the relevant age group (13.1 percent), though somewhat lower than the percentage of blacks in the active-duty military (19.1 percent). No serious case can be made that blacks suffer undue casualties in America's wars and military interventions.

Differences between the Army and Nonmilitary Organizations

To meet our goal of studying the ways in which the army's experience can be transferred to the civilian sector, we should look at the obvious and important differences between the army and nonmilitary organizations. In this regard, compared with most private-sector organizations, the

Table 10.2. Blacks as percentage of those killed in action in U.S. military operations since Vietnam

Operation	Blacks Killed (%)	Total Killed	Blacks Killed
Mayaguez (1975)	7.1	14	1
Lebanon (1983)	18.1	254	46
Grenada (1983)	—	18	0
Panama (1989)	4.3	23	1
Gulf War (1991)	15.4	182	28
Somalia (1992–93)	6.9	29	2
Saudi Arabia (1996)	10.5	19	2
Total	**14.8**	**539**	**80**

Notes: Blacks comprised 12.1 percent of 47,193 combat deaths in the Vietnam War. Blacks were 13.1 percent of the twenty- to thirty-four–year-old U.S. population in 1990. Blacks averaged 19.1 percent of active-duty military personnel during 1975–95.

army has an obvious advantage. The army can maintain standards while still promoting African Americans at all levels because of the large number of black personnel within the organization. The army's experience with a plenitude of qualified black personnel illuminates an important lesson. When not marginalized, African American cultural patterns can add to the effectiveness of mainstream organizations. The overarching point is that the most effective and fairest way to achieve racial equality of opportunity in the United States is to increase the number of qualified African Americans available to fill positions. Doing so is no small task, as it will require large expenditures and new educational approaches. But as an objective and basic principle, it is infinitely superior to a system under which blacks in visible positions of authority are presumed to have benefited from relaxed standards and white resentment is stoked by that perception.

The notion that African Americans cannot succeed without lowering standards is built on the paradigm of black failure. The army's experience can help move us toward eliminating that paradigm.

Desegregation of the Armed Forces

This is not the place to give a full history of blacks in the military, but some background information may be useful.[4] Black Americans have a noble tradition of service in our country's armed forces. From colonial times to World War II, involvement by blacks resurfaced in two related and pre-

---

[4] Historical studies of blacks in the American armed forces are quite extensive. The standard work is Nalty (1986). See also Nalty and MacGregor (1981) and Mershon and Schlossman (1998). An excellent account of black women soldiers in World War II is B. Moore (1996). Bibliographies of blacks in the military are Davis and Hill (1985) and Department of the Army (1993).

dictable ways: increased use of blacks when manpower shortages demanded, followed by a regression of rights once the conflict was over. This recruit-retain-reject pattern was broken only when segregation ended.

A major threshold was crossed when some twenty-five hundred blacks volunteered for the Battle of the Bulge in the winter of 1944–45, serving in all-black platoons within white companies. The black soldiers' excellent combat performance, coupled with a lack of serious friction from white troops, made the experiment an unqualified success. Significantly, survey data collected showed that the more contact white soldiers had with black troops, the more favorable was their reaction toward racial integration. This became one of the landmark findings of *The American Soldier* and was used to buttress later desegregation decisions (Star, Williams, and Stouffer 1949).

The first step toward desegregation of the armed forces was the executive order issued by President Truman in 1948. Racial integration really began with the Korean War and was de facto accomplished by the early 1950s. The period between the wars in Korea and Vietnam was one of relative racial calm in the armed forces. With the Vietnam War, however, white-black polarization heightened with racial clashes occurring worldwide throughout the services. Racial conflict did not disappear in 1973 with the end of the draft and the Vietnam War. In many ways it grew worse. Fights between black and white soldiers were endemic in the mid- and late 1970s, an era now remembered as the "time of troubles."

The military took a hard look at its enlistment procedures. In the early 1980s, recruitment was aided immeasurably by the introduction of post-service educational benefits which were capped by the Montgomery G.I. Bill in 1985. The new enlistment incentives turned the army around. When recent veterans are asked how important G.I. Bill benefits were in their enlistment decision, 51 percent of blacks (32 percent of whites) answer "important" or "very important" (Westat, Inc. 1986). The greatest long-term avenue of equal opportunity in America may be the G.I. Bill benefits offered by the army.

Another significant development was the increase in the number of black officers in the army. Among commissioned officers, the proportion of blacks went from 3 percent in 1970 to 7 percent in 1980 and to 11 percent in 1990, a figure that has remained fairly constant ever since. Racial integration of leadership brought the army out of its time of troubles. The 1989 appointment of Colin L. Powell to chairman of the Joint Chiefs of Staff, the most powerful military position in the world, was a significant step.

Can We Really Draw Lessons from the Army?

Even if we grant that racial integration and black achievement have gone farther in the army than in any other institution, can any lessons be drawn for civilian life? Surely the differences in formal organization and culture are so great that little can be applied from the army to the larger society. Here we present three arguments, in ascending order of difficulty, that critics might make for why the army cannot be used as a model:

1. The army has at its command methods of surveillance and coercion unavailable to civilian institutions.
2. All persons in the army enjoy a modicum of economic security as well as decent housing and medical facilities.
3. Soldiers come from a segment of society that excludes the very bottom rungs; thus, they do not bring the most severe social problems into the army.

In responding to these objections, our intent is not in any way to deny the significant differences between military and civilian life, but to argue that the army's ability to change its way of doing things has broadly applicable implications for overcoming "race" in America.

The Army's Social Structure

Certainly the army is not a democracy—but few other organizations are either. To be sure, the army relies more strongly on round-the-clock accountability than do most civilian organizations. But accountability and control cannot in and of themselves force good race relations. The racial situation is far worse in prisons, where coercive authority weighs much more heavily than in the military. Let us also not forget that racist norms and behavior can prevail in large-scale organizations including those with quasi-military structures. We need only mention the raw racist words on a tape of retired Los Angeles police detective Mark Fuhrman in connection with the initial O. J. Simpson trial and the continuing controversies over racism in local police departments. Even more telling were the racist signs and paraphernalia at the annual "Good Ol' Boys Roundup," a Tennessee gathering of federal law enforcement officials and others from around the country ("Good Ol' Boys Roundup Video Genuine," *The Washington Times,* December 7, 1995, A4).

There is a more definitive rejoinder to those who state that it is the unique hierarchical conditions of military service that account for its positive race relations. We must remember and stress that the same authority structure existed in the army of the 1970s when racial turbulence was endemic. What allowed the army to move from a racially tense situation to the relative harmony of the present period? Something other than submersion of individual rights must be involved.

Soldiers' Economic Security

It is also true that soldiers enjoy at least a modicum of economic well-being. Once in the army, even the lowest soldier is not "underclass." A private receives base pay of $12,000 a year, in addition to room and board, medical care, and other benefits. A master sergeant earns about $40,000 plus medical benefits for himself and his family, and is eligible for a pension of 50 percent of base pay after twenty years service. A mid-level officer has similar benefits with base pay of about $55,000 a year. Again, however, we must ask why the army of the 1970s was so torn by racial strife, when real earnings and benefits were practically identical to what they are today. Likewise, why are race relations generally better in the army than in the other services which all have nearly identical systems of authority and compensation?

The solid economic status of most soldiers does not explain the dynamics of race relations in the army. After all, racial tensions have sharpened in society at large at all income levels. Indeed, the "rage" (in Ellis Cose's evocative term) of the black middle class in a racist American society is an increasingly dominant theme in the current literature.[5]

Exclusion of the Bottom Rung

The most salient of the objections to the army as a model for race relations is that the army, while not drawing from America's elite youth, does exclude the very bottom rungs of American society. As measured by test scores and school credentials, the army effectively precludes the bottom one-third of black youths and the bottom one-fourth of white youths. This is a valid point and must be addressed seriously. After all, if it is simply the quality of youth that matters, then all the army's racial experiences and equal opportunity programs are largely irrelevant.

The rebuttal to this argument is that race relations are better in the armed forces than in institutions that presumably recruit the highest quality youths in America—our colleges and universities. We have some pertinent data on this question. In 1993, we conducted a survey on racial attitudes among soldiers and among undergraduates at Northwestern University, a highly selective school with a relatively positive racial atmosphere. As shown in Table 10.3, soldiers, both black and white, were much more likely to say that they got along better with other races since joining the army than were the students since arriving on campus.

---

[5] Cose (1993). The manner in which race persists in defining relations within middle-class and professional circles has a growing literature (see also Bell 1992; Benjamin 1992; Hochschild 1995; Nelson 1993; Staples 1994). For observations of the treatment of upper-middle-class blacks in public settings, see Graham (1995). For a sociological context, see Landry (1987).

Table 10.3. Racial attitudes of soldiers and university students by race

Since being [in the army/at this university], I get along with people of other races:	Black Students (%)	White Students (%)	Black Soldiers (%)	White Soldiers (%)
Better	9	18	25	38
Same as Before	73	77	70	53
Worse	18	5	5	9
Total	**100**	**100**	**100**	**100**

Source: 1994 army survey by the authors: black *N* = 1,282, white *N* = 1,824; 1994 Northwestern University survey by the authors: black *N* = 89, white *N* = 542.

Indeed, twice as many black students said that they got along worse with other races since arriving on campus than those who said they got along better. The black soldiers present an entirely different story. Three times as many said they got along better with other races than those who said they got along worse. Similar, if less pronounced, attitudes are found among the white soldiers. These data should put to rest the argument that it is the quality of recruits that accounts for the generally successful race relations in the army.

In fact, one could easily produce arguments showing why race relations should be worse in the army than on campus. The army, after all, is populated overwhelmingly by young males, the group most prone to get into trouble. It enforces constrained living conditions, with little outlet for private expression. Also, it sends young people into harm's way, a likelihood that should aggravate rather than reduce social tensions. How these negatives become positives is the key to the army model.

What then can be learned? We suggest a broad principle. Race relations can best be transformed by an absolute commitment to nondiscrimination, coupled with uncompromising standards of performance. To maintain standards, however, paths of opportunity must be created—through education, training, and mentoring—for those who otherwise would be at a disadvantage.

Overcoming Race: A Primer

Analogies between military and civilian organizations have obvious limitations, especially in matters of race. How, then, do we transfer the army's successes to nonmilitary settings? Although obvious differences between military and civilian settings preclude exact comparisons, we can articulate the key principles of the army experience. Comprehension of how race relations work in the army does suggest the following ten concrete lessons.

Lesson One: Blacks and Whites Will Not View Opportunities and Race Relations the Same

Even in the army, the most successfully racially integrated institution in American society, blacks and whites still have disparate views of equal opportunity. Blacks consistently view racial matters in a less favorable light than do whites. This cuts across gender and rank. There is no foreseeable situation in any American institution, much less society as a whole, where this is likely to change. What the army does show, however, is that black and white social attitudes can become significantly closer in egalitarian settings with shared experiences. It also shows that blacks and whites do not have to hold identical views of the racial situation in order to succeed together.

Lesson Two: Focus on Black Opportunity Channels Rather than Eradicating Racism

Better to have blacks in substantial numbers in leadership positions in an organization with some white racists than to have an organization with few blacks and fewer black leaders where racial bigots are absent (or, more likely, invisible). The proclivity in civilian organizations, notably the university world, is to foster a better racial climate through eradication of racist statements and symbols. Such efforts are meaningful only when accompanied by concrete steps to expand the pool of qualified students and faculty. Likewise, in governmental and corporate structures, the emphasis must continually be on opening avenues of opportunity for black participation and movement into leadership roles.

The presence, even if not in any great number, of white racist "skinheads" in the army points to a profound and counterintuitive lesson. The focus first and foremost should always be on avenues that promote black achievement rather than on the rhetoric of nonracism. Of course, the aim must always be both to maximize the avenues of the opportunity and to combat overt and covert racism. If there must be a trade-off between, on the one side, black advancement coexisting with white racists and, on the other, few blacks in a presumed nonracial setting, we firmly come down on the side of the former. In terms of genuine racial opportunity, this means we opt for the realities of the army model over the state of affairs at most elite universities where antiracism is promulgated but where the African American presence is limited.

Lamentable as the presence of white racists may be, it is not the core issue. Indeed, African American history is eloquent testimony to how black accomplishment can occur despite pervasive white racism. In no way should the absence of white racists be considered a precondition for African American achievement. This is one of the most significant morals of the army experience.

Lesson Three: Be Ruthless against Discrimination

Although formal efforts to prohibit racist expressions can be a way organizations avoid a genuine opening up of channels for black advancement, this lesson does not imply a retreat from antidiscrimination. Racist behavior cannot be tolerated within the leadership of an organization. Individuals who display such tendencies must not be promoted to positions of responsibility. Racist behavior in the army effectively terminates one's career. That one rarely hears racial remarks among army NCOs and officers, even in all-white groups, reflects how much this norm is adhered to. Whether formal or informal, the promotion criteria must include sensitivity on racial matters. Shelby Steele's proposal to criminalize racial discrimination (though not his proposal to do away with affirmative action) has, in a manner of speaking, been accomplished de facto in the military (Steele 1995).

Lesson Four: Create Conditions So That White and Black Youth Can Serve on an Equal Basis to Improve Their Social and Civic Opportunities

The intense cooperation required to meet certain ends often found in military life has a democratizing effect. This echoes Gordon W. Allport's classic statement written almost four decades ago: "Prejudice . . . may be reduced by equal status contact between majority and minority groups in the pursuit of common goals. The effect is greatly enhanced if this contact is sanctioned by institutional supports . . . and provided it is of the sort that leads to the perception of common interests and common humanity between members of the two groups."[6] The "equal contact" thesis is long-standing and hard-wearing.

Some form of civilian national service is the only likely means of restoring the opportunities for young people, opportunities that were reduced by the end of conscription and compounded by the current military drawdown. During the peacetime draft years between the wars in Korea and Vietnam, close to half of black males reaching age eighteen served in the

---

[6] Allport (1954, 263). This principle was generated by the research on race relations reported in *The American Soldier.*

armed forces, a figure that remained about the same during the Vietnam era. After the end of the Vietnam War and the draft in 1973, the proportion declined to 15 percent. With the end of the cold war and the accompanying drawdown, the proportion of black men entering the military in 1995 has fallen to 8 percent.

The connection between the demise of the draft and the growth of an underclass is a plausible hypothesis and deserves examination. The critical point is that sharing the obligations of citizenship will act as a solvent for many of the differences among the various participants. That all participants will be living at not much more than subsistence levels and that all will be equally eligible for post-service educational benefits underscore the egalitarianism of the national service proposal. We encourage a public debate about the merits of youth service in either civilian or military capacities, whether compulsory, voluntary, or contingent on benefits.

National service would open avenues never before available to deprived young people; existing local and state youth corps show overwhelming enrollment by poor and minority youths. A national youth service corps linked to post-service educational benefits, the functional equivalent of the draft army, would offer an opportunity for college or vocational training to large numbers of youths who otherwise would be trapped in a dead-end existence. Much as the original G.I. Bill provided a "way up" for many veterans, so would educational benefits for civilian youth service do the same for young men and women today. AmeriCorps, President Clinton's youth service program, has about twenty thousand enrollees annually. African Americans constituted 31 percent of the membership—a figure almost identical with the proportion of blacks in the army's enlisted ranks.

Lesson Five: Affirmative Action Must Be Linked to Standards and the Qualified Pool

The army eschews promotion quotas, but it does set goals. These goals are based on the relevant pool of qualified candidates, not on the proportion of blacks in the entire organization, much less on general population figures. Failure to meet goals must be explained, but "timetables" do not exist. This "soft" affirmative action contrasts with the quota-driven programs that have characterized federal agencies (Holmes 1995). Indeed, the promotion lag of blacks compared with whites at certain levels, especially from captain to major, indicates that army promotions are not bound to goals.

The goals in the army promotion process are based not on the number of minority members in the army, but on the number of minority members in the pool of potential promotees to the next higher rank. This criterion cuts through much of the thicket that surrounds affirmative action in civilian life, and allows for some picking and choosing among numerous minority candidates. Beyond the numbers implied in goals, however, there must be a longer range aim—placing blacks in those junior positions that serve as launching pads for future promotions. The army does not elaborately disguise its goals or its methods for attaining them because it does not have to deal with the fundamental fact that drives the quota system in civilian institutions: the dearth of qualified blacks. In simple terms, enough blacks must be present in the promotion pool to make affirmative action work well.

To get a better idea of how these policies work in practice, consider how they might work in the academic world. In that case, hiring committees would strive to hire a proportion of minority new assistant professors in a given field roughly equal to the minority proportion of recent Ph.D.'s in that field. Correspondingly, the proportionate number of associate professors should approximate the number of assistant professors, and the number of full professors should aim for the same percentage as found among associate professors. (Blacks accounted for 3.5 percent of all Ph.D.'s awarded in 1995; excluding doctorates in education, they accounted for 2.4 percent of all Ph.D.'s [National Center for Educational Statistics 1997].) The impact of such a policy is to focus long-term equal opportunity efforts on expanding the number of minority candidates entering the pipeline, rather than struggling to fill a proportionate number of slots with a disproportionately small number of qualified candidates.

Maintenance of common standards for promotion may cause short-term turmoil, as it did in the army of the 1970s, but it also means that those who attain senior positions are fully qualified. Any set of standards must also take into account, as does the army's, such "whole-person" qualities as initiative, perseverance, leadership, and commitment to organizational goals. That the army contained few putative liberals willing to rationalize an initial drop in standards allowed those blacks who were promoted in the early days to become the strongest defenders of standards for their own black subordinates. An organization that promotes the less qualified to buy temporary peace only invites long-term disaffection.

Lessons Six: Affirmative Action Must Follow a "Supply-Side" Not a "Demand-Side" Model

In practical terms, the army has developed an affirmative action program based on "supply." This contrasts with the "demand"—and more typical—version of affirmative action in which goals and quotas are established without prior efforts to enlarge the pool of qualified people.

We interject here an object lesson on an affirmative action program—one based on the demand-side model—that seems destined not to work. In 1995, the navy announced a "12/12/5" goal, which it wants to reach by 2000. By that date, the navy wants to attain an officer accession composition that is at least 12 percent black, 12 percent Hispanic, and 5 percent Asian or Pacific Islander ("Navy Sets New Diversity Goals for Officer Accessions," *Navy Times* May 1, 1995, 14). (In time, that figure should become the standard for the total officer composition.) To reach that goal, the percentage of officers in the designated racial categories would have to double within four years.

When queried as to where the "12/12/5" figure came from, a very senior navy official told one of the authors that this was the projected racial composition of the United States and that the "Navy should look like America." Toward this goal, the navy has introduced initiatives that allow recruiters certain leeway in offering navy Reserve Officer Training Corps (ROTC) scholarships to minority members. Yet, the navy goals are untenable unless accompanied by new programs to expand the pool of minorities who could be raised to meet commissioning standards. Unlike the army, for example, the navy has a small presence in the ROTC programs in historically black colleges. In light of the navy's insistence that standards "will not be dropped," the navy's "12/12/5" goals appear unrealistic.

The lesson here is simple: diversity in and of itself is not a rationale for affirmative action. Indeed, under the 1995 U.S. Supreme Court ruling in *Adarand Construction v. Pena,* affirmative action for the purpose of reflecting racial and ethnic diversity for its own sake is unconstitutional. Diversity as a goal not only obscures the proper goal of redressing historical and contemporary racial discrimination but also increasingly bypasses African Americans. Much better to build up avenues of equal opportunity rather than concoct numbers to correspond with notions of diversity based on gross population numbers.

Good affirmative action acknowledges that compensatory action may be needed to help members of disadvantaged groups to meet the standards of competition. Bad affirmative action suspends those standards. The objective always should be to prepare members of a historically disadvantaged population to compete on an equal footing with the more privileged. These precepts are very much in accordance with core American values (Williams 1970).[7]

Lesson Seven: A Level Playing Field Is Not Always Enough

The army shows how youths with deficient backgrounds can meet demanding academic as well as physical standards. The army has success-

---

[7] On how Americans support compensatory action but not ethnic/gender quotas, see Lipset (1995).

fully introduced internal programs to bring young people up to enlistment standards, to raise enlisted soldiers to noncommissioned officer standards, to bring undergraduates up to officer commissioning standards, and to raise high school graduates to West Point admission standards. These programs are not targeted exclusively to minority soldiers, but the participants are disproportionately African American.

The army's success in producing black leaders occurs because it recognizes that a level playing field is not always enough. And this points to another army lesson for civilian society: rather than compromise standards, soldiers are raised to meet competitive standards. Toward this end, the army has established far-reaching educational programs that emphasize mathematics, reading, and writing.

At the enlisted level this involves one of the largest continuing education programs in the world. In 1995, some sixty thousand soldiers were enrolled in Functional Academic Skills Training (FAST), of whom 60 percent were black. Of the forty-one standard lessons, twenty-three deal with mathematics, eleven with reading, and seven with writing. Without FAST, the strong black representation in the NCO corps would be impossible.

The U.S. Military Academy at West Point remains the most prestigious source of commissions in the army. Almost half of the black cadets who enter West Point are products of one of the most unusual secondary schools in America—the U.S. Military Academy Preparatory School. The ten-month program, in effect a thirteenth year of high school, has a sole academic emphasis on reading, writing, and mathematics. Without the "Prep School," as it is known in army circles, the number of black cadets would be perilously low. Remarkably, black "prepsters" are just as likely (74 percent) to graduate from West Point as white direct-admitees (75 percent).

Evaluating programs designed to boost academic skills and test scores is fraught with difficulty. But there is sufficient evidence from the army experience to show that "intelligence"—as measured by achievement tests—can be raised significantly through programs that are well staffed, have motivated participants, and adopt a military regimen. Residential programs away from the participant's home area seem to be the most effective way to resocialize young people toward productive goals. As is done in the army, such programs should emphasize mathematics, reading, and writing.

There are no easy ways to upgrade the skills of students with academic weaknesses, but the programs described here—some expensive, some less so—offer lessons. First, they all emphasize reading, writing, and mathematical skills. Although they include physical training and a military ethos, the "three Rs" remain paramount. In addition, completion of the program has a direct and clear payoff: promotion to an NCO, an officer's commission, or admission to West Point. In the end, there are no real losers for anyone who stays the course.

If liberals must learn that white racism is not the central point, conservatives have something to learn, too. The skill-boosting programs that produce so many black leaders in the army are costly. These programs require a big commitment of money and resources. Sometimes, as in the army's remedial programs, "throwing money" at a social problem does solve it.

Lesson Eight: Affirmative Action Should Be Focused on African Americans

The army's racial affirmative action is geared de facto to blacks. We hold that this principle should be generalized throughout the society. The basic social dichotomy in our society is black versus white and even, if we are frank, increasingly black versus nonblack. The core reality is that blacks have both a sense of identity and of grievance with America that is unique and far exceeds that of any other ethnic group.[8] (Perhaps the Native American story comes closest.) The confluence of race, slavery, and segregation is unparalleled. Affirmative action for African Americans is required as much for current social reality as for historical treatment. Multiculturalism ultimately trivializes the distinct history and predicament of black Americans. The African American story is singular and of such magnitude that it ought not to be compared to the experiences of other American ethnic, especially immigrant, groups.[9] The American black experience is neither like the immigrants of yesterday nor the ones of today.

Affirmative action based on class or income is a chimera.[10] Not only is it much more difficult to operationalize than affirmative action based either on race/ethnicity or on gender, but the nonblack poor would soon displace blacks in affirmative action procedures. More to the point, we argue that race overrides class as a source of ingrained prejudice in our country. (Ask yourself: Would the child of a white ditch digger or that of a black physician cause more upset marrying into a white family?) Affirmative action based on class or income, paradoxically enough, would work against black Americans, the very group for which affirmative action is most justified. African Americans are increasingly apprehensive that the "wide net" approach to affirmative action is another way of excluding blacks from channels of opportunity. A policy of class-based affirmative action would only confirm these apprehensions.

[8] The authoritative work on the state of African Americans is Jaynes and Williams (1989).
[9] On the noncomparability of black Americans and other ethnic groups, we follow Lieberson (1980) and Huggins (1995, 148–57).
[10] A sophisticated argument for class-based affirmative action is Kahlenberg (1996).

Terminology on affirmative action is instructive. When the issue was defined originally as focusing on African Americans, the preferred term was "equal opportunity." "Multiculturalism" and "diversity" as affirmative action concepts entered the vocabulary only after nonblack groups came to be included in affirmative action programs. The decline of African Americans in affirmative action priorities corresponded directly with the replacement of equal opportunity with the rhetoric of multiculturalism and diversity.

Lesson Nine: Recognize Afro-Anglo Culture as the Core American Culture

An unquantifiable component in the army's success in race relations is that the organization is multiracial, but unicultural—and the uniculture is Afro-Anglo. Our central argument here is that something similar must occur in American society as a whole. One of the most striking effects of racial integration in the army is that enlisted life has become somewhat African Americanized. In terms of vocabulary, humor, and musical tastes, white enlisted soldiers become attuned and partially assimilated into African American cultural patterns. This phenomenon has a message for civilian society.

We need a reconstructed interpretation of American history that stresses how much our nation's culture and moral vision derive from the African American experience.[11] White Americans must recognize the African American elements in our bedrock culture; equally, black Americans must recognize their contributions to the common American culture and resist the lure of an Afro-centric curricula that too easily obscures the contribution of African Americans to our national heritage.

We use the term Afro-Anglo in a special sense. The "Anglo" refers to the obvious British heritage that Americans, whatever their own ethnicity, recognize as the core of our country's culture—notably our language, our social customs, and especially our legal and political traditions. We must recognize that our nation's culture also has a core "Afro" element—moral vision, rhetoric, literature, music, and Protestant Christianity. Certainly immigrants have shaped our national identity, but the bedrock culture remains Afro-Anglo. Leaving aside black majority countries, few countries (Brazil? Cuba?) have been influenced more strongly by African culture than our own. It would be hard to overstate how strongly a numerically small racial minority has influenced a dominant racial majority, indeed the

[11] Jaynes and Williams, in *Common Destiny*, make the special point that economic and political facets of race relations should not overshadow the important tasks of "social integration and cultural maintenance" (1989, 32).

culture of the dominant nation on the world scene. The very rhetoric of the American creed has been shaped largely by African American formulations of equality (Condit and Lucaites 1993).

We think the army offers an important model for how we ought to consider the African American component in our culture. Black history rather than being held apart (as the multicultural establishment seems to prefer) should be seen as an original and shaping component of core American culture. Rather than a multicultural view of America, we need a unified American national identity whose core is recognized as Afro-Anglo (Moskos 1997). A group that for too long has felt alienated from what it imagined to be the mainstream of American culture must now realize that they have long been part of that mainstream.

If America is to be truly a world leader, its message must not be empty of moral content. An invocation of our black heritage, which has deepened and enhanced the American Dream, is as important as our economic and military might. Our own civil rights struggle has become part of the world movement toward freedom. John Hope Franklin, the dean of black historians, puts it succinctly: "The role of the Negro in America is not only significant in itself but central in the task of fulfilling the nation's true destiny" (Franklin 1989). The crux of American exceptionalism may well be the influence of black Americans on the total culture.

Certainly there has been a duality in black thought on whether blacks are essentially outsiders with strong African connections or are quintessential Americans. To the question "are blacks Americans?" the army experience offers a resounding "yes." It also means, in the sense of shared culture, that "Americans are part black." This may be the only way to lance the boil of a black "oppositional" culture. Just as we now recognize our shared American religious culture as Judeo-Christian in origin, we hope for an acknowledgment of our common Afro-Anglo heritage.

We must abandon the mind-set that being "black" and being "American" are somehow mutually exclusive. This is a false dichotomy even though it is often held by many black nationalists and most whites. The relationship between being black and being American is not "either-or" but "both-and." The titles of the two autobiographies of black generals are informative: Benjamin O. Davis, Jr., *American* (1991) and Colin L. Powell, *My American Journey* (1995).

Lesson Ten: Enhancing Black Participation
Is Good for Organizational Effectiveness

The blunt truth is that the way most Americans see it, the greater the black proportion in an organization, the poorer its effectiveness. The armed forces are the welcome exception. That the disproportionately black army stands out as one of the most respected organizations in American society has profound meaning. So does the fact the General Colin L. Powell occupies the pinnacle of American esteem. Not only has the military played a central role as an avenue of black achievement, it has also shown that a large African American presence has been conducive for the smooth operation of a major American institution.

Indeed, as the proportion of blacks increased, there was a corresponding increase in the standing and effectiveness of the army. Other variables also surely accounted for this improved state of affairs, but the military's signaling of its concern with equal opportunity, its early implementation of affirmative action, and its enhancement of black achievement was certainly a necessary condition. Ultimately, any program of engineered race relations must meet a single test. In the not-so-long run, does it improve the performance of the organization in which it is implemented?

The military of the 1970s recognized that its race problem was so critical that it was on the verge of self-destruction. That realization set in motion the steps that have led to today's relatively positive state of affairs. As racial division grows in American society at large, will we come to the same realization?

CHAPTER ELEVEN

War's Legacy in Men's Lives

Glen H. Elder, Jr., and Christopher Chan

Older veteran claims "he survived war but found his life in ruins."
　　—D. Botting, *From the Ruins of the Reich: Germany, 1945–1949*

War mobilization represents a pervasive and varied experience across successive birth cohorts of American men in the twentieth century. The rate of military involvement peaked during World War II, with over 70 percent of American men born in the early 1920s serving in active duty.[1] Efforts to understand the personal impact of military service have centered mainly on exposure to life disruptions and the traumatic events of combat (Clipp and Elder 1996; Herman 1992), with emphasis on experiences with death and the dying. But the nature of this influence depends on the fit between military experience and the lives of recruits. The meaning of recruitment and wartime events is contingent on *when* they occur in a person's life, as detailed in life-course theory (Elder 1998). The likelihood of disruption increases with age at entry, and later entry was especially common in the manpower mobilization of World War II.

---

[1] One of the most useful sources of information on the pervasiveness of military service and its life-course effects is provided by Dennis Hogan's reanalysis of a nationwide mobility data set (1981). Hogan uses one-year cohorts that are sensitive to historical changes in experience and options.

This chapter explores the lifelong consequences of entry into the Second World War at an older age, examining the consequences for marriage, career, health, and retirement patterns. Our analysis draws on studies of approximately eight hundred men from the Stanford-Terman study who were born between 1900 and the 1920s (Holahan and Sears 1995). The study began in 1922 and has continued across thirteen waves of data. Despite the men's advanced age in 1940, over 40 percent entered the service before the war ended. We compare the life-course effects of an older age at entry with a younger age at entry (thirty-three years or older versus twenty-nine years or younger) across the postwar years. We have excluded the middle group (ages thirty to thirty-two) to highlight the impact of truly late mobilization.

Background

Military Recruitment in World War II

Basic training is a time when a great diversity of people are subjected to equalizing forces. Basic training regimes under the universal scope of recruitment became one of the best examples of both diversity and the search for common ground. A veteran observed that he encountered people he didn't even know existed and soon "found himself living among fellows from all over the country . . . when you talk these things over with them and get their slant on things, it sort of opens up your horizons" (Havighurst et al. 1951, 188). Willard Waller, in his seminal essay *War and the Family*, reflected on the social mixing wrought by mobilization: "[P]eople are thrown together who have never seen one another before and will never see one another again; regions, culture groups, and classes are all mixed as they are at no other period in life" (1940, 14).

This building of equality and mutual ties in basic training eliminated the social advantages (or disadvantages) that recruits brought to the service. Brotz and Wilson refer to induction and basic training as the "knifing-off" of past experience and the minimization of background diversity: "Nothing in one's past seems relevant unless, possibly, a capacity for adaptation and the ability to assume a new role" (1946, 374). Because wars are fought, won, and lost by military units, not by soldiers acting alone, basic training seeks to build group cohesiveness and equality at the expense of individuality. It does so through a regime that makes prior identities irrelevant, requires uniform dress and appearance, minimizes privacy, and rewards performance on the basis of group achievement: "A spirit of comradeship emerges as individuality is subordinated to the welfare of the unit" (Elder and Clipp 1988, 179).

No matter how effective basic training is in creating a sense of commonality, it could not ensure common experience across the war years (in the combat zone, see Williams 1984).[2] Indeed, soaring manpower needs during World War II significantly increased the age heterogeneity of military recruits from age eighteen to age thirty-eight or so, a span of twenty years or more. By comparison, relatively few men who served in Vietnam entered the service after the age of twenty-three. The age heterogeneity of World War II recruits markedly increased their diversity and inequality of life outcomes. World War II expanded the educational prospects of veterans through provisions of the G.I. Bill (Olson 1974) and enlarged access to life opportunities through skill training in the military (Sampson and Laub 1996). However, these benefits were most available and useful to men who were in the formative phase of adult life, especially during the years after high school. For example, the G.I. Bill was primarily crafted for men and women who were younger than than twenty-five years of age, the traditional time for higher education.

Men who enter military service at a young age have the stamina for military service and typically lack obligations to family and work. Their entry shortly after the completion of high school comes before serious commitments to higher education, family, and work. Their war experiences can give them training and maturity that enhance life-course choices and options. Two studies of men who came of age in the Great Depression generally show these lifetime benefits of mobilization at a young age during the Second World War (Elder 1987; Sampson and Laub 1996). Their lives were timed well to maximize the benefits of service training.

The extraordinary age span of military recruitment in World War II placed men on a wide range of life-course trajectories. This age diversity in life experience produced unanticipated life-course inequalities. With survey information that extends back in time before World War II, the Stanford-Terman data archive is unusually well suited to an assessment of the lifetime effects of military timing and especially that of entry at an older age (see Elder, Pavalko, and Clipp 1993).

The Stanford-Terman Study

The Terman longitudinal study began data collection in 1922 under the direction of Lewis Terman, then professor of psychology at Stan-

[2] Robin M. Williams, Jr., was also a co-author of the two volumes of *The American Soldier,* a study of soldiers in World War II, one of the first projects of large-scale social science based on social surveys. The first volume focused on the adjustment of men to army life, the second on the implications of combat. See Stouffer, Suchman, et al. 1949; Stouffer, Lumsdaine, et al. 1949.

ford University. Initially, 1,528 third to eighth graders were recruited from large public schools in California on the basis of high scores on intelligence assessments (Terman and Oden 1959). They were questioned by mail-in surveys on matters of family, education, and work at four points before World War II (1922, 1928, 1936, and 1940). Military experience was the main subject of questionnaires administered in 1945 and 1950. Since then, survey data have been collected in seven waves, timed approximately five to ten years apart, for a total of thirteen waves of data spanning seventy-two years. Postwar questionnaires collected data on work, marriage, and achievement as well as details regarding aging and life review.

The archives are composed of cross-sectional records for each of the data collection points. This information, supplemented with qualitative data, served as the basis for constructing life-history records for all respondents (see Elder, Pavalko, and Clipp 1993). We draw on trajectories of work careers and physical and emotional health as well as information on divorce and retirement. Space restrictions preclude giving a detailed account of the measures here, but it is available elsewhere.[3]

Because the respondents' ages ranged from twenty to thirty-seven in 1940 and almost half were recruited for service in World War II, the sample is especially appropriate for studying age variations in the timing of military service. The subsample used in this study consists of all men for whom time of entry into the service is known. Veterans were divided into three categories defined by age of entry: younger entrants, ages eighteen to twenty-nine years ($N = 107$, nearly all entered after age twenty-three); middle entrants, ages thirty to thirty-two years ($N = 112$); and older entrants, ages thirty-three to forty-one years ($N = 105$). The middle entrants are not included in this study of late entry. Our discussion compares the youngest and oldest entrants; the nonveterans are included in some cases for contrast. In some cases, we compare veterans in the sample by birth cohort: an older cohort of men born before 1911 and a younger cohort of men born later.

Because the Stanford-Terman longitudinal study was designed for high-ability children, the level of educational attainment of respondents is high: 48 percent of the men report a professional or graduate degree, and only a handful claim less than a college degree. Virtually all are white and come from middle-class to upper-middle-class households. Despite these limitations in the sample's socioeconomic and racial breadth, its age coverage and in-depth questions on military service and health make it a

---

[3] Three prior analyses of the Terman data are drawn on in our account of wartime experience and its lifetime effects: a study of the impact of World War II on the marital instability of the Terman men (Pavalko and Elder 1990); a study of the late-life careers of the Terman men (Elder and Pavalko 1993); and the life-course effects of military timing (Elder, Shanahan, and Clipp 1994).

Table 11.1. Work, family, and the life course: the Terman men in 1940

	Nonveterans (N) (N = 381–404)	Younger Entrants (Y) (N = 77–100)	Older Entrants (O) (N = 81–107)	Significant Differences
Family				
Married (%)	87	36	83	O>Y, N>Y
With Children (%)	65	10	60	O>Y, N>Y
Work				
Average Years of Education	13	13	15	O>N
Average Years of Work Experience	8	3	9	O>Y, N>Y
With Upward Career Trajectory (%)	47	42	50	
Supervisors (%)	18	11	20	N>Y
In School (%)	22	31	16	O<Y

Note: Total N varies from variable to variable because of missing cases. The last column reports the results from standard two-tailed T-tests for differences between means or proportions.
Source: Authors' tabulations from the Terman archive.

unique resource for studying the long-term effects of military service on a broad range of outcomes.

Life Experiences during the Second World War

Table 11.1 summarizes the life-course stages of the younger and older Terman men at the start of the war. Although the men in the Terman study were nearing the age of thirty (on average), their older age did not exclude them from mobilization for active duty. Slightly more than 45 percent were inducted before the end of the war, with a large majority donning uniforms in 1942 and 1943.

Those who entered military service at a young age were unlikely to be married or with children. Typically they married during or after active duty, usually becoming parents only after demobilization. These men averaged thirteen years of schooling, and many were still in school when recruited. By contrast, older entrants were pulled from established family roles. Most were already married and a majority had become parents before active duty. The average length of education for this group is fifteen years. The older entrants were deeply involved in their careers, as indicated by a higher average number of work years and more upwardly mobile trajectories in 1940.

Table 11.2 summarizes life-course experiences of the younger and older Terman men before, during, and just after their service. One significant difference is their occupational experiences. Over a fifth of younger entrants reported a new job or occupation that was very different from their prewar

Table 11.2. Wartime experiences of Terman veterans by age at entry into military service

	Younger Entrants (%) (N = 72–105)	Older Entrants (%) (N = 76–100)	Significant Differences
Timing of Marriage and Service			
Marriage before Service	42	88	
Marriage during Service	46	8	
Marriage after Service	12	3	***
Timing of Parenthood and Service			
Parenthood before Service	17	66	
Parenthood during Service	35	17	
Parenthood after Service	49	17	***
Career Discontinuity			
Prewar to Postwar	21	6	***
Military Experience			
Served Overseas	83	67	***
Officer at Entry	45	62	***
Officer at Exit	76	72	ns
Killed	1	1	ns
Injured	6	9	ns
Exposed to Death and Dying	42	31	***
Exposed to Combat	71	55	***
Combat Duration (in weeks)	52	20	***

Note: N varies from variable to variable because of missing cases. The last column reports results from standard T-test of differences between proportions or chi-square tests for association (*** = p<.01; ns = not significant).
Sources: Authors' tabulations (Killed, Injured, and Exposed to Death and Dying) and Table 1 in Elder, Shanahan, and Clipp (1994).

positions. However, older entrants were more likely to return as best they could to the types of work they were engaged in before the war. Some of the older entrants even returned to less desirable circumstances in the same line of work. One of the veterans, an assistant professor before the war, found that he was no longer competitive with younger colleagues when he returned after four years abroad. By contrast, the younger entrants had not yet made investments in their occupations. They learned new skills while in the service and this gave them the flexibility to enter new occupations.

Although war mobilization was less disruptive for younger entrants (in that it was less disruptive of their work and family lives), they were more likely to end up overseas and in combat situations. These younger men were typically favored for combat units: younger entrants averaged fifty-two weeks of combat experience compared to only twenty weeks for the older entrants. Only a small handful of Terman veterans were injured during the war and practically none were killed. However, the younger entrants were more likely to report exposure to death.

Overall, these figures show that military mobilization represents a very different experience for men who entered military roles at different times in their lives. Entry into the service disrupted the lives of older entrants by separating them from family and established career paths. For the younger recruits, military service was less disruptive of work and family but more stressful in terms of exposure to combat, death, and dying. As we shall see, these diverse wartime experiences created different pathways for the Terman men, pathways that led to inequalities in family, work, and health.

The Long-Term Effects of War

Next we look in more detail at the consequences of military service for marriage, career, health, and retirement patterns. We compare each of these outcomes among men who entered the war at an older age (thirty-three years and older) and those who entered at a younger age (twenty-nine years or younger).

Divorce

Historical records in the United States show an increase in divorce following the Civil War, World War I, World War II, and the Vietnam War.[4] The Terman veterans were subject to the same pressures during the Second World War. As a whole, only 15 percent of the Terman men who were ever married experienced divorce during their lifetime, but the chances of divorce were one and a half times higher for veterans compared to the nonveterans in the study. Moreover, the mechanism that increased the risk of divorce *differed* for the younger and older entrants (Pavalko and Elder 1990). While some younger entrants had high divorce rates because of stress from intense combat, many older entrants were subject to divorce because the timing of their marriage created unexpected stresses and uncertainties.

These diverse effects appear in Figure 11.1, which compares divorce probabilities by 1955 for marriages established before and during the war and for marriages among combat and noncombat veterans. Unions established between 1942 and 1945 (as were most younger entrants' marriages) were half as likely to end in divorce compared to marriages begun before 1940 (as were most older entrant's marriages). Combat experience (which was greater for younger entrants) tripled the likelihood of divorce. Duration of combat does not alter either of these results, and neither do variations in education, age at first marriage, or age at service entry. Thus, both younger

---

[4] Jacobsen (1959) has carried out the most comprehensive survey of war effects on divorce, and South (1985) provides supplementary information.

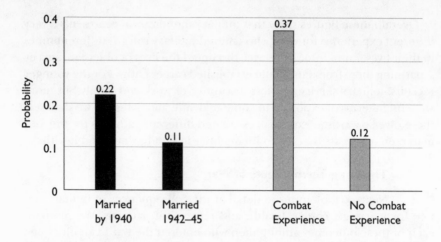

Figure 11.1 Divorce probabilities of Terman veterans by marriage cohort and combat experience. Expected probabilities based on logistic regression models of the logged-odds of divorce by 1955 for all Terman men and for Terman men married at military entry (from Table 2 in Pavalko and Elder 1990). Calculated probabilities are the expected values for veterans with sixteen years of schooling who first married when they were twenty-four years old.

and older entrants were subject to divorce pressures because of their war experiences but the specific mechanisms differed for the two groups.

Why were prewar marriages more at risk than war marriages? One explanation claims that prewar marriages were not established with full knowledge of wartime stresses; these stresses were not part of the "calculus of marital commitment." When mass recruitment began, wives were wholly unprepared for the pain of lengthy separation, for the dreadful uncertainty and unending loneliness, and for the ever-mounting sexual pressures and family burdens. By contrast, men and women who fell in love and married during the war did so knowing that separation and substantial risks were likely elements of their relationships in the foreseeable future. In sum, couples who married during full-scale war mobilization were likely to make this decision with an awareness of wartime realities while prewar marriages encountered the stresses of war with no anticipation of their effects.

The link between men's combat experience and the probabilities of divorce suggests that the intensity of war undermined family stability after the veterans returned home. Many of them faced a long-term struggle with symptoms of post-traumatic stress due to heavy combat, symptoms including an inability to feel emotion and closeness to others, immobilizing anxiety and depression, hyper-alertness and reactivity to sounds, intrusive memories of battle scenes during the day, and sleep disturbed by combat nightmares (Brill and Beebe 1956). A 1965 report cites accumulating evidence "that many veterans have retained their original combat symptoms of startle reaction, recurrent nightmares, and irritability largely unchanged" (Archibald and Tuddenham 1965, 475; see also Herman 1992). Acute startle reactions were expressed in exaggerated responses to noise, for example, and to a wife's efforts to rouse her husband from sleep in the morning. Irritability became explosiveness under the pressures of family and work.

These types of traumatic memories of combat adversely affected the marriages of World War II veterans as they did the marriages of Korean and Vietnam veterans (Pavalko and Elder 1990; Laufer and Gallops 1985; Kulka et al. 1990). One of the Terman men who served in the Italian campaign acknowledged in later life that his prewar marriage was not strong before he left home and that, on his return, his wife could not accommodate his unpredictable rages and sullen moods. His three-year separation made the postwar reunion very difficult under even the best of circumstances.

Work Careers

The Terman study's lifetime information on occupations and earnings enabled us to examine how age at mobilization influenced the earnings of veterans after the war. Previous studies that show an earnings advantage for World War II veterans compared with nonveterans have not taken age at entry into account (cf. Little and Fredland 1979). We compared the earnings curves of younger and older entrants with similarly aged nonveterans in order to show whether service entry resulted in any advantages or disadvantages. Relative income loss was greatest among the older entrants (recall that they were mobilized during the career advancement stage of their lives). In fact, these men generally lost more in expected lifetime earnings than did nonveterans. On the other hand, young entrants *surpassed* the earnings of similarly qualified nonveterans. These two results are shown in Figure 11.2. Many other studies have found similar results (Villemez and Kasarda 1976; Browning, Lopreato, and Poston 1973). Although these differences in earnings may indicate that the younger veterans are more talented in ways that elude our measurements, none of the differences were due to preservice attributes, such as father's occupational status, preservice career characteristics, or IQ.

Five years out of a man's career in his thirties is more damaging than the same loss of work time in his twenties. Especially for the college educated, most people experience a rapid growth of earnings in their thirties. Men who miss this growth period because of war service show lower life-

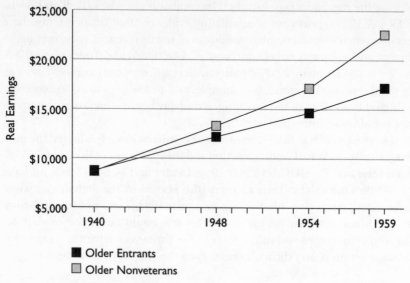

■ Older Entrants
☐ Older Nonveterans

Younger Entrants and Younger Nonveterans

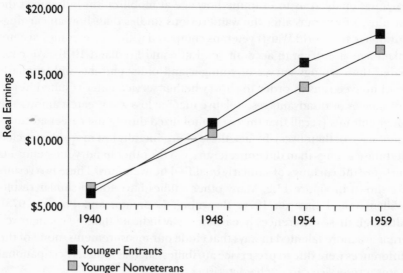

■ Younger Entrants
☐ Younger Nonveterans

Figure 11.2 Earnings curves of Terman men. Earnings are in 1959 constant dollars. We found statistically significant differences in earnings (all years combined) between younger entrants and young nonveterans ($t = 2.07$; $p = .04$) and between older entrants and older nonveterans ($t = 3.12$; $p = .002$).

time earnings. For example, a research chemist in the older entrant group illustrates the personal economic costs of entering the draft late (at age thirty-two). In 1945, he spoke about how his term in the army had changed his plans and left him behind on technical skills. Ten years after the war, he still felt gaps in his professional development and shortly thereafter decided to shift into administration. Another veteran remembered feeling obsolescent in his old job of university teaching and research. Five years in the service had been costly at his level of expertise. This same career disruption actually forced an older recruit to give up his budding career in music. He had been away too long from the practice of his craft.

Changes in functional lines of work are another discontinuity that may have accounted for these career trajectories (Wilensky 1961). Men who were mobilized in the armed forces were frequently assigned tasks functionally unrelated to their civilian work. For example, a young academic in the humanities was assigned to a radar unit in northern England. Another example is a general medical doctor who ended up in a communications unit in Southeast Asia because he had grown up in Indonesia.

The implications of this double disjuncture (time out from one's prewar career and possibly a change in line of work) were presumably more damaging for the older men. Younger men could afford to experiment and to discard a career of very short duration because they had most of their productive lives ahead. By contrast, the older entrants lacked degrees of freedom and could be "untracked" by their war service, suffering impaired earnings for the remainder of their lives.

Not only were younger entrants' careers less disrupted by war service, they were also more likely to benefit economically from military service directly. In their case, war served as a bridge to greater social and economic opportunity through general and occupational military training (Hastings and Elder 1988). Veteran status also gave them access to benefits such as the educational and housing components of the G.I. Bill. These skills and benefits were especially useful to younger entrants who joined the service as early as they could.

The Experience of Military Physicians

We should note that not all members of the older cohort were adversely affected by military service. Though typically members of the older cohort, physicians occupied a favored position relative to military service because so many of them were mobilized into a system in desperate need of highly trained medical personnel. In some cases, physicians' military careers entailed greater challenge and managerial responsibility. Consider the experience of a surgeon who received his medical degree in the depths of the Great Depression from an Ivy League university. In a letter to Lewis Terman shortly after the war, he recounted his military career:

> On 10 January 1942, my unit, the 5th General Hospital was activated, and six weeks later I arrived in the United Kingdom. . . . Shortly before D-day I was . . . made Chief of the Surgical Service of the 22nd General, a 1500 bed hospital. Except for a short period of ill health, the following year was the best of my life . . . I had very considerable responsibilities, and was as busy as I have ever been, with rarely less than 1000 patients under my care. Our service made a very good record, and many members somehow found time to make contributions to the literature of war surgery.

This experience strengthened his commitment to the orthopedic surgery of trauma and, partly as a result of his war record, he was elected to the American Association for the Surgery of Trauma in 1946. After being challenged to the hilt during the war, he and some of his colleagues felt sadly unfulfilled by their postwar employment. But his work in orthopedic surgery led to notable medical appointments and productive self-employment into the 1960s and 1970s.

The transition into a more demanding field of responsibilities is one of the most common themes across the life histories of physicians who were mobilized into World War II. Another surgeon who completed his medical degree in the mid-1930s obtained a reserve commission in the U.S. Army Medical Corps and was ordered to active duty in the midst of his last year of residency in surgery. Within a period of several months, he found himself chief of Surgical Service at a large general hospital in Manila with a capacity of two thousand beds. More than thirty years later, after a highly successful practice and research career in surgery, he viewed his five years of U.S. Army experience as a turning point, one that entailed a dramatic increase in responsibility for a young man who had not yet completed his internship in surgery. He also saw negatives—the delay in launching a practice and in starting a family. But the *positives* were far more numerous. When he assessed the best and worst periods of his life 1986, he rated his military service as an eight on a scale from one to ten, the best of all times.

Health Experiences

Did social disruptions due to war mobilization have a lasting adverse effect on the physical and emotional health of the Terman men? To answer this question, we constructed a typology of physical and emotional health trajectories between 1945 and 1986. Ph.D. coders trained in medical fields assigned respondents to one of six trajectories on the basis of their overall phys-

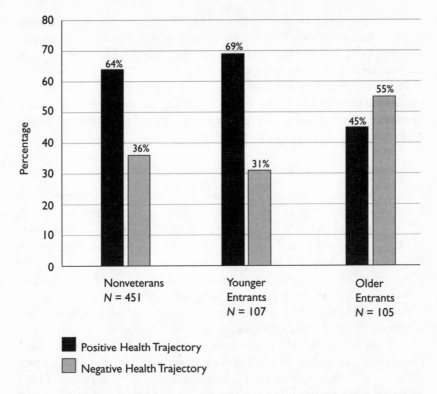

Figure 11.3 Physical health history of Terman men by veteran status and age of entry. Positive trajectory includes those who experienced "constant good health" and "decline with recovery." Negative trajectories are "decline at end of life," "sporadic," "linear decline," and "constant poor health." (Adapted from Elder, Shanahan, and Clipp 1994, Table 3.)

ical health ratings for cross-sections and intervals: constant good health (35 percent), decline at the end of life (25 percent), linear decline (14 percent), decline and recovery (22 percent), and constant poor health (39 percent) (Elder, Pavalko, and Clipp 1993). We consider "constant good health" and "decline and recovery" as positive health trajectories and the rest as negative.

Previous studies have shown that in general veteran status is not a significant factor in physical health (Elder, Shanahan, and Clipp 1994). However, Figure 11.3 shows that age at entry into the war does matter. The older entrants experienced more negative health trajectories compared to nonveterans in the study. By contrast, the younger entrants exhibited slightly more *positive* health trajectories than nonveterans. Exposure to combat, which is more common among the younger men, does not reduce this difference. These findings hold even after adjustments for education, entry, and age, and are consistent with how the Terman men viewed their wartime service from the perspective of later life.

How can we make sense of the negative health trajectories of the older entrants? There are two plausible explanations: that the stress of life-course disruptions *and* the unhealthy repression of wartime experience increased their risk of physical decline in later life.

Health Cost of Life-Course Disruptions

Previous studies have shown that social coherence and integration are important for reducing an individual's morbidity and mortality (Antonovsky 1979). Qualities such as a willing and sympathetic listener, the coherence of a family unit, and a family's social support and unconditional acceptance were diminished among men who went to war, especially when they left wives and children behind. Many veterans also experienced the disorganization of work in terms of lost coworkers and unfinished careers.

It is possible that these life-course disruptions accelerated the decline of veterans' health, and more so for the older entrants. Though little is known about the actual mechanisms by which social disruption affects physical health, Cohen and Williamson observed that "there is sufficient evidence to convince us that stress influences the immune system" (1991, 8). Social integration clearly matters for psychological and physical well-being, as documented by studies of social support (Cohen and Syme 1985; House, Landis, and Umberson 1988); and the adverse consequences of social breakdown for health are revealed in a number of studies, including Kai Erikson's (1976) study of Buffalo Creek.[5] Other studies have also shown that veterans are at risk of physical illness through negative affective and physiological states (e.g., feelings of loss of control) over an unspecified period of time (Kiecolt-Glaser and Glaser 1991; van der Kolk, McFarlane, and Weisaeth 1996). Reassembling one's social support network after the war was sometimes difficult. A navy veteran observed (in a 1950 interview) that "numerous changes brought about by the war made it impossible to pick up where" he had left off, and so he had to "start all over again." He recalled that new start as "quite a task."

---

[5] This study (Erikson 1976) documents the social devastation of an Appalachian community after it was hit by a wall of water from a collapsed dam. A heavy loss of life, the total destruction of housing, and ill-conceived relocation efforts that separated family members and neighbors heightened feelings of demoralization and psychosocial trauma. A follow-up of adult survivors (Green et al. 1990) 14 years after the event found significant psychopathology in approximately one-fourth of the sample.

The quality of social relationships also plays an important role in how the immune system functions. For example, in discussing the relationship between life events and cancer, Paykel and Rao (1984) have linked individual disorders to external social stressors such as the lack of a confidant. The climate of postwar America did not favor the communication and sharing of wartime traumas and dislocations. For many people impatiently trying to get on with their lives, the war became a repressed past. In this context, veterans learned to bury within their psyches the lingering stresses and emotions of war.

The long-term health costs of this delay in working through war trauma could be significant. In their theory of inhibition, Pennebaker and Sussman (1988, 327; see also Herman 1992) conclude that "the work of inhibition serves as a low level but cumulative stressor. As will all cumulative stressors, inhibition over time is associated with increases in stress-related diseases." This theory suggests that people who experience wartime disruptions (such as the older entrants) encounter more adverse health effects later on in life because they have not shared the experience. Failure to talk about wartime experience may have tangible negative health effects. (Younger entrants, by contrast, had to deal more frequently with the stresses of combat.)

Retirement: General Trends

As we turn to retirement patterns, we note the growing complexity of retirement behavior in general. Simple distinctions between fully employed and fully retired are no longer adequate because they oversimplify the retirement process. Studies show that anywhere from one-fourth to two-thirds of men in recent cohorts are using some form of partial retirement such as "bridge jobs" between the end of a career and a full exit out of the labor force.[6] The careers of the Terman men during later life also exhibited diverse patterns of work exit.

The Terman study's detailed work histories enabled us to identify four patterns of retirement based on changes in the temporal pattern of time worked:

1. Gradual—almost half of the men in the sample exited from the workforce through a gradual reduction in the amount of time worked.

---

[6] The accumulating evidence on this pattern of late-life careers comes from a number of studies (Reimers and Honig 1989, Ruhm 1990, Beck 1986, Burkhauser and Quinn 1989, Gustman and Steinmeier 1984).

2. Abrupt—the second largest group of men (30 percent) retired through an abrupt exit. These men were working full time and then exited the labor force in a single transition.
3. Sporadic—approximately 16 percent were defined as having a sporadic pattern since they reduced their worktime by 50 percent or more and then substantially increased it at a later point in time. The majority of men in this category were those who completely exited and then reentered the labor force.
4. No Transition—finally, 8 percent of the men belong to the category "no transition" because they did not have a 15 percent or more reduction in their work time when last observed.

The relatively high percentage of men in the "gradual" category reflects the predominance of professional or executive positions among the Terman men. In general, these workers are more likely to have options for time reductions in their career or for transferring work skills to a less demanding job, such as consulting. Remarkably, the percentages are similar to those reported by Reimers and Honig (1989) in their analysis of the Retirement History Survey, a national study. They found that 35 percent of the men followed a traditional path, moving from full employment to full retirement in one step (analogous to our "abrupt exit" category). Fifteen percent returned to the workforce after partial or full retirement at some point in their retirement history (analogous to our "sporadic" category). They did not identify a gradual type of exit but concluded that 37 percent of the men spent at least some time in a state of partial retirement.

Retirement: Comparison of Younger and Older Entrants

How did military mobilization shape these patterns of work exit in later life? A strong possibility is that an increased likelihood of health problems among older entrants increased their risk of an abrupt exit from the labor force. Simultaneously, the relative earnings losses they experienced may prevent them from gradually reducing their work time during old age. Many in this group may have had to remain in the labor force full time during their later years to ensure pension support and make up for lost time. By contrast, younger entrants may have been better able to gradually reduce their work time during their later years because service entry did not have serious negative consequences for their health or their material well-being. Retirement patterns for this subgroup should match those in the nonveteran category.

Results in Figure 11.4 support these expectations. Across all of the groups, the typical path is gradual retirement through reductions in work time. However, the proportion who chose this pathway to retirement is low-

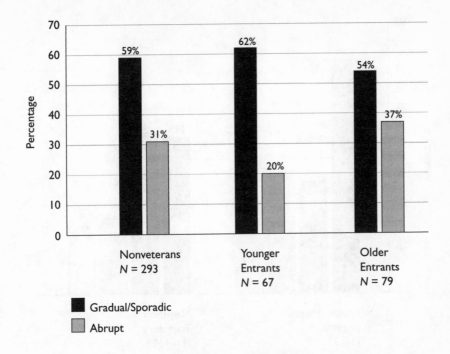

Figure 11.4 Retirement patterns of Terman men by veteran status and age at start of military service. $\chi^2(9,519) = 14.85$, p<.10. (Based on authors' tabulations from the Terman Archive.)

est among older entrants. These results are consistent with our hypothesized links between negative health, earnings losses, and patterns of work exit. Indeed, Figure 11.5 shows the strong influence of health on retirement patterns. Men who experienced negative health trajectories were more likely to exit abruptly from the labor force. (The lack of detailed information on assets, pensions, and social security benefits prevents us from considering other mechanisms that might link wartime service to retirement behavior through income histories.)

Conclusion

Using the unparalleled resources of the Stanford-Terman archive, we have compared men who entered military service before their thirtieth birthday and those who entered after the age of thirty-two years. The two cohorts are similar in family background and IQ, but the older entrants were further along in their life course at time of entry. They had more edu-

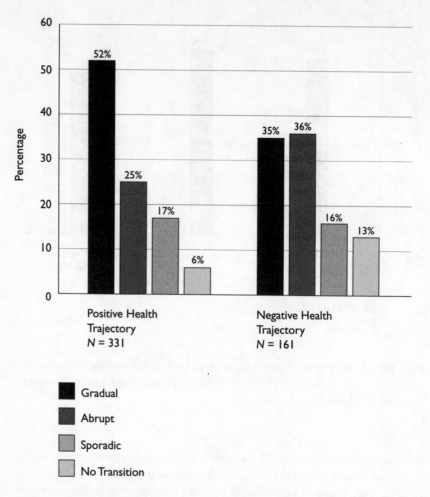

Figure 11.5 Retirement patterns of Terman men by physical health trajectory. $\chi^2(3, 492) = 18.1$, p<.001. (Based on authors' tabulations from the Terman archive.)

cation and were more likely to be married and have children before the war. We have shown that

1. The older entrants experienced a higher risk of divorce and separation.
2. Their careers were disrupted, and they had lower lifetime earnings than nonveterans, whereas younger entrants achieved higher earnings than nonveterans.

3. They experienced more negative health outcomes than nonveterans, whereas younger entrants experienced more positive health outcomes than nonveterans.

4. They were more likely than younger entrants to leave the workforce abruptly (possibly due to declining health), whereas a more gradual pattern of retirement typifies the late-life careers of younger entrants.

The contemporary significance of the experiences of older recruits from World War II can be seen in the policy decision to mobilize the U. S. Army Reserves for duty in the Gulf War of 1991. Reservists who served overseas typically had job and family obligations. Mobilization may well have disrupted their lives in ways that could have long-term adverse effects as well. Although these costs are likely to have been greater for veterans in the Second World War (owing to the greater duration of their service and overseas duty—the Terman veterans were in the service for at least three years, and often longer), these contemporary disruptions may have measurable effects.

With due caution for the generalizability of results based on a sample of talented men, this analysis has shown that *age differentiation produces cumulative disadvantages and advantages across the life course.* In the armed forces of World War II, recruits aged eighteen to twenty-eight were at a timely point in their lives to enter military service and derive benefits from it. But with the possible exception of military physicians, entry after age thirty-two placed men at greater risk of family instability, work-life and earning setbacks, and declining physical health.

C H A P T E R   T W E L V E

Diversity and Consensus:
What Part Does Religion Play?

J. Milton Yinger

What part does religion play in maintaining diversity and consensus in society? To provide a background for answering this question, I describe religious trends in the United States, noting that the United States is a surprisingly religious country with a great diversity of faiths. I then look at the effect on consensus of some of the peculiarities of religion in the United States: the separation of church and state; the rise of the religious right; how a religious "free market" increases religious participation and also consensus; and the role of a sort of "civil religion" that exists here.

Although there are some unifying trends, diversity of religion appears to be growing. One might expect that this is leading to less consensus, but paradoxically, even diversity can support a kind of consensus. I use the example of African American religion to explore this idea.

I conclude with some thoughts on how, through our mutual dependence on freedom of religion, we can begin to climb the steps of the ecumenical ladder, steps that include tolerance, conversation, cooperation.

Religion in the United States

Our ultimate task is to answer the question, "Is religion an important part of American consensus, or is it, due to the great diversity of faiths, a divisive influence?" Let us begin by looking at religion in the United States.

How Religious Is the United States?

The United States is widely regarded, by its people and by others, as a religious society—more than other urban, industrial societies by most measures. What are some of the facts that support this assessment? Church membership, which was about 17 percent in 1776, is now more than 60 percent (Finke and Stark 1992). In a series of cross-national surveys, adult samples from twenty countries were asked about the future importance of religion. The proportion who said it would be more important was lowest in France (13.4 percent) and highest in the United States (49.2 percent) (Campbell and Curtis 1996).

Numerous polls taken by Gallup and by the General Social Survey (G.S.S.) (1994) have found that more than 90 percent of Americans believe in God. *Free Inquiry*, a secular, humanistic magazine, believing that these polls were not accurate, commissioned a poll of its own. The result: 92 percent stated their belief in God ("Religious Belief in America: A New Poll," *Free Inquiry* 1996;16[3]).

Not all of such data, of course, should be taken as the gospel truth. The polling agencies involved have excellent records, but some sampling error is inevitable. More important, the temptation for respondents to give socially correct answers is quite strong. For many years in several polls, it has been found that 40 percent or more of Americans attend religious services at least once a week—three or four times the rates in Europe (Princeton Religious Research Center 1992; Smith 1991a). The G.S.S. polls from 1972 to 1982 found that 35 percent attended religious services nearly every week, every week, or several times a week. The 1988–94 percentages were slightly lower: 34 percent (adapted from the codebook, G.S.S. 1994). Using a variety of measures, Hadaway, Marler, and Chaves (1993) found the rates to be about half of the widely accepted 40 percent level. This is still significantly higher, one should note, than the rates for most European countries. On this question of America's difference, however, we would be wise to reserve judgment and wait for further study (Caplow 1998).

Diversity of Religion in the United States

The United States is often described as a society based on the Judeo-Christian tradition. I do not want to disagree strongly with that assertion. Some qualifications, however, are needed: The Judeo-Christian tradition has enormous variation and internal contradictions. Like all religions, it is influenced by its social, cultural, and geographical environments. Early Calvinism's "saved by God's election" may now resonate less strongly than Emerson's doctrine of self-reliance, at least in the middle and upper classes. "The expectation of a Holy Commonwealth to be brought into being on these shores by an act of God was restated as a vote of political confidence in the average man and his corporate ability to achieve a democratic Utopia" (Sperry 1946, 250; see also Hatch 1991). As Sperry put it, "God himself became republican."

Some of the founders of the United States were strongly influenced by the Deists and Encyclopediaists, with their intellectual and, indeed, naturalist leanings. Native American and imported African religious elements were important in the lives of some of the earliest Americans. There were, and are, some subtle influences from those traditions among Americans of European background. Some of us listen with appreciation to the Indian-Christian blend of Vine Deloria, Jr.: "Who will find peace with the lands? . . . Who will listen to the trees, the animals and birds, the voices of the places of the land? . . . The invaders of the North American Continent will finally discover that for this land God is Red" (1973, 66ff).

What, then, is the current mix of religions in the United States? Once again, lacking census data, we are dependent on sample surveys. The G.S.S. has regularly inquired about religious preferences in their interviews of English-speaking, noninstitutional-living persons eighteen years of age or older. Table 12.1 provides the results in broad categories.

By extrapolation, we can use these numbers as rough approximations of the religious self-identification among the 266 million Americans (as of October 1996). Perhaps we can smooth the approximations by noting several qualifying factors. Because the interviews were only with English speakers eighteen years of age and older, newcomers to the United States are underrepresented. We need also to note that the demographic mix in the years ahead, with associated religious preferences, will change quite drastically due to changing age pyramids. In 1995, the U.S. Bureau of the Census estimated that 15 percent of the elderly were of African American, Asian, Hispanic, or Native American backgrounds. However, 26 percent of those of working age came from those same groups, as did 33 percent of children under eighteen. When immigration from Hispanic and Asian countries is factored in, we realize that the relative stability of the religious mix noted in Table 12.1 may not be matched in the next twenty-five years.

There can be no question that diversity is a major element in the religious scene of the United States. America is home to

- more Roman Catholics than Italy;
- more Protestants than all of Europe, if Orthodoxy is seen as a Christian division separate from Protestantism;

Table 12.1. Religious preferences in the United States

	1972–82 (%)	1988–94 (%)
Protestants	64	62
Catholics	25	25
Jews	2	2
None	7	7
Other	1	3

Source: Adapted from General Social Survey 1994.

- 40 percent or more of the Jews of the world;
- rapidly growing numbers of Muslims, Buddhists, and Hindus who, within a decade, will probably number ten million or more;
- new religions by the dozens, some of them home grown, some imports from Asia, Europe, or Africa; and
- a syncretist Native American Church and scores of tribal religions.

And of course there is diversity within as well as among these divisions (Shurden 1993): Jesse Helms and Jesse Jackson are both Baptists.

Ethnicity Doesn't Necessarily Match Religious Preference

One often cannot trust one's intuitions about religion in the United States. For example, not all Americans of Asian background are Buddhists, Muslims, or Hindus. Perhaps 40 percent of Korean immigrants, for example, are Christians. Twenty percent of Hispanics are Protestants, reflecting the rapidly growing number of Protestants in Latin America (Martin 1990). There are about two thousand Catholic priests of Hispanic background in the United States, but Southern Baptists claim twenty-three hundred Hispanic pastors (Suro 1989). A large majority of the immigrants from the Philippines are Christians.

There are other indications that ethnicity and national background do not match closely with religious preference. Americans of German origin can be Protestants, Catholics, or Jews. Somewhat over half of the Irish in the United States are Protestants (albeit, most of their ancestors moved to Ireland from Scotland or England three hundred or more years ago). Most African Americans are Protestants, but 5 percent or more are Catholics, perhaps 2 percent Muslims, and 1 percent Jews.

It is important to remember that the 3 percent in the "other" category in Table 12.1, most of them in the three major Asian religions, represent eight million people. That will expand rapidly, perhaps double, as the total population of Americans of Asian origin is expected to expand in the next twenty-five years.

To get the full sense of the diversity of religions, we need to recognize how heterogeneous are these broad categories. Unitarians and Southern Baptists are listed as Protestants, as are Mormons and the Serbian Orthodox—to suggest the range. Black American members of the Nation of Islam are listed with immigrants from Turkey, North Africa, and Pakistan. Buddhist migrants from Taiwan, Sri Lanka, and Malaysia bring varying religious perceptions as well as other cultural differences to America.

Stereotypes sometimes hide this diversity. As we read the stories—or rumors—of Islamic terrorists, for example, we need also to study the adaptation of the three million or more Muslim Americans to life in the United States and the thoughtful reexaminations of Islamic faith. (e.g., Moore 1996; Arkoun 1994).

Trends

There are several trends we should note regarding religion in the United States. Differential birth rates, immigration, conversions (in almost every possible direction), intermarriages, new religions, surging membership in some churches and decline in others are dramatically affecting the American religious scene and its implications for consensus.

The small decline in the proportion of Protestants in recent years (from 64 to 62 percent), has not affected denominations equally. The so-called "mainline" churches (the older, more established denominations, with mainly middle- and upper-class members) have declined by 10 percent or more. Evangelical churches, particularly the more fundamentalist among them, have increased in number and membership (Marty and Appleby 1994, 1995).

These trends, however, have been moderated in recent years with losses being reduced, or even reversed, and the fundamentalists' gains being qualified by some sharp internal divisions (Niebuhr 1998). We need also to note that when G.S.S. respondents were asked about their general religious views—whether they were fundamentalist, moderate, or liberal—there was only a small shift to the right, if I may use that term, and a somewhat larger shift to the left, with the middle ground losing rather sharply (Table 12.2).

We get a somewhat different picture when the respondents were asked how they were raised, using the same three categories and combining the whole series. More indicated a conservative upbringing than are currently fundamentalist (a loss of 1.2 percent); more indicated a moderate religious background than their current views show (a loss of 1.9 percent);

Table 12.2. Religious views among Americans

	1972–82 (%)	1983–87 (%)	1988–94 (%)	Change in Percentage
Fundamentalist	29.1	33.6	33.4	+ 4.3
Moderate	51.5	41.9	39.7	–11.8
Liberal	19.1	24.5	26.9	+ 7.8

Source: Adapted from General Social Survey 1994.

but more called themselves liberal in their views than noted a liberal background (a gain of 3.1 percent). Along with the attention paid to the fundamentalist Christian Coalition, we need, in light of these data, to notice such events as the "Summit on Ethics and Meaning," which brought twelve hundred participants to Washington, D.C. (April 1996), to reinvigorate religious liberals.

One cannot know the number of individual changes from these data. Ten percent may have shifted into the fundamentalist category, for example, while 11.2 percent shifted out. On balance, however, these samples show a small shift in preference toward a liberal label. Perhaps we have not had a fundamentalist wave so much as a natural growth in size due to higher birth rates, slightly reduced by a shift in the liberal direction.

The number of Jews in the United States has grown, during the last quarter of a century, a little less rapidly than the total population. Low birth rates have not been entirely balanced out by immigration; gains from conversions have been somewhat smaller than losses (many associated with intermarriage). Meanwhile, their denominational preferences have changed somewhat. Several times during the 1988–94 period, the G.S.S. asked Jewish respondents not only for their denominational preferences, but also for the denomination in which they were raised (Table 12.3).

In recent years, we have heard often of the wave of "new religions" and new variations of established religions sweeping across America and other parts of the world (see, e.g., Miller 1997). Perhaps we need to see them against a historical background, not of an overwhelmingly dominant Puritan, or Puritan and Anglican, or even Puritan-Anglican-Methodist-Baptist background, but against a background of greater diversity. Catholics were among the earliest European settlers in North America, including some parts of what is now the United States. The first Jews came early in the seventeenth century. And we need now to add the increase, particularly since 1965, in the number of Muslims, Buddhists, and Hindus.

Table 12.3. Changes in denominational preferences among Jews 1988–94

	Preferences (%)	How Raised (%)	Change in Percentage
Orthodox	3	15	−12
Conservative	36	39	−3
Reform	42	34	+ 8
None of These	20	12	+ 8

Source: Adapted from General Social Survey 1994.

Equally important for a history relevant to the diversity and consensus theme is the repeated appearance of new religions proclaiming their "outsiderism," in a "language of dissent," as Moore put it. These new religions see themselves—in a paradoxical way—as part of America's consensus on freedom, arguing for the right to diversity (Moore 1986; see also Bainbridge 1996; Marini 1982; Robbins and Palmer 1997; Yinger 1982, Chapter 11). This interpretation may overcorrect American religious history. It does, however, pose a basic question: Does American religious diversity, built upon continuous early and recent waves of denominations, sects, and cults, contribute to or weaken American cultural consensus?

Is Religion a Source of Consensus?

Defining Consensus

First, what shall we mean by the word consensus? The dictionaries give us a wide choice. It is harmony, cooperation; it is unanimity or general agreement in matters of opinion or evidence, or a unifying trend. Consensus denotes a general connection between the different parts of a nation's civilization. Surely we must treat it as a variable, not as an attribute; and that opens the possibility of examining the ways in which the various kinds of diversity in a society weaken consensus or contribute to it.

Several years ago I suggested that we might gain important insights into ecumenical trends by seeing them along a range, or as steps on a ladder from toleration to conversation, cooperation, federation, and integration. It may be useful to think of consensus in the same way. We can also draw on the ideas of Robin M. Williams, Jr., who transforms the term "consensus" into a valuable sociological concept by such observations as these:

> Several factors weaken consensus: sharp differentiation in occupations and
> class; diverse cultural backgrounds; the indirect and quasi-anonymous nature

of many activities [what E. A. Ross called long-distance sin against persons distant and unknown]; and rapid changes in the social structure. (Williams 1970, 602–604)

Common values are not enough to maintain consensual behavior. Both consensus and the reliable application of sanctions are required. Or, as Williams put it in a different context, consensus rests not only on common values but also on the recognition of interdependence. This statement may summarize his point of view: "The main kind of agreement upon values that remains possible is a consensus not upon specific ends and particular actions, but upon relatively generalized principles, or upon inclusive and relatively unexplicit symbols" (Williams 1970, 241).

Traditional View That Religion Increases Consensus

The belief that religion is a source of consensus and of integration in a society is at least as old as Confucius. Rites bind the multitudes together and "serve as dikes against the excesses to which people are prone." Millennia later, many philosophers, anthropologists, and sociologists—probably thinking of religiously homogeneous and sometimes quite isolated societies—shared this view. The primary function of religion, to Durkheim, is a preservation of social unity: "So everything leads us back to this same idea: before all, rites are means by which the social group reaffirms itself periodically" (1947, 387).

This is not to say, I must add, that any particular religion is good, even if it is a unifier. It may help to preserve a social order that from an outside perspective is quite unacceptable, due, for example, to its support of human sacrifice, slavery, gross inequalities, or holy warfare.

Church and State

Moving beyond Confucius, and even Durkheim, two topics appear when we examine the integrative influence of religion in the United States or other urban, industrial, heterodoxical societies: What is the relationship of church and state? And is there a "civil religion" that to some degree bridges over the lines separating the several religions? Here I can scarcely more than ask these questions.

The First Amendment to the U.S. Constitution states that "Congress shall make no law respecting an establishment of religion, or prohibiting the free exercise thereof." Jefferson spoke of "this loathsome combination of church and state." Tocqueville believed that, by the First Amendment, the United States strengthened religion and smoothed the relationships between religion and politics.

While a Durkheimian might claim that religious diversity undercuts faith and social influence by reducing the plausibility of each of the faiths, a stronger case can be made that in the United States the opposite effect is true. The universalistic religions, at least, are seriously constrained by close connection with the state (Yinger 1970, Chapter 19). Weber's analysis of this relationship is regularly confirmed: Where religious values collide with the demands of statehood, religion will almost always lose. "The state's absolute end is to safeguard (or to change) the external and internal distribution of power; ultimately this end must seem meaningless to any universalistic religion of salvation. . . . It is absolutely essential for every political association to appeal to the naked violence of coercive means in the face of outsiders as well as in the face of internal enemies" (Weber 1968, 334).

Kenneth Thompson makes a similar point from a religious perspective rather than from Weber's analytic perspective: "Men and Women yearn for a perspective that transcends all the fragmentary purposes of human existence. Politics and nationalism remain fragmentary endeavors" (1986, 14). One suspects that Thompson is expressing his hopes rather than what he has observed. Today we see that political dominance is sought by Hindu extremists, Buddhist nationals in Southeast Asia, Muslim fundamentalists in Iran, where they are in power, and in many other lands where they seek such power. We also see Jewish fundamentalists in Israel, surrounded by sharply opposing Islamic states, and Orthodox Serbians (seeking statehood in Bosnia) who have no fear of the constraining effect of Christian universalism.

The evidence, I believe, is clear. At least when judged by democratic standards, the separation of church and state is essential. Demerath and Straight put it well: "[T]he logic behind a secularly neutral state with a free-ranging religious polity is that each *complements and constrains* the other" (1997, 50, italics added). We should not forget that the absence of an established church does not mean the absence of state influence on religion. In many ways the state affects religion—some of them intended, but most of them unintended and unexamined. The state exerts its influence by laws, court decisions, taxation rulings, welfare policies, support or neglect of education, military actions, and in other ways (see Wuthnow 1988).

Rise of the Religious Right

Is the United States in danger of consensus-shattering religious nationalism? Are the small breaks in the wall of separation of church and state that have occurred likely to be greatly enlarged by the highly visible Christian Coalition? For generations, the federal government, at least, was dominated by upper-middle-class and upper-class white Protestants, who are still heavily represented among the cultural and power elites (Davidson, Pyle, and Reyes 1995). They have had no specifically religious agenda, however, nor does their cultural world seem to be shattering.

This is not how it seems to the lower-middle-class and working-class fundamentalists, however. G.S.S. data in the early 1980s indicated that about 25 percent of the respondents were part of the "Moral Majority," as they were often called at that time, whether or not they were members of the organization by that name. They expressed dismay at what they saw as cultural degradation. Direct political actions, however, were seldom taken. They were more likely, in fact, to criticize such actions (Bromley and Shupe 1984).

By the late 1980s, a "Christian Coalition," part of the "religious right," drastically modified that point of view by organized political activity. I will not try to assess the reasons for the recent convergence of interests between some fundamentalist Christians and some politicians. There are observers who see this increased political involvement as an effort on the part of the religious right to respond to modernization, urbanization, and globalization. In this view, the Christian Coalition is a direct descendant of the Moral Majority, but is more sophisticated or perhaps just more dismayed at what they see as moral decay. Others see the religion-politics connections as a case of conservative secular elites and their ideological spokesmen "hoodwinking" some religious conservatives into working against their own interests, with little to show for their efforts (for a range of views see Lind 1996; Hodgson 1996; Wilcox and Rozell 1995; Marty and Appleby 1997; Davis and Robinson 1996; Manza and Brooks 1997; Lienesch 1993).

From the large and diverse literature on this topic we can draw several conclusions relevant to our interest in consensus and diversity: The 25 percent of respondents to various polls who could be classified as part of a religious right has not increased in number, although it has become much more visible. We should not, however, draw too sharp a line between fundamentalists and others with regard to values and attitudes (Dimaggio, Evans, and Bryson 1996; Davis and Robinson 1996). We should recognize that the religious right is not a monolithic movement. Politics is the art of compromise; and those seeking to protect a treasured ideology will respond in different ways to the dilemmas that are faced when politics and ideology meet. The actions of leaders are not routinely supported by the less articulate members. Catholic and Protestant fundamentalists are very uncertain political allies, because Catholics, who tend to agree with the fundamentalists on cultural questions, are more likely to agree with progressive Protestants on economic and social issues. When the Catholic bishops issued a pastoral letter, in 1984, endorsing government efforts to guide the economy and to provide welfare, the Rev. Jerry Falwell saw the letter as pointing the way to communism. A religiously diverse set of critics (George

Will, Charles Krauthammer, and Norman Podhoretz) were equally critical of the pastoral letter (Steinfels 1985; see also McBrien 1982; Canadian Conference of Catholic Bishops 1988).

The free expression of the fundamentalists' political views is as legitimate, in my view, as expression by Quakers, Unitarians, and the social action committees of many Protestant denominations. The slightly cracked wall between church and state may, as a result of recent politically oriented activity by the Christian Coalition, lose a few more chips (Wilcox and Jelen 1995). I believe, however, that consensus on the First Amendment remains quite strong. Meanwhile, as the country struggles with the stress produced by continuous and major social and cultural change, tolerance, conversation, and cooperation—steps up the ladder of consensus—remain of critical importance. There is a fairly strong consensus, for example, on the belief that abortion, although often the lesser of two evils, is not a positive good. While preserving the right to an abortion, would not a wise policy emphasize the need for strengthening programs to reduce the number of infant and maternal deaths, unwanted pregnancies, and neglected children? Such programs can be supported by both opponents and supporters of the right to an abortion, except for those for whom even the first level of consensus—toleration—is unacceptable.

A Religious Free Market

To return to the theme of this section, we can ask: Has the separation of church and state weakened religion in the United States, perhaps due to the lack of a powerful supporter and defender? Williams has written: "Added empirical support and conceptual elaboration has been given to the hypothesis that religious pluralism [which almost by definition implies such separation]—at least in the United States and most Western European nations—strengthens organized religion by providing a 'quasi-ethnic' collectivity as a focus of identity and social location" (1973, 180). That hypothesis is still being studied and upheld. Finke, Guest, and Stark further document the fact that a religious free market—pluralism and competition—increases religious participation (1996).

In light of the sharp controversies among religious groups and the political activism of some, are we in the early stage of breaking down the constraining-supporting relationship of free religion and democratic politics? I think not. Yet "eternal vigilance" is required on the part of all who seek a democratic polity *and* an unconstrained religious context. If this is true, societies that are putting severe limits on the range of permitted religious expressions (e.g., China, Iran, Russia, Israel, India—at varying levels of intensity) are at the same time limiting—in some cases by intent—the development of democratic polity. There are, of course, countercurrents and ambiguities in each of these situations. This is true particularly of India, with its 120 million Muslims, millions of Buddhists and Christians, the great diversity among its Hindus, and the continuing influence of the Gandhi tradition.

An established or dominant church, with prohibition, repression, and even persecution of other faiths, does not prevent diversity. It creates oppositional groups that are likely to match intolerance with intolerance. Diversity that protects a common interest in freedom of religion encourages tolerance, conversation, and cooperation.

One thinks of a story told by James Zogby, president of the Arab-American Institute. As a leader of the political-action group for Arab Americans he was having difficulty, although a Democrat, making contact with Bill Clinton's campaign. So Zogby called Senator Lieberman, an Orthodox Jew, who arranged a contact with George Stephanopoulos, Clinton's communication director, through whom he secured a meeting with Clinton, to everyone's satisfaction. As reported by David Broder, "Zogby made the obvious point: 'Only in America would an Arab American spokesman call a Jewish American senator to call a Greek Orthodox campaign operative to let us help a Southern Baptist get elected president'" (Broder 1992).

A Civil Religion of the United States

Does a "civil religion" help maintain the separation of church and state while bringing a kind of overarching religious consensus to the United States? Robert Bellah sees a "religious dimension of political life" that provides "a transcendent goal for the political process," which stands under the judgment of a higher law (Bellah 1992, 1967). The Supreme Court has held that "we are a religious people whose institutions presuppose a Supreme Being" (Raab 1964, 16), a view spoken or inferred by most presidents. "You cannot otherwise explain our government except on the basis of a deeply felt religious faith" (President Eisenhower, quoted in Raab 1964, 16). After the Gulf War, President Bush declared, "I should have made more clear that God is our rock and our salvation" (Walker 1991).

None of this refers, of course, to a particular institution or doctrine. "The propitious smiles of Heaven can never be expected on a nation that disregards the eternal rules of order and right which Heaven itself has ordained" (quoted by Bellah 1967, 7–8). Those, of course, are the words of George Washington in his first inaugural address. President Eisenhower was agreeing with his predecessor, but when he added to his statement about the need for a religious faith "and I don't care what it is" he made some staunch churchmen shudder. Does it make no difference, they wondered, what faiths are embraced? I imagine that Eisenhower was not being casual or indifferent. He was suggesting that the American way of life was based on a shared foundation of religious values. That has always been a questionable assumption. It has become more problematic, I believe, as America has become more diverse. We can see, however, that even this greater diversity can support the consensus on religious freedom.

I will not extend this comment on civil religion further except to say that civil religions, even if anchored in a kind of general understanding, have a strong tendency to drift toward a religious nationalism, to proclamations in one language or another of "Gott mit uns"—proclamations that undercut any consensus that rests upon religious universalism (Bellah 1992; Gehrig 1979; Hughey 1983; Juergensmeyer 1993; O'Brien 1988).

Unifying Trends in the Midst of Diversity

As noted, diversity is a major element of religion in the United States. At the same time social forces are softening the lines of separation and modifying the diversity of religion in America. There are splits, but also interdenominational consultations and denominational unions that tie together, for example, locally separate black and white churches. The United Methodist Church routinely assigns its black bishops without reference to the racial makeup of their jurisdictions. Black-white separation is the norm in local congregations, but the G.S.S. reports that 40 percent of their respondents attend church with persons from the other race (most commonly a small number).

On the individual level, religious intermarriage both reflects and affects the softening of the lines of separation. A special census report in 1957, based on a sample of thirty thousand, found that 12.1 percent of Catholics, 4.5 percent of Protestants, and 3.7 percent of Jews were intermarried (U.S. Bureau of the Census 1958). Studies by the National Opinion Research Center indicate a very large increase: about 40 percent among Catholics and 18 percent among Protestants. (The numbers are about equal, but because there are about two and a half times as many Protestants as Catholics, the percentage of intermarriages is lower.) A survey made by the Council of Jewish Federations reported that before 1965, 9 percent intermarried; for those married since 1985, the rate was 52 percent (Steinfels 1992; Smith 1991b). In about half of these marriages, one of the partners converted to the faith of the other. Several million persons raised as Protestants are now Catholics or married to Catholics. Several million persons raised as Catholics are now Protestant or married to Protestants. The numbers are smaller with reference to Jews, but hundreds of thousands are involved.

What do these numerous religious intermarriages mean for American diversity and consensus? Do they indicate a decline in the strength of religious commitments, making it easier to intermarry? Does it show an increase in toleration, a reduction of prejudice? Does it show some convergence in polity and doctrine as diverse churches adapt to the changing American scene? I believe that all of these statements are true, although I cannot judge their comparative or their collective weights.

One might think that by softening the lines of separation, these group and individual unions are reducing the diversity of religion in America. However, the trend toward diversity noted earlier is a much stronger force. Is this diversity a barrier to consensus? Not necessarily. There are several components to consensus, some of which diversity supports but others that it inhibits. Diversity discourages consensus thought of as harmony and unanimity, but it makes possible consensus in the form of cooperation and common purpose among people with very different interests.

An Example: African American Religion

A glance at religion among African Americans can help us to test this proposition—that diversity actually *supports* consensus building. The experience of slavery powerfully affected African American religion; and as it developed, African American religion powerfully affected the experience of slavery. The resulting beliefs, practices, institutional structures, and patterns of leadership have been major influences, even as they have been adapted to freedom, industrialization, and urban life.

Early studies emphasized what I call the "shield element" in the religion of African Americans. It developed as a way of protecting its adherents from the cruel blows of slavery. A common theme is that suffering is only a prelude to ultimate victory and reward; power comes from suffering.

More recent studies have emphasized not only adaptive but also aggressive elements in black religion. It was a sword as well as a shield. "We must be struck by the appearance of one or another kind of messianic preacher in almost every slave revolt on record" (Genovese 1970, 34–35; see also Raboteau 1978).

After emancipation, the protest theme was muted in the churches of small towns and rural areas; but among the growing urban population it became more and more prominent. It became a vital part of the civil rights movement, not only through the lives of the major leaders, but also through the courage of thousands of nameless participants. I will not try to document but will only assert that African American churches and their leaders, often hand in hand with white churches and leaders, have been major players in that movement during the last half century (Baer and

Singer 1988; King 1963; Lehman 1988; Lincoln 1984; Lincoln and Mamiya 1990; Murphy, Melton, and Ward 1993; Lewis and D'Orso 1998).

Even if the present mood of the country inclines many toward the belief that the movement for racial justice has stalled, perhaps even gone into reverse, we need not deny the reduction of prejudices nor the improvement in educational, economic, and political opportunities for some black Americans. The figures on the rate of unemployment (persistently twice as high for blacks) and on income (60 percent of the white rate) are well known. We need, however, to put them alongside the gains: an expanding middle class; an increase from three to thirty-nine black members of Congress in forty years; an increase from 51 percent (1980) to 73 percent (1994) of black men and women finishing high school; an increase from 8 percent (1980) to 13 percent (1994) of blacks earning college degrees.

Preceding and leading the legal and political changes was the civil rights movement. Gary Wills gives an eloquent description: "There is no nobler sequence of events in American modern history than the marches and sermons and jailings that brought about the end of Jim Crow laws in the South. Men, women, and children, blacks and whites together, ministers, rabbis, priests, and nuns joined hands for a moment to protest without violence. Their stunning challenge to society was this: 'We have more will to go on being beaten than you have will to keep beating us.' They backed up that defiance with patient suffering, enduring jeers, spittle, dogs, blows, hoses, jails, and death" (1996, 62).

The Role of the Dissident

You may agree with my emphasis on the consensus-building influence of a diverse group, with many of the members religiously motivated, if the reference is to Martin Luther King, Jr., Andrew Young, or even the more combative Jesse Jackson. But what are we to do with Louis Farrakhan? He broke with the American Muslim Mission when it began to speak in a less harshly separatist tone to emphasize Muslim tolerance (Lee 1996; Mamiya 1982; McCloud 1995; Muhammad 1980; Whitehurst 1980). "I could understand this shift," Farrakhan declared, "if the White man had improved just a little. But the devil hasn't changed. If anything, he's gotten worse" (Muhammad 1978). Farrakhan has recently hailed Gadhafi as a brother and champion of human rights.

"The simplest thing is to attack Farrakhan as an uncivilized man. The wisest thing may be to see him as an early (or even late) warning signal— a kind of fever marking the course of a serious illness in American society" (Yinger 1994, 269). The conditions that lifted him into prominence, winning some followers and many others who, judging from their own experience, believe he is telling it like it is, are still widespread, despite significant improvement (Patterson 1997; Shipler 1997; Wilson 1996). The conditions for the poorest third are desperate. If we can't hear Farrakhan's shrill message, we can listen to Emile Durkheim, who emphasized how a society can learn from its deviants. Cultural deviation in a complex society, despite its divisive effects, can be part of a process whereby old inequities are broken, neglected standards renewed, and new values given a field for growth. Can we learn, from such deviant responses as those of Farrakhan, to reassess the prevailing standards and the degree of their neglect? On the whole, the media and the rest of us have done the simplest thing: forget the sources of the discontent and attack the messenger. Instead let's listen to Shakespeare, through the words he gives to King Henry V:

> There is some soul of goodness in things evil,
> Would men observingly distill it out . . .
> Thus we may gather honey from the weed,
> And make a moral of the devil himself.

This example from African American religion shows how diverse groups can cooperate with each other when confronted with a common purpose, and even dissident voices can play a valuable role. Taking a look at the bigger picture, do the diverse religions in the United States as a whole have similar common ideals?

Conclusion: How to Get Along with Each Other

How can culturally and structurally different religious groups live together in the same society and contribute to a conflict-reducing consensus? Let me offer a few sweeping generalizations—even more sweeping than some I have already made.

The rock-bottom requirement—if the consensual influence is to outweigh the divisive influence—is religious tolerance. "Toleration makes difference possible; difference makes tolerance necessary" (Walzer 1997, xii). This does not come easily to some of those who see the United States as simply a Christian country. Tolerance does have wide cultural support, however, and other steps up the ecumenical ladder—conversation, cooperation, federation, and even integration—are not uncommon.

Further adaptation to life in an urban, heterogeneous, and rapidly changing society on the part of all religions may bring them closer together. This may require a readiness to accept very different histories, myths, and metaphors as deeply similar ways of responding to the human condition (Marty and Appleby 1997). Is it possible to be religiously modest?

The development of more conflict resolution practices that prevent differences from escalating into sharp antagonisms is essential. This requires a recognition of common interests and common problems.

Consensus might be strengthened by an overarching civil religion that is not tied to an historical and often imaginary past of religious homogeneity and, more importantly, is not an instrument of the state. This would require far more support and nourishment from those who emphasize universalism in religion than is now common. The temptation to bend a civil religion to the purposes of the state and party are enormous.

Such developments as these, I believe, are possible only to the degree that social and religious ignorance, discrimination, and the great inequalities of power and income are reduced.

From my point of view, moreover, we ought not to assume that a very high level of consensus is, ipso facto, good. Nor ought we to assume that diversity is good only if it is somehow folded into the larger set of understandings by a kind of anthropological appreciative understanding.

These judgments rest on several observations:

The cultures and practices of all societies contain, along with their glorious elements, the flotsam and jetsam of the historical passage. These harmful residues may be accepted, even fought for, as part of a sacred tradition, a consensus, by diverse members of a society.

Dissidents in a society can point clearly, for those who would see, to the weaknesses in culture and the failures to live up to acclaimed standards. We do not have to like Louis Farrakhan or agree with him, as I have suggested, to learn from him. It is easier, however, to create enemies, the Other, or—if I can stretch the meaning of the word—witches in an effort to reinforce a narrow consensus to which the majority have become accustomed and from which we profit. Dissidents can make it more difficult for us to do that.

Changes in the modern world are so continuous and so dramatic that we are as much in need of established techniques of adaptation and reformation as we are in need of substantial consensus. We cannot secure the latter without developing the former.

Even were there a much fuller consensus in the United States than we have now, the question of how to live with great diversity would still be with us, for we are tied as never before into global structures where consensus often means only that we have laboriously attained a small set of mutual concessions. Nationally and internationally, the great need is for increased skill in climbing up the ecumenical ladder to tolerance, conversation, and cooperation.

Hang on. We're in for a strenuous ride.

C H A P T E R   T H I R T E E N

Diversity in American Families

Judith Treas

ociologists who study America's families used to emphasize common features of form and function. For much of the twentieth century, sociologists described families as conjugal units—married with children—that went about the business of getting income, supporting constituents, socializing children, and rooting individuals in a broader context of class and community. Sociology textbooks enshrined this particular family type, as their titles reveal: *The Family: A Dynamic Interpretation* (Waller 1938), *The Family: From Institution to Companionship* (Burgess and Locke 1953), and *The Family: Its Structure and Function* (Coser 1964). Textbooks pointed out that some U.S. groups would not or could not meet middle-class norms, but textbook treatment of these exceptions tended to underscore the unitary logic of American family life in much the same way as did textbook chapters on the Chinese or Russian family.

Today, privileging a single family type has gone out of fashion. Books bear titles that are nonjudgmental, inclusive, or noncommittal, as evidenced by *Families: What Makes Them Work* (Olson and McCubbin 1983), *Marriages and Families in a Diverse Society* (Wolf 1996), and *New Families, No Families?* (Goldscheider and Waite 1991). These semantic changes recognize that many Americans live in something bearing little resemblance to "the family" described in out-of-print textbooks. Changes in academic sociology also acknowledge that the hallmarks of family life—enduring social bonds, emotional ties, and supportive relationships—also characterize many other types of intimate arrangements.

How these changes in the scholarly portrayal of American family life came about speaks as much to political and ideological currents as to demographic and behavioral ones. What began as a feminist critique of the patriarchal family came to embody demands for greater appreciation of a wide variety of family arrangements. Although there has been a numerical shift away from the most common residential family type (i.e., husband-wife families with children) in favor of other living arrangements, Americans remain divided as to whether family changes are all for the better or represent some disturbing new development. Not even family experts agree (Stacey 1996). For better or worse, diversity in American families is an empirical fact.

This chapter begins by reviewing demographic changes in American family life in the second half of the twentieth century. Many trends point to greater diversity, but others maintain family continuities. Unmarried cohabitation, for example, has affected the household categories of couples far more than activities and relationships within households. Today, immigrants, whose behavior is shaped by practical opportunities and constraints as well as by cultural tradition, offer intriguing examples of accommodation and resistance to assumptions about how family life is organized. Law, blood, adoption, and co-residence underpin conventional definitions of family. Because these definitions are increasingly inadequate to describe Americans' families, many people are pressing to expand definitions of kith and kin in keeping with broad legal developments favoring greater choice in family life.

Trends since Mid-Century

Fewer and fewer people reside in a family consisting of a bread-winning father, homemaking mother, and two or more children. As McLanahan and Casper (1995) point out, the family depicted in 1950s situation comedies has become increasingly rare. The nuclear family celebrated in early television series was a historical anomaly in many ways. The one-earner family became possible only after economic affluence and the "living wage" permitted an ordinary male breadwinner to earn enough to support wife and children. Also, this married-with-children stage in the life course engaged so many Americans only because the 1950s had unusually high rates of early marriage and baby-boom levels of fertility (Cherlin 1992). Even in the 1950s, not everyone lived in families like the Nelson's or the

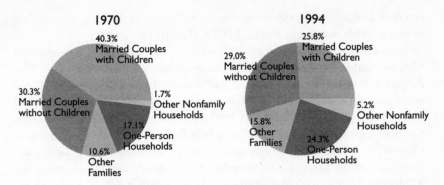

Figure 13.1 American households by type: 1970 and 1994. (Adapted from Rawlings and Saluter 1995, vii.)

Cleaver's. The childless Mertzes drawn into Lucy's domestic intrigues were a reminder that many Americans lived different family lives.

Today's families are apt to involve dual-earner couples, with or without children, married or not, same sex or heterosexual. There are also unmarried adults, including many single parents raising children. Figure 13.1 shows that as recently as 1970, 40 percent of households consisted of husband, wife, and one or more of their own children under eighteen years of age. By 1994, married couples with children had declined to 26 percent of all households. A growing proportion of households with children did not contain a married couple, and more adults lived outside families altogether. Almost a quarter of households consisted of one person living alone.

Slow to Marry, Quick to Divorce

Buoying 1950s families were young Americans who were quick to the altar and then had their first child early in marriage. Today, single people are slower to marry, and married ones are slower to have children. Although marriage and parenthood were once graduation requirements for adulthood, these expectations have weakened, and more Americans move through the life course without taking on these family obligations. Among women aged thirty to thirty-four, those who had *never* married climbed from 6 to 20 percent between 1970 and 1994; among men of these ages, the figure rose from 9 to 30 percent (Saluter 1996, v). Americans also put off parenthood. In 1992, 41 percent of women aged twenty-five to twenty-nine had never borne a child. Among forty- to forty-four-year-old women (those nearing the end of their childbearing years), 16 percent remained childless. These women were half again as likely to be childless as comparable women in the mid-1970s (Bachu 1993, xii).

If Americans are slower to marry, they are quicker to divorce. Compared with the following decades, 1950s divorce rates were relatively low. The divorce rates rose steeply from the 1960s to the 1980s (Cherlin 1992), and some demographers predicted that one in every two marriages would end in divorce (Martin and Bumpass 1989). At nearly half of weddings today, the bride, groom, or both have been married previously (U.S. Bureau of Census 1995, Table 143). At one in every seven weddings, one or both partners has tied the knot at least twice before. Thus, remarriage often creates a "blended" family with an elaborate web of kinship, support, and custody. Due to increases in divorce and in out-of-wedlock births, fewer than three-fourths of American children in 1991 were living with two parents; only half resided in nuclear families composed of only their two biological parents and perhaps full siblings (Furukawa 1994, 3).

Rise in Cohabitation

The rise in cohabitation is another remarkable change. For every one hundred married couples in 1970, there was only one heterosexual unmarried twosome living together; by 1994, there were seven unmarried couples per one hundred married ones (Saluter 1996). With more Americans living together, surveys reported that American public opinion became more tolerant toward cohabitation (Thornton 1989) and premarital sex in general (Smith 1994). Once, only poor folks and bohemian youth lived together outside marriage. But today, well-educated professionals freely cohabit as do middle-aged divorced people and the occasional senior citizen (Gronveld-Hatch 1995). By the late 1980s, half of Americans aged thirty to thirty-four reported having cohabited (Bumpass and Sweet 1989).

Changes in Women's Lives

Changes in families are no more impressive than changes in the lives of women in families. In the midst of the 1950s baby boom, married women often devoted themselves to full-time homemaking. American women today are apt to combine paid work outside the home with unpaid housework. Women's workforce involvement has risen, notably for mothers of young children, mothers who were most likely to be occupied at home. In 1975, 67 percent of married mothers with children under three years of age were outside the labor force; by 1994, 60 percent of women with young children were in the labor force (U.S. Bureau of Census 1995, Table 639). Married-couple families increasingly rely on two earners to make ends meet, and work offers women greater rewards—better jobs and better pay—than in the past (Bianchi 1995).

Of course, there are trade-offs. Many two-earner couples are more strapped for time than they are for money (Hochschild 1997). The most popular campaign promise in the 1996 presidential election offered new mothers a twenty-four-hour hospital stay to rest up after the birth of a child. Married couples' time together has declined (Kingston and Nock 1987), and shift work accommodating child care has increased (Presser 1995). Domestic multitasking is the order of the day, as cellular phones make it possible to schedule the plumber from the sidelines of the child's baseball game! When it comes to money, dual-earner families do offer children more economic security. In families in which both parents work full time, only 2 percent of children newborn to age seventeen are poor compared with 10 percent when the father works full time and the mother is a full-time homemaker (Hogan and Lichter 1995). Worst off financially are children in single-parent families: Even if the parent works full time, 13 percent of youngsters in father-headed families and 19 percent in mother-headed families fall below the poverty line.

Documenting family changes is relatively easy. Explaining them is more difficult. Take divorce. One argument holds that women's increased economic opportunities fostered an "independence effect" (Cherlin 1992). No longer dependent on a husband's paycheck, a working woman could afford to put off marriage, to divorce, or to raise her children on her own. Without much evidence, conservative political commentators argue that welfare programs extended this "independence" even to the poor. Others blame men for a wholesale retreat from commitment (Ehrenreich 1983); it may be that young men's eroding economic prospects make it harder for them to take on a family breadwinner role like their fathers or grandfathers did in the 1950s (Wilson 1987; Oppenheimer 1994). Clearly, a number of forces—economic, demographic, and ideological—have been acting on America's families, and their effect has been an increase in their diversity.

Countercurrents

There is no question that people today have more choices about family life and are subject to fewer normative constraints. They can marry or not, have children in and out of wedlock or not, find love with partners of the same or opposite sex. If their choices do not meet with everyone's approval, they can join communities and social worlds where they are more welcome. The focus on diversity, however, may lead us to miss several issues: areas of continuity in family; life stages where living arrangements point to greater uniformity; and diversifying trends that have turned back on themselves.

There will probably always be some constituency for family conventions. Although the freedom to choose invites experimentation with family form, some still prefer to follow well-worn paths as they grow up and grow older. Just as many people buy their clothes off the rack, their personal computers with a standard software package, and their autos without optional equipment, many Americans opt for familiar family arrangements. They move predictably from stop-gap singles arrangements to married couple to husband-wife families with children to empty-nest couple to widowed, single-person household. While some chafe at clear-cut expectations for age, gender, and sexual relations in conventional family life, others are comforted by this predictability.

Cohabitors' and Older Americans' Greater Uniformity

Nor have innovations in family life been as revolutionary as was once hoped or feared. Despite the increase in couples living together outside marriage, much basic family building—rather than being derailed by cohabitation—is still on track. When cohabitors are added to the numbers married, young people are almost as likely to have paired off as in the past (Bumpass, Sweet, and Cherlin 1991). Divorced people move on to new unions about as rapidly as in the past, even if these unions are often cohabitations (Cherlin 1992). About half of the increase in families headed by single fathers is due to cohabitation; that is, to the fact that unmarried couples with children are categorized as families headed by an unmarried man (Garasky and Meyer 1996). While cohabitors hold less-conventional views of marriage than married people, heterosexual cohabitors are nearly as likely to expect sexual exclusivity of their partners (94 percent versus 99 percent) (Treas and Giesen 1996). Nor is cohabitation a long-term marital alternative: Most cohabitors go on to either marry or break up, and Americans also tend to trade cohabitation for marriage before—or shortly after—the birth of a child. While cohabitation has reshuffled household types, the activities and relationships we associate with couples remain remarkably intact in these unions.

The growth of the older segment of Americans has, of course, shifted the population away from the younger ages that populated 1950s sitcom families. The resulting increase in childless husband-wife and single-person households certainly diversified American families. A focus on later life, however, shows that older Americans have actually achieved greater uniformity in their own family arrangements. Thanks in large part to the growth of Social Security and Medicare, older adults are the one segment of American society that has become more economically secure. With fewer financial constraints, older people can now afford to realize their preferred living arrangements—residing independently rather than making their homes with grown children or others. Typically, older couples live together until one dies, and then the survivor carries on alone. Almost *all* community-dwelling Americans sixty-five or older are living in their *own* homes. In 1990, 84 percent of older women were either the householder or the spouse of the householder—an increase of 30 percent over 1950. Similarly, more than nine out of ten older men lived in their own homes (Treas and Torrecilha 1995). Given the experience of America's elders, might younger Americans also settle into more uniform family arrangements if their economic prospects improved?

Diversity in Reverse

Most trends run out of steam sooner or later, putting another brake on diversity. While virtually everyone recognized the increase in divorce, how many noted when the divorce rate topped out in the 1980s (Cherlin 1992)? Even the pendulum of public policy can retrace its path. For better or worse, there are legislative initiatives in several states to repeal "no fault" divorce statutes in a perhaps futile effort to make more married couples stay together. Demographic trends often turn back on themselves. After the baby boom, many wondered whether low fertility signaled a full retreat from childbearing. The fertility decline could not be sustained indefinitely, however. In 1992, total fertility had climbed to a level not seen since the early 1970s (U.S. Bureau of the Census 1995, Table 93). Another reversal is evident for out-of-wedlock births, where increases in births to unmarried teenagers have been followed by recent declines (Shogren 1996). Of course, if trends are sustained long enough, behavior associated with a minority becomes the dominant pattern. The increase in married women's labor force participation has made two-earner couples the norm, even in privileged social classes where historically wives did not work for pay.

Greater diversity in family structure dominates trends, but diversifying trends coexist with countervailing forces. As occurred for older people, Americans might achieve more uniformity at some points in the life course if improved economic prospects reduced financial constraints on family choices. This is especially plausible for young adults, because rising age at marriage, coupled with cohabitation, means that many couples' first big purchase is the wedding itself. If trends peak (or bottom out) or new modal patterns of family behavior emerge, the mix of family types may also change.

Immigrant Families

The counterculture of the 1960s inspired cohabitation. In the 1990s, it is the immigrant population that has introduced innovations in family life. The past thirty years have seen record numbers of immigrants arrive in the United States. Unlike earlier waves of immigrants, these new-comers are an economically diverse group that hales from non-European origins, particularly Asia and the Western Hemisphere (Fix and Passel 1994). Bringing their own cultural notions about how domestic life should be organized, they also adapt in novel ways to the new needs, opportunities, and constraints they face in the United States. They adapt not by copying conventional American family forms, but by creating new—perhaps temporary—family arrangements (Blank 1998).

However much immigrants might like to replicate their previous family patterns in the United States, they face many impediments. One constraint is demographic. Immigrants, particularly new ones, are hard put to reconstruct kinship connections in the United States—the combination of parents and children, aunts and cousins that formed their original family. The general pattern in international immigration is for one family member to establish a beachhead, gradually bringing kin to the United States after becoming sufficiently established (Zhou 1997a). Of course, refugee families, torn by war and political repression, face particular hardships in reconstituting families. Separations and sacrifices associated with the immigrant experience also disrupt family building. To get a financial toehold in the United States, save up money, or support family members abroad, marriage may be postponed. Childbearing may also be deferred (Massey and Mullan 1984).

Even when kin are close at hand, there may be good reasons to organize family life in new ways. Elderly people who have looked forward to a bed by the fire in the middle of family activities may not relish an "in-law" apartment over the garage in an American suburb lacking places to walk to, good public transportation, and neighbors who speak a familiar language. Subsidized senior housing among co-ethnics may be more attractive than residing with grown children who are too busy making a living to offer companionship. According to anecdotal evidence (Matloff 1996), even very filial immigrant communities may have elderly people live apart from kin to qualify for public benefits (Treas 1997), because the practice frees up money to buy a home, send grandchildren to college, and otherwise advance the family fortunes. Whether an elderly newcomer winds up residing with adult children or not, living arrangements in the United States reflect unique constraints and opportunities posed by this society, not just cultural expectations formulated in a distant homeland.

Complex Households

Immigrants, particularly newcomers, adopt an assortment of non-family, multifamily, and extended family arrangements characterized by complexity and crowding. For example, a dozen male day laborers—perhaps from the same Mexican village—may share a single motel room in a transient neighborhood, economizing on rent so they can save up the money they need to return home more quickly. Where housing costs are high, unrelated families, cooking in shifts, may crowd a three-bedroom house. Elsewhere, a new immigrant makes his home with his cousin's family until he learns the ropes, gets a job, makes friends, and moves out on his own. In poor neighborhoods, the households burst at the seams, and their residents spill out into makeshift living quarters in garages or garden sheds.

Newcomers' living arrangements have captured public attention, even sparking legal efforts to limit the number of residents per household. None of these living arrangements are new to American society, however. Complex households are time-tested ways that immigrants have coped with unfamiliar cultures, limited resources, and absence of closest kin. Immigrants' objective conditions make complex households necessary. The nonfamily, multifamily, and extended family arrangements they adopt are not necessarily preferred even in their countries of origin (Blank 1998), but culture may shape their choices in other ways. To the extent that immigrants hold different standards for privacy, hospitality, and personal space, they may well be more accepting of complex living arrangements than are native-born Americans.

The adaptation of newcomers stands in contrast to trends for the rest of the population. Recent generations of native-born Americans have not had to put up with crowded living conditions and complex households. Although boarders were once a common feature in American households (Modell and Hareven 1973), affluence has permitted Americans to enjoy more private and spacious accommodations (Myers and Wolch 1995). At the same time, leases, zoning regulations, and building codes have thrown up legal impediments to expanding households to make room for new circumstances and new members. Most Americans' complex living arrangements are largely confined to transitions of relatively short duration that punctuate the life course (e.g., friends sharing housing while launching careers or the newly divorced returning briefly to the parental home). Our reluctance to take shelter together may contribute to the growth of the homeless population. Immigrants' acceptance of big, complex households facilitates their survival and incorporation into American society.

Parachute Children

Although the large, complex households of recent immigrants are usually a response to low incomes, not all immigrants are poor. Affluent immigrants have adopted their own practices to meet family needs. At both ends of the age spectrum are intriguing examples of innovative family practices that reflect a characteristic accommodation of material aspirations and family ties.

Consider the young immigrants called "parachute kids" (Chou 1996). Estimates based on visa applications put their numbers at more than forty thousand arriving since the 1980s (Hamilton 1993). Living and studying in the United States, these youngsters go about their lives without the close family supervision that Americans deem appropriate for juveniles (Zhou 1997b). Under the legal guardianship of a complete stranger, two teenage brothers from Taiwan live together in a large, if sparsely furnished, house while attending high school in a wealthy California suburb. A twelve-year-old student from Korea is left in the care of an elderly housekeeper. While parents pay children's expenses, they cannot directly monitor offspring's homework, friends, or well-being, because they continue to live and work outside the United States.

These arrangements allow children to obtain U.S. educations. American schooling is accessible and prestigious, leading to English proficiency and a successful professional career. Parents expect children to study hard and gain admission to an elite university. Only on rare occasions do parachute kids come to the attention of the general public, perhaps because they become involved in gangs, neighbors complain about noisy parties, or school officials grow concerned about their welfare. Although their age calls attention to their circumstances, parachute kids are part and parcel of a more general ethos of immigrant family life. Separations from loved ones and other hardships are tolerated because of a shared commitment to advancing the family's prospects. The result is often a transnational family with a foot in two or more nations.

Bicontinental Grannies

Aspirations for economic advancement also underpin a global diaspora of highly educated technicians, scientists, and professionals from the developing world—a development that creates transnational families with branches in several continents. The aging widow who resides with her son in Delhi may have a daughter in San Diego, a son in Toronto, and another son in London. Elderly Iranians and Taiwanese find themselves in similar situations. The matriarchs and patriarchs of transnational families often live lives unimaginable in the days before air travel.

Affluent immigrant offspring can afford not only to send money home to parents, but also to bankroll their parents' trips to visit them. Because elderly retirees have more flexible schedules than do kin working and studying in the United States, older people's visits can be timed for special occasions (e.g., weddings) or periods when it is nice to have extra help (e.g., the birth of a baby or children's summer vacations). Nor are parents' visits necessarily once-in-a-lifetime affairs. Arriving on a six-month visitor's visa, the elderly become semipermanent members of the household—enjoying American amenities and returning home only long enough to tend to business, visit friends, shop for ethnic staples, and obtain another visitor's visa.

Older people with several offspring living abroad sometimes move seasonally from home to home, living first with one family for a few months and then with another. When queried about these arrangements, their U.S.-born grandchildren assert that the attention lavished on elderly relations is part of their ethnic culture and that their families are very traditional. Only when pressed will they allow that traditional family arrangements would find their grandmother firmly planted in the home of her eldest son, not crossing continents to rotate between the households of various offspring. Cyclical residential moves across long distances are taken for granted in many ethnic communities in the United States. In developing countries, having an elderly person rotate residences is a support adopted only by those in extreme poverty. The routinized and extended visits of the elderly are an example of novel adaptations that immigrant families—in this case relatively well-off ones—make to their lives in the United States.

Rethinking the Family

Conventional notions of household and family—established definitions and typologies based on legal relationships, common residence, and/or biological links—are useful for charting changes, but they cannot capture the rich variations in American family life. Among our intimate "family" circle, many of us number individuals who do not qualify as close family members by blood, marriage, adoption, or co-residence.

Personal Definitions of Family

In the African American community, an extended family network may include people—some even favored with kinship terms like "aunt"—who are not relatives, strictly speaking (Stack 1974). Lesbians and gays insist on families of their own choosing, constituted of partners, friends, ex-lovers, and kin with whom they share strong personal ties (Weston 1991). More and more people talk about coworkers with affection once reserved for close relatives (Hochschild 1997). In store displays of Mother's Day cards, the "Like a Mother to Me" section stands as testimony to family feeling for non-kin. When divorce and remarriage create "blended" families uniting people with indirect ties, a child may have more contact with her stepbrother's grandparents than her own. Even our understanding of families in nature is being revised to recognize that family groups can transcend taken-for-granted arrangements. Among the gibbons of northern Sumatra, what seems a conventional nuclear family turns out to be a widower, a female who has deserted her mate, and two unrelated, adolescent runaways whom they have taken in (Small 1995, 18).

Personal definitions of family—unencumbered by rigid roles or kinship rules—hold considerable appeal. They offer expanded behavioral options and the flexibility for people to work out arrangements to meet their individual needs, preferences, and constraints. Although new definitions of family sometimes encounter resistance in American society, the notion is far from revolutionary. Expanded choices in family life are consistent with the evolution of family law and social mores. In the past, whether and whom one married were constrained by parental consent requirements, by ecclesiastical incest rules applied even to distant kin, or by prohibitions against mixed-race marriages. Most of these barriers to marriage have been gradually eliminated (Glendon 1989, 35–84). Similarly, instead of a few narrow grounds for divorce, marriages today can be ended for any reason by either partner. Rights to parent have also increased: Disability is no longer regarded as a good excuse for involuntary sterilization, and poverty is no longer seen as a good enough reason to remove children from the parental home.

At Odds with Official Family Designations

While there is greater acceptance of individual choice in family life, more than personal relationships are at stake in the social construction of who is and isn't family. Given relationships confer specific rights and obligations. These relationships determine who is admitted during hospital visiting hours and who is not. They say who must give court testimony against a defendant and who can decline to do so. They specify who is obliged to provide financial support. In the event of death, they fix who inherits in the absence of a will, who qualifies for Social Security survivor benefits, who can claim the body, and who can attend the funeral without loss of pay. They determine who can authorize a minor to participate in a school field trip and who will be covered under employer-provided health insurance plans. They spell out who can join immigrant kin in the United States and who is shut out.

As American families become more diverse, we confront more questions about what relationships qualify as family ones; what sorts of relationships merit interventions, protections, or benefits; what constitutes a creative adaptation to new social circumstances and what constitutes a social problem. Bureaucracies charged with protecting children, paying benefits, or administering estates want clear-cut rules to follow in settling competing claims and assigning responsibility. Husband-wife and parent-child relationships are universally recognized and easy to verify. Courts, schools, insurance agencies, welfare departments, and personnel offices prefer these sorts of formal kinship categories over the informal relations many of us favor in our daily lives. If only as a money-saving measure, governments and employers limit family benefits to kin that they designate, not the more expansive and perhaps expensive "families we choose." Public agencies and private businesses have been slow to validate relationships that are not already universally accepted.

Seeking Greater Rights

With so much riding on official family designations, we all have a stake in having "our" particular relationships recognized—above and beyond desires for dignity, legitimacy, and social validation. "Is it fair," ask people whose lives don't fit bureaucratic categories, "to privilege some relationships and some family forms above others?" Contesting narrow definitions of kinship, people with "orphaned" relationships want formal standing for unions that have not been legally acknowledged in the past. They want to extend to their relationship the rights already enjoyed by other family members. Cohabitors demand to register their unions with city bureaus, and lesbians and gays mobilize to have same-sex marriage recognized by church and state. While grandparents' place in the family tree is secure, they, too, have been seeking greater rights. All fifty states have passed laws affirming grandparents' right to contact with minor grandchildren. Ironically, the older generation has also lobbied to be classified with non-kin in order to be paid for their grandchildren's foster care. Grandparents' demands, of course, reflect other changes in family life, such as more divorce in the middle generation and growing numbers called on to raise grandchildren when troubles arise in their children's lives (Furukawa 1994).

Protection of Minors versus Rights of Minors

If they include minors, families—especially unconventional ones— are pressured to demonstrate that they meet children's needs. After all, our families are those that adults choose, but children have little choice but to go along (Rapoport 1989, 65). Regrettably, there is little agreement in American society as to what sorts of families are best (or even minimally adequate) for kids, and concerned adults won't find easy answers in scholarly research. We are told that organized child care is fine *if* it is quality care. Divorce is better for kids *if* the marriage is characterized by a great deal of open conflict. Furthermore, many Americans do not have the luxury of choosing the family arrangements that they think optimal. They struggle to make the best of what they have, perhaps sharing housing or putting up with kin who have obvious shortcomings. Their family preferences are constrained by the circumstance of their lives.

There are surely limits to free choice in families just as there are limits to free speech, but it is not always clear where to draw the line. In one California county, for example, the social service department had been quietly helping pregnant teens marry their babies' fathers (Lait 1996a). In one case, everyone involved favored marriage to ensure the baby would be supported by a young man with a steady job. The couple, who shared a room in his mother's home, were devoted to one another. The young woman testified that her partner's concern had gotten her out of gangs, off of drugs, and into school. Her mother, a struggling single parent unable to provide much supervision and security at home, approved of the match.

The difficulty was that the pregnant bride was a fourteen-year-old junior high school student. Her fiancé was twenty-two, and sex with a minor is a criminal offense. Some officials urged that he be prosecuted, but others reasoned that he would not be able to support his family if he went to jail. The observation that the girls encouraged to wed were all Hispanic sparked further controversy. The social service department said it was only respecting Mexican culture, one where early marriage is accepted. Others charged the agency with racism in treating Latinas differently than other pregnant teens and in stereotyping a poor, immigrant population.

Is the pregnant teen a child who needs to be protected from predatory adults or a precocious woman who should be free to choose her family? How much weight should be given to the opinions of the couple's parents? Is the baby better served by a single mother or married parents? Can a grown man who has sex with a girl be trusted to support her and their child? Will the girl's age leave her powerless and vulnerable to marital abuse? Do poverty and the risks to unsheltered teens in low-income neighborhoods justify compromising ideals about family life? Should immigrants have to conform to American family norms or should cultural differences be recognized? And, who is to say what constitutes a genuine cultural difference anyway? The social service agency ultimately chose to abandon matchmaking in favor of legal prosecution, even as a successful married couple in an upscale community stepped forward to reveal that they, too, had once been teen parents with doubtful futures (Lait 1996b).

Conclusion

The family of breadwinning father, homemaking mother, and their children has declined numerically since its brief heyday in the 1950s. Working moms, single parents, and unmarried couples now command our attention. Today, immigrants are a source of innovation in family life, because their family preferences are shaped by new opportunities in the United States as well as by the constraints of immigrant experience. Growing diversity has introduced new possibilities for the organization of families and loosened the normative constraints that once dictated a fairly narrow range of behavioral options. Realizing preferences does not invariably lead to more diversity, however. The family lives of older people have become more uniform, because greater economic security permitted more older Americans to realize their preference for independent living.

While many changes in American family life have been neatly captured by conventional definitions of family, new developments have opened up discourse on what counts as family and who counts as kin. Expansive definitions of family—with caring as a common denominator—are consistent with many aspects of our lives. Family innovations, however, have to contend both with the requirements of bureaucracies and with concerns about how well they can provide for children. Especially when the interests of adults, kids, and the state collide, new issues outpace cultural consensus on the right thing to do.

C H A P T E R   F O U R T E E N

Television and Diversity:
The Quantum Leap Model

James Lowell Gibbs, Jr.

The persistent diversity *and* division of the American people are strongly stamped in our nation's television viewing habits. A recent BBDO special report[1] reveals a trend toward strongly compartmentalized viewing habits and niche-oriented programming: Blacks watch shows targeted to a black audience and whites watch shows intended for a white, "mainstream" audience. Some view this trend as celebrating our society's diversity, while others view it as perpetuating its divisions. Is compartmentalized viewing inevitable? Or, can television programming support commonality and consensus, or lessen divisiveness?[2] Only a few television shows in the past decade have had significant appeal to both black and white audiences. This chapter explores lessons from a popular television series that chalked up such crossover appeal, yet had further, unexploited crossover potential, *Quantum Leap*.

---

[1] BBDO (1997a). The unnamed author of the BBDO report is Doug Alligood, Senior Vice President, Special Markets, BBDO.

[2] Rich sources on the ways in which African Americans and African American culture are treated in the media are Dates and Barlow (1990) and Gray (1995). The latter focuses specifically on television and includes chapters on individual television shows that have wide appeal to black audiences: *A Different World, Frank's Place,* and *In Living Color.* Another excellent, more focused, source is Jhally and Lewis (1992), which presents a very detailed analysis of *The Cosby Show.*

Compartmentalized Viewing

For twelve years the New York office of BBDO, a large advertising agency, has issued an annual report on black television viewing. For the last seven of these years, the report has tracked a strong split between the viewing preferences of black American households and total American households (BBDO 1997a, 1). Widely reported in the general media, the findings of the 1997 BBDO report revealed that, in the 1996–97 prime-time network television season, "only one of the top 10 and four of the top 20 most popular shows in *black* households are among the most popular with total viewers" (BBDO 1997a, 2, emphasis added). The crossover show among the top ten of black viewers is (number 9) *NFL Monday Night Football* (BBDO 1997a, 2). The other three crossover programs are further down, being in the black top twenty. They are *Walker, Texas Ranger* (number 14); *Cosby* (number 15); and the *NBC Monday Night Movie* (number 18) (BBDO 1997a, 2). When the top twenty shows among black viewers are perused for how they rank with *total* viewers, a *very wide gap* in black versus total (mainstream) preferences emerges (BBDO 1997a, 2).[3] "Black primetime network TV viewers . . . continue to demonstrate strong preferences for shows pertinent to the black experience" (BBDO 1997a, 4).

[3] "For example, *Living Single* ranked 1st in black households but only 84th with total households; *New York Undercover,* 2nd in black households, was 87th in total households; and *Moesha,* 5th in black households, was 103rd in total households. Similarly, *Seinfeld,* 2nd in total households, was 68th in black households (BBDO 1997a, 2).

I would like to acknowledge the support of Phyllis Moen and Donna Dempster-McClain of Cornell's Bronfenbrenner Life Course Center, organizers of the symposium honoring Robin M. Williams, Jr., and editors of this book. I would also like to thank Prof. Williams for his encouragement, friendship, and colleagueship extending back some forty years.

Thanks also go to my colleague, Sonya A. Greier of the Graduate School of Business, Stanford University, who guided me to obscure print sources on the media, to a timely television special on black/white viewing patterns, and, thereby, to sources for Nielsen ratings on *Quantum Leap.* John Carman of *the San Francisco Chronicle* also provided a useful hard-to-find piece of information.

Early helpful clues for sleuthing Nielsen ratings were provided by Allan Johnson of the *Chicago Tribune.* Barry Cook, Vice President of Communications at Nielsen Media Research, also was helpful in this regard. Nielsen ratings for *Quantum Leap* were provided by Tim Brooks, Director of Research, USA Network; by Horst Stipp, Director of Social Development of the National Broadcasting Company; and by Jeff Dellin of Universal TV. I'm grateful to all of them for their crucial assistance.

Norma Sessler and Tracy Snyder of the Media Department and Public Relations Department of BBDO New York enabled me to receive the *BBDO Special Report* quoted here and the news release pertaining to the report.

Drafts of this paper were read by Jewelle Taylor Gibbs, Shirlee Taylor Haizlip, and Katherine L. Armstrong. It benefited from their comments and observations, for which I am highly appreciative.

As Doug Alligood, author of the report, observes, "[B]lack viewers want to see themselves represented on the TV screen" (BBDO 1997b, 4). And, as Allan Johnson points out, "[T]he top five shows in black households each . . . features a predominantly black or multiracial cast, unlike the counterparts on the mainstream list of TV shows" (Johnson 1997).[4]

In 1996 and 1997 the top ten shows among black viewers, in rank order were (1) *Living Single,* (2) *New York Undercover,* (3) *Martin,* (4) *Family Matters,* (5) *Moesha,* (6) *Malcolm and Eddie,* (7) *The Jamie Foxx Show,* (8) *Boy Meets World,* (9) *NFL Monday Night Football,* and (10) *The Wayans Bros* (BBDO 1997a, 2).

However, it's not that blacks simply want to see black performers or black roles *per se.* "Dramas like 'ER,' 'NYPD Blue,' 'Law and Order' and 'Homicide' all feature African-Americans as part of the ensemble cast. These black characters are important parts of their respective shows. But . . . none of these programs shows up among the 20 shows favored by blacks" (Johnson 1997).

Thus, most shows top-rated in black households had black performers in prominent or starring roles. Alligood (cited in Johnson 1997) tellingly uses "two shows (with) premises of friends hanging out together *[Friends* and *Living Single]* as examples of how simply placing blacks in supporting roles won't necessarily pull black audiences in."

Not surprisingly, the 1992 BBDO report revealed that "blacks are turned off by shows that feature embarrassing racial stereotypes and situations" (Maines 1992, 9). But, paradoxically, there are stereotyped dimensions to some of the roles and many of situations in the shows top-rated in black households (O'Connor 1997, 46). But, then, stereotypes of one sort or another are diagnostic of sitcoms and many popular television genres (cf. Gray 1995; Hass 1998).

Compartmentalization by Age

The 1997 BBDO report singles out three important new trends in the compartmentalization of black and total television viewing habits. The first relates to age. In the 1996–97 television season, in contrast to past years, the viewing preferences of blacks generally did not vary by age. The notable exception is the viewing preferences of blacks older than fifty in their top twenty list of preferred shows. Among this age group

[4] On the matter of the basis on which blacks make their viewing preferences, Abby Kearse, who wrote and produced the MTV half-hour TV special "Black and White TV" (MTV News 1997), observed that "the biggest issue or common theme that we found is that people have been making their choices based on the need for identity and being able to relate or identify with the characters that they're watching" (cited in Johnson 1997, 3).

Walker, Texas Ranger (number 1) leads *Cosby* (number 2) on a list dominated by other CBS shows including *Touched By An Angel* (tied for third), *60 Minutes* (number 7), *Early Edition* (number 13), *Promised Land* (number 14), *Dr. Quinn, Medicine Woman* (tied for fifteenth), *Ink* (tied for fifteenth), *Diagnosis Murder* (number 18), and *Moloney* (tied for twentieth). (BBDO 1997a, 3)

We can conclude that black viewers over age fifty are less compartmentalized in their viewing than younger viewers.

Compartmentalization by Network

The fact that the list of top twenty shows preferred by blacks over age fifty is dominated by CBS programs becomes particularly significant when set against the second new trend laid out in the 1997 Alligood report: "Fox, UPN [United Paramount Networks], and WB [Warner Brothers channel] network programs dominate the overall black household top 20 with a combined total of 12 shows" (BBDO 1997b, 1). As Tim Brooks has observed, since cable television has become a more significant player vis-à-vis the broadcast networks, the *network itself* (especially the cable networks) is what is targeted at a particular audience (Brooks, personal communication, April 1997). The network rather than the show aims to be the viewer's television "home" (cf. Brooks and Marsh 1995, xx–xxi).

Crossover Appeal to Younger Viewers

The third trend presented in the BBDO report concerns an additional relationship between age and viewing patterns. Shows "pertinent to the black experience . . . [especially those] with plots revolving around situations that are predominantly black" are popular with black viewers under age fifty (BBDO 1997b, 4). These same shows also have crossover appeal to many younger *nonblack* viewers (age twelve to twenty-four) (BBDO 1997b, 4). "Perhaps because of style, [and] language and attitudes toward 'the establishment,' [these] shows appeal to many younger viewers, regardless of race" (BBDO 1997a, 4). Elsewhere the report's author observes: "As for young people, they are more racially aware and often more tolerant than previous generations. Their popular culture is more ethnically inclusive and color is not as important an issue for them" (Alligood 1993, 74). In short, younger people are more willing to cross racial boundaries in their television viewing, in their music listening, and in their fashions (cf. Hass 1998, 37).

The crossover choices of older (age fifty and over) blacks and younger (age twelve to twenty-four) whites remind us that *demographic attributes other than race* also shape alternative viewing habits. They challenge the notion that racially compartmentalized viewing is inevitable. But, if it is not necessarily inevitable, what can be said of its future?

What Is the Future of Compartmentalized, Segmented Viewing?

There can be two primary responses to the increase in compartmentalized, segmented viewing patterns.

The Pluralist View: Embracing Diversity

The first view is rooted in the pluralist view of American society. It sees compartmentalized viewing as reflecting the reality of American society and the distinctive life styles that characterize races and ethnic groups. But we should not accept this position uncritically. Thus, Alligood notes that black viewing preferences should not be taken as reflective of *actual* black life *per se* but, rather, as "a measure of preference [made] from the programs [actually] available to viewers who watch prime time network TV" (BBDO 1997a, 4). While the selection of shows pertinent to the black experience available today is greater than in past decades, they still present only certain dimensions of black life and concerns (Gray 1995).

Among the dimensions of African American life little represented on the television screen is the life of professionals in fields other than medicine—say law, accounting, or academia. Serious (as opposed to comedic) treatment of family also largely is lacking. A historically critical institution, slavery has not been examined in depth, particular from the inside point of view. Here, the contrast with the treatment of the holocaust is noteworthy. *Overrepresented* on television is the role in black life of athletics and the world of rappers and entertainers. These shortcomings notwithstanding, shows rated in the top twenty by black viewers play an important role in affirming African American identity (cf. footnote 4).

Another View: Divisive Segregation

The second response to compartmentalized viewing patterns is not to accept these viewing patterns as a given, but to question their long-run value:

In recent years, the movement from broadcasting to narrow casting, from mass markets to "niche" or target markets, and the rise of new media, has led to a new form of segregation: programming targeted at exclusive clusters of demographic characteristics; reconstructed media ghettos demarcated along age, ethnic, class and life-style lines. These markets are increasingly segregated publics; how will anybody know how the "other half" lives? (Duncombe and Mattson 1995, 1)

Will compartmentalized viewing patterns hold as the demographic profile of the American population changes drastically in the next century to become one with a nonwhite majority? Given the facts, reported above, that black viewers over age fifty are less compartmentalized in their viewing than younger viewers and that younger viewers of all races are more prone to crossover spectatorship, what will overall viewing habits look like as baby boomers and, thus, the entire population ages (cf. Alligood 1993)? Will compartmentalized viewing and niche-oriented programming simply perpetuate diversity and division, or can they also support consensus and commonality?

Quantum Leap as a Broader Model for Diversity-Enhancing Programming

Can the large, diverse viewing audience that characterizes the United States share a common television focus other than *NFL Monday Night Football* or the *NBC Monday Night Movie?* The crossover success of *The Cosby Show* in the 1980s and the less spectacular success of the 1990s *Quantum Leap,* a show profiled below, both suggest "yes."

One element of *The Cosby Show*'s appeal was its base in universal themes, themes characteristic not just of black families, but of all families (Jhally and Lewis 1992; Alligood 1993). Yet, because *The Cosby Show* sites its universal theme in a black family context, the show has particular appeal to black families, who seem themselves reflected in it (Jhally and Lewis 1992; Alligood 1993). Because *Quantum Leap*'s episodes focus on more than one ethnic group, its *potential* crossover appeal would seem to be greater than that of any other show, including *The Cosby Show.*

Quantum Leap: A Case Study

Quantum Leap is a science fiction series that ran for three years on NBC. Using an unusual premise, it enables viewers to identify with both the hero, a white male, *and* others of varying ethnicity and gender. By doing so, it attracts white, "mainstream" viewers as well as black viewers and helps them to appreciate diversity itself.[5]

The hero in *Quantum Leap* is a white, midwestern physicist, Dr. Samuel Beckett, played by Scott Bakula. Dr. Beckett, or "Sam," invents a time machine

---

[5] Following the thrust of the BBDO report and much reporting of compartmentalized viewing in the media, the black/white polarity is used for the moment. Later it will be noted that nonblack viewers of *Quantum Leap* are not just whites but, significantly, persons of all ethnicities and races.

that can transport him into different decades. He travels through time, "leaping" into the bodies and identities of persons facing life crises to set things right, after which he is propelled into his next challenge.

At the beginning of each episode, Sam discovers himself in another person's body and identity. Typically, he does not know who he is until he sees himself in a mirror or other reflecting surface. Those around him see and hear him as the persona into whom he has leapt. For the purposes of this chapter, we'll call this person the "leapee." In his leaps, Sam is accompanying by an observer, Al, played by Dean Stockwell. Al is a hologram invisible and inaudible to all but Sam, small children, and certain animals. He is the link between Sam and the master computer, Ziggy, that controls the leaps and transmits information about the leapee and that person's life, including the "odds and reasons for Sam's current situation" (Brooks and Marsh 1995, 847; Wiggins 1993). This information, relayed by Al, helps Sam to figure out not only what problem in the leapee's life he is supposed to set right, but how to do so without changing history—a stricture under which he must operate.

The first innovation of the *Quantum Leap* concept is that the transformation of Sam's leaps is not simply to experience the identity of the other, as in the Hollywood genre referred to as racial transformation films (Gibbs 1996), which includes films as diverse as *Black Like Me* (1964) and *Trading Places* (1983). Rather, the leaps have an *ethical* intent (Wiggins 1993).[6] Sam leaps into another person in order to make a life-altering intervention. In doing so, he not only fixes a problem in the leapee's life, *he imparts a lesson to the audience.* The *Quantum Leap* episodes are nothing if not morality tales. They combine some of the entertainment value and adventure of, say, *Magnum, P.I.* with the moral uplift of *The Waltons*.

Quantum Leap Episode "The Color of Truth"

Many of the *Quantum Leap* episodes deal with racial issues. One of them, "The Color of Truth,"[7] apparently was inspired by the film *Driving Miss Daisy* (1989). In it, set in North Carolina in 1955, "Sam leaps in as an elderly black man, Jessie Tyler, the chauffeur of a prominent white woman. Unaware that he is black, Sam sits at a white lunch counter and sets off a

---

[6] Wiggins presents an excellent, detailed analysis of the ethical issues treated in the *Quantum Leap* series and characterizes the "ethical stance of the show [as] liberal egalitarianism" (1993). A strength of her paper is the detailed way in which it documents how that governing stance is played out in the various ways that episodes treat a range of ethical issues that confront our society.

[7] This episode and several other episodes from the *Quantum Leap* series are available for sale or rental in VHS videotape format from several commercial outlets. And, as of this writing, they still are in syndication on the Sci-Fi Channel.

chain of events leading to a near-death and forcing Jessie's employer to champion the cause of equality between the races" (Wiggins 1993, 112).

In contrast to racial transformation films, *Quantum Leap* does not accept the racial hierarchy as a given. Because the series is moralizing at heart, each episode that deals with race imparts the lesson that racial prejudice should be fought and the equality of all people recognized (Wiggins 1993, 112).

It should be noted that *Quantum Leap*'s implicit stance on the causes of durable inequalities in American society is almost naive. The series' emphasis is on the responsibility of *individuals* for ethical actions rather than on the faults of institutions or the dominant structures of society. Thus, *Quantum Leap* does not directly criticize the institutions of American society. Rather, it suggests how individuals can behave more ethically within those institutions.[8]

The second striking innovation of the *Quantum Leap* concept is that the persons into whose identities Sam leaps are diverse, not only in race, but in gender, ethnicity, religion, age, occupation, class, sexual orientation, and ability/disability.[9] Sam becomes a very wide variety of personas including, for example, a rabbi, a Mafioso, a mentally retarded young man, a young woman who has been raped, a mother of teens, a gay naval cadet, a college professor, even a laboratory chimp!

In having Scott Bakula play a completely different "leapee" character in each episode, the series employs an "anthology" format. This is one of its dramatic strengths.

Why did *Quantum Leap* take this particular tack of featuring a diversity of roles when other television shows did not? Part of the answer lies in the diverse creative and production staff of the show. Donald P. Bellasario, who is the executive producer and main creative force (and also the creator of the television series *Magnum P.I.*) (Chunovic 1993, 156) has an Italian background. Deborah Pratt, who is *Quantum Leap*'s co-executive producer, writer, and occasional director of episodes (and is also Bellasario's wife) is African American (Chunovic 1993, 156). In many of the episodes that she directed, located in a narrative with a feminist thrust, Sam leapt across the gender line into a woman. The multiracial, mixed gender composition of the producers, writers, and actors contributes to the authenticity and power of *Quantum Leap* as a vehicle for portraying the life of the Other.

---

[8] Katherine L. Armstrong has suggested that the American public's concern with *individual responsibility* is a key element underlying the popularity of the current television series *Touched by an Angel*. (Katherine L. Armstrong, personal communication, March 1997.) Each episode, like *Quantum Leap*, carries a moral. In addition, the fact that a lead character, the head angel, is a black woman also bears its own diversity-related moral.

[9] There is at least one episode of *Quantum Leap* centered on each of these enumerated themes.

Quantum Leap Episode "A Song for the Soul"

In another relevant episode, Sam leaps in as Cheree, a young black woman who is a member of a singing group similar to The Supremes, as they were first getting started. Sam saves Lynette, one of the trio, from being raped by a would-be promoter who is a pimp. He also persuades her not to leave school to make it as a singer and reconciles her with her minister father.

In episodes like this one, in which Sam's leap crosses the gender line, the transformation effect for the average viewer is engaging and transfixing. Perhaps because of this, the transgender leaps are a powerful vehicle for imparting ethical messages about gender issues such as sexual harassment and discrimination against women.

The transformation mechanism in *Quantum Leap* is more intense than in Hollywood's racial transformation films (cf. Gibbs 1996). In contrast to those films, Sam does not simply "pass" or put on blackface or whiteface. He actually *becomes* another persona—in both body and identity. It is the very intensity of this kind of transformation that creates its power as a vehicle for the vicarious experiencing of diversity.[10] Trying on first one race and then another, then one gender and the other, one age and then another, and so on, the *Quantum Leap* audience is exposed to the experiential dimension of the lives of many different Others. On a deeper level, some of their fears about difference and the piercing of racial or other boundaries may be alleviated *or* exacerbated through identification with the experience of the hero on the television screen. The *Quantum Leap* audience is exposed to the diversity of this society in a way that few people are in everyday life.

The hypothesis argued here is that fears are alleviated, that the series takes the audience not only to enhanced understanding of diversity, but to greater *acceptance* of it. This is because the episodes use the absorption generated by the narrative and its leap as a "teachable moment" when a moral can be imparted tellingly. The Walton-like moral increases the possibility of an episode leaving a viewer with greater acceptance of the kind of Other who is the focus of the narrative. Some of the intrapersonal dynamics that underlie the effects of this outcome are listed in the approaches for the

[10] Even *Star Wars* has been shown to involve a powerful quasi-racial transformation. From Guerrero's work we know that science fiction is not always as egalitarian in its stance as *Quantum Leap*. In an insightful analysis, he details how *Star Wars* can be read as a racial allegory. In that film, he notes: "[W]hite people, particularly white males, are constructed as the sole and sovereign human norm, contrasted to 'wookies' and assorted myriad of exotic creatures and humanoids, especially as depicted in the film's memorable bar scene" (Guerrero 1993, 117–18).

He goes on to observe: "Race figures as Manichaean allegory, with the construction of whiteness as good and most specifically associated with Princess Leia in her flowing white gown, as contrasted with evil, symbolically concentrated in the black armor of the nefarious Darth Vader and his black space station, the Death Star" (118).

reduction of intergroup hostility laid out in Chapter 15.[11] Reflecting the "valuing diversity" argument cited in the Introduction to this book, *Quantum Leap* operates by "recognizing and 'privileging' the unique beliefs, values, etc., of distinct cultural (or racial) groups" (8).

The Expected Audience for Quantum Leap

Who would one expect to make up the audience for *Quantum Leap*? Given its science fiction thrust, and the linked action emphasis as Sam leaps from one time period to another, the program naturally appeals to the young and others who are attracted to adventure shows. Besides adventure, science fiction has an intellectual, technological component. So, *Quantum Leap* also should appeal to "techies," who usually belong to the more educated segment of the television audience.

Quantum Leap's emphasis on "human interest," the little dramas of people's everyday lives, suggests that the program would appeal to women. Specifically, many of the episodes emphasize what, traditionally, have been thought of as "women's issues." These involve themes such as family tensions (including tensions between the generations, or between spouses— as in domestic abuse); the problems of single parents; and discrimination against women. Additional episodes center on other human interest and ethical concerns such as the impact of the war in Vietnam; discrimination against homosexuals and against those of various nonwhite races; and discrimination against those with disabilities such as mental retardation, visual impairment, or hearing impairment. Another aspect of *Quantum Leap*, mentioned earlier, which appeals to women, is its delivery of Walton-like morals. The morality tale dimension of the series also appeals to blacks who, stereotypes of black women as "welfare queens" notwithstanding, often are traditional on matters like family values and social justice. Blacks would be drawn to the series for another reason as well: its frequent treatment of race as the focus for its episodes and their moral point.[12]

---

[11] Williams's approaches (see Chapter 15) to reducing intergroup hostility whose intrapersonal dynamics underlie the hypothesized effects of regular viewing of *Quantum Leap* include (52) resolution of conflict by indirection; (60) more effective hostility reduction when those being educated feel that they are not under attack; (62) prejudice effectively being reduced when learners feel they actively participate in gathering the relevant information; (66) effectiveness of propaganda which makes an "emotional" appeal; and (70) appeals to conscience or ethics. Some of Williams's propositions involving intergroup collaboration and contact also apply to this chapter's hypothesis. They include (81) increased concrete knowledge of the life of a minority group; and, in a sense, (84) reverse role taking.

[12] Besides "The Color of Truth" mentioned earlier, some of the other *Quantum Leap* episodes that focus on race include "So Help Me God," "Pool Hall Blues," "Black and White on Fire," "The Leap between the States," and "Justice." In the latter, Sam leaps into a Ku Klux Klan initiate and faces the strongest test of all of his own personal values. These episodes are summarized briefly in Chunovic (1993) and more fully in Wiggins (1993).

Sam, *Quantum Leap*'s protagonist, is from the Midwest—Kansas—and he is very Middle American, indeed "All-American," in his outlook. Thus, for example, by and large, he eschews sex outside of marriage and, generally, is a very decent fellow. So, one would expect Middle America to identify with him as one of their own.

A key feature of *Quantum Leap* which undoubtedly pulls viewers from all of the several categories mentioned above is the program's narrative linchpin, the fantasy of magically becoming someone else. Teens, women, people of color, homosexuals, and those with disabilities all, from time to time, must wonder what it would be like to be free of that role attribute which often causes them to be the object of oppression or discrimination or to be considered disabled. But watching a *Quantum Leap* episode enables them to go beyond mere *wondering* and, vicariously, to try on the role of an Other. It involves a transformation fantasy, racial or otherwise. In short, for those viewers, experiencing *Quantum Leap* episodes can foster a kind of projection that is cathartic or compensatory in nature and, therefore, psychically satisfying.

The potential of *Quantum Leap* to satisfy intrapsychic needs undoubtedly is an element in the program's attraction for mainstream Middle Americans (including even older white males) as well. Here, the psychic mechanism may be somewhat different. The identification may be not only with the Other whom Sam becomes, but, perhaps, with Sam *qua* Sam, the All-American good guy hero. Nonmainstream viewers may also experience a double identification while watching *Quantum Leap*. They, too, may identify not only with the persona into whom Sam leaps, but with Sam himself. As Horst Stipp (personal communication, April 1997) has commented, it is very difficult to predict which of the many aspects of a particular television program or series predisposes a given individual to view it. Thus, it would be intriguing to see research conducted on the kinds of psychic outcomes that are hypothesized here as playing out for viewers *of Quantum Leap*.[13]

Checking the Ratings: The Actual Audience for *Quantum Leap*

Quantum Leap Ratings on NBC

Quantum Leap was popular enough to run for three seasons (1989–90 to 1991–92) on a national broadcast network, NBC, the National Broadcasting Company. Although it was not among the top twenty shows, it

---

[13] Bacon-Smith (1992) is a study providing insights into the dynamics of varying psychological outcomes of television spectatorship.

placed well. In its peak season, 1991–92, with a 10.8 average Nielsen rating, it ranked sixty-second among all programs, being watched in a typical week by 9,671,000 households (Tim Brooks, personal communication 1997).[14]

As we predicted here, when it ran on NBC, *Quantum Leap* was popular with teens (8.9 rating). It rated higher (11.3) in households where the household head had one or more years of college than in households where the head had no college (9.2). Finally, it was more popular with women than with men, being most highly rated among young adult women and middle-aged women.[15]

Quantum Leap's appeal to Middle America was shown by the fact that it had its second highest ratings in the West Central geographical area (13.1) and in midsized counties (11.0) rather than in the counties that comprise the twenty-one largest U.S. metropolitan areas (9.9) or in the smallest ones (10.7). Similarly, on the income dimension, its highest ratings were in middle-income households.[16]

Quantum Leap Ratings on Cable Television

The popularity of the *Quantum Leap* series did not end with its network run. Since that run ended in 1992, the series has been in syndication on two American cable networks. It ran daily on weekdays on the USA Network for a few years, and also on the Sci-Fi Channel (also owned by the USA Network), where it initially ran daily and, since then, has run several times a month. *Quantum Leap* also runs in syndication overseas.[17] Because cable TV, unlike broadcast television, is not free, but involves a user fee, the long run of *Quantum Leap* in syndication is a tangible measure of its popularity.

Cable networks have aired *Quantum Leap* in more than one time slot, in contrast to the NBC pattern of a single prime-time evening hour. Thus, because Sci-Fi Channel programs are not staggered in the different time zones, when *Quantum Leap* is telecast at 6 P.M. Eastern Standard Time it is viewed at 3 P.M. in the Pacific Time Zone.

[14] A Nielsen rating is "the percent of all television-equipped homes tuned to a program on an average night as measured by the A. C. Nielsen Company" (Brooks and Marsh 1995, 1258). Thus, a rating of 16.0 for the *NFL Monday Night Football* in 1996 and 1997 means that on the average, 16 percent of all homes that had a television set were tuned to this show.

[15] In November 1991, the Nielsen rating for women 18–34 was 9.3; for women 18–49 and for women 25–54, it was 9.0; but for women 18–54 it was 7.7; and for women 55+ it was 5.1.

[16] The highest ratings (12.7) in November 1991 were in households whose income was in the $30,000–$39,999 bracket. For those in the $20,000–$29,999 range the rating was 10.3, while in the $40,000–$49,999 bracket it was 11.6. For households with incomes of $60,000 and above, it was 11.8.

[17] *Quantum Leap* is popular in several other countries: the United Kingdom, Germany, France, Peru, and Australia. Fans of the program, known as "Quantum Leapers" stay in touch via the Internet on several sites located in various countries.

Interestingly, the Nielsen ratings for *Quantum Leap* as it ran in syndication on the USA Network and the Sci-Fi Channel reveal that audience composition varies greatly according to the *time of day* the program airs. Thus, when *Quantum Leap* aired on the USA Network at 1 P.M. (EST) on October 9, 1993, the strongest ratings were among *males*.[18] But when it aired at midnight (EST) on October 18, 1995, the gender discrepancy in viewing was more marked *and* the strongest ratings were among *females*.[19]

It would be interesting to know whether *ethnic* viewing patterns of *Quantum Leap* on cable vary from group to group as they do from one gender to the other. But data showing Nielsen ratings of cable showings of *Quantum Leap* by ethnic/racial households are not publicly available. However, what these ratings might be can be inferred from other data. For example, the USA Network does well compared to similar cable networks in pulling in black viewers. So, one would expect the black viewership of *Quantum Leap* on the USA Network to be *at least as good as* viewership among non-black households viewing the program on that particular network.

By and large, cable networks, more than the broadcast networks, have catered to niche ethnic and racial audiences. Fox, UPN, and WB efforts in this regard were cited earlier. This niche targeting is rooted in the pluralist model of American society. It responds to ethnic and racial groups' desire for programming that reflects their unique values, beliefs, and lifestyles. But niche-oriented programming can cut two ways. It can support ethnic and other components of America's diversity in the quest to honor and valorize their identities. But, to the extent that it uses and reinforces stereotypes, it can devalue diversity, sustain durable inequalities, and divide society (cf. Jhally and Lewis 1992; Gray 1995).

In the move to niche programming, the USA Network was "the first basic-cable network to devise a comprehensive, nationally-oriented marketing campaign targeting minority audiences that do not subscribe to cable," partially because cable penetration of the general market had leveled off (Miller 1992, 17). Thus, Andrew Besch, senior vice president of marketing at USA said, "We know that USA is very popular with minorities, especially within the Hispanic community," as he pointed to the lure of the network's action-adventure shows and made-for-TV movies (Miller 1992, 86).[20]

---

[18] Strongest male ratings (33.5) were among those aged 18–49. Strongest female ratings (13.5) were in the same age group.

[19] Strongest ratings among females (57.3) were among those ages 18–49. Strongest males figures (17.9) were in the same age group.

[20] Besch observed further that the network "may also create campaigns targeting Asian viewers for its new Sci-Fi Channel; the network's research shows that genre [to be] popular with Asians" (Miller 1992, 86).

Tellingly, the cable networks have not acted on the implications of this position. Thus, the producers of *Quantum Leap* and the cable network which has its syndication rights, the USA Network, have not exploited the full of range of audiences to which the series appeals. The specific audiences to which various episodes of *Quantum Leap* speaks apparently were not identified and targeted. These audiences include, particularly, women, African Americans and other people of color, teenagers, senior citizens, the developmentally disabled, and, to a lesser extent, gays and persons concerned with animal rights. Evidently, the only niche audience to which the series has been marketed is science fiction fans!

Latent in the complex cosmopolitanism of American diversity lie two other targetable audiences. Both the *Quantum Leap* series as a whole and specific episodes could be marketed to the audience of people interested in or curious about diversity *per se*. This group includes the crossover audiences of older blacks and younger *non*blacks identified in the 1997 BBDO report. A related audience is those persons not only interested in or curious about various Others, but morally or ideologically *committed* to honoring and promulgating diversity. That latter niche audience, cosmopolites, crosscuts many races, ethnic groups, religions, both genders, various sexual orientations, and political orientations. It is a group critical to the nation's civic welfare.

Quantum Leap as a model for diversity-enhancing programming need not be conceptualized concretely and narrowly in terms of a science-fiction anthology format whose focus changes with each episode. It can be conceptualized more broadly, in terms of the series' previously identified underlying dimensions: utilization of universal themes played out in a culturally specific context and imparting a moral lesson. This template fits television series such as *Frank's Place*, *I'll Fly Away*, and the James Earl Jones vehicle, *Under One Roof*. These series, while set in an African American context, treat concerns that are broader and generalizable to other ethnicities. They also have significant crossover potential.

This template also would fit a similar noncomedic series that did not use African America as the culturally specific context, but, say, Mexican America or Japanese America, and so on. Notably, though, no such series have yet played on network television.

Frank's Place, *I'll Fly Away*, and *Under One Roof*, while critical successes, did not attract a large enough following on network television to last more than a short time. Significantly, they have not been picked up in syndication by the for-profit cable networks, although *I'll Fly Away* has rerun on public television. The data reported here suggest that, with aggressive marketing, these series could acquire a larger niche African American audience *and* a probable crossover audience because their themes are ethnically specific *and* universal.

In their ethnic-oriented niche-programming the cable networks, by and large, have emphasized sitcoms for black audiences and melodramas for Hispanic ones. But they have not showcased as much as they could serious dramas such as the African American–focused ones mentioned above. This is regrettable because such shows, with their authentic, real-life qualities and implied morality themes, offer ethnic audiences a more valorizing mirror of themselves. And, when more broadly marketed, they can stimulate other, mainstream audiences also to encounter and embrace diversity.

Conclusion

The key argument in this chapter is that viewers who follow *Quantum Leap* identify with the hero, Sam Beckett. Through Sam's leaps, viewers also identify with persons having varied, diverse attributes. As viewers vicariously experience the lives of various Others, in time they come to understand and appreciate diversity itself. This outcome is most attractingly realized in a series like *Quantum Leap,* with its anthology format, in which there is a different focus (and different characters) each week. *Quantum Leap* leaps viewers into diversity.

A more subtle argument, derived from the first one, concerns the value of a more standard niche-oriented series that focuses on a particular segment of our diverse society, a series such as *I'll Fly Away.* This type of show can *also* be a vehicle through which the viewer vividly experiences the role of the Other and, ultimately, acquires an appreciation for diversity.

Cable television can play a dual role vis-à-vis American diversity. Its programming can be and is a vehicle though which segments of our diverse society view and affirm their identity and lifeways. But, *at the same time,* with imaginative program concepts, writing, and bold marketing, cable television can enable and encourage all of our citizens to engage in *crossover* viewing. They can experience the life of the Other and come to appreciate and value the diversity which is so uniquely and valuably American.

PART FOUR

AFTERWORD

CHAPTER FIFTEEN

The Reduction of Intergroup Tensions

Robin M. Williams, Jr., with a preface by Peter I. Rose

Preface

Robin M. Williams, Jr.'s long out of print monograph, The Reduction of Intergroup Tensions: A Survey of Research on Problems of Ethnic, Racial, and Religious Group Relations, *published in 1947 by the Social Science Research Council, has never been out of date. It was and remains one of the most comprehensive and significant documents ever to address the dilemmas associated with diversity in our often fragmented society.*

The bulletin's introduction began with Williams's describing why group hostility is such a problem in modern American society. It set the context for examining "research needs and opportunities involved in the problem of reducing tensions among, ethnic, racial, and religious groups, especially in the United States" (Williams 1947, 1). Williams followed with an appraisal of programs dealing with intergroup relations in the immediate post–World War II period. Then came the most important chapter of all, "Propositions on Intergroup Hostility and Conflict." With permission of the author and the Social Science Research Council, the introduction, all of the proposi-

Excerpts from Robin M. Williams, Jr.'s *The Reduction of Intergroup Tensions: A Survey of Research on Problems of Ethnic, Racial, and Religious Group Relations* are reprinted here with permission of the Social Science Research Council.

*tions that focus on reducing intergroup hostility and conflict, and part of the con-
cluding chapter, "Summary and Prospect," are reprinted here. Williams's contribution is at once a period piece and a timeless classic.*

*While some of the language may seem a bit arcane (Williams used the then-
preferred term "Negro" instead of African American), the conceptual framework is
as timely today as it was more than fifty years ago. Indeed, many younger social scientists, unfamiliar with the bulletin, will be struck by how much of what its author
wrote then has become a part of the vernacular of "race relations discourse." This is
especially noteworthy in Williams's classic definitions and explications of the concepts of prejudice, discrimination, and group conflict. Also useful are his theorems
about social action in general. He discusses the principles, working hypotheses, and
assumptions relating to the origins and prevalence of hostility. He reviews studies of
the reactions of minority groups to their degradation, segregation, and exclusion,
and suggests approaches to redress legitimate grievances to bring us "toward a more
perfect union." Still, central to the bulletin were the now-famous "propositions." In
the pages that follow, we focus on the propositions that Williams put forth to reduce
intergroup conflict. With the exception of bracketed material, which the editors have
included to ensure clarity, continuity, and stylistic consistency with the other contributions to this volume, the text is as Williams published it in 1947.*

*It should be noted that the original Social Science Research Council monograph
included a chapter on "Selected Possibilities for Research," many of which are still
timely a half century after they were outlined. Finally, Williams began his summary
chapter with a comment that is, sadly, all too relevant today: "Intergroup tensions
in the United States are persistent, widespread, and serious" (Williams 1947, 105).*

Group Hostility as a "Problem"

Few things are more obvious in present day society than the
great prevalence and intensity of hostility and conflict among various
types of social groups.[1] On the one hand, there have been [in the twentieth century] two world wars, a number of major revolutions, and dozens
of undeclared wars, insurrections, rebellions, coups d'état, and other
disorders of a mass-political character. On the other side, during this
comparatively short period of recent history there has occurred an enormous proliferation of race riots, anti-Semitic disturbances, strikes and
other labor-management conflicts, ethnic group clashes, and many disruptive movements based on systematic philosophies of hate and violence. Hardly anywhere in the major societies of the world could one
find today a person who has not been touched by the crosscurrents of
intergroup antagonism and conflict.

[1] This section reproduces text from Chapter 1, "Introduction" (Williams 1947). [Eds.]

Hostilities and conflicts among intra-national groups have evoked serious thought in recent years. When such hostility has taken the form of ethnic, religious, or racial cleavages it has had a particularly sharp impact because of its incompatibility with some of the most important historical values and cultural axioms of Western society. The incongruities are very clear in the United States. In the value-system which has been at least nominally dominant throughout most of American national history, a central element has been what may be called a "universal" ethic. This ethic formally enjoins certain important rules of behavior which are supposed to apply to everyone regardless of his particular status or group membership. At its most explicit level this type of principle appears in the Golden Rule, in the categorical value placed on honesty and fair play, in Constitutional and other legal requirements which stress rights and duties regardless of color, creed, class, [gender,] or national origin. It is manifest likewise in the belief that individuals should be rewarded according to their personal qualities and achievements, rather than on the basis of birth in a particular group or class. Its ramifications can be traced in such seemingly unrelated things as competitive examinations for civil service positions, the one-price system, the code of being a good loser in competitive activities, the disapproval of nepotism and favoritism in public office, and a great variety of other beliefs and practices which are generally taken for granted. Discrimination and hostility among intra-national groups identified on the basis of race, national origin, or religion thus come into conflict with a central theme of what Myrdal has called the American Creed.[2]

The marked development of sentiments of nationalism in the modern world has likewise sharpened awareness of internal conflict as a problem. But the unifying sentiment that "we are all Americans" has often met qualifying and divisive definitions when applied to particular subgroups and classes: Negroes, Mexican or Spanish Americans, Jews, Catholics, Japanese Americans and many others. Aside from their importance in such considerations of unity, intergroup relations within the United States have possible repercussions in international relations. The role of the United States in the international scene may be profoundly affected by developments in the relations of domestic groups. American statesmen who deal with world problems have to contend with world-wide press coverage of intergroup relations in the United States.

All these facets of intergroup tensions are colored by their distinctive American context, a central aspect of which is the extraordinary heterogeneity of the people. All Americans, save the American Indians, are recent immigrants—as Will Rogers aptly pointed out with reference to the *Mayflower*

[2] Gunnar Myrdal, *An American Dilemma* (New York: Harper & Row, 1944).

tradition when he said that his ancestors "met the boat." The varied cultures from which our population stocks have come have made intergroup tolerance, at least, not just a virtue but in some senses a societal necessity. Insofar as the melting pot is a mythical concept—and certainly there is far from complete assimilation of all groups into a homogeneous way of life— some basis for intergroup tolerance and collaboration has been essential for the nation's existence as a social system.

In the case of many population elements a gradual process of assimilation is blurring and erasing group differences. But certain other groups remain distinctive, either because of physical traits or because cultural traits of high visibility have been retained. Meanwhile, the national economy and social organization are beginning to exhibit traits of "maturity" and rigidity. In this situation intergroup tensions stand out with particular sharpness and, partly because of this, the impression that wholly new problems are emerging tends to develop.

The recognition of group conflicts in recent years has thus led to a sense of crisis which must be evaluated against historical perspective. There is a strong tendency in American thought to ignore or minimize the very considerable amount of intra-national group conflict which has appeared in various periods of our history. Yet an examination of the record [shows] that internal hostilities and disorders have been by no means infrequent.[3]

In this connection the title of [this chapter] requires some comment. Concentration of attention upon means for "reducing group hostility" may seem to rest upon an implicit value-premise: that the reduction of hostility is in itself a desirable goal regardless of other considerations. To take such an unqualified position in a publication of this nature would be both unnecessary and naive. The only necessary assumption is that under *some* circumstances certain individuals and groups find it desirable to attempt to reduce hostility or conflict or both. Insofar as this is true, there is a social raison d'être for scientific study directed toward testing the results of various means used in these attempts. On the other hand, any mature research orientation in this field will explicitly recognize the possibility that from the standpoint of certain principles and values, a measure of intergroup hostility and con-

---

[3] Representative sources include: Bennett M. Rich, *The Presidents and Civil Disorder* (Washington: The Brookings Institution, 1941); A. F. Raper, *The Tragedy of Lynching* (Chapel Hill: University of North Carolina Press, 1933); Chicago Commission on Race Relations, *The Negro in Chicago* (University of Chicago Press, 1922); J. G. Miller, *The Black Patch War* (Chapel Hill: University of North Carolina Press, 1936); Arthur M. Mowrey, *The Dorr War* (Providence: Preston and Rounds, 1901); Leland D. Baldwin, *Whiskey Rebels* (Pittsburgh: University of Pittsburgh Press, 1939); Gustavus Myers, *History of Bigotry in the United States* (New York: Random House, 1943); Harvey Wish, "American Slave Insurrections before 1861," *Journal of Negro History* 22:299–320 (1937).

flict may sometimes be unavoidable, if not on occasion actually a means to the attainment of highly valued purposes. It is certain that instances can be pointed out, as for example in Negro-white relations, in which temporary intensification of conflict has led to changes which are widely regarded as improvements in terms of major values of American society. At the same time it can scarcely be doubted that much intergroup hostility is extremely costly, often in terms of standards accepted by all or most of the parties involved. There is at least a possibility that adequate solutions can sometimes be achieved at less social cost through avenues other than conflict. The extent to which techniques can be developed and utilized to reach such solutions will have much to do with the whole future of American-and world-society.

Reducing Intergroup Hostility and Conflict

Preliminary Considerations

It is essential to distinguish at least three aspects of negative interaction: prejudice (hostility), discrimination, and conflict.[4] Although often closely connected in life situations, these elements have a considerable range of independent variation. Accordingly, the implied therapies are not necessarily the same when the aim is, e.g., to remove prejudice as when it is merely to minimize conflict.

Prejudice

In its broadest meaning prejudice may be considered simply as a *prejudgment* of individuals on the basis of some type of social categorization. A prejudice is thus a generalization which operates in advance of the particular situation in which it is manifested. An illustration is a stereotype which attributes a cluster of traits to individuals as representative of a group; it is thus in one aspect a cluster of cognitive judgments, implying a set of behavioral expectations. In another aspect it involves a set of evaluations. That is, the prejudice is not simply a set of expectations; it is also a set of evaluations of good and bad, superior and inferior. Thus a prejudiced individual brings to the immediate situation certain beliefs as to the traits of others, coupled with a positive or negative predisposition toward these traits.

Prejudice, in this general sense, is an inevitable and universal feature of social life. What is significant as a variable is the basis upon which any par-

---

[4] The material in this section is drawn from Chapter 3, "Propositions on Intergroup Hostility and Conflict" (Williams 1947). We retain the original numbering of propositions for the reduction or control of hostility and conflict (46–66, 68–102). We omit propositions 1–45, which treat other issues, for example, the origins of conflict, and proposition 67. [Eds.]

ticular prejudice rests. The crucial distinction lies between prejudices which are based upon functional position in the social order or real differences in values, and those which emphasize stereotypes centered on symbols such as skin color which have no intrinsic functional importance. Thus, all prejudices represent action-sets of a categorical rather than situational or ad hoc character. But there is a great difference between "prejudices" against social positions such as employers, ministers, labor leaders, radio commentators, bootleggers, professors, landlords, etc., on the one hand, and prejudices against racial or cultural groups, on the other.

The particular type of prejudice which is important in understanding hostility and conflict among ethnic, racial, or religious groups is *a negative attitude which violates some important norms or values nominally accepted in the culture.* There is prejudice based on conformity to the social customs of a group as against the prejudice, anchored in deep aggressive needs in the personality, which may persist even in the face of group pressure. There is the prejudice of economic or political opportunism, often calculating and impersonal, in contrast to the fanaticism of the religious or cultural zealot. There is the prejudice manifest in a specific idée fixe concerning a particular group, on the one hand, and the prejudice expressive of generalized antipathy to out-groups, on the other. Even the prejudice which arises primarily out of individual psychological needs appears in many forms; it may serve, for example, as a projection of repressed hatreds and other "antisocial" urges of the individual, a prop for ego-level or sense of self-esteem, a defense against repressed sexual drives, or a method of winning group approval.[5]

Discrimination

It is clear from comparative study of situations involving intergroup relations that prejudice is not perfectly correlated with discrimination or conflict. Discrimination in some degree always accompanies prejudice, but a given state of prejudice may be accompanied by greatly varying degrees and types of discrimination. The latter may be generally defined as the *differential treatment of individuals considered to belong to a particular social group.* Like prejudice, discrimination in this sense is an inevitable and universal feature of social life. The social groups may or may not have a biological basis, and if they have, the biological referents may or may not be functional. The "discrimination" against women in public life, for example, is based in part on [beliefs about] a biologically

[5] Cf. Fritz Redl's discussion in *Intercultural Education News,* 7(4):3–5 (1946); also G. W. Allport, *ABC's of Scapegoating* (Chicago: Central Y.M.C.A. College [1943]), pp. 15–23.

functional referent. Discrimination against Negroes, on the other hand, is based upon the culturally imputed significance of certain traits such as skin color which have no demonstrated relevance to biological function. Again, there is discrimination against religious, occupational, ethnic, and other groups which have no real or assumed biological referents. To arrive at a definitive view of discrimination it must be pointed out that in the context of intergroup relations the word ordinarily refers not merely to selective or differential behavior, but to such behavior *insofar as it violates important institutional standards* which usually are obligatory in certain areas of conduct. Thus, except for the probable deviations around such social norms, it is expected in our society that occupational opportunity will be available on the basis of merit or ability, that all citizens are entitled to specified legal rights, that economic transactions will be carried out according to the rules of the market. Discrimination may be said to exist to the degree that individuals of a given group who are otherwise formally qualified are not treated in conformity with these nominally universal institutionalized codes.

Conflict

A high level of active hostility shading into open intergroup *conflict* is still a third type of problem, not necessarily coextensive with the other two. Prejudice unquestionably is sharpest just prior to, during, and sometimes immediately after a conflict situation. But prejudice may exist in the absence of direct contact between groups, as formerly against the "terrible Turk" when there was no actual opportunity for direct conflict.[6] Also, it must be remembered that a firmly established caste system, which in some respects represents a maximum of prejudice, may operate with little open conflict.[7]

Now taking conflict alone as the final expression of prejudice-hostility, we may distinguish at least three major types of "realistic" conflict, which differ

[6] Here Williams refers to the well-documented tendency of individuals to express antipathy toward nonexistent groups and groups with whom they have little or no contact (e.g., Turks). [Eds.]
[7] This example is enough to demonstrate that the mere minimization of *conflict* alone is not the goal of most groups concerned with intergroup relations in the United States. The problem is much more complicated. What many representatives of minority groups are actually seeking is a minimum of prejudice, together with a minimum of conflict, and a minimum of discrimination. At least in the short run, these objectives are not necessarily mutually compatible. For instance, the attempt to eliminate discrimination often leads directly to increases in hostility and conflict; efforts to avoid conflict, conversely, may perpetuate or reinforce patterns of discrimination. [Conflict over the implementation and, now, the dismantling of affirmative action programs is a case in point. Eds.]

in their bases of origin: conflict of interests, of values (cultural conflict), of personality types.[8] Any intergroup conflict ordinarily involves all three types in varying proportions. With groups which are already culturally identified by clear symbols, the competition of members of the different groups for wealth, work, power, and various symbols of status and success defines a "realistic" conflict of interests. Similarly, there are often real intergroup differences in values, beliefs, personal habits, and customs. Such cultural differences may and often do lead to tangible disagreements on matters of considerable emotional importance to individuals; and both parties may be convinced of the rightness of their own positions. Third, because of varying modal patterns of family conditioning and perhaps other factors, different groups may contain different proportions of various personality types—a fact which does not appear to be wholly reducible to differences in the formal content of group culture. Insofar as such differences exist, interpersonal contacts may lead to irritation, hostility, and conflict.

Unrealistic Bases of Conflict

In addition to these three main bases of "realistic" conflict, group hostility typically involves certain "unrealistic" components. At least three may be considered to have practical importance: *ignorance and error, deflected hostility, historical tradition* [emphasis added].

The influence of ignorance is widely recognized and is the object of much educational effort. Sheer unawareness of other groups' characteristics, especially lack of acquaintance with individuals, is conducive to exaggeration of intergroup differences and to receptivity to hostile propaganda. Erroneous judgments may be made even with fairly complete knowledge, if incorrect inferences are drawn from known facts. This is especially important in the case on imputations of "responsibility," e.g., when a decline in material rewards arising from complex forces in our economic system is imputed to specific groups which do not have any significant casual role in the situation.

Deflected hostility takes two main forms: projection and displacement. In the first, unacceptable elements in the personality are attributed to others; thus it is the other group which is said to be hostile, or scheming to exploit, and so on. In the second, hostility is directed against a source other than that which originally created it. In intergroup relations deflected hostility may result in "over-determined" reactions in which the hostility is out of all proportion to the realistic basis. This situation depends upon a complex set of factors but an essential element is the existence of much hostility which can-

---

[8] Adapted from Gustav Ichheiser, "The Jews and Anti-Semitism," *Sociometry* 9:92–108 (1946).

not be directly expressed or otherwise dissipated within the groups in which it originates.[9] The persistence and virulence of intergroup hostility is certainly not explicable without taking deflected aggression into account.

The factor of historical tradition must be accorded the status of a variable. Old rivalries, conflicts, and traumas are remembered, and traditional prejudices may tend to be perpetuated well beyond the point at which they cease to have any intrinsic relevance to current situations.

Mutually Reinforcing Sources of Conflict

To appraise the relative importance of realistic and unrealistic components or of interests versus values in intergroup tension would be a very hazardous undertaking at the present stage of our understanding, although such appraisals are often given with surprising confidence and conviction. We can be reasonably sure, however, that any explanation of intergroup hostility in terms of a single factor like "purely economic competition" represents an oversimplification which is likely to encourage ill conceived action. Further, the known facts create a strong presumption that a main source of the persistence of intergroup hostility is precisely the *interlocking and mutual reinforcement* of cultural differences, other visible differences, realistic interests, deflected aggression, and other factors. In short, the most important questions may concern not the influence of particular factors but the way in which mutual reinforcement operates, and determination of the strategic factors in a plan for shifting the resultant pattern. In this connection, there is a definite possibility that the factors which are most important in producing hostility and conflict are by no means the same as those which are most important *for control purposes.* Thus, the roots of intergroup hostility may lie in the early socialization of children in the home. But this process is so inaccessible to direct external control that other, even seemingly far removed, approaches may be much more promising for immediate action.

---

[9] An important factor in racial or ethnic conflict is the pattern of *deflected aggression.* Some of the conditions defining this pattern are (a) frustrations or deprivations imposed by sources which are either: (1) difficult to define or locate, or (2) persons or organizations in a position of power or authority over the individual, or (3) persons to whom the individual is closely tied by affectional bonds; (b) aroused hostilities [that] are blocked from direct expression against the sources of frustration; and (c) substitute objects of aggression [that] are available and are: (1) highly *visible,* and (2) *vulnerable,* i.e., not in a position to retaliate. It appears that in the case of direct aggression there is always some displaced aggression accompanying it and adding additional force to the rational attack (Dollard, 1939, 55, p. 19).

This is a widespread, recurrent, and important pattern of emotional structuring in human society and is widely recognized on the level of common-sense observation. Ordinary examples are legion: the child punished by his parents destroys a toy or maltreats his pet; the employee humiliated by his supervisor "takes it out" on his family; the defeated small businessman joins an anti-minority movement.

Such considerations as those sketched above are essential to fruitful orientation of research on techniques for reducing or controlling intergroup hostility. They indicate clearly, for example, that action programs may deal with either realistic or unrealistic components or both, and that the predicted effects may be expected to vary with the choices made. To take another application, the present analysis implies that even complete intergroup knowledge could not by itself eliminate group hostility. It implies, also, that indirect approaches which attack the realistic bases of conflict, perhaps without even ostensibly dealing with intergroup relations as such, have as valid a claim for consideration as do direct education or propaganda approaches.

Most of the propositions about relations among racial, ethnic, and religious groups which are listed hereinafter are current in the literature,[10] although the present wording is usually synthetic rather than drawn from any one source. In some instances in which the hypothesis was not found in explicit form in published material, the present statement represents an inference necessary to "make sense" of actions or statements which have been observed. The total listing may be regarded as a series of notes on problems needing further research. The present formulations can only be tentative and it is certain they fall far short of exhausting the questions which could be raised, even on the basis of present knowledge. The sole aim of the compilation is to bring together in compact and convenient form a sampling of what is known and surmised in this field. To whatever degree further thinking may be stimulated or research possibilities suggested, the compilation will have served its purpose.

Propositions Concerning the Reduction or Control of Hostility and Conflict

General Orientation

46. The two extreme "solutions" for eliminating a given group conflict are: (a) complete insulation, e.g., geographic exclusion, and (b) complete assimilation.

47. The main theoretical possibilities for minimizing a given group conflict are: (a) actual reduction in hostility, (b) no change in hostility level, but

---

[10] Representative sources and quotations are given to illustrate a number of propositions. However, many of the propositions listed have been put forward in essentially congruent form by many different students of this field. It has not seemed expedient, therefore, to attempt any elaborate or systematic documentation. Incidentally, one of the striking impressions gained from a review of available literature is the existing consensus on a considerable number of basic hypotheses—along with the usually recognized divergences of viewpoint.

a re-channelization to substitute targets (in the extreme case, diffusion to a variety of objects), [or] (c) no change in hostility level and retention of major object-fixation, but repression of overt conflict.

48. The reduction of intergroup conflict depends upon: (a) reduction of hostility, which depends upon minimization of frustrations and insecurities and their attendant anxieties, [or] (b) proper canalization of existing hostilities, through sanctions, diversions, redefinition of situations, etc.

49. An individual does not act only in *more* or *less* prejudiced ways: he acts in *different* ways depending upon the function of the basic value structure in his personality in action.

50. Any given pattern of intergroup hostility and conflict varies in its intensity and in its implications depending upon whether it is (a) traditional and sanctioned as a "legitimate" channel for aggression-release, or (b) in opposition to nominally dominant value-patterns.

51. Simultaneous direct attack on every form of intergroup discrimination is likely to intensify the reaction it attempts to stop. Programs aimed against discrimination will be least likely to set off unmanageable "nativistic" reactions by proceeding one point at a time, and by starting with items of lowest negative symbolic potential.

52. A general principle of approach is that, except in acute crisis situations, problems of group conflict are usually most readily resolved by indirection rather than by frontal assault. In propaganda, for example, direct arguments tend to present a sharp issue which arouses maximum resistance; a more effective procedure is to emphasize common aims and suggest group integration as a means for their attainment.

Insofar as possible, if it is desired to avoid defensive hostility, guided changes in intergroup relations must be made in such a way as to avoid or minimize the interpretation that they threaten security with regard to those things in which the groups have important emotional commitments. (It should be clear, however, that various gradualistic ameliorative proposals for reducing hostility or conflict do not directly reach the problem of "interested," calculated discrimination or the conscious use of group visibility as a means for perpetuating a privileged social and economic position).

53. Where strong prejudice is present in a group which is highly self-conscious, and strongly bound together, outside criticism of its prejudice is likely to be taken as an attack on the group; and *one* immediate effect is to strengthen the prejudice, which by virtue of the attack becomes a symbol of in-group membership and solidarity. (Two historical cases are especially good illustrations: Northern criticism of race relations in the Southern states; outside criticism of the Afrikaans-speaking whites in the Union of South Africa).

Information and Education

54. The likelihood of conflict is reduced by education and propaganda emphases upon characteristics and values *common* to various groups rather than upon intergroup *differences*. (But there is danger that attitudes thus created may lead to expectation of greater similarity than later experience demonstrates, and this can lead to disillusionment and secondary reinforcement of hostility. A second qualification is that some persons holding to a doctrine of cultural pluralism advocate awareness of differences on the assumption that acceptance of differences comes only after a transitional period, which may involve temporary intensification of hostility.)

55. Favorable attitudes and the extent of information about given groups are positively, but slightly, correlated; effects are not clearly proven in detail but the general evidence is positive.

56. The effects of imparting a given type of information about minority groups—under given circumstances—differ, depending upon the extent and degree to which the recipients already have favorable or unfavorable attitudes toward the group or groups in question.

57. The mere giving of objective general information in print or by lecture about a group which is the object of hostility has only a slight effect, or no effect, in reducing hostility—at least in the short run.

58. Even with a uniform body of instructional materials about a given group or groups, the effects of instruction upon recipients will vary appreciably with the basic attitudes and "personality" of the instructor.

59. Insofar as education or propaganda reduces hostility toward any specific group or toward out-groups in general, it does so largely by re-channelizing aggressive impulses rather than removing them.

60. Attempts to reduce intergroup hostility by education will be the more effective, (a) the more the learners are convinced in the beginning that they themselves are not under attack for their opinions; and (b) the more the learners are allowed initially to express freely their verbal hostilities to instructors who maintain an atmosphere of calm objectivity.

61. Educational programs will have maximum effects, all other things being equal, when information is presented as part of the ordinary action of a group in carrying out its usual social function (e.g., as part of general teacher training, job training for public officials, conferences of industrialists, labor leaders, merchants, real estate dealers, etc.).

62. Prejudices are most likely to be changed by the imparting of information about the object of prejudice when the learners themselves actively participate in gathering the relevant information.

63. Changing the attitudes of *groups* rather than isolated individuals is the more effective approach for breaking up intergroup stereotypes and prejudices.

64. Hostility is decreased by any activity which leads members of conflicting groups to identify their own values and life-activities in individuals of the other group. To be most effective this requires devices for including *personal* identification before the introduction of group labels.

Direct Reorientation of Values

65. In intergroup relations, word-of-mouth propaganda, especially that which appears spontaneous and informal, is more effective than visual or formal propaganda in influencing attitudes and behavior.

    So far as specific media are concerned, the scanty evidence suggests this general order of effectiveness: (1) direct personal communication (speeches, lectures, etc.); (2) [television,] radio; (3) printed materials. However, the research results also suggest that the order of effectiveness varies with the subject matter, the type of appeal, and the type of audience.

66. In intergroup relations, propaganda which makes an "emotional" (value-oriented) appeal is likely to be more effective than that which is restricted to factual appeal.

    But this plausible assertion may be countered with the view that such appeals arouse relatively uncontrolled emotions which are not likely to lead to tolerant or humane behavior. It certainly appears that there are sufficient dangers in strongly emotional propaganda to warrant careful testing with different types of audiences.

68. Propaganda which appeals for minority rights on the basis of the group's achievements tends beyond a certain point to arouse insecurity—hostility in the dominant group by stressing group differences and competitive success. [See Walker, Chapter 3 in this volume.]

69. It is dangerous technique to employ *mass* propaganda emphasizing "rising tides of prejudice" as a means intended to mobilize defenders of minority rights and good intergroup relations. Such propaganda is likely to have a boomerang effect upon slightly prejudiced or wavering elements: it creates the presumption of group support for hostile actions.

70. Appeals to conscience or ethics must be carefully handled, if they are to diminish rather than intensify hostility. In general, such appeals are probably most effective in reinforcing the sentiments of persons who are already convinced; they are probably not effective (immediately, at least) with militant anti-ethnics, and may even result in increased hostility as a reaction to guilt-feelings.

71. Appeals to local pride are sometimes useful in motivating leaders to prevent open conflict. Mass violence is widely regarded in America as bringing discredit upon the community in which it occurs.

72. Conflict is discouraged by providing, through sources of high general prestige, for specific public commendation of individuals of the dominant group who work for toleration, minority rights, mutual understanding, and the like.

73. An effective propaganda approach in intergroup relations is that which emphasizes national symbols and common American achievements, sacrifices, destinies, etc., while unobtrusively indicating the common participation of minority group members.

74. Other things being equal, the blocking of hostile impulses and their deflection into harmless channels is facilitated by any devices which strongly remind individuals of commonly acknowledged cultural prescriptions against hostility to other groups. Examples of such devices are: (a) pronouncements by representatives of moral and political authority; (b) dramatic ceremonial affirmation of the relevant patterns and values; [or] public reward and (sometimes) punishment.

75. Conflict and hostility are rendered less probable by any activity which leads individuals to take for granted the other groups (e.g., [movies] show Negroes as members of various kinds of groups, where the emphasis of presentation is upon what the group is doing).

76. Individuals who have been exposed to strongly religious training, or who participate in organized religious activities, do not necessarily manifest less hostility or greater tolerance than individuals not having these characteristics. Only certain types of religious training are effective in lessening intergroup hostility.

77. The effects of public refutation of hostile rumors vary with the nature of the refutation and with the type of rumor and attendant situation, e.g.:
   (a) *In chronic but relatively stable and mild intergroup tensions,* rumors are probably best ignored, or refuted only by indirection and propaganda of the deed [or actions that render them false].
   (b) *Rumors of unusual character, intensity, or prevalence* (e.g., role of minorities in the armed forces in war) probably should be met by "official" propaganda. However, publicizing the rumors themselves should be avoided; the refutation should be as indirect (nonmanifest) as is consistent with the necessity of gaining attention.
   (c) *In crisis situations* (pre-riot, etc.) refutation of rumors of hostile intentions or of hostile actions of opposing groups, weakness of control forces, and the like tends to check conflict.[11]

---

[11] Contrary assumptions are also advanced by experienced authorities. Almost nothing is definitely established on these propositions.

Intergroup Contact and Collaboration

78. Lessened hostility will result from arranging intergroup collaboration, on the basis of personal association of individuals as functional equals, on a common task jointly accepted as worthwhile.

79. [The effectiveness of] personal contacts between members of different groups in producing friendly relations [vary with a host of factors including] relative economic and social status, and similarity of interests and tastes.

80. Personal association of members of different groups is most effective in reducing hostility and increasing understanding when the focus of interaction is upon a common interest, goal, or task rather than upon intergroup association as such. (The converse hypothesis, that such association should explicitly stress the purpose of promoting group understanding, is often acted upon.)

81. Increased concrete knowledge of the life of a minority group, especially of particular persons whose behavior does not fit stereotyped conceptions, tends to break up rigid stereotypes and under some conditions to diffuse or decrease hostility.

82. Prejudice is reduced by arranging for personal, intimate contacts of members of different groups who share important tastes and interests in common. (Prejudice is usually only increased by casual, public contacts, especially in urban situations).

83. Diminution of hostility may be expected when it is possible to arrange for ritualized conflict or competition between groups which cut across ethnic or racial lines (e.g., a local athletic team which includes an "ethnic" playing against a rival team which is also multi-ethnic).

84. Hostility is reduced by arranging for reverse role-taking in public drama or ceremony (e.g., an anti-Negro person plays a realistic Negro role). Retraining in intergroup relations among highly prejudiced persons is facilitated by arranging "rehearsal" situations in which initial contacts with out-group members may be made without the feeling of "playing for keeps." To change permanently and to stabilize behavior patterns, however, the "players" must be led through increasingly realistic participations.

85. Participation in public rituals and ceremonies re-affirming solidarity and pledging cooperation works toward inhibition of tendencies for intergroup conflict.

86. Formation of committees of mixed membership to deal with local problems tends to reduce the likelihood of conflict for the time being.

87. In any integration of minority members into a work *situation on the initiative of higher control-groups in an organization*, acceptance is facilitated by arranging for representation of the minority in the upper as well as the

lower levels of the organization. This arrangement is necessary to forestall accusations that workers are forced to accept that which the control-group itself will not tolerate.

88. The introduction of minority group members into new areas or activities is most effective in securing compliance with a minimum of conflict:

    (a) With gradual introduction of selected individuals, with a minimum of prior discussion or announcement in cases in which there are relatively tolerant initial attitudes in the majority population.

    (b) With statements that the minority will be introduced, accompanied by a considerable volume of information, exhortation, and discussion prior to the change itself in populations having relatively strong initial prejudice.

    (c) The least effective method is polling, or otherwise determining wishes of the majority group, in advance of the change—the results being understood to constitute a binding decision. (This may be done either with or without an information and discussion program.)

Legislation and Law Enforcement

89. The existence of laws protecting the rights of minorities and court decisions upholding these laws tend, in the long run, to decrease conflict over the rights involved.

90. Whenever there is sufficient flexibility in public attitudes, the abolition of legal discrimination and disabilities in the long run will reduce hostility and conflict.

91. A general expectation of authoritative intervention and the possibility of punishment for acts of violence, whether in group conflict or in individual incidents, will decrease the probability of open conflict.

    (a) Tendencies toward open conflict are inhibited by the publicized presence of effective, well disciplined, and impartial law-enforcement agencies.

    (b) Mixed police forces, with careful indoctrination in handling conflict situations, can deal most effectively with open conflict, and the presence of such forces may decrease the likelihood of conflict.

92. In the event of open conflict the resolution of the crisis with a minimum of violence, damage, and residue of hostility is facilitated by: (a) prompt and full publicity to allay fears and to stress the control agencies' capacities to control, (b) assurances of strict and impartial justice, (c) special distribution of police to danger spots, (d) provision for prompt summoning of military or other outside order-maintaining forces, (e) enlisting cooperation of neighborhood leaders, (f) personal public appeal by

high officials, (g) the presence of high officials in danger areas—with full dramatization of their presence, [and] (h) minimum use of force.

Social Organization

93. Possibilities of conflict are lessened by the establishment of clear, detailed, and widely recognized patterns for interpersonal relationships in situations of casual contact (e.g., in public conveyances).
94. In America a minority ethnic or racial group struggling for improved status, or for the alleviation of intergroup hostility, will be most successful if it relies upon a variety of organizations rather than one overall organization.
95. Mediation between groups in conflict is possible only when effective appeal can be made to a superior value-consensus which transcends group differences, e.g., the preservation of a larger community, common larger "interests," basic religious values, shared mores, etc.
96. Open conflict is rendered less likely by providing regularized leisure-time activities for those population elements most susceptible to riot-forming influences (e.g., adolescent males of lower class groups).
97. The device of *official* committees concerned with intergroup relations (e.g., Mayors' committees) will not ordinarily originate pressure for change but may be useful in transmitting pressure from more militant groups to official political leaders.
98. Outside agencies coming into a local community to stimulate, initiate, or otherwise affect programs directed toward intergroup relations will meet minimum resistance when they: (a) work through local persons and established local groups; (b) avoid extensive publicity for themselves; (c) adapt techniques and organization to local circumstances rather than propose a rigid scheme prepared in advance.
99. Aggressive needs, arising out of internal group structure, are lessened by arrangements providing for the necessary authority and coordination through group consensus rather than through rigid hierarchical organization.
100. Dispersion of minorities as individuals or small groups (*not* as communities) throughout a wide area and in various positions in the social structure tends to diffuse hostility and in the long run to reduce it.
101. A vulnerable minority can itself help to reduce hostility and conflict insofar as there is group control over individual members, by: (a) educating its members to an understanding of the dominant group's reaction to the minority's values and behavior, (b) careful study of the behaviors of its own members which are regarded as objectionable by other groups, (c) minimizing conspicuous display of traits of marked negative symbol value,

[and] (d) participation *as individuals* in wider community activities which are widely regarded as necessary in the common welfare.

102. All other things being equal, the probability of intergroup conflict is reduced by any measures which facilitate the internal differentiation of minorities, insofar as this serves to remove the objective basis for rigid social categorization.

It is believed that these propositions constitute a reasonably solid base of reference from which future research may depart. It is believed also that they constitute a challenge of the first order to social sciences and social action in these times.

Summary and Prospect

The application of science to practice is usually made possible only by slow and arduous *cumulation* of findings over long periods of time.[12] Literally millions of man-hours of research precede the current practical applications of a science like physics. There is certainly no reason to suppose that any less work will be required to reach comparable levels of applicability of social science.

Where research does not provide an unequivocal basis for positive prediction, it still offers at least two extremely important possibilities for contributing to understanding and action. First, there is much to be gained from demonstration of the sheer range of possible actions and their accompaniments and consequences. If a particular propaganda effort were made on the assumption that certain effects would be obtained, research on the problem might well find the situation recalcitrant to any positive prediction in the mode of "If you do A, then B and only B will follow." It might be possible however, to demonstrate a whole series of unanticipated effects; careful study might show not only effect B (say, greater awareness of admirable qualities in a minority group), but also effect C (enhanced fear of competition), effect D (greater awareness of intergroup cultural differences) and so on. Precisely this sort of demonstration may be of inestimable value to practitioners in evaluating possibilities of action. Second, there is the possibility of what may be called negative prediction. Generalizations in this mode will be in such forms as "Under these conditions, X will *not* appear," or "This action will not have as one of its effects" or "This action is impossible because of factors X, Y, and Z in the situation." If research in certain instances can do no more that state the probable lim-

---

[12] This section reprints material from Chapter 5, "Summary and Prospect" (Williams 1947). [Eds.]

its of particular types of programs or specify the results definitely not to be anticipated, it will have performed a socially vital function in diverting effort away from blind alleys and from the attempt to fulfill wishful but erroneous anticipation.

Finally, in focusing upon purposive "techniques" or "approaches" for reducing intergroup tensions there is no necessary implication that group hostility is subject to elimination or anything approximating complete control by these methods, within the framework of our present culture and society. It is certainly possible that unplanned and essentially non-controllable features of modern society make a relatively high level of intergroup hostility unavoidable. This is a question less likely to be answered by empirical research than by the larger developments of the times. However, hostility and conflict are not either present or completely absent but manifest a wide range of variation and, consequently, purposive attempts at control must be evaluated in terms of resulting increases or decreases rather than presence or absence. [I have] tried to document the fact that there are specific problems which lend themselves to research testing. It is submitted that the potential results hold considerable promise for scientific advance and social integration.

CHAPTER SIXTEEN

Long Time Passing: Race, Prejudice, and the Reduction of Intergroup Tensions

Peter I. Rose

R obin M. Williams, Jr.'s thoughts and analyses of American values, norms, and social institutions, especially education, and his research on intergroup relations, desegregation, and true integration, were not only pioneering, they were rarely to be challenged. More often than not, what he wrote about thirty, forty, and even fifty years ago provided extremely useful guides for social action. This remains so.

The Reduction of Intergroup Tensions (the core of which is reprinted in Chapter 15) was singular in its comprehensiveness, offering a review of the then-extant literature, an assessment of the post–World War situation, possibilities and guidelines for research, and, most important, Williams's empirically based and clearly formulated proposals for resolving racial, ethnic, and religious conflicts. It was and remains a unique document in the annals of social research.

Four Studies

Since the late 1940s, in addition to his monumental work in the study of American culture and society (1955, 1960, 1970), Williams continued to contribute to the study of race relations. Of particular interest are four co-authored books examined in this chapter: *Schools in Transition* (1954), *Strangers Next Door* (1964), *Mutual Accommodation* (1977), and *A Common Destiny* (1989). The appendix to Williams's Social Science Research Council monograph ends with an important theme that appears throughout this work:

> Too much time and talent can be diverted to the elaboration and refinement of devices for observation and measurement. Or, research workers may be too timid about attacking important problems merely because ideal tools are not available. . . . Techniques are tools for purposive action rather than materials for intellectual chess-playing; on the other hand, research does not necessarily lose its scientific status by reason of a focus on practical affairs. (1947, 134)

Whether working alone or in collaboration with others, Williams never drifted from the three Comtian goals of combining theory, research, *and* praxis.

Schools in Transition (1954)

Among the best known of the early empirical works, and one that demonstrates Williams's combination of theory, research, and application, is *Schools in Transition,* written with Margaret Ryan and published by the University of North Carolina Press in 1954. It was one report among several funded by the Fund for the Advancement of Education and the Ford Foundation, a volume directed toward "the informed citizen, whether school official or teacher or interested member a community" (Williams and Ryan 1954, v) on the experiences of those in twenty-four cities in various parts of the country undergoing various phases of desegregation.

Schools in Transition is a synthesis of the field reports of a number of researchers and, like so many of Williams's studies, ends not only with a summary but with a set of "lessons," in this instance about the unevenness of change and the significance of social contexts. The book concludes on a hopeful note:

> The experience now at hand shows that where desegregation has been tried, the typical outcome has been its eventual acceptance. While the ease of transition varies greatly from community to community and some resist the move more than others, the direction of change is clearly toward the acceptance of educational integration as public policy. (Williams and Ryan 1954, 248)

Most reviewers, including the young lawyer Marion Thompson Wright (now Marion Wright Edelman), found the book (and its companion volume, *The Negro and the Schools,* by Harry Ashmore) informative and instructive. "The evidence presented embodies the hope for a future which building upon a past and the present will be characterized by an even greater improvement in race relations in both school and non-school social worlds" (Wright 1955). Another commentator, L. Joseph Stone, writing in *Social Research,* described the book as "a most valuable compilation: a mine of highly specific hypotheses for the researcher, and of hunches regarding the best procedures for political and educational practitioners who must prepare to act on the desegregation and ultimate integration of the races in our public school systems" (1955, 120). Most others agreed (Hickey and Scott 1955; Lovejoy 1955; Miller 1955; Rendeiro 1956).

Strangers Next Door (1964)

Ten years after *Schools in Transition, Strangers Next Door* was published by Prentice-Hall. In *Strangers Next Door,* there is a clear expansion of ideas and the testing and modification of some of the propositions presented in 1947 in *The Reduction of Intergroup Tensions* as well as one of the basic premises expressed by Herbert Blumer in his article "Race Prejudice as a Sense of Group Position" published a year later (1958, 6).

Strangers Next Door, which Williams wrote in collaboration with John Dean and Edward Suchman, is a comprehensive summary of what many informally called "The Elmira Study." It was the culmination of ten years of research—and another half-decade to pull everything together—using a variety of techniques (observations, reconnaissance surveys, interviews, questionnaires) on black-white and Jewish-gentile relations in four middle-sized cities: the baseline town of Elmira (called "Hometown") and three other code-named places: "Valley City" in the Southwest, "Southport" in the Deep South and "Steelville" in the Midwest. The book includes adaptations from the dissertations and reports of Lois Dean, Bob Eichhorn, Manet Fowler, Bob Johnson, Mel Kohn, Pauline Moller, Don Noel, Alphonso Pinkney, Alice Rossi, and others skillfully interwoven into its ten chapters on racial and ethnic relations, ethnocentrism, prejudice, patterns of segregation, social interaction and intergroup attitudes, situational variation, and other matters. Among the most noteworthy is a long chapter called "The World of Minorities," with its oft-cited subsection, "The Nature of the Negro Subcommunity," adapted from Bob Johnson's dissertation, "The Nature of the Minority Community." Also noteworthy is "Sociological Correlates of Social-Distance Feelings among Negroes," based on Don Noel's "Correlates of Anti-White Prejudice."

In the last chapter, "Structures and Processes in Multigroup Society," Williams and his colleagues closely examine the significance of "ethnic groupings," which they define as "distinctive subcultures that emerge and exist alongside and, often, interconnected to one or more other systems of invidious ranking," such as those based on kin, class, and community, or neighborhood structure (Williams, Dean, and Suchman 1964, 357–58).

The section "The World of Minorities" is my favorite, and a favorite even of far more critical reviewers (for example, Grimshaw 1964, 495–96). Reading through this section once again, I was suddenly transported back in time, nearly forty years, to a dank settlement house in Elmira where fellow graduate student Katie Huggins and I spent long afternoons interviewing teenage African American boys. We then would spend long evenings in after-interview colloquies when she and I would discuss whether a white person like me could ever get the same information from our subjects as a black person like her and how much difference our genders had on the same process.

Like *Schools in Transition,* published in the year of the *Brown v. Board of Education* decision, 1954, *Strangers Next Door* was also published at the end of an era, in 1964. In even more obvious ways, it was a watershed volume. By the time it appeared, those referred to as "Negroes" in its pages—and those young men Katie and I interviewed—were Negroes no more. The rising call for Black Power and the move for a distinct and distinctive black consciousness had already signaled the beginning of a new age in race relations. Some reviewers, sensitive to the changes, urged Williams and his colleagues to bring their book up to date and "thus increase its immediate relevance for decision makers" (Kushnick 1966, 322). Others, Alma Taeuber among them, saw other flaws in the volume, citing too loose a connection between data and discussion; the raising of many questions but the providing of too few answers; and the failure to capitalize on "the most commendable feature of the research design—its explicitly comparative approach [which] remains largely unexplored" (Taeuber 1966, 236).

Reexamining the volume, I am far more inclined to agree with those who saw *Strangers Next Door* as sounder methodologically—and theoretically—than the likes of Taeuber would have their readers believe. Perhaps the best counter to her arguments is to be found in J. Milton Yinger's assessment, published in the *American Sociological Review* in 1965, in which he indicates the triple-tiered significance of the book: its solid descriptiveness; its usefulness in understanding relationships between groups; and its relevance to the broader analysis of the way a complex society like ours functions from more than a single vantage point. Yinger was one of the few to point out that "[a]ltogether, this book keeps the study of ethnic relations—seen from the perspective of both majority and minority—within the framework of a theory of society" (1965, 440).

The book was not only, as J. Milton Yinger predicted, "likely to serve as a source of both data and interpretation for many years to come" (1965,

440), it also continues to evoke postmonitions of a period of excitement, challenge, and opportunity to test ideas.

Mutual Accommodation (1977)

A decade later, *Mutual Accommodation* was published by the University of Minnesota Press. It was the third major study of interracial and interethnic conflict and cooperation in this country in which Williams was the driving force. It was also the most controversial (see, for example, Katznelson 1979; Eisinger 1978). Written with Madelyn Rhenisch, the report detailed the results of the dismantling of the United States' massive system of racial segregation, the abolition of many restrictions on immigration, the removal of discriminatory barriers to public facilities, and the enactment of "one of the most sweeping set of national laws to be found in any nation concerning civil and political rights of minorities" (Williams 1977, 3).

Williams and Rhenisch offered a generally hopeful view that America's dilemma might finally be resolved. This optimistic, though frequently qualified view—but not qualified sufficiently to satisfy such critics as Ira Katznelson (1979, 723)—was based on summaries and comparisons of a number of nationwide surveys. The findings included substantial evidence of cultural changes, structural changes, and a challenge to many conventional wisdoms about how reactionary and racist white Americans *really* are. The investigators found "increased cosmopolitanism" in the populace. This was attributed to education (both an increase in the educational level of the respondent and the content of what he or she was being taught), to changes in media treatment of African Americans and other minorities, and to desegregation of the armed forces and other major social institutions. They found further evidence of interracial accommodation in residential neighborhoods in a variety of cities.

In a foreword to *Mutual Accommodation,* Marvin Bressler noted, "The concept of success . . . is always equivocal, and inflated expectations must be constrained by the recognition that advances in intergroup relations are invariably partial and uneven" (Williams 1977, ix) Bressler's words were both cautionary and prophetic.

A Common Destiny (1989)

In a much more recent volume, *A Common Destiny: Blacks and American Society* (1989), Gerald David Jaynes and Robin Williams implicitly return to several cautionary notes in Williams's early monograph, *The Reduction of Intergroup Tensions* (1947), by indicating that there is still a long way to go.

Jaynes and Williams's book is the final report of the Committee on the Status of Black Americans of the National Research Council, which

Williams chaired in the late 1980s. Its pages are filled with comparisons of blacks and whites in almost every sphere of life.

The editors began with a statement of how far our society had come in dealing with the issue of "race" as well as a commentary on how far we had yet to go. "Just five decades ago, most black Americans could not work, live, shop, eat, seek entertainment, or travel where they chose. Even a quarter of a century ago—100 years after the Emancipation Proclamation of 1863— most blacks were effectively denied the right to vote"; they went on to point out that "[a] large majority of blacks lived in poverty and very few black children had the opportunity to receive a basic education; indeed, black children were still forced to attend inferior and separate schools in jurisdictions that had not accepted the 1954 decision of the Supreme Court declaring segregated schools unconstitutional" (Jaynes and Williams 1989, 3). At the time they were writing, they noted that the situation was very different. Still,

the great gulf that existed between black and white Americans in 1939 has only been narrowed; it has not been closed. One of three blacks still live in house-holds with incomes below the poverty line. Even more blacks are in areas where ineffective schools, high rates of dependence on public assistance, severe problems of crime and drug use, and low and declining employment prevail. Race relations, as they affect the lives of inhabitants of these areas, differ considerably from black-white relations involving middle class blacks. Lower status black have less access to desegregated schools, neighborhoods, and other institutions and public facilities. Their interactions with whites frequently emphasize their subordinate status—as low-skilled employees, public agency clients, and marginally performing students. The status of black Americans today can be characterized as a glass that is half empty—if measured by persisting disparities between black and white Americans since the early 1970s. (Jaynes and Williams 1989, 3–4)

The question that the Committee on the Status of Black Americans sought to address concerned the reasons for "the continuing distress of large numbers of black Americans . . . despite the victories of the civil rights movement" (Jaynes and Williams 1989, 4). The answers are methodically presented in ten chapters that examine the history of interaction and participation of blacks in various social institutions since the baseline era of 1935–45; the attitudes of blacks and whites about race; patterns of residential segregation; the social structure of black communities; the family and the issue of identity; services rendered through schools and social agencies; health and welfare; and black involvement in politics, the economy, and the criminal justice system. Although the institution of religion is handled in a separate chapter, matters of faith, organization, participation, and the role of the church in the past and present are found in many parts of the overall report.

Both *Mutual Accommodation* and *A Common Destiny* challenge deeply engrained "truths." For example, in the last volume the researchers report several results that are contrary to popular belief. "The evidence does not support some popular hypotheses that purport to explain female-headed households, high birth rates to unmarried women, low labor force participation by males, or poor academic performance solely on the basis of government support programs or, more generally, on the existence of a 'culture of poverty' among the black poor" (Jaynes and Williams 1989, 10). They also report that the findings of increasing tolerance reported in *Mutual Accommodation*, while challenged in a variety of ways, *had not been reversed*. Indeed, they say, "Black-white cultural differences have narrowed since 1960, not widened" (Jaynes and Williams 1989, 10).

Despite this "good news," I found the most recent report disturbing. (Although I saw the report quite differently than R. J. Herrnstein [1990], who wrote a lengthy attack on *A Common Destiny*. Not surprisingly, he found Jaynes and Williams's "Discrimination Model" wanting for failing to take into account race "differences.") It is disturbing not in how it was written or in its emphasis on discrimination instead of what Herrnstein calls a "Distributional Model," but in what it says about *continuing* discrimination. It is also disturbing about some of the reversals (that belie the larger generalization), such as the resegregation of urban neighborhoods and the place of many blacks in the uneven development of American capitalism. These two issues are discussed by Ira Katznelson in his critical review (1979, 724) of Williams's previous book, *Mutual Accommodation*. Again, with an uneasy sense of déjà vu, I read that many changes in recent years "have been most detrimental to the fortunes of blacks, and opportunities were curtailed most for blacks of lowest status" (Jaynes and Williams 1989, 11). This finding puts Williams and his colleagues into the very epicenter of the debate about the issue of the "urban underclass" (Wilson 1978, 1987). William Julius Wilson, who was a member of the task force that helped to prepare the report on *A Common Destiny* (and is author of Chapter 7 in this volume), has more to say about such findings as cited in Jaynes and Williams's book and about the opportunity structure as spelled out in his own book (Wilson 1996).

I, for one, would like to see Williams and Jaynes speak to a related and, I believe, compounding issue: the role of new immigrants in the context of their latest assessments of intergroup relations and the broader issue of competition in American society.

Today, the presence of new minorities from Asia and Latin America is seen by many as again thwarting the progress of those, borrowing phrases from Lipset and Raab (1969), who are predominantly white "once hads" and predominantly black "never hads." A follow-up to *A Common Destiny* might well add another dimension to the overall understanding of the politics of resentment and the sociology of intergroup relations. This follow-up should address the very large and very heterogeneous third force of nonwhite, nonblacks who have been entering the United States since 1965 and constitute a presence of their own. Their relationships to African Americans and other old minorities should be studied (Rose 1993). This study should also include an analysis of the relationship between the black migrants from the rural South and earlier immigrants, mainly from eastern and southern Europe, whom they met and sometimes competed against. This analysis could then be compared to today's situation where the blacks' competitors are more apt to be Latino or Asian.

Conclusion

In 1994, Williams published an essay, "The Sociology of Ethnic Conflicts: Comparative International Perspectives," in the *Annual Review of Sociology*. His abstract for that piece ends with a characteristic Williamsesque coda:

> Research in this field contends with many difficulties, and one-sided theories do not fare well. Yet abundant descriptive materials are available, statistical techniques are improving, conceptual clarification continues, and substantive knowledge does accumulate. Accordingly, there is hope for better understanding of some of the most destructive and tragic conflicts of our times.

The words were written in the mid-1990s but might have been written fifty years ago. Indeed, going back to *The Reduction of Intergroup Tensions,* one can find similar sentiments in similar language: the reluctance to put all eggs in one theoretical basket, the belief that it is important to use all available data, the admonition always to sharpen the focus of the ever-changing conceptual lenses, and, above all, the reasonable decency, the kind of humanism that infuses every fiber of Williams's being and is evident even in his most formal writing.

Bibliography

Ahrne, Göran. 1994. *Social Organizations: Interaction inside, outside, and between Organizations.* London: Sage.
——. 1996. "Civil Society and Civil Organizations." *Organization* 3:109–20.
Alba, Richard. 1985. *Italian Americans: Into the Twilight of Ethnicity.* Englewood Cliffs, NJ: Prentice Hall.
——. 1990. *Ethnic Identity: The Transformation of White America.* New Haven: Yale.
Alba, Richard, Nancy Denton, John Logan, and Shu-yin Leung. 1995. "Neighborhood Change under Conditions of Mass Immigration: The New York City Region, 1970–1990." *International Migration Review* 29 (Fall):625–56.
Alba, Richard, and John Logan. 1991. "Variations on Two Themes: Racial and Ethnic Patterns in the Attainment of Suburban Residence." *Demography* 28 (August):431–53.
Alba, Richard, John Logan, and Paul Bellair. 1994. "Living with Crime: The Implications of Racial/Ethnic Differences in Suburban Location." *Social Forces* 73 (December):395–434.
Alba, Richard, John Logan, and Kyle Crowder. 1997. "White Ethnic Neighborhoods and Assimilation: The Greater New York Region, 1980–1990." *Social Forces* 75 (3):883–912.
Alba, Richard, John Logan, Brian Stults, Gilbert Marzan, and Wenquan Zhang. 1999. "Immigrant Groups and Suburbs: A Reexamination of Suburbanization and Spatial Assimilation." *American Sociological Review.* In press.
Alexander, C. Norman, and Mary G. Wiley. 1981. "Situated Activity and Identity Formation." In *Social Psychology: Sociological Perspectives,* edited by M. Rosenberg and R. H. Turner, 269–89. New York: Basic.
Allen, James, and Eugene Turner. 1997. *The Ethnic Quilt: Population Diversity in Southern California.* Northridge: Center for Geographical Studies, California State University.
Alligood, Doug. 1993. "Blacks Are Gravitating to Programs with Black Themes That Relate to Them." *Broadcasting and Cable* 123:74.
Allport, Gordon. 1943. *ABC's of Scapegoating.* Chicago: Central Y.M.C.A. College.
——. 1954. *The Nature of Prejudice.* Reading, MA: Addison-Wesley.
Alwin, Duane F., and Robert M. Hauser. 1975. "The Decomposition of Effects in Path Analysis." *American Sociological Review* 40 (February):37–47.
Anderson, Grace M. 1974. *Networks of Contact: The Portuguese and Toronto.* Waterloo, Ontario: Wilfrid Laurier University.

Antonovsky, A. 1979. *Health, Stress, and Coping.* San Francisco: Jossey-Boss.

Archibald, H. C., and R. D. Tuddenham. 1965. "Persistent Stress Reaction after Combat: A 20-Year Follow-Up." *Archives of General Psychiatry* 12:475–81.

Arkoun, Mohammed. 1994. *Rethinking Islam: Common Questions, Uncommon Answers.* Boulder, CO: Westview.

Bachu, Amara. 1993. "Fertility of American Women: June 1992." In *Current Population Reports,* 20–470. Washington, DC: U.S. Government Printing Office.

Bacon-Smith, Camille. 1992. *Enterprising Women: Television Fandom and the Creation of Popular Myth.* Philadelphia: University of Pennsylvania Press.

Baer, Hans A., and Merrill Singer (guest eds.). 1988. *Black American Religion in the Twentieth Century.* Review of Religious Research 4(29): entire issue.

Bainbridge, William Sims. 1996. *The Sociology of Religious Movements.* New York: Routledge.

Baldwin, Leland D. 1939. *Whiskey Rebels.* Pittsburgh: University of Pittsburgh Press.

Bales, Robert F. 1950. *Interaction Process Analysis: A Method for the Study of Small Groups.* Reading, MA: Addison-Wesley.

Baltzell, E. Digby. 1964. *The Protestant Establishment: Aristocracy and Caste in America.* New York: Vintage.

Barringer, Herbert, Robert W. Gardner, and Michael Levin. 1993. *Asians and Pacific Islanders in the United States.* New York: Russell Sage.

Barth, Fredrik. 1981. *Process and Form in Social Life. Selected Essays of Fredrik Barth.* Vol. 1. London: Routledge & Kegan Paul.

Bayer, R. 1981. *Homosexuality and American Psychiatry: The Politics of Diagnosis.* Princeton, NJ: Princeton University Press.

BBDO. 1997a. Special Markets. *Special Report* 2(2) February.

BBDO. 1997b. "BBDO's 12th Annual Report on Black TV Viewing Finds Seven-Year Trend in Split Viewing Preference between Black and Total Households Continues." New York. News Release, February 21.

Beale, Calvin L. 1995. "Noneconomic Value of Rural America: Value or Rural America." Paper presented at the USDA expert's conference, Washington, DC, May.

———. 1996. "The Ethnic Dimension of Persistent Poverty in Rural and Small Town Areas." In *Racial and Ethnic Minorities in Rural Areas,* edited by L. L. Swanson, AER 731:26–32. Washington, DC: USDA-ERS.

Bean, Frank, and Marta Tienda. 1987. *The Hispanic Population of the United States.* New York: Russell Sage.

Beck, S. H. 1986. "Mobility from Preretirement to Postretirement Job." *The Sociological Quarterly* 27(4):515–31.

Bell, Derrick. 1992. *Faces at the Bottom of the Well.* New York: Basic.

Bellah, Robert N. 1967. "Civil Religion in America." *Daedalus* 96:1–21.

———. 1992. *The Broken Covenant: American Civil Religion in Time of Trouble.* Chicago: University of Chicago Press.

Bem, Sandra L. 1993. *The Lenses of Gender: Transforming the Debate on Sexual Inequality.* New Haven, CT: Yale University Press.

Benjamin, Lois. 1992. *The Black Elite.* Chicago: Nelson-Hall.

Berger, Joseph, Bernard P. Cohen, and Morris Zelditch, Jr. 1966. "Status Characteristics and Expectation States." In *Sociological Theories in Progress,* edited by J. Berger, M. Zelditch, Jr., and B. Anderson, 29–46. Boston: Houghton-Mifflin.

Berger, Joseph, M. Hamit Fisek, Robert Z. Norman, and Morris Zelditch, Jr. 1977. *Status Characteristics and Social Interaction: An Expectation States Approach.* New York: Elsevier.

Bianchi, Suzanne. 1995. "Changing Economic Roles of Women and Men." In *State of the Union: America in the 1990s,* edited by R. Farley, 1:107–54. New York: Russell Sage.

Blackstone, W. 1979. *Commentaries on the Laws of England.* Chicago: University of Chicago Press.

Blank, Susan. 1998. "Hearth and Home: Three Explanations for the Living Arrangements of Mexican Immigrants and U.S.-Born Mexican-Americans." *Social Forum* 13:35–59.

Blau, Peter M., and Otis Dudley Duncan. 1967. *The American Occupational Structure.* New York: John Wiley.

Blauner, Robert. 1972. *Racial Oppression in America.* New York: Harper & Row.

Blumer, Herbert. 1958. "Race Prejudice as a Sense of Group Position." *The Pacific Sociological Review* (Spring):6.

———. 1969. *Symbolic Interactionism: Perspective and Method.* Englewood Cliffs, NJ: Prentice-Hall.

Bonacich, Edna. 1972. "A Theory of Ethnic Antagonism: The Split Labor Market." *American Sociological Review* 37:547–59.

Botting, D. 1985. *From the Ruins of the Reich: Germany, 1945–1949.* New York: Crown.

Bourdieu, Pierre. 1965. *Travail et Travailleurs en Algerie.* Paris: Editions Mouton.

Bourgois, Philippe. 1995. *In Search of Respect: Selling Crack in El Barrio.* New York: Cambridge University Press.

Brazziel, William, and Marion Brazziel. 1980. *Recent College and University Enrollment Patterns of Black Students in States Affected by Adams-Califano Litigation.* Albany, GA: Southern Education Foundation.

Brill, N. R., and G. W. Beebe. 1956. *A Follow-Up Study of War Neuroses.* Washington, DC: U.S. Government Printing Office.

Broder, David S. 1992. "A Stand-Up Guy Who Thinks of Himself as Unpredictable." *The Cleveland Plain Dealer*, December 13, D3.

Bromley, David G., and Anson Shupe, eds. 1984. *New Christian Politics.* Macon, GA: Mercer University Press.

Brooks, Tim, and Earle Marsh. 1995. *The Complete Directory to Prime Time Network and Cable TV Shows: 1946–Present.* New York: Ballantine Books.

Brotz, H., and E. Wilson. 1946. "Characteristics of Military Society." *American Journal of Sociology* 51:371–75.

Brown, David L. 1998. "Enhancing the Spatial Policy Framework with Ecological Analysis." In *Continuities in Sociological Human Ecology*, edited by M. Miklin and D. L. Poston, 195–213. New York: Plenum.

Brown, David L., Glenn V. Fuguitt, Tim B. Heaton, and Saba Waseem. 1997. "Continuities in Size of Place Preferences in the United States, 1972–1992." *Rural Sociology* 62 (4):408–28.

Brown, David L., and Thomas A. Hirschl. 1995. "Household Poverty in Rural and Metropolitan-Core Areas of the United States." *Rural Sociology* 60(1):44–66.

Brown, Rupert. 1995. *Prejudice.* Oxford, U.K.: Blackwell.

Browning, H. L., S. C. Lopreato, and D. L. Poston, Jr. 1973. "Income and Veteran Status: Variations among Mexican Americans, Blacks, and Anglos." *American Sociological Review* 38(1):74–85.

Bumpass, Larry L., and James A. Sweet. 1989. "National Estimates of Cohabitation." *Demography* 26:615–25.

Bumpass, Larry L., James A. Sweet, and Andrew Cherlin. 1991. "The Role of Cohabitation in Declining Rates of Marriage." *Journal of Marriage and the Family* 53:913–27.

Burgess, Ernest W. 1925. "The Growth of the City: An Introduction to a Research Project." In *The City*, edited by R. E. Park, E. W. Burgess, and R. D. McKenzie, 47–62. Chicago: University of Chicago Press.

Burgess, Ernest W., and Harvey J. Locke. 1953. *The Family: From Institution to Companionship.* New York: American.

Burke, Peter J., and Donald C. Reitzes. 1981. "The Link between Identity and Role Performance." *Social Psychology Quarterly* 44:83–92.

Burke, Peter J., and Judy C. Tully. 1977. "The Measurement of Role Identity." *Social Forces* 55:881–97.

Burkhauser, R. V., and J. F. Quinn. 1989. "American Patterns of Work and Retirement." In *Redefining the Process of Retirement: An International Perspective,* edited by W. Schmahl, 91–113. Berlin: Springer.

Burtless, Gary. 1985. "Are Targeted Wage Subsidies Harmful? Evidence from a Wage Voucher Experiment." *Industrial and Labor Relations Review* 39(1):105–14.

Campbell, Karen E., Peter V. Marsden, and Jeanne S. Hurlbert. 1986. "Social Resources and Socioeconomic Status." *Social Networks* 8:97–117.

Campbell, Karen E., and Rachel Rosenfeld. 1986. "Job Search and Job Mobility: Sex and Race Differences." *Research in the Sociology of Work* 3:entire issue.

Campbell, Robert A., and James E. Curtis. 1996. "The Public's View on the Future of Religion and Science: Cross-National Survey Results." *Review of Religious Research* 37(3):260–67.

Canadian Conference of Catholic Bishops. 1988. "A Statement of Social Policy." *Dissent* Summer:314–21.

Caplow, Theodore. 1998. "A Symposium on Church Attendance in the United States." *American Sociological Review* 63(February):43–58.

Carter, Stephen L. 1993. *The Culture of Disbelief.* New York: Basic.

Center on Budget and Policy Priorities. 1996a. *The Administration's $3 Billion Jobs Proposal.* Washington, DC: Center on Budget and Policy Priorities.

———. 1996b. *The Depth of the Food Stamp Cuts in the Welfare Bills.* Washington, DC: Center on Budget and Policy Priorities.

Cherlin, Andrew. 1992. *Marriage, Divorce, Remarriage.* Cambridge, MA: Harvard University Press.

Chicago Commission on Race Relations. 1922. *The Negro in Chicago.* Chicago: University of Chicago Press.

Chiswick, Barry, and Teresa Sullivan. 1995. "The New Immigrants." In *State of the Union: America in the 1990s,* edited by R. Farley, 2:211–70. New York: Russell Sage.

Chou, Jeremy. 1996. "The Outsider among the Outsiders." *The Los Angeles Times,* September 28, B11.

Chunovic, Louis. 1993. *The Quantum Leap Book.* New York: Citadel.

Clawson, Dan. 1995. "From the Editor's Desk." *Contemporary Sociology* 24(2):ix.

Clipp, E. C., and G. H. Elder, Jr. 1996. "The Aging Veteran of World War II: Psychiatric and Life Course Insights." In *Aging and Post-Traumatic Stress Disorder,* edited by P. E. Ruskin and J. A. Talbott, 19–51. Washington, DC: American Psychiatric Press.

Clipp, E. C., E. K. Pavalko, and G. H. Elder, Jr. 1992. "Trajectories of Health: In Concept and Empirical Pattern." *Behavior, Health, and Aging* 2(3):159–79.

Clotfelter, Charles T., Ronald G. Ehrenberg, Malcolm Getz, and John T. Siegfried. 1991. *Economic Challenges in Higher Education.* Chicago: University of Chicago Press.

Coase, Ronald. 1992. "The Institutional Structure of Production." *American Economic Review* 82:713–19.

Cohen, Elizabeth G. 1972. "Interracial Interaction Disability." *Human Relations* 25:9–24.

Cohen, Elizabeth G., and Susan S. Roper. 1972. "Modification of Interracial Interaction Disability: An Application of Status Characteristic Theory." *American Sociological Review* 37:643–57.

Cohen, S., and S. L. Syme, eds. 1985. *Social Support and Health.* Orlando, FL: Academic.

Cohen, S., and G. M. Williamson. 1991. "Stress and Infectious Disease in Humans." *Psychological Bulletin* 109(1):5–24.

Condit, Celeste Michelle, and John Louis Lucaites. 1993. *Crafting Equality: America's Anglo-African Word.* Chicago: University of Chicago Press.

Constantine, Jill M. 1995. "The Effect of Attending Historically Black Colleges and Universities on Future Wages of Black Students." *Industrial and Labor Relations Review* 48(3):531–46.

Corcoran, Mary, Linda Datcher, and Greg J. Duncan. 1980. "Most Workers Find Jobs through Word of Mouth." *Monthly Labor Review* August:33–35.

Cornell, Stephen. 1988. *The Return of the Native.* New York: Oxford.

Cose, Ellis. 1993. *The Rage of a Privileged Class.* New York: Harper Collins.

Coser, Rose Laub. 1964. *The Family: Its Structure and Functions.* New York: St. Martin's.

Couch, Carl. 1992. "Toward a Formal Theory of Social Processes." *Symbolic Interaction* 15:117–34.

Cox, Oliver C. 1948. *Caste, Class, and Race: A Study in Social Dynamics.* Garden City, NJ: Doubleday.

Danziger, Sheldon H., and Peter Gottschalk. 1995. *America Unequal.* Cambridge, MA: Harvard University Press.

Dates, Jannette L., and William Barlow, eds. 1990. *Split Image: African-Americans in the Mass Media.* Washington, DC: Howard University Press.

Davidson, James D., Ralph E. Pyle, and David V. Reyes. 1995. "Persistence and Change in the Protestant Establishment, 1930–1992." *Social Forces* 74(1):157–75.

Davis, Benjamin O., Jr. 1991. *American.* Washington, DC: Smithsonian Institution Press.

Davis, James A., and Tom W. Smith. 1994. *General Social Survey, 1994.* Chicago: National Opinion Research Center.

———. 1996. *General Social Survey, 1996.* Chicago: National Opinion Research Center.

Davis, Lenwood G., and George Hill, compilers. 1985. *Blacks in the American Armed Forces, 1776–1983.* Westport, CT: Greenwood.

Davis, Nancy J., and Robert V. Robinson. 1996. "Are the Rumors of War Exaggerated? Religious Orthodoxy and Moral Progressivism in America." *American Journal of Sociology* 103(3):756–87.

de Beauvoir, Simone. 1952. *The Second Sex.* New York: Knopf.

De Schweinitz, Dorothea. 1932. *How Workers Find Jobs. A Study of Four Thousand Hosiery Workers in Philadelphia.* Philadelphia: University of Pennsylvania Press.

Deloria, Vine, Jr. 1973. *God Is Red.* New York: Dell.

Demerath, N. J., III, and Karen S. Straight. 1997. Religious Politics and the State: Cross-Cultural Observations. *Cross Currents* Spring: 43–58.

D'Emilio, J. 1983. *Sexual Politics, Sexual Communities: The Making of a Homosexual Minority in the United States, 1940–1970.* Chicago: University of Chicago Press.

D'Emilio, J., and E. B. Freedman. 1988. *Intimate Matters: A History of Sexuality in America.* New York: Harper & Row.

Department of the Army. 1993. *Black Americans in the Military.* Washington, DC: Pentagon Library.

DiMaggio, Paul, John Evans, and Bethany Bryson. 1996. "Have Americans' Social Attitudes Become More Polarized?" *American Journal of Sociology* 102(3):690–755.

Dollard, John. 1939. *Frustration and Aggression.* New Haven: Yale University Press.

Dornbusch, Sanford M., and W. Richard Scott. 1975. *Evaluation and the Exercise of Authority.* San Francisco: Jossey-Bass.

Duncan, Beverly, and Otis Dudley Duncan. 1968. "Minorities and the Process of Stratification." *American Sociological Review* 33(3):356–64.

Duncan, Otis Dudley. 1961. "A Socioeconomic Index for All Occupations." In *Occupations and Social Status,* edited by Albert J. Reiss, Jr., 109–38. Glencoe: Free Press.

———. 1969. "Inheritance of Poverty or Inheritance of Race." In *On Understanding Poverty,* edited by D. P. Moynihan, 85–110. New York: Basic.

Duncombe, Stephen, and Andrew Mattson, eds. 1995. *Black and White Television: African Americans and Early TV.* Primary Documents in Media and Social History. Old Westbury, NY: American Studies Program, State University of New York.

Durkheim, Emile. 1947. *The Elementary Forms of the Religious Life.* New York: Free Press.

———. [1893] 1964. *The Division of Labor in Society.* Glencoe, IL: Free Press.

Ehrenberg, Ronald G., and Donna S. Rothstein. 1994. "Do Historically Black Institutions of Higher Education Confer Unique Advantages on Black Students? An Initial Analysis." In *Choices and Consequences: Contemporary Policy Issues in Education*, edited by R. G. Ehrenberg, 89–137. Ithaca, NY: ILR Press.

Ehrenreich, Barbara. 1983. *In the Hearts of Men.* New York: Doubleday.

Eisinger, Peter K. 1978. "Review of *Mutual Accommodation* by R. M. Williams, Jr." *Political Science Quarterly* 93:344–45.

Elder, G. H., Jr. 1987. "War Mobilization and the Life Course: A Cohort of World War II Veterans." *Sociological Forum* 2(3):449–72.

——. 1998. "The Life Course and Human Development." In *Handbook of Child Psychology*. Vol. 1. *Theoretical Models of Human Development*, edited by R. M. Lerner, 939–91. New York: Wiley.

Elder, G. H., Jr., and E. C. Clipp. 1988. "Wartime Losses and Social Bonding: Influences across 40 Years in Men's Lives." *Psychiatry* 51:177–98.

Elder, G. H., Jr., and E. K. Pavalko. 1993. "Work Careers in Men's Later Years: Transitions, Trajectories, and Historical Change." *Journal of Gerontology* 48(4):S180–S191.

Elder, G. H., Jr., E. K. Pavalko, and E. C. Clipp. 1993. *Working with Archival Data: Studying Lives.* Newbury Park, CA: Sage.

Elder, G. H., Jr., M. J. Shanahan, and E. C. Clipp. 1994. "When War Comes to Men's Lives: Life Course Patterns in Family, Work, and Health." *Psychology and Aging*, Special Issue 9(1):5–16.

Erickson, Bonnie H. 1996. *The Structure of Ignorance.* Charleston, SC: International Sunbelt Social Network Conference.

Erikson, K. T. 1976. *Everything in Its Path: Destruction of Community in the Buffalo Creek Flood.* New York: Simon and Schuster.

"Ex-G.I. Gets Life Term in Racial Killings." 1997. *The New York Times*, March 7, A8.

Farkas, George D., Randall Olsen, Ernst W. Stromsdofer, Linda C. Sharpe, Felicity Skidmore, D. Alton Smith, and Sally Merrill. 1984. *Post-Program Impacts of the Youth Incentive Entitlement Pilot Projects.* New York: Manpower Demonstration Research.

Farkas, George D., D. Alton Smith, Ernst W. Stromsdofer, Gail Trask, and Robert Jerrett, III. 1982. *Impacts of the Youth Incentive Entitlement Pilot Projects.* New York: Manpower Demonstration Research.

Farley, Reynolds. 1996. *The New American Reality: Who We Are, How We Got Here, Where We Are Going.* New York: Russell Sage.

Farley, Reynolds, and Walter R. Allen. 1987. *The Color Line and the Quality of Life in America.* New York: Russell Sage.

Farley, Reynolds, and William H. Frey. 1994. "Changes in the Segregation of Whites from Blacks during the 1980s." *American Sociological Review* 59:23–45.

Fausto-Sterling, A. 1993. "The Five Sexes: Why Male and Female Are Not Enough." *The Sciences* 33(2):19–24.

Featherman, David, and Robert Hauser. 1976. "Changes in the Socioeconomic Stratification of the Races, 1962–1973." *American Journal of Sociology* 82(3):621–51.

Finke, Roger, Avery M. Guest, and Rodney Stark. 1996. "Mobilizing Local Religious Markets: Religious Pluralism in the Empire State, 1855–1865." *American Sociological Review* 61(2):203–18.

Finke, Roger, and Rodney Stark. 1992. *The Churching of America: Winners and Losers in Our Religious Economy.* New Brunswick, NJ: Rutgers University Press.

Fischer, Claude S., Michael Hout, Martin Sanchez Jankowski, Samuel R. Lucas, Ann Swidler, and Kim Voss. 1996. *Inequality by Design: Cracking the Bell Curve Myth.* Princeton, NJ: Princeton University Press.

Fix, Michael, and Jeffery S. Passel. 1994. *Immigration and Immigrants: Setting the Record Straight.* Washington, DC: Urban Institute.

Fixico, Donald L. 1986. *Termination and Relocation: Federal Indian Policy, 1945–1960.* Albuquerque: University of New Mexico Press.

Fordyce, Hugh. 1993. *1992 Statistical Report.* Atlanta: United Negro College Fund.

Franklin, John Hope. 1989. "The New Negro History." In *Race and History: Selected Essays 1938–1998,* by John Hope Franklin, 41–48. Baton Rouge: Louisiana State University.

Frazier, E. Franklin. 1932. *The Negro Family in Chicago.* Chicago: University of Chicago Press.

Freud, S. [1905] 1962. *Three Essays on the Theory of Sexuality.* New York: Basic.

——. [1920] 1959. "The Psychogenesis of a Case of Homosexuality in a Woman." In *Sigmund Freud: Collected Papers,* edited by E. Jones, 2:202–31. New York: Basic.

——. [1925] 1959. "Some Psychological Consequences of the Anatomical Distinction between the Sexes." In *Sigmund Freud: Collected Papers,* edited by E. Jones, 5:186–97. New York: Basic.

Fuguitt, Glenn V., and Calvin L. Beale. 1996. "Recent Trends in Nonmetropolitan Migration: Toward a New Turnaround?" *Growth and Change* 27:156–74.

Fuguitt, Glenn V., David L. Brown, and Calvin L. Beale. 1989. *Rural and Small Town America.* New York: Russell Sage.

Furukawa, Stacy. 1994. "The Diverse Living Arrangements of Children: Summer 1991." In *Current Population Reports,* 38–70. Washington, DC: U.S. Government Printing Office.

Gans, Herbert J. 1979. "Symbolic Ethnicity: The Future of Ethnic Groups and Cultures in America." *Ethnic and Racial Studies* 2 (January):1–20.

Garasky, Steven, and Daniel R. Meyer. 1996. "Reconsidering the Increase in Father-Only Families." *Demography* 33:385–93.

Gehrig, Gail. 1979. *American Civil Religion: An Assessment.* Monograph Series 3. Provo, UT: Society for the Scientific Study of Religion.

Gellner, Ernest. 1969. *Thought and Change.* Chicago: University of Chicago Press.

General Social Survey (G.S.S.). 1994. *Cumulative Codebook, 1972–1994.* Chicago: National Opinion Research Center.

Genovese, Eugene D. 1970. *The World the Slaveholders Made.* New York: Pantheon.

Gibbs, James Lowell, Jr. 1996. "Dream or Nightmare? The Hollywood Racial Transformation Film." Unpubl. manuscript, Dept. of Anthropology, Stanford University.

Giddens, Anthony. 1979. *Central Problems in Social Theory.* London: Macmillan.

Gilman, Charlotte Perkins. 1971. *The Man-Made World or Our Androcentric Culture.* New York: Johnson Reprint.

Glazer, Nathan, and Daniel Patrick Moynihan. 1970. *Beyond the Melting Pot.* Cambridge, MA: MIT Press.

Glendon, Mary Ann. 1989. *The Transformation of Family Law: State, Law, and Family in the United States and Western Europe.* Chicago: University of Chicago Press.

Goffman, Erving. 1959. *The Presentation of Self in Everyday Life.* New York: Doubleday.

Goldberger, Arthur S., and Charles F. Manski. 1995. "Review Article: *The Bell Curve* by Herrnstein and Murray." *Journal of Economic Literature* 33 (June):762–76.

Goldscheider, Frances K., and Linda J. Waite. 1991. *New Families, No Families?* Berkeley: University of California Press.

"Good Ol' Boys Roundup Video Genuine." 1995. *The Washington Times,* December 7, A4.

Gordon, Milton M. 1964. *Assimilation in American Life.* New York: Oxford University Press.

Gottdiener, Mark. 1987. "Space as a Force of Production." *International Journal of Urban and Regional Research* 11 (3):405–16.

Graham, Lawrence Otis. 1995. *Member of the Club: Reflection on Life in a Racially Polarized World.* New York: Harper Collins.

Granovetter, Mark. 1985. "Economic Action and Social Structure: The Problem of Embeddedness." *American Journal of Sociology* 91:481–510.

——. 1995. *Getting a Job: A Study of Contacts and Careers.* Chicago: University of Chicago Press.

Gray, Herman. 1995. *Watching Race: Television and the Struggle for Blackness*. Minneapolis: University of Minnesota Press.

Greeley, Andrew. 1974. *Ethnicity in the United States: A Preliminary Reconnaissance*. New York: Wiley.

———. 1978. *Ethnicity, Denomination, and Inequality*. Beverly Hills: Sage.

Green, B. L., J. D. Lindy, M. C. Grace, G. C. Gleser, A. C. Leonard, M. Korol, and C. Winget. 1990. "Buffalo Creek Survivors in the Second Decade: Stability of Stress Symptoms." *American Journal of Orthopsychiatry* 60(1):43–54.

Greenberg, D. E. 1988. *The Construction of Homosexuality*. Chicago: University of Chicago Press.

Grimshaw, Allen D. 1964. "Research on Intergroup Relations and Conflict: A Review [of *Strangers Next Door*]." *Journal of Conflict Resolution* 8:492–503.

Gronveld-Hatch, Rebecca. 1995. *Aging and Cohabitation*. New York: Garland.

Grusky, David, and Thomas DiPrete. 1990. "Recent Trends in the Process of Stratification." *Demography* 27:617–37.

Gueron, Judith M. 1984. *Lessons from a Job Guarantee: The Youth Incentive Entitlement Pilot Projects*. New York: Manpower Demonstration Research.

Guerrero, Ed. 1993. *Framing Blackness: The African-American Image in Film*. Philadelphia: Temple University Press.

Guinier, Lani. 1994. *The Tyranny of the Majority*. New York: Free Press.

Gundlach, James, and Alden Roberts. 1978. "Native American Indian Migration and Relocation: Success or Failure." *Pacific Sociological Review* 12:117–28.

Gustman, A. L., and T. L. Steinmeier. 1984. "Partial Retirement and the Analysis of Retirement Behavior." *Industrial and Labor Relations Review* 37(3):403–15.

Hadaway, C. Kirk, Penny Long Marler, and Mark Chaves. 1993. "What the Polls Don't Show: A Closer Look at U.S. Church Attendance." *American Sociological Review* 58(6):175–86.

Hamilton, Denise. 1993. "A House, Cash—and No Parents." *The Los Angeles Times*, June 24, 1.

Han, Shin-Kap, and Phyllis Moen. 1999. "Clocking Out: Temporal Patterning of Retirement." *American Journal of Sociology* 105(1): In press.

Han, Shin-Kap, and Phyllis Moen. 1999. "Work and Family in Temporal Context: A Life Course Approach." *The Annals of the American Academy of Political and Social Science* March:98–110.

Hannan, Michael T. 1979. "The Dynamics of Ethnic Boundaries in Modern States." In *National Development and the World System*, edited by M. T. Hannan and J. W. Meyer, 253–75. Chicago: University of Chicago Press.

Hass, Nancy. 1998. "A TV Generation Is Seeing beyond Color." *The New York Times*, February 22, 38.

Hastings, T. J., and G. H. Elder, Jr. 1988. *War Mobilization and Earnings in Men's Lives*. Atlanta: American Psychological Association.

Hatch, Nathan O. 1991. *The Democratization of American Christianity*. New Haven, CT: Yale University Press.

Hauser, Robert M. 1995. "Review of *The Bell Curve*." *Contemporary Sociology* 24:149–53.

Hauser, Robert M., and John Robert Warren. 1997. "Socioeconomic Indexes of Occupational Status: A Review, Update, and Critique." In *Sociological Methodology 1997*, edited by A. Raftery, 177–298. Cambridge, U.K.: Blackwell.

Havighurst, R. J., J. W. Baughman, E. W. Burgess, and W. H. Eaton. 1951. *The American Veteran Back Home*. New York: Longmans Green.

Hawley, Amos. 1971. *Urban Society: An Ecological Approach*. New York: Ronald.

Healy, Patrick. 1995a. "A Federal Judge Has Delayed His Recent Order to Mississippi Public Colleges to Adopt Tougher Admission Standards." *Chronicle of Higher Education*, April 28, A58.

———. 1995b. "Georgia's Proposed Admission Requirements Stir Fears of Big Enrollment Drops at Black Colleges." *Chronicle of Higher Education*, April 21, A36.

———. 1996a. "Mississippi Colleges Await Results of Tougher Admissions Standards." *Chronicle of Higher Education*, July 12, A30.

———. 1996b. "Black Enrollments Fall Sharply at Mississippi Public Colleges." *Chronicle of Higher Education*, September 27, A46.

Hechter, Michael. 1975. *Internal Colonialism*. London: Routledge & Kegan Paul.

Heckman, James J. 1995. "Lessons from *The Bell Curve*." *Journal of Political Economy* 103 (October):1091–1120.

Heise, David R. 1979. *Understanding Events: Affect and the Construction of Social Action*. New York: Cambridge University Press.

Henderson, Vivian. 1975. "Race, Economics, and Public Policy." *Crisis* 83(Fall):50–55.

Herman, J. L. 1992. *Trauma and Recovery*. New York: Basic.

Herrnstein, Richard J. 1971. "I.Q." *Atlantic Monthly* September:43–64.

———. 1990. "Still an American Dilemma." *Public Interest* (Winter):3–17.

Hernnstein, Richard J., and Charles Murray. 1994. *The Bell Curve: Intelligence and Class Structure in American Life*. New York: Free Press.

Hickey, Philip, and James A. Scott. 1955. "Growing Together, Review of *Schools in Transition* by R. M. Williams, Jr., and Margaret W. Ryan." *Christian Century* 72:792–93.

Higham, John. 1970. *Strangers in the Land: Patterns of American Nativism, 1860–1925*. New York: Atheneum.

Hill, Susan. 1984. *The Traditionally Black Institutions of Higher Education, 1860 to 1982*. Washington, DC: National Center for Education Statistics, U.S. Department of Education.

Hirschl, Thomas A., and Mark R. Rank. 1999. "Community Effects on Welfare Participation." *Sociological Forum* 14(1):159–178.

Hirschman, Charles. 1980. "Theories and Models in Ethnic Inequality." In *Research in Race and Ethnic Relations*, edited by C. B. Marrett and C. Leggon, 2:1–20. Greenwich, CT: JAI Press.

———. 1983. "The Melting Pot Reconsidered." *Annual Review of Sociology* 9:397–423.

Hirschman, Charles, and Morrison G. Wong. 1984. "Socioeconomic Gains of Asian Americans, Blacks, and Hispanics: 1960–1976." *American Journal of Sociology* 90(3):584–607.

Hirschmann, Albert O. 1958. *The Strategy of Economic Development*. New Haven: Yale University Press.

Hoch, Irving, Julie Hewitt, and Vicky Virgin. 1984. *Real Income, Poverty, and Resources*. Washington, DC: Resources for the Future.

Hochschild, Arlie Russell. 1997. *The Time Bind*. New York: Metropolitan.

Hochschild, Jennifer L. 1995. *Facing up to the American Dream: Race, Class, and the Soul of a Nation*. Princeton, NJ: Princeton University Press.

Hodgson, Godfrey. 1996. *The World Turned Right Side Up: A History of the Conservative Ascendancy in America*. Boston: Houghton-Mifflin.

Hoffman, Charlene M., Thomas D. Snyder, and Bill Sonnenberg. 1992. *Historically Black Colleges and Universities, 1976–90*. Washington, DC: U.S. Government Printing Office.

Hofmeyr, Isabel. 1987. "Building a Nation from Words: Afrikaans Language, Literature, and Ethnic Identity, 1902–1924." In *The Politics of Race, Class, and Nationalism in Twentieth-Century South Africa*, edited by S. Marks and S. Trapido, 95–123. London: Longman.

Hogan, Dennis P. 1981. *Transitions and Social Change: The Early Lives of American Man*. New York: Academic.

Hogan, Dennis P., and Daniel T. Lichter. 1995. "Children and Youth: Living Arrangements and Welfare." In *State of the Union: America in the 1990s*, edited by R. Farley, 2:93–139. New York: Russell Sage.

Holahan, C. K., and R. R. Sears. 1995. *The Gifted Group in Later Maturity*. Stanford, CA: Stanford University Press.

Holmes, Steven A. 1995. "Once-Tough Chief of Affirmative-Action Agency Is Forced to Change Tack." *The New York Times,* August 6, A-13.

Holzer, Harry J. 1987. "Informal Job Search and Black Youth Unemployment." *American Economic Review* 77:446–52.

——. 1996. *What Employers Want: Job Prospects for Less-Educated Workers.* New York: Russell Sage.

Horowitz, Donald L. 1975. "Ethnic Identity." In *Ethnicity: Theory and Experience,* edited by N. Glazer and D. P. Moynihan, 111–40. Cambridge, MA: Harvard University Press.

Horton, John. 1995. *The Politics of Diversity: Immigration, Resistance, and Change in Monterey Park, California.* Philadelphia: Temple University Press.

House, James S. 1981. "Social Structure and Personality." In *Social Psychology: Sociological Perspectives,* edited by M. Rosenberg and R. H. Turner, 525–61. New York: Basic.

House, James S., K. R. Landis, and D. Umberson. 1988. "Social Relationships and Health." *Science* 241:540–45.

Hout, Michael, and Daniel P. Dohan. 1996. "Two Paths to Educational Opportunity: Class and Educational Selection in Sweden and the United States." In *Can Education Be Equalized? The Swedish Case in Comparative Perspective,* edited by R. Erikson and J. O. Jonsson, 207–31. Boulder, CO: Westview.

Hoxie, Frederick E. 1984. *A Final Promise—The Campaign to Assimilate the Indians, 1880–1920.* Lincoln: University of Nebraska Press.

Huggins, Nathan Irving. 1995. "Ethnic Americans." In *Revelations: American History, American Myths,* 148–57. New York: Oxford University Press.

Hughes, Everett C., and Helen M. Hughes. 1952. *Where Peoples Meet: Racial and Ethnic Frontiers.* Glencoe, IL: Free Press.

Hughey, Michael. 1983. *Civil Religion and Moral Order: Theoretical and Historical Dimensions.* Westport, CT: Greenwood.

Ichheiser, Gustav. 1946. "The Jews and Anti-Semitism." *Sociometry* 9:92–108.

Inkeles, Alex. 1998. *One World Emerging?: Convergence and Divergence in Industrial Societies.* Boulder, CO: Westview.

Jackson, Kenneth. 1985. *Crabgrass Frontier: The Suburbanization of the United States.* New York: Oxford University Press.

Jacobson, P. H. 1959. *American Marriage and Divorce.* New York: Rinehart.

James, David R. 1998. "The Transformation of the Southern Racial State: Class and Race Determinants of Local-State Structures." *American Sociological Review* 53(2):191–208.

Jasso, Guillermina. 1991. "A Mechanism Possibly Implicated in the Origin of Gender Inequality: Framework and an Initial Theorem." Unpubl. manuscript, Dept. of Sociology, Univ. of Iowa.

Jaynes, Gerald David, and Robin M. Williams, Jr., eds. 1989. *A Common Destiny: Blacks and American Society.* Washington, DC: National Academy Press.

Jencks, Christopher, Susan Bartlett, Mary Corcoran, James Crouse, David Eaglesfield, Gregory Jackson, Kent McClelland, Peter Mueser, Michael Olneck, Joseph Schwartz, Sherry Ward, Jill Williams. 1979. *Who Gets Ahead: The Determinants of Economic Success in America.* New York: Basic.

Jencks, Christopher, Marshall Smith, Henry Acland, Mary Jo Bane, David Cohen, Herbert Gintis, Barbara Heyns, and Stephen Michelson. 1972. *Inequality: A Reassessment of the Effects of Family and Schooling in America.* New York: Basic.

Jensen, Leif, and Yoshimi Chitose. 1997. "Will Workfare Work? Job Availability for Welfare Recipients in Rural and Urban America." *Population Research and Policy Review* 16:383–95.

Jensen, Leif, and Marta Tienda. 1989. "Nonmetropolitan Minority Families in the United States: Trends in Racial and Ethnic Economic Stratification, 1959–1986." *Rural Sociology* 54(4):509–32.

Jhally, Sut, and Justin Lewis. 1992. *Enlightened Racism: The Cosby Show Audiences and the Myth of the American Dream.* Boulder, CO: Westview.

Johnson, Allan. 1997. "The Difference between Black and White Viewers—A Study in Contrast." *Chicago Tribune*, April 18, 1, 3.

Johnson, Kenneth, and Calvin L. Beale. 1994. "The Recent Revival of Widespread Population Growth in Nonmetropolitan Areas of the United States." *Rural Sociology* 59(4):435–44.

Jordan, Winthrop. 1974. *The White Man's Burden: Historical Origins of Racism in the United States.* New York: Oxford University Press.

Juergensmeyer, Mark. 1993. *The New Cold War? Religious Nationalism Confronts the Secular State.* Berkeley: University of California Press.

Kahlenberg, Richard. 1996. *The Remedy: Class, Race, and Affirmative Action.* New York: Basic.

Kallen, Horace M. 1924. *Culture and Democracy in the United States.* New York: Boni and Liveright.

Karoly, Lynn. 1993. "The Trend in Inequality among Families, Individuals, and Workers in the United States: A Twenty-Five Year Perspective." In *Uneven Tides: Rising Inequality in America,* edited by S. Danziger and P. Gottschalk, 19–97. New York: Russell Sage.

Kasarda, John D. 1993. "Inner-City Concentrated Poverty and Neighborhood Distress: 1970–1990." *Housing Policy Debate* 4(3):253–302.

Katz, Lawrence. 1996. *Wage Subsidies for the Disadvantaged.* Cambridge, MA: National Bureau of Economic Research.

Katznelson, Ira. 1979. "Review of *Mutual Accommodation* by R. M. Williams, Jr." *Journal of Politics* 41:723–24.

Kiecolt-Glaser, J. K., and R. Glaser. 1991. "Stress and Immune Function in Humans." In *Psychoneuroimmunology,* 2d ed., edited by R. Ader, D. L. Felten, and N. Cohen, 849–67. New York: Academic.

King, Martin Luther, Jr. 1963. *Why We Can't Wait.* New York: Harper & Row.

Kingston, Paul William, and Steven L. Nock. 1987. "Time Together among Dual Earner Couples." *American Sociological Review* 73(2):391–400.

Kohn, Melvin L. 1963. "Social Class and Parent-Child Relationships: An Interpretation." *American Journal of Sociology* 68(January):471–80.

———. 1977 [1st ed. 1969]. *Class and Conformity: A Study in Values, with a Reassessment,* 2d ed. Chicago, IL: University of Chicago Press.

———. 1980. "Job Complexity and Adult Personality." In *Themes of Work and Love in Adulthood,* edited by N. J. Smelser and E. H. Erikson, 193–210. Cambridge, MA: Harvard University Press.

———. 1989. "Social Structure and Personality: A Quintessentially Sociological Approach to Social Psychology." *Social Forces* 68:26–33.

———. 1996. "Review Essay: *The Bell Curve* from the Perspective of Research on Social Structure and Personality." *Sociological Forum* 11(June):395–411.

Kohn, Melvin L., Atsushi Naoi, Carrie Schoenbach, Carmi Schooler, and Kazimierz M. Slomczynski. 1990. "Position in the Class Structure and Psychological Functioning in the United States, Japan, and Poland." *American Journal of Sociology* 95:964–1008.

Kohn, Melvin L., and Carrie Schoenbach. 1983. "Class, Stratification, and Psychological Functioning." In *Work and Personality: An Inquiry into the Social Stratification,* by M. L. Kohn and C. Schooler (with collaboration of Joanne Miller, Karen A. Miller, Carrie Schoenbach, and Ronald Schoenberg), 154–89. Norwood, NJ: Ablex.

Kohn, Melvin L., and Carmi Schooler. 1978. "The Reciprocal Effects of the Substantive Complexity of Work and Intellectual Flexibility: A Longitudinal Assessment." *American Journal of Sociology* 84:24–52.

Kohn, Melvin L., and Carmi Schooler (with collaboration of Joanne Miller, Karen A. Miller, Carrie Schoenbach, and Ronald Schoenberg). 1983. *Work and Personality: An Inquiry into the Impact of Social Stratification.* Norwood, NJ: Ablex.

Kohn, Melvin L., and Kazimierz M. Slomczynski (with the collaboration of Carrie Schoenbach). 1990. *Social Structure and Self-Direction: A Comparative Analysis of the United States and Poland.* Oxford, U.K.: Basil Blackwell.

Kohn, Melvin L., Kazimierz M. Slomczynski, Krystyna Janicka, Valeri Khmelko, Bogdan W. Mach, Vladimir Paniotto, Wojciech Zaborowski, Roberto Gutierrez, and Cory Heyman. 1997. "Social Structure and Personality under Conditions of Radical Social Change: A Comparative Analysis of Poland and Ukraine." *American Sociological Review* 62:614–38.

Korenman, Sanders, and Christopher Winship. 1996. *A Reanalysis of* The Bell Curve. Cambridge, MA: National Bureau of Economic Research.

Kulka, R. A., W. E. Schlenger, J. A. Fairbank, R. L. Hough, B. K. Jordan, C. R. Marmar, and D. S. Weiss. 1990. *Trauma and the Vietnam War Generation: Report of Findings from the National Vietnam Veterans Readjustment Study.* New York: Brunner/Mazel.

Kushnick, Louis. 1966. "Review of *Strangers Next Door* by R. M. Williams, Jr., et al." *Race* 7:321–22.

Kwawer, J. 1980. "Transference and Countertransference in Homosexuality: Changing Psychoanalytic Views." *American Journal of Psychoanalytic Therapy* 34:72–80.

Lait, Matt. 1996a. "O. C. Agency Helped Underage Mothers to Wed." *The Los Angeles Times*, September 1, A1.

———. 1996b. "No Simple Solutions." *The Los Angeles Times*, September 29, A3.

Landry, Bart. 1987. *The New Black Middle Class.* Berkeley: University of California Press.

Laufer, R. S., and M. S. Gallops. 1985. "Life-Course Effects of Vietnam Combat and Abusive Violence: Marital Patterns." *Journal of Marriage and the Family* 47(4):839–53.

Laumann, Edward O. 1973. *Bonds of Pluralism. The Form and Substance of Urban Social Networks.* New York: Wiley Interscience.

Laurence, Janice H. 1994. *The Military: Purveyors of Fine Skills and Comportment for a Few Good Men.* Philadelphia: National Center on the Educational Quality of the Workforce, University of Pennsylvania.

Lederman, Douglas. 1998. "High Court Declines to Review Mississippi Desegregation Case. *Chronicle of Higher Education*, January 30, A28.

Lee, Martha F. 1996. *The Nation of Islam: An American Millenarian Movement.* Syracuse, NY: Syracuse University Press.

Lehman, Edward C., Jr. 1988. "Religion and Race in the United States." *Review of Religious Research* 30(2):entire issue.

Lenski, Gerhard. 1966. *Power and Privilege: A Theory of Social Stratification.* New York: McGraw-Hill.

Levy, Frank. 1995. "Incomes and Income Inequality." In *State of the Union: America in the 1990s*, edited by R. Farley, 1:1–58. New York: Russell Sage.

Lewis, John, and Michael D'Orso. 1998. *Walking with the Wind: A Memoir of the Movement.* New York: Simon and Schuster.

Lieberson, Stanley. 1980. *A Piece of the Pie: Black and White Immigrants since 1880.* Berkeley: University of California Press.

Lieberson, Stanley, and Mary Waters. 1988. *From Many Strands: Ethnic and Racial Groups in Contemporary America.* New York: Russell Sage.

Lienesch, Michael. 1993. *Redeeming America: Piety and Politics in the New Christian Right.* Chapel Hill: University of North Carolina Press.

Lin, Nan. 1982. "Social Resources and Instrumental Action." In *Social Structure and Network Analysis*, edited by P. V. Marsden and N. Lin, 131–45. Beverly Hills, CA: Sage.

Lin, Nan, and Mary Dumin. 1986. "Access to Occupations through Social Ties." *Social Networks* 8:365–85.

Linard, André. 1996. "La Pêche, Enjeu de Toutes Les Convoîtises." In *Conflits Din de Siècle*, edited by I. Ramonet, C. D. Brie, and A. Gresh, 29. Paris: Le Monde Diplomatique, Manière de Voir.

Lincoln, C. Eric. 1984. *Race, Religion, and the Continuing American Dilemma.* New York: Hill and Wang.

Lincoln, C. Eric, and Lawrence H. Mamiya. 1990. *The Black Church in the American Experience.* Durham, NC: Duke University Press.

Lind, Michael. 1996. *Up from Conservatism: Why the Right Is Wrong for America.* New York: Free Press.

Lipset, Seymour Martin. 1995. *Equality and the American Creed.* Washington, DC: Progressive Policy Institute.

Lipset, Seymour Martin, and Earl Raab. 1969. *The Politics of Unreason.* New York: Harper & Row.

Lipset, Seymour Martin, and Stein Rokkan. 1967. *Party Systems and Voter Alignments.* New York: Free Press.

Little, R. D., and J. E. Fredland. 1979. "Veteran Status, Earnings, and Race: Some Long-Term Results." *Armed Forces and Society* 5(2):244–60.

Lobao, Linda. 1996. "A Sociology of the Periphery versus a Peripheral Sociology: Rural Sociology and the Dimensions of Space." *Rural Sociology* 61(1):77–102.

Local Community Fact Book for Chicago—1950. 1953. Chicago: Community Inventory, University of Chicago.

Local Community Fact Book for Chicago—1960. 1963. Chicago: Community Inventory, University of Chicago.

Logan, John. 1996. "Rural America as a Symbol of American Values." *Rural Development Perspectives* 1(1):24–28.

Logan, John, and Reid Golden. 1986. "Suburbs and Satellites: Two Decades of Change." *American Sociological Review* 51(June):430–37.

Lovejoy, Albert E. 1955. "Review of *Schools in Transition* by Robin M. Williams, Jr., and Margaret W. Ryan." *Social Forces* 34:94.

MacKinnon, C. A. 1987. "Difference and Dominance: On Sex Discrimination (1984)." In *Feminism Unmodified: Discourses on Life and Law,* edited by C. MacKinnon, 32–45. Cambridge, MA: Harvard University Press.

Maines, John. 1992. "Black and White in Color." *American Demographics* 14:9.

Mamiya, Lawrence H. 1982. "From Black Muslim to Bilalian." *Journal for the Scientific Study of Religion* 12:138–52.

Mandal, Ernest. 1976. "Capitalism and Regional Disparities." *Southwest Economy and Society* 1:41–46.

Manski, Charles, and Stephen Lerman. 1977. "The Estimation of Choice-Based Probabilities from Choice-Based Samples." *Econometrica* 45:1977–88.

"Many Seek Security in Private Communities." 1995. *The New York Times,* September 3, 1.

Manza, Jeff, and Clem Brooks. 1997. "The Religious Factor in U.S. Presidential Elections, 1960–1992." *American Journal of Sociology* 103(1):38–81.

Marini, Stephen A. 1982. *Radical Sects of Revolutionary New England.* Cambridge, MA: Harvard University Press.

Markovsky, Barry, LeRoy F. Smith, and Joseph Berger. 1984. "Do Status Interventions Persist?" *American Sociological Review* 49:373–82.

Marsden, Peter V., and Jeanne S. Hurlbert. 1988. "Social Resources and Mobility Outcomes: A Replication and Extension." *Social Forces* 66:1038–59.

Marshall, T. H. 1949. *Citizenship and Social Class.* Cambridge, U.K.: Cambridge University Press.

Martin, David. 1990. *Tongues of Fire: The Explosion of Protestantism in Latin America.* Oxford, U.K.: Basil Blackwood.

Martin, Teresa Castro, and Larry L. Bumpass. 1989. "Recent Trends in Marital Disruption." *Demography* 26:37–61.

Marty, Martin E., and R. Scott Appleby, eds. 1994. *Accounting for Fundamentalisms: The Dynamic Character of Movements.* Chicago: University of Chicago Press.

———. 1995. *Fundamentalism Comprehended.* Chicago: University of Chicago Press.

——. 1997. *The One and the Many*. Cambridge, MA: Harvard University Press.

Massey, Douglas S. 1985. "Ethnic Residential Segregation: A Theoretical Synthesis and Empirical Review." *Sociology and Social Research* 69:315–50.

Massey, Douglas S., and Nancy Denton. 1987. "Trends in Residential Segregation of Blacks, Hispanics, and Asians: 1970–1980." *American Sociological Review* 52:802–25.

——. 1988. "Suburbanization and Segregation in U.S. Metropolitan Areas." *American Journal of Sociology* 94:592–626.

——. 1993. *American Apartheid: Segregation and the Making of the Underclass*. Cambridge, MA: Harvard University Press.

Massey, Douglas S., and Brendan P. Mullan. 1984. "A Demonstration of the Effect of Seasonal Migration on Fertility." *Demography* 21:501–17.

Matloff, Norman. 1996. *Welfare Use among Elderly Chinese Immigrants*. Testimony to the Senate Judiciary Committee Subcommittee on Immigration. 104th Cong., 2d sess.

McBrien, Richard P. 1982. "Roman Catholicism: E. Pluribus Unum." *Daedalus* 111(1):73–83.

McCloud, Aminah Beverly. 1995. *African American Islam*. New York: Routledge.

McGranahan, David, and Kathleen Kassel. 1996. "Education and Rural Minority Job Opportunities." In *Racial and Ethnic Minorities in Rural Areas*, edited by L. L. Swanson, AER 731:5–25. Washington, DC: USDA-ERS.

McLanahan, Sara, and Lynne Casper. 1995. "Growing Diversity and Inequality in the American Family." In *State of the Union: America in the 1990s*, edited by Reynolds Farley. 1–45. New York: Russell Sage.

McMahon, Anne M., Barbara C. Ilardi, and Henry A. Walker. 1994. "The Organizational Enactment of Social Identities." Unpubl. manuscript, Williamson School of Business Administration, Youngstown State University.

Mead, George H. 1934. *Mind, Self, and Society*. Chicago: University of Chicago Press.

——. 1938. *Philosophy of the Act*. Chicago: University of Chicago Press.

Mershon, Sherie, and Steven Schlossman. 1998. *Foxholes and Color Lines*. Baltimore: Johns Hopkins University Press.

Miller, Dan E., Robert A. Hintz, Jr., and Carl J. Couch. 1975. "The Elements and Structure of Openings." In *Constructing Social Life*, edited by C. J. Couch and Robert A. Hintz, Jr., 1–25. Champaign, IL: Stipes.

Miller, Donald E. 1997. *Reinventing American Protestantism: Christianity in the New Millennium*. Berkeley: University of California Press.

Miller, J. Erroll. 1955. "Immediate versus Gradual Desegregation, Review of *Schools in Transition*, by Robin M. Williams, Jr., and Margaret W. Ryan." *Phylon* 16:106–8.

Miller, J. G. 1936. *The Black Patch War*. Chapel Hill: University of North Carolina Press.

Miller, Joanne, Carmi Schooler, Melvin L. Kohn, and Karen A. Miller. 1979. "Women and Work: The Psychological Effects of Occupational Conditions." *American Journal of Sociology* 85:66–94.

Miller, Joanne, Kazimierz M. Slomczynski, and Melvin L. Kohn. 1985. "Continuity of Learning-Generalization: The Effect of Job on Men's Intellective Process in the United States and Poland." *American Journal of Sociology* 91:593–615.

Miller, Karen A., Melvin L. Kohn, and Carmi Schooler. 1985. "Educational Self-Direction and the Cognitive Functioning of Students." *Social Forces* 63(June):923–44.

——. 1986. "Educational Self-Direction and Personality." *American Sociological Review* 51:372–90.

Miller, Stuart. 1992. "USA Makes Major Effort to Draft Minority Auds." *Variety* 349(4):17, 86.

Mills, Charles Wright. 1959. *The Sociological Imagination*. New York: Oxford University Press.

Modell, John, and Tamara Hareven. 1973. "Urbanization and the Malleable Household." *Journal of Marriage and the Family* 35:467–79.

Moen, Phyllis. 1998. "Recasting Careers: Changing Reference Groups, Risks, and Realities." *Generations* 22(1):40–45.

Moen, Phyllis, Donna Dempster-McClain, and Robin M. Williams, Jr. 1989. "Social Integration and Longevity: An Event History Analysis of Women's Roles and Resilience." *American Sociological Review* 54(August):635–47.

———. 1992. "Successful Aging: A Life Course Perspective on Women's Roles and Health." *American Journal of Sociology* 97(6):1612–38.

Montgomery, James D. 1994. "Weak Ties, Employment, and Inequality: An Equilibrium Analysis." *American Journal of Sociology* 99:1212–36.

Moore, Brenda L. 1996. *To Serve My Country, To Serve My Race.* New York: New York University Press.

Moore, Cathleen M. 1996. *Al-Mughtaribun: American Law and the Transformation of Muslim Life in the United States.* Albany, NY: SUNY Press.

Moore, R. Laurence. 1986. *Religious Outsiders and the Making of Americans.* New York: Oxford University Press.

Mortimer, Jeylan T., Jon Lorence, and Donald S. Kumka. 1986. *Work, Family, and Personality: Transition to Adulthood.* Norwood, NJ: Ablex.

Mortimer, Jeylan T., Ellen Efron Pimentel, Seongryeol Ryu, Katherine Nash, and Chaimun Lee. 1996. "Part-Time Work and Occupational Value Formation in Adolescence." *Social Forces* 74(June):1405–18.

Moskos, Charles C., and John Sibley Butler. 1996. *All That We Can Be: Black Leadership and Racial Integration the Army Way.* New York: Basic.

Moskos, Peter C. 1997. "Afro-Anglo: America's Core Culture." *National Journal of Sociology* 7:131–39.

Mowrey, Arthur M. 1901. *The Dorr War.* Providence: Preston and Rounds.

MTV News. 1997. "Black and White TV." Half-hour television special.

Muhammad, Askia. 1978. "Disputes Rend Nation of Islam." *Cleveland Plain Dealer,* November 15, 27.

Muhammad, Wallace Deen. 1980. *As the Light Shineth from the East.* Cedarhurst, NY: WMD Publications.

Murphy, Larry G., J. Gordon Melton, and Gary L. Ward. 1993. *Encyclopedia of African American Religions.* New York: Garland.

Murray, Stephen O., Joseph H. Rankin, and Dennis W. Magill. 1981. "Strong Ties and Job Information." *Sociology of Work and Occupations* 8:119–36.

Mutran, Elizabeth, and Linda K. George. 1982. "Alternative Methods of Measuring Role/Identity: A Research Note." *Social Forces* 60:866–76.

Myers, Dowell, and Jennifer Wolch. 1995. "The Polarization of Housing Status." In *State of the Union: America in the 1990s,* edited by R. Farley, 1:269–334. New York: Russell Sage.

Myers, Gustavus. 1943. *The History of Bigotry in the United States.* New York: Random House.

Myrdal, Gunnar. 1944. *An American Dilemma.* New York: Harper & Row.

———. 1957. *Rich Lands and Poor.* New York: Harper & Row.

Nagel, Joanne. 1996. *American Indian Ethnic Renewal.* New York: Oxford.

Nalty, Bernard C. 1986. *Strength for the Fight: A History of Black Americans in the Military.* New York: Free Press.

Nalty, Bernard C., and Morris J. MacGregor. 1981. *Blacks in the Military: Essential Documents.* Wilmington, DE: Scholarly Resources.

Naoi, Atsushi, and Carmi Schooler. 1985. "Occupational Conditions and Psychological Functioning in Japan." *American Journal of Sociology* 90:729–52.

National Center for Educational Statistics. 1997. *Digest of Education Statistics, 1997.* Washington, DC: U.S. Department of Education.

———. *High School and Beyond.* 1980. Ann Arbor, MI: Inter-university Consortium for Political and Social Research.

"Navy Sets New Diversity Goals for Officer Accessions." 1995. *Navy Times,* May 1, 14.

Nee, Victor, and Jimy Sanders. 1985. "The Road to Parity: Determinants of the Socioeconomic Achievements of Asian Americans." *Ethnic and Racial Studies* 8(1):75–93.

Neidert, Lisa S., and Reynolds Farley. 1985. "Assimilation in the United States: An Analysis of Ethnic and Generational Differences in Status and Achievement." *American Sociological Review* 50(6):840–50.

Nelson, Jill. 1993. *Volunteer Slavery*. Chicago: Noble.

Niebuhr, Gustav. 1998. "Make-Up of American Religion Is Looking More Like Mosaic, Data Say." *The New York Times*, April 12, 12.

Noiriel, Gerard. 1996. *The French Melting Pot: Immigration, Citizenship, and National Identity*. Translated by Geoffroy de Laforcade. Minneapolis: University of Minnesota Press.

Nord, Mark. 1996a. *Do State AFDC Benefit Levels Reflect a Racial or Urban Bias?* Working Paper 10. Madison, WI: Department of Rural Sociology, Rural Poverty Information Series.

———. 1996b. *Living near the Poverty Line: Nonmetropolitan Poverty and Income, 1995*. Working Paper 12. Madison, WI: Department of Rural Sociology, Rural Poverty Information Series.

O'Brien, Conor Cruise. 1988. *God Land: Reflections on Religion and Nationalism*. Cambridge, MA: Harvard University Press.

O'Connor, John. 1997. "If Whites Can Be Silly, Why Can't Blacks Cut Up?" *The New York Times*, April 19, 46.

Ogletree, Charles J., Jr. 1996. "The Case for Affirmative Action." *Stanford* 24(5):68–69.

O'Hare, William P. 1988. *The Rise of Poverty in Rural America*. Washington, DC: Population Reference Bureau.

Olson, David H., and Hamilton McCubbin. 1983. *Families: What Makes Them Work*. Beverly Hills, CA: Sage.

Olson, K. W. 1974. *The G.I. Bill, the Veterans, and the Colleges*. Lexington: University Press of Kentucky.

Olzak, Susan. 1992. *The Dynamics of Ethnic Competition and Conflict*. Stanford: Stanford University Press.

Omi, Michael, and Howard Winant. 1994. *Racial Formation in the United States: From the 1960s to the 1990s*. New York: Routledge.

Oppenheimer, Valerie. 1994. "Women's Rising Employment and the Future of the Family in Industrial Societies." *Population and Development Review* 20:293–42.

Ortiz, Vilma. 1996. "The Mexican-Origin Population: Permanent Working Class or Emergent Middle Class?" In *Ethnic Los Angeles*, edited by R. Waldinger and M. Bozorgmehr, 247–77. New York: Russell Sage.

Park, Robert E. 1950. *Race and Culture*. Glencoe, IL: Free Press.

Park, Robert E., and Ernest Burgess, eds. [1921] 1969. *Introduction to the Science of Sociology*. Chicago: University of Chicago Press.

Park, Robert E., Ernest Burgess, and Roderick McKenzie. 1925. *The City*. Chicago: University of Chicago Press.

Parsons, Talcott. 1951. *The Social System*. Glencoe, IL: Free Press.

Patterson, Orlando. 1997. *The Ordeal of Integration: Progress and Resentment in America's "Racial" Crisis*. Washington DC: Civitas/Counterpoint.

Pavalko, E. K., and G. H. Elder, Jr. 1990. "World War II and Divorce: A Life Course Perspective." *The American Journal of Sociology* 95(5):1213–34.

Paykel, E. S., and B. M. Rao. 1984. "Methodology in Studies of Life Events and Cancer." In *Psychosocial Stress and Cancer*, edited by C. L. Cooper, 73–89. New York: Wiley.

Pennebaker, J. W., and J. R. Susman. 1988. "Disclosure of Traumas and Psychosomatic Processes." *Social Science Medicine* 26(3):327–32.

Portes, Alejandro, and Robert L. Bach. 1985. *Latin Journey: Cuban and Mexican Immigrants in the United States*. Berkeley: University of California Press.

Portes, Alejandro, and Ruben Rumbaut. 1996. *Immigrant America*. Berkeley: University of California Press.

Powell, Colin L. 1995. *My American Journey*. New York: Random House.

Presser, Harriet B. 1995. "Job, Family, and Gender: Determinants of Nonstandard Work Schedules among Employed Americans in 1991." *Demography* 32:577–98.

Princeton Religious Research Center. 1992. "Church Attendance Constant." *Emerging Trends* 14(3):4.

Raab, Earl, ed. 1964. *Religious Conflict in America: Studies in the Problems beyond Bigotry.* Garden City, NY: Anchor.

Raboteau, Albert J. 1978. *Slave Religion: The "Invisible Religion" in the Antebellum South.* Oxford, U.K.: Oxford University Press.

"Race Disparities in Federal Civil Service." 1995. *The Washington Post,* April 10, 1.

Raper, Arthur F. 1933. *The Tragedy of Lynching.* Chapel Hill: University of North Carolina Press.

Rapoport, Rhona. 1989. *Ideologies about Family Forms: Towards Diversity.* London: Routledge.

Rawlings, Steve W., and Arlene F. Saluter. 1995. "Households and Family Characteristics: March 1994." *Current Population Reports* Series P-20-483, vii. Washington, DC: U.S. Dept. of Commerce.

Redl, Fritz. 1946. *Intercultural Education News* 7(4):3–5.

Reimers, C., and M. Honig. 1989. "The Retirement Process in the United States: Mobility among Full-Time Work, Partial Retirement, and Full Retirement." In *Redefining the Process of Retirement: An International Perspective,* edited by W. Schmahl, 115–31. Berlin: Springer.

Reischauer, Robert, and R. Kent Weaver. 1995. "Financial Welfare: Are Block Grants the Answer?" In *Looking Before We Leap: Social Science and Welfare Reform,* edited by R. Kent Weaver and William T. Dickens, 13–26. Washington, DC: Brookings Institution.

"Religious Belief in America: A New Poll." 1996. *Free Inquiry* 16(3).

Rendeiro, Pamela. 1956. "Review of *Schools in Transition* by R. M. Williams, Jr. and Margaret W. Ryan." *Social Education* 20:190–191.

Research Triangle Institute. 1981. *Longitudinal Study: Base Year (1972) through Fourth Follow Up, 1979.* Washington, DC: National Center for Education Statistics.

Rich, Bennett M. 1941. *The Presidents and Civil Disorder.* Washington, DC: Brookings Institution.

Ridgeway, Cecilia L. 1991. "The Social Construction of Status Value: Gender and Other Nominal Characteristics." *Social Forces* 70:367–86.

Ridgeway, Cecilia L., and Henry A. Walker. 1995. "Status Structures." In *Sociological Perspectives on Social Psychology,* edited by K. S. Cook, G. A. Fine, and J. S. House, 281–310. Boston: Allyn and Bacon.

Robbins, Thomas, and Susan Palmer, eds. 1997. *Millennium, Messiahs, and Mayhem: Contemporary Apocalyptic Movements.* New York: Routledge.

Robinson, Jerry W., Jr., and James D. Preston. 1976. "Equal-Status Contact Modification of Racial Prejudice: A Reexamination of the Contact Hypothesis." *Social Forces* 54:911–24.

Roper Organization, Inc. 1992. *Public Attitudes toward Rural America and Rural Electric Cooperatives.* Washington, DC: National Rural Electric Cooperatives Association.

Rose, Peter I. 1993. "'Of Every Hue and Caste': Race, Immigration, and Perceptions of Pluralism." In *Interminority Affairs in the U.S.: Pluralism at the Crossroads,* edited by Peter I. Rose. *Annals of the American Academy of Social and Political Science* 530:187–202.

———. 1997a. *Tempest-Tost: Race, Immigration, and the Dilemmas of Diversity.* New York: Oxford University Press.

———. 1997b. *They and We: Racial and Ethnic Relations in the United States.* New York: McGraw-Hill.

———. 1998. *Professional Passions.* New York: Smith.

Rothberg, Joseph M., Paul T. Bartone, Harry C. Holloway, and David H. Marlowe. 1990. "Life and Death in the U.S. Army." *Journal of the American Medical Association* 265:2241–44.

Rowan, Carl. 1993. *Breaking Barriers: A Memoir*. Boston: Little, Brown.

Rudenstine, Neil L. 1996. "Why a Diverse Student Body Is So Important." *The Chronicle of Higher Education*, April 19, B1.

Ruhm, C. J. 1990. "Career Jobs, Bridge Employment, and Retirement." In *Bridges to Retirement: Older Workers in a Changing Labor Market*, edited by P. B. Doeringer, 92–107. Ithaca, NY: ILR Press.

Rural Sociological Society Task Force on Persistent Rural Poverty. 1993. *Persistent Poverty in Rural America*. Boulder, CO: Westview.

Rutten, Rosanne. 1994. "Courting the Workers' Vote in a Hacienda Region: Rhetoric and Response in the 1992 Philippine Elections." *Pilipinas* 22:1–34.

Saluter, Arlene. 1996. "Marital Status and Living Arrangements: March 1994." In *Current Population Reports*, Series P20–484, A7. Washington, DC: U.S. Government Printing Office.

Sampson, R. J., and J. H. Laub. 1996. "Socioeconomic Achievement in the Life Course of Disadvantaged Men: Military Service as a Turning Point, Circa 1940–1965." *American Sociological Review* 61(3):347–67.

Sanchez, George. 1993. *Becoming Mexican American: Ethnicity, Culture, and Identity in Chicano Los Angeles, 1900–1945*. New York: Oxford University Press.

Sayer, Andrew. 1993. *Method of Social Science: A Realist Approach*. London: Routledge.

Schlesinger, Arthur M., Jr. 1992. *The Disuniting of America*. New York: Norton.

Schroedel, Jean Reith. 1985. *Alone in a Crowd: Women in the Trades Tell Their Stories*. Philadelphia: Temple University Press.

Schultz, Theodore W. 1953. *The Economic Organization of Agriculture*. New York: McGraw-Hill.

Schwartzman, David. 1997. *Black Unemployment: Part of Unskilled Unemployment*. Westport, CT: Greenwood.

Sheppard, E. 1996. "Site, Situation, and Social Theory." *Environment and Planning A* 28:1339–44.

Shipler, David K. 1997. *A Country of Strangers: Blacks and Whites in America*. New York: Knopf.

Shogren, Elizabeth. 1996. "Birthrate for Unwed Women Shows Decline." *The Los Angeles Times*, October 5, A1.

Shurden, Walter B., ed. 1993. *The Struggle for the Soul of the SBC: Moderate Responses to the Fundamentalist Movement*. Macon, GA: Mercer University Press.

Simmel, Georg. [1908] 1971. "How Is Society Possible?" In *Georg Simmel: On Individuality and Social Forms*, edited by D. N. Levine, 6–22. Chicago: University of Chicago Press.

Simon, Curtis J., and John T. Warner. 1992. "Matchmaker, Matchmaker: The Effect of Old Boy Networks on Job Match Quality, Earnings, and Tenure." *Journal of Labor Economics* 10:306–31.

Skocpol, Theda. 1979. *States and Social Revolutions*. Cambridge, MA: Cambridge University Press.

Small, Meredith F. 1995. *What's Love Got to Do With It? The Evolution of Human Mating*. New York: Doubleday.

Smith, Neil. 1990. *Uneven Development*. Cambridge, MA: Basil Blackwell.

Smith, Tom W. 1991a. *GSS Social Change Report Counting Flocks and Lost Sheep: Trends in Religious Preference since World War II*. Chicago: National Opinion Research Center.

———. 1991b. *What Do Americans Think about Jews*. New York: American Jewish Committee.

———. 1994. "Attitudes toward Family Issues in the United States." In *Sexuality across the Life Course*, edited by A. Rossi, 63–97. Chicago: University of Chicago Press.

Smith-Lovin, Lynn, and David Heise. 1988. *Analyzing Social Interaction: Advances in Affect Control Theory*. New York: Gordon and Breach.

Smothers, Ronald. 1995. "Mississippi Mellows on Issues of Bias in State Universities." *The New York Times*, March 13, 14.

Snipp, C. Matthew. 1989. *American Indians: The First of the This Land*. New York: Russell Sage.

Snipp, C. Matthew, and Gary Sandefur. 1989. "Earnings of American Indians and Alaska Natives: The Effects of Residence and Migration." *Social Forces* 66:994–1008.

Social Security Administration. 1996. *Social Security Bulletin Annual Statistical Supplement 1996*. Washington, DC: Social Security Administration.

Soja, Edward W. 1989. *Postmodern Geographies*. New York: Verso.

South, S. J. 1985. "Economic Conditions and the Divorce Rate: A Time-Series Analysis of the Postwar United States." *Journal of Marriage and the Family* 47(1):31–41.

Sowell, Thomas. 1994. *Race and Culture*. New York: Basic.

Sperry, Willard. 1946. *Religion in America*. New York: Macmillan.

Stacey, Judith. 1996. *In the Name of the Family: Rethinking Values in the Postmodern Age*. Boston: Beacon.

Stack, Carol B. 1974. *All Our Kin: Strategies for Survival in a Black Community*. New York: Harper & Row.

Staples, Brent. 1994. *Parallel Time*. New York: Pantheon.

Star, Shirley A., Robin M. Williams, Jr., and Samuel A. Stouffer. 1949. "Negro Soldiers." In *The American Soldier*, Vol. 1, *Adjustments during Army Life*, edited by Stouffer, Samuel A., Edward A. Suchman, Leland C. DeVinney, Shirley A. Star, and Robin M. Williams, Jr., 486–599. Princeton, NJ: Princeton University Press.

Steele, Shelby. 1995. "Affirmative Action Must Go." *The New York Times*, March 1, A13.

Steinfels, Peter. 1985. The Bishops and Their Critics. *Dissent*. 176–82.

Stinchcombe, Arthur L. 1990. "Work Institutions and the Sociology of Everyday Life." In *The Nature of Work. Sociological Perspectives*, edited by K. Erikson and S. P. Vallas, 99–116. New Haven, CT: Yale University Press.

Stone, L. Joseph. 1955. "Review of *Schools in Transition*, by R. M. Williams, Jr., and Margaret W. Ryan." *Social Research* 22:18–20.

Storper, Michael, and Richard Walker. 1989. *The Capitalist Imperative: Territory, Technology, and Industrial Growth*. New York: Basil Blackwell.

Stouffer, Samuel. A., A. A. Lumsdaine, M. H. Lumsdaine, R. M. Williams, Jr., M. B. Smith, I. L. Janis, Shirley A. Star, and L. S. Cottrell, Jr. 1949. *The American Soldier*. Vol. 2, *Combat and Its Aftermath*. Princeton, NJ: Princeton University Press.

Stouffer, Samuel A., Edward A. Suchman, Leland C. DeVinney, Shirley A. Star, and Robin M. Williams, Jr. 1949. *The American Soldier*. Vol. 1, *Adjustment during Army Life*. Princeton, NJ: Princeton University Press.

Stryker, Sheldon. 1981. "Symbolic Interactionism: Themes and Variations." In *Social Psychology: Sociological Perspectives*, edited by M. Rosenberg and R. H. Turner, 3–29. New York: Basic.

Suro, Roberto. 1989. "Switch by Hispanic Catholics Changes Face of U.S. Religion." *The New York Times*, May 14, Late City Final Edition.

Taeuber, Alma F. 1966. "Review of *Strangers Next Door* by R. M. Williams, Jr., et al." *Social Service Review* 40:233–36.

Takaki, Ronald. 1993. *A Different Mirror*. Boston: Little, Brown.

Taubman, Paul J. 1991. "Discrimination within the Family: The Treatment of Daughters and Sons." In *Essays on the Economics of Discrimination*, edited by E. P. Hoffman, 25–42. Kalamazoo, MI: W. E. Upjohn Institute for Employment Research.

Taylor, Howard F. 1995. "Review of *The Bell Curve*." *Contemporary Sociology* 24:153–58.

Terman, L. M., and M. H. Oden. 1959. *Genetic Studies of Genius*. Vol. 5. *The Gifted Group at Mid-Life: Thirty-Five Years of Follow-up of the Superior Child*. Stanford, CA: Stanford University Press.

Thompson, Kenneth W. 1986. "Religion and Politics: An Overview." *Annals of the American Academy of Political and Social Science* 483:12–24.

Thornton, Arland. 1989. "Changing attitudes toward Family Issues in the United States." *Journal of Marriage and the Family* 51:873–93.

Thurow, Lester. 1990. "The Crusade That's Killing Prosperity." *American Prospect* March/April:54–59.

Tilly, Charles. 1974. *Urban World*. Boston: Little, Brown.

Tolbert, Charles, Patrick M. Horan, and E. M. Beck. 1980. "The Structure of Economic Segmentation: A Dual Economy Approach." *American Journal of Sociology* 85:1095–116.

Tomaskovic-Devey, Donald, and Vincent J. Roscigno. 1977. "Uneven Development and Local Inequality in the U.S. South: The Role of Outside Investment, Landed Elites, and Racial Dynamics." *Sociological Forum* 12(4):565–97.

Tönnies, Ferdinand. 1957. *Community and Society*. Translated and edited by Charles P. Loomis. East Lansing, MI: Michigan State University.

Treas, Judith. 1997. "Older Immigrants and Welfare Reform." *International Journal of Sociology and Social Policy* 17:8–33.

Treas, Judith, and Deirdre Giesen. 1996. "Cheatin' Hearts and Rational Choice: Marriage, Cohabitation, and Infidelity in the U.S." Paper presented at the annual meeting of the American Sociological Association, New York, NY, August 16–20.

Treas, Judith, and Ramon Torrecilha. 1995. "The Older Population." In *State of the Union: America in the 1990s*, edited by R. Farley, 2:47–92. New York: Russell Sage.

U.S. Bureau of the Census. 1958. *Current Population Reports*. Series P-20. Washington, DC: U.S. Department of Commerce, Bureau of the Census.

———. 1959–97. *Current Population Reports*. Consumer Income Series P-60. Washington, DC: U.S. Department of Commerce, Bureau of the Census.

———. 1973, 1983, 1993. *Census of the Population*. Public Use Microdata Sample files. Washington, DC: U.S. Department of Commerce, Bureau of the Census.

———. 1973. *Census of Population: 1970*. Vol. 1. *Characteristics of the Population*, Part 50, *West Virginia*. Washington, DC: U.S. Government Printing Office.

———. 1983. *1980 Census of Population*. Vol. 1. *Characteristics of the Population*, Chapter C, *General Social and Economic Characteristics*, Part 50, *West Virginia*. Washington, DC: U.S. Government Printing Office.

———. 1993. *Census of Population: Detailed Characteristics of the Population*. Washington, DC: U.S. Government Printing Office.

———. 1995. *Consolidated Federal Funds County Data File, 1994*. Washington, DC: U.S. Department of Commerce, Bureau of the Census.

———. 1995. *Statistical Abstract of the United States, 1995*. 115th ed. Washington, DC: U.S. Government Printing Office.

———. 1998. *March 1997 Current Population Survey*. Washington, DC: U.S. Department of Commerce, Bureau of the Census.

———. 1998. *Small Area Income and Poverty Estimates: 1993 State and County Income and Poverty Estimates*. Revised January 1998. World Wide Web URL: www.census.gov/hhes/www/saipe93.html.

U.S. Department of Agriculture. 1996. *Rural Conditions and Trends* 7(1):Appendix Table 3.

———. 1996. *Rural Conditions and Trends* 8(3):Appendix Table 8.

U.S. Department of Defense. 1998. *Semi-Annual Occupational Profile*. Packer Air Force Base, FL: Defense Equal Opportunity Management Institute, Research Division.

van der Kolk, B. A., A. C. McFarlane, and L. Weisaeth, eds. 1996. *Traumatic Stress: The Effects of Overwhelming Experience on Mind, Body, and Society*. New York: Guilford.

Venkatesh, Sudhir. 1996. "Private Lives, Public Housing: An Ethnography of the Robert Taylor Homes." Ph.D. dissertation., University of Chicago.

Villemez, W. J., and J. D. Kasarda. 1976. "Veteran Status and Socioeconomic Attainment." *Armed Forces and Society* 2(3):407–20.

Wagner, David G., Rebecca S. Ford, and Thomas W. Ford. 1986. "Can Gender Inequalities Be Reduced?" *American Sociological Review* 51:47–61.

Waldinger, Roger. 1989. "Immigration and Urban Change." *Annual Review of Sociology* 15:211–32.

——. 1996. *Still the Promised City? African-Americans and New Immigrants in Post-Industrial New York.* Cambridge, MA: Harvard University Press.

Waldinger, Roger, and Mehdi Bozorgmehr. 1996. *Ethnic Los Angeles.* New York: Russell Sage.

Walker, Henry A. 1992. "Legitimating Social Behavior: Developments and Prospects." Paper presented at the annual meeting of the American Sociological Association, Pittsburgh, PA, August 20–24.

Walker, Henry A., and Morris Zelditch, Jr. 1993. "Power, Legitimacy, and the Stability of Authority: A Theoretical Research Program." In *Theoretical Research Programs: Studies in the Growth of Theory,* edited by J. Berger and Morris Zelditch, Jr., 364–81. Stanford: Stanford University Press.

Walker, Richard. 1991. "Bush Adds Religion to Arsenal against Iraq." *St. Petersburg Times,* February 9, 3E.

Waller, Willard. 1938. *The Family: A Dynamic Interpretation.* New York: Dryden.

——. 1940. *War and the Family.* New York: Dryden.

Walzer, Michael. 1997. *On Toleration.* New Haven, CT: Yale University Press.

Waters, Mary C. 1990. *Ethnic Options: Choosing Identities in America.* Berkeley: University of California Press.

Weber, Max. 1968. *Economy and Society,* edited by G. Roth and C. Wittich. Berkeley: University of California Press.

Wesolowski, Wlodzimierz. 1979. *Classes, Strata, and Power.* London: Routledge and Kegan Paul.

Westat, Inc. 1986. *The 1985 Army Experience Survey: Tabular Descriptions of First-Term Separatees,* Vol. 1. Alexandria, VA: U.S. Army Research Institute for the Behavioral and Social Sciences.

Weston, Kath. 1991. *Families We Choose: Lesbians, Gays, Kinship.* New York: Columbia University Press.

Whitehurst, James E. 1980. The Mainstreaming of Black Muslims: Healing the Hate. *Christian Century* February 27:225–29.

Wicker, Tom. 1968. *"Introduction" Report of the National Advisory Commission on Civil Disorders.* New York: Bantam.

Wiggins, Kayla McKinney. 1993. "Epic Heroes, Ethical Issues, and Time Paradoxes in *Quantum Leap.*" *Journal of Popular Film and Television* 21:111–20.

Wilcox, Clyde, and Ted G. Jelen. 1995. *Public Attitudes toward Church and State.* Armonk, NY: M. E. Sharpe.

Wilcox, Clyde, and Mark J. Rozell, eds. 1995. *God at the Grass Roots: The Christian Right in the 1994 Elections.* Lanham, MD: Rowman and Littlefield.

Wilensky, H. L. 1961. "Orderly Careers and Social Participation in the Middle Mass." *American Sociological Review* 24:836–45.

Williams, Robin M., Jr. 1946. "Some Observations on Sociological Research in Government during World War II." *American Sociological Review* 11:573–77.

——. 1947. *The Reduction of Intergroup Tensions: A Survey of Research on Problems of Ethnic, Racial, and Religious Group Relations.* New York: Social Science Research Council.

——. 1951. *American Society: A Sociological Interpretation.* New York: Alfred A. Knopf.

——. 1960. *American Society: A Sociological Interpretation.* New York: Alfred A. Knopf.

——. (with John P. Dean, and Edward A. Suchman). 1964. *Strangers Next Door: Ethnic Relations in American Communities.* Englewood Cliffs, NJ: Prentice-Hall.

——. 1970. *American Society: A Sociological Interpretation.* New York: Alfred A. Knopf.

——. 1973. "Continuity and Change in Recent Research on Social Institutions." *Annals of the American Academy of Political and Social Science* 406:171–82.

——. (with Madelyn Rhenisch). 1977. *Mutual Accommodation: Ethnic Conflict and Cooperation.* Minneapolis: University of Minnesota Press.

———. 1984. "Field Observations and Surveys in Combat Zones." *Social Psychology Quarterly* 47(2):186–92.
———. 1989. "The American Soldier: An Assessment, Several Wars Later." *Public Opinion Quarterly* 53:153–74.
———. 1994. "The Sociology of Ethnic Conflicts: Comparative International Perspectives." *Annual Review of Sociology* 20:49–79.
Williams, Robin M., Jr., and Margaret W. Ryan. 1954. *Schools in Transition: Community Experiences in Desegregation.* Chapel Hill: University of North Carolina Press.
Williamson, Jeffrey. 1965. "Regional Inequality and the Process of National Development: A Description of Patterns." *Economic Development and Cultural Change* 13:3–45.Willits, Fern K., Robert C. Bealer, and Vincent L. Timbers. 1990. "Popular Images of 'Rurality': Data from a Pennsylvania Survey." *Rural Sociology* 55:559–78.
Willits, Fern K., Robert C. Bealer, Vincent L. Timbers. 1990. "Popular Images of 'Rurality': Data from a Pennsylvania Survey." *Rural Sociology* 55:559–78.
Wills, Gary. 1996. A Tale of Three Leaders. *The New York Review of Books* 43(14):61–74.
Wilson, William Julius. 1978. *The Declining Significance of Race: Blacks and Changing American Institutions.* Chicago: University of Chicago Press.
———. 1987. *The Truly Disadvantaged: The Inner City, The Underclass, and Public Policy.* Chicago: University of Chicago Press.
———. 1996. *When Work Disappears: The World of the New Urban Poor.* New York: Alfred A. Knopf.
Wirth, Louis, ed. [1928] 1965. *On Cities and Social Life.* Chicago: University of Chicago Press.
Wish, Harvey. 1937. "American Slave Insurrections before 1861." *Journal of Negro History* 22:299–320.
Witte, Rob. 1996. *Racist Violence and the State: A Comparative Analysis of Britain, France, and the Netherlands.* London: Longman.
Wolf, Robin. 1996. *Marriages and Families in a Diverse Society.* New York: Harper Collins.
Wright, Erik Olin. 1978. *Class, Crisis, and the State.* London: New Left.
Wright, Marion Thompson. 1955. "Review of *Schools in Transition* by R. M. Williams, Jr." *Journal of Negro History* 40:85–90.
Wuthnow, Robert. 1988. *The Restructuring of American Religion: Society and Faith since World War II.* Princeton, NJ: Princeton University Press.
Yinger, J. Milton. 1965. "Review of *Strangers Next Door* by R. M. Williams, Jr., et al." *American Sociological Review* 30:439–40.
———. 1970. *The Scientific Study of Religion.* New York: Macmillan.
———. 1982. *Countercultures: The Promise and the Peril of a World Turned Upside Down.* New York: Free Press.
———. 1985. "Ethnicity." *Annual Review of Sociology* 11:151–80.
———. 1994. *Ethnicity: Source of Strength? Source of Conflict?* Albany, NY: SUNY Press.
Zhou, Min. 1992. *Chinatown: The Socioeconomic Potential of an Urban Enclave.* Philadelphia: Temple University Press.
———. 1997a. "Growing Up American: The Challenge Confronting Immigrant Children and Children of Immigrants." *Annual Review of Sociology* 23:63–95.
———. 1997b. "'Parachute' Kids and 'Astronaut Parents': The Educational Experience of Chinese Children in Transitional Families." Los Angeles: Department of Sociology, UCLA.

Contributors

RICHARD ALBA is Professor of Sociology and Public Policy at the State University of New York at Albany. The seeds of his interest in ethnicity were sown during his childhood in the Bronx of the 1940s and 1950s and nurtured intellectually at Columbia University, where he received his undergraduate and graduate education. His books include *Ethnic Identity: The Transformation of White America, Italian Americans: Into the Twilight of Ethnicity,* and *Right versus Privilege: The Open Admissions Experiment at the City University of New York* (co-author). He has published numerous articles in sociology journals, most recently with John Logan and others on racial and ethnic residential patterns in the metropolitan United States. He is currently working on a book, with Victor Nee of Cornell University, that will attempt to extend assimilation theory to new immigrant groups.

SANDRA LIPSITZ BEM is Professor of Psychology and Women's Studies at Cornell University, where she also served as Director of Women's Studies from 1978 through 1985 and as Senior Sexual Harassment Counselor from 1993 through 1995. For her early work on androgyny and gender schema theory, she was awarded a Distinguished Scientific Award for an Early Career Contribution to Psychology by the American Psychological Association in 1976 and a Young Scholar Award from the American Association of University Women in 1980. More recently, her book *The Lenses of Gender: Transforming the Debate on Sexual Inequality* was selected as the Best Book in Psychology for 1993 by the Association of American Publishers. She has also written a memoir entitled *An Unconventional Family.*

DAVID L. BROWN is Professor and Chair of the Department of Rural Sociology at Cornell University. His publications focus on migration and population redistribution, rural poverty, and community sociology. His current research is concerned with residential preferences and population redistribution in the United States and with household livelihood strategies in rural Hungary. Before joining the Cornell faculty, Professor Brown conducted and directed social science research for the U.S. Department of Agriculture. He served for one year as a consultant to the White House Domestic Policy Staff with a particular focus on rural development policy.

JOHN SIBLEY BUTLER is the Dallas TACA Centennial Professor of Liberal Arts (Sociology) and the Arthur James Douglass Centennial Professor of Entrepreneurship and Small Business (Graduate School of Business) at the University of Texas at Austin. He is also the Sam Barshop Fellow at the IC2 Institute. His research is in the area of organizational behavior (military) and entrepreneurship. His books include *Entrepreneurship and Self-Help among Black Americans: A Reconsideration of Race and Economics, All That We Can Be: Black Leadership and Racial Integration the Army Way* (with Charles Moskos), and *Immigrant and Minority Entrepreneurship: The Economic Rebuilding of American Communities* (with George Kozmetsky).

CHRISTOPHER CHAN is Assistant Professor of Sociology at Florida State University, where he is also a Research Affiliate in the Pepper Institute on Aging and Public Policy. His research and teaching interests are in aging, social inequality, and the family.

DONNA DEMPSTER-MCCLAIN is Associate Director of the Bronfenbrenner Life Course Center and Senior Lecturer in the Department of Human Development at Cornell University. Her research and teaching interests focus on social gerontology and life course transitions. She served as Project Director for the Cornell Women's Roles and Well-Being Study from 1985 to 1992 and was an Associate Professor of Child and Family Development at California State University, Long Beach, from 1970 to 1983.

RONALD G. EHRENBERG is the Irving M. Ives Professor of Industrial and Labor Relations and Economics at Cornell University. He also is Director of the Cornell Higher Education Research Institute and Co-director of Cornell's Institute for Labor Market Policies. From July 1, 1995, to June 30, 1998, he served as Cornell's Vice President for Academic Programs, Planning, and Budgeting.

GLEN H. ELDER, JR., is Howard W. Odum Distinguished Professor of Sociology and Research Professor of Psychology at the University of North Carolina at Chapel Hill, where he co-directs the Carolina Consortium on Human Development and manages a research program on life course studies. He also has served on the faculties of the University of California, Berkeley, and Cornell University. His books (authored, co-authored, and edited) include *Children of the Great Depression, Life Course Dynamics, Children in Time and Place, Families in Troubled Times,* and *Developmental Science.*

JAMES LOWELL GIBBS, JR., is Martin Luther King, Jr., Centennial Professor of Anthropology Emeritus at Stanford University, where he has been since 1966 and where he has been cited for his service to undergraduate education. He is co-producer and co-director of the award-winning ethnographic film "The Cows of Dolo Ken Paye" and producer of the video sequel, "Dolo Ken Paye's People Go to the Movies." He is an Africanist and editor of and contributor to the now classic *Peoples of Africa* and co-author of *Law in Radically Different Cultures.*

CHARLES HIRSCHMAN is Professor in the Department of Sociology at the University of Washington. Before his appointment at the University of Washington, he taught at Duke University (1972–81) and Cornell University (1981–87). His major research interests are in social and demographic change in Southeast Asia and ethnic stratification in the United States. He currently chairs the SSRC Committee on International Migration and is directing a project on household economic and demographic change in Vietnam.

MELVIN L. KOHN, currently Professor of Sociology at the Johns Hopkins University, received his Ph.D. from Cornell University (under the supervision of Robin M. Williams, Jr.) in 1952. His research on social structure and personality, research that provides the perspective on which his essay is based, has been published in *Class and Conformity: A Study in Values; Work and Personality: An Inquiry into the Impact of Social Stratification* (co-authored with Carmi Schooler); and *Social Structure and Self-Direction: A Comparative Analysis of the United States and Poland* (co-authored with Kazimierz M. Slomczynski), as well as in journal articles. His current research focuses on social structure and personality under conditions of radical social change—a comparative study of Poland and Ukraine, being done in collaboration with sociologists from those countries.

MARLENE A. LEE is an Assistant Professor in the Department of Rural Sociology at the University of Wisconsin at Madison. Her current research focuses on self-employment, employment transitions, and welfare reform.

PHILIP E. LEWIS is the Harold Tanner Dean of the College of Arts and Sciences at Cornell University. A graduate of Davidson College, he received a Ph.D. in French Literature from Yale, where he was a Woodrow Wilson fellow and a Danforth fellow. He has published extensively on various aspects of seventeenth-century French literature and on contemporary criticism. His book on La Rochefoucauld was published by Cornell Press in 1977, and his book on Charles Perrault was published by Stanford University Press in 1996. He has received fellowships from the Cornell Society for the Humanities, the Camargo Foundation, and the National Endowment for the Humanities.

JOHN LOGAN is Professor of Sociology at the University at Albany. He is coauthor (with Harvey Molotch) of *Urban Fortunes: The Political Economy of Place* and (with Glenna Spitze) *Family Ties: The Enduring Relations between Parents and Their Grown Children.* His current research deals with minority and immigrant groups in the United States since the turn of the century.

PHYLLIS MOEN is Ferris Family Professor of Life Course Studies and Professor of Sociology and of Human Development at Cornell University, where she is a founding director of the Bronfenbrenner Life Course Center. Her research focuses on gender and aging over the life course, including work/family transitions and trajectories, and is funded by the National Institute on Aging and the Alfred P. Sloan Foundation for life course research. Her books include *Working Parents, Women's Two Roles,* and, as coauthor, *Examining Lives in Context* and *The State of Americans.*

CHARLES MOSKOS, a former draftee, is Professor of Sociology at Northwestern University and Chairman of the Inter-University Seminar on Armed Forces and Society. His books include *The Military—More Than Just a Job?, The New Conscientious Objection, A Call to Civic Service, All That We Can Be,* and *The Postmodern Military.* His research with American combat soldiers has taken him to Vietnam, Panama, Saudi Arabia, Somalia, Haiti, and Bosnia. He has been a fellow at the Woodrow Wilson International Center for Scholars and a Guggenheim fellow. His writings have been translated into sixteen languages.

ROBERT B. OLSEN (Ph.D. from Cornell University in labor economics) is an economist at Mathematica Policy Research in Washington, D.C. He has researched several topics in the economics of education, such as the nonpecuniary benefits of attending college and the impact of financial aid offers on the decision to attend Cornell. His current research focuses on wage inequality across education groups and industries.

PETER I. ROSE, sociologist (Ph.D. from Cornell, 1959), is Sophia Smith Professor and Director of the American Studies Diploma Program at Smith College and a member of the Graduate Faculty of the University of Massachusetts. He is the author of *They and We, The Subject is Race, Strangers in Their Midst, Mainstream and Margins,* and *Tempest-Tost* and editor of *The Study of Society, The Ghetto and Beyond, Nation and Nations, Seeing Ourselves, Americans from Africa, Working with Refugees,* and *Interminority Affairs and Professional Passions.*

DONNA S. ROTHSTEIN is a research economist at the U.S. Bureau of Labor Statistics in the Office of Employment Research and Program Development.

C. MATTHEW SNIPP is a Professor of Sociology at Stanford University. He is the author of numerous publications dealing with racial and ethnic inequality in the United States and has focused much of his work on the status of American Indians. He has been a fellow at the Census Bureau and the Center for Advanced Study in the Behavioral Sciences. He is currently an advisor to the Census Bureau and the President's Initiative on Race.

BRIAN J. STULTS is a doctoral student in the Department of Sociology at the University of Albany. In addition to his interest in patterns of residential attainment and suburbanization, he also focuses on aggregate relationships between race and crime in neighborhoods, including effects of social threat and racial discrimination.

CHARLES TILLY is the Joseph L. Buttenwieser Professor of Social Sciences at Columbia University. His most recent books are *Roads from Past to Future, Work under Capitalism* (with Chris Tilly), *Durable Inequality,* and *Transforming Post-Communist Political Economies* (co-edited with Joan Nelson and Lee Walker). He is now writing *Contention and Democracy in Europe* and (with Doug McAdam and Sidney Tarrow) *Dynamics of Contention,* both for Cambridge University Press.

JUDITH TREAS is Professor of Sociology at the University of California, Irvine. She earned a Ph.D. in Sociology from the University of California, Los Angeles, and served on the faculties of Sociology and Gerontology at the University of Southern California. A specialist on topics of aging, family, and population, she has published over fifty research articles and chapters and is the author of *Older Americans in the 1990s and Beyond*. Her current research investigates the determinants and consequences of sexual infidelity among married and cohabiting Americans.

HENRY A. WALKER is Professor of Sociology at Cornell University and a specialist in theoretical methods and experimental sociology. He earned his Ph.D. in Sociology at Stanford. His recent publications focus on power and legitimation processes and on gender status in task groups.

ROBIN M. WILLIAMS, JR., has been a professor at Cornell University for over fifty years (since 1946). He was Henry Scarborough Professor of Social Sciences from 1967 to 1985 and is currently Professor Emeritus. He is also part-time Visiting Professor at University of California, Irvine (1992–present). His co-authored books include *The American Soldier* (Vols. 1–2), *Schools in Transition*, and *What College Students Think*. His other major writings include *The Reduction of Intergroup Tensions, Strangers Next Door: Ethnic Relations in American Communities, American Society: A Sociological Interpretation*, and *Mutual Accommodation: Ethnic Conflict and Cooperation*. He is also co-editor, with Gerald David Jaynes, of *A Common Destiny: Blacks and American Society*. He is past president of the American Sociological Association, the Eastern Sociological Society, and the Sociological Research Association, and he is an elected member of the National Academy of Sciences.

WILLIAM JULIUS WILSON is the John P. and Linda L. Geyser University Professor at Harvard University. He has been elected to the National Academy of Sciences, the American Academy of Arts and Sciences, and the American Philosophical Society. He is past president of the American Sociological Association and is a MacArthur Prize fellow. He is the author of numerous publications, including *The Truly Disadvantaged* and *When Work Disappears: The World of the New Urban Poor*.

J. MILTON YINGER (Ph.D. from the University of Wisconsin) has held teaching positions at Ohio Wesleyan University (1941–47) and at Oberlin College (1947–87) with brief visiting professorships at the Universities of Michigan, Washington, and Hawaii. He has written many articles and books including *Religion in the Struggle for Power, Racial and Cultural Minorities* (with George E. Simpson; Anisfield-Wolf Award, 1958), *Toward a Field Theory of Behavior, The Scientific Study of Religion, Middle Start: An Experiment in the Educational Enrichment of Young Adolescents* (with several colleagues), *Countercultures*, and *Ethnicity: Source of Strength? Source of Conflict*. His professional activities include Council Member, Secretary, and President of the American Sociological Association.

WENQUAN ZHANG is a Ph.D. student in the Department of Sociology at the State University of New York at Albany. His research interests include minority/majority relations, the assimilation of new immigrants, racial and ethnic segregation, and application of geographic information systems in sociological studies.

Index